EIGHTEEN
UPBUILDING DISCOURSES

KIERKEGAARD'S WRITINGS, V

EIGHTEEN UPBUILDING DISCOURSES

by Søren Kierkegaard

Edited and Translated
with Introduction and Notes by

Howard V. Hong and
Edna H. Hong

PRINCETON UNIVERSITY PRESS
PRINCETON, NEW JERSEY

Copyright © 1990 by Howard V. Hong

Published by Princeton University Press
41 William Street, Princeton, New Jersey 08540
In the United Kingdom: Princeton University Press, Oxford

Library of Congress Cataloging-in-Publication Data

Kierkegaard, Søren, 1813-1855.
[Atten opbyggelige taler. English]
Eighteen upbuilding discourses / by Søren Kierkegaard ; edited and translated with
introduction and notes by Howard V. Hong and Edna H. Hong.
p.   cm. — (Kierkegaard's writings ; 5)
Translation of: Atten opbyggelige taler.
Includes bibliographical references.
ISBN 0-691-07380-5 (alk. paper) :
1. Spiritual life. I. Hong, Howard Vincent, 1912-   . II. Hong, Edna Hatlestad,
1913-   . III. Title. IV. Title: 18 upbuilding discourses. V. Series: Kierkegaard, Søren,
1813-1855. Works. English. 1978 ; 5.
BV4505.K3713 1990
248.4—dc20   90-34571

ISBN 0-691-07380-5

Preparation of this volume has been made possible in part by a grant from
the Division of Research Programs of the National Endowment
for the Humanities, an independent federal agency

Princeton University Press books are printed
on acid-free paper, and meet the guidelines for
permanence and durability of the Committee on
Production Guidelines for Book Longevity
of the Council on Library Resources

Designed by Frank Mahood

Printed in the United States of America by Princeton
University Press, Princeton, New Jersey

1 3 5 7 9 10 8 6 4 2

CONTENTS

One Who Prays Aright Struggles in Prayer
and Is Victorious—in That God Is Victorious
377

HISTORICAL INTRODUCTION

A few years after the publication of his six small volumes of upbuilding[1] discourses (1843-1844), Søren Kierkegaard was faced with the question of whether to publish *The Point of View for My Work as an Author.*[2]

If I do nothing at all directly to assure a full understanding of my whole literary production . . . then what? Then there will be no judgment at all on my authorship in its totality, for no one has sufficient faith or time or competence to look for a comprehensive plan [*Total-Anlæg*] in the entire production. Consequently the verdict will be that I have changed somewhat over the years.

So it will be. This distresses me. I am deeply convinced that there is another integral coherence, that there is a comprehensiveness in the whole production (especially through the assistance of Governance), and that there certainly is something else to be said about it than this meager comment that in a way the author has changed.[3]

Part of the evidence that there is a comprehensive plan or structure in the whole variegated authorship and that the author was not one who changed essentially as he became older is the publication pattern of the six volumes of discourses.

Signed Upbuilding Discourses	Pseudonymous Works
	Either/Or . . . February 20, 1843
Two Upbuilding Discourses . . . . . . May 16, 1843	
	Fear and Trembling and
Three . . . . . . October 16, 1843	*Repetition* . . . October 16, 1843

[1] On this term, see p. 5 and note 3.
[2] Published posthumously in 1859.
[3] *JP* VI 6346 (*Pap.* X¹ A 116).

Four ...... December 6, 1843
Two .... March 5, 1844
Three .... June 8, 1844

                          Philosophical Fragments
                          .... June 13, 1844
                          The Concept of Anxiety and
                          Prefaces .... June 17, 1844
Four .... August 31, 1844

                          Postscript ... February 27, 1846
Christian Discourses
.... April 26, 1848

                          The Crisis and a Crisis in
                          the Life of an Actress
                          .... July 24-27, 1848

At the heart of the coherent, comprehensive plan, despite many differences among the published works and within the types of writings, is a common intention: to make aware.[4]

The category for my undertaking is: to *make persons aware* of the essentially Christian, but this accounts for the repeated statement: I am not that, for otherwise there is confusion. My task is to get persons deceived—within the meaning of truth—into religious commitment, which they have cast off, but I do not have authority; instead of authority I use the very opposite, I say: the whole undertaking is for my own discipline and education. This again is a genuinely Socratic approach. Just as he was the ignorant one, so here; instead of being the teacher, I am the one who is being educated.[5]

Although there are a comprehensive plan and a common aim in the published writings, there is also a great variety in theme, form, and tone. Indeed, the preface to *The Lily in the Field and the Bird of the Air*, after particular reference to the pair

[4] See, for example, *Philosophical Fragments, or A Fragment of Philosophy*, p. 93, *KW* VII (*SV* IV 256); *The Point of View for My Work as an Author*, in *The Point of View*, *KW* XXII (*SV* XIII 494, 496, 501, 537-40); *JP* VI 6577, 6712 (*Pap.* X² A 375, 742).
    [5] *JP* VI 6533 (*Pap.* X² A 196).

Either/Or and *Two Upbuilding Discourses* (1843), quotes the preface to *Two Upbuilding Discourses* (1844), which states that the work " 'is offered with the right hand'—in contrast to the pseudonyms, which were held out and are held out with the left hand."[6] The distinction is reiterated in *Point of View*: "The duplexity is there from the very beginning. *Two Upbuilding Discourses* is concurrent with *Either/Or*. The duplexity in the deeper sense, that is, in the sense of the whole authorship, was by no means that about which there was talk at the time: the first and second parts of *Either/Or*. No, the duplexity was: *Either/Or* and *Two Upbuilding Discourses*."[7]

The distinction between two series of published works—the pseudonymous works and the upbuilding discourses—is not incompatible with the stress upon a comprehensive plan and a common aim that embrace the variety of kinds, levels of development, and modes of approach. An analogous variety is evident also within the range of each of the two series. The essential commonality and the particular differences between the upbuilding discourses and the pseudonymous works, and also between the early and late works in each series, are epitomized by certain characteristics and emphases found in the discourses.

The most obvious difference is that whereas the pseudonymous works from *Either/Or* through *Concluding Unscientific Postscript* are indirect communication, the signed discourses from first to last are direct.[8] But the two modes of communication have ultimately the same aim: "to **make aware** of the religious, the essentially Christian."[9] To accomplish this, Kierkegaard used two procedural modes in the *Total-Anlæg*.

---

[6] *Without Authority*, KW XVIII (*SV* XI 5). The works of the right hand appeared with Kierkegaard's name as author. See *Kierkegaard: Letters and Documents*, Letter 240, *KW* XXV; *Point of View*, *KW* XXII (*SV* XIII 526).

[7] *Point of View*, *KW* XXII (*SV* XIII 522).

[8] The last pseudonymous works, *The Sickness unto Death* and *Practice in Christianity*, under the distinguishing new pseudonym Anti-Climacus and with Kierkegaard as editor, are also direct. "Anti" in Anti-Climacus means not "against" but "above" or "before" Johannes Climacus in level or rank.

[9] *On My Work as an Author*, with *Point of View*, *KW* XXII (*SV* XIII 501).

In "The Accounting," in *On My Work as an Author*, he describes the relation of the two approaches:

> But just as that which has been communicated (the idea of the religious) has been cast entirely into reflection and taken back again out of reflection, so also the *communication* has been decisively marked by *reflection*, or the form of communication used is that of reflection. "Direct communication" is: to communicate the truth directly; "communication in reflection" is: *to deceive into the truth*. But since the movement is to arrive at the simple, the communication in turn must sooner or later end in direct communication. It began **maieutically** with esthetic works,* and the whole pseudonymous production is *maieutic* in nature. Therefore, these works were also pseudonymous, whereas the directly religious—which from the beginning was present in the glimmer of an indication—carried my name. The directly religious was present from the very beginning; *Two Upbuilding Discourses* (1843) are in fact concurrent** with *Either/Or*. And in order to safeguard the concurrence of the directly religious, every pseudonymous work was accompanied concurrently by a little collection of "upbuilding discourses" until *Concluding Postscript* appeared, which poses the issue, which is "the issue" κατ' ἐξοχήν [in the eminent sense] of the whole authorship: "becoming a Christian."***

* The maieutic lies in the relation between the esthetic productivity as the beginning and the religious as the τέλος [goal]. It begins with the esthetic, in which possibly the majority have their lives, and then the religious is introduced so quickly that those who, moved by the esthetic, decide to follow along, are suddenly standing right in the middle of the decisive qualifications of the essentially Christian, are prompted at least to become *aware*.

** This also serves to prevent the illusion that the religious is something one turns to when one has become older. "One begins as an esthetic author and then when one has become older and no longer has the powers of youth, then one becomes a religious author." But if an author *con-*

currently begins as an esthetic and a religious author, the religious productivity certainly cannot be explained by the incidental fact that the author has become older, inasmuch as one certainly cannot concurrently be older than oneself.

***The situation* (becoming a "Christian" in "Christendom," where consequently one is a Christian)—the situation, which, as any dialectician sees, casts everything into reflection, also makes an indirect method necessary, because the task here must be to take measures against the illusion: calling oneself a Christian, perhaps deluding oneself into thinking one is a Christian, when one is not. Therefore, the one who introduced the issue did not *directly* define himself as being Christian and the others not; no, just the *reverse*—he denies being that and concedes it to the others. This Johannes Climacus does. —In relation to pure receptivity, like the empty jar that is to be filled, *direct* communication is appropriate, but when illusion is involved, consequently something that must first be removed, direct communication is inappropriate.[10]

Within the series of signed direct discourses, there is a distinction between the initial six volumes of the first period (terminated by the publication of *Concluding Unscientific Postscript,* 1846) and the writings of the second period. The eighteen discourses Kierkegaard calls the indication of the directly religious. The second period was a time of exclusively religious productivity[11] (the review of *Two Ages* he regarded as writing without involving him as an author[12]). The exception was his piece on the actress Luise Heiberg titled *The Crisis and a Crisis in the Life of an Actress,* which nevertheless also had and has its place in the *Total-Anlæg.*

But in order inversely to recall the beginning (corresponding to what *Two Upbuilding Discourses* was at the beginning, when the larger works were esthetic), there appeared at the

---

[10] Ibid. (495-97).
[11] Ibid. (496).
[12] See *JP* V 5877 (*Pap.* VII¹ A 9).

end (when for a long period the productivity was exclusively and voluminously religious) a little esthetic article by
Inter et Inter in the newspaper *Fædrelandet*, 188-91, July
1848. The flash of the two upbuilding discourses at the beginning meant that it was actually this that should advance,
this at which it was to arrive; the flash of the little esthetic
article at the end was meant, by way of a faint reflection, to
bring to consciousness that from the beginning the esthetic
was what should be left behind, what should be abandoned.[13]

Other distinctions are made at the beginning of the preface[14]
in each of the six volumes that make up the eighteen upbuilding discourses: "this little book (which is called 'discourses,'
not sermons, because its author does not have authority to
preach, 'upbuilding discourses,' not discourses for upbuilding,
because the speaker by no means claims to be a *teacher*)." The
first distinction, between discourses and sermons, rests primarily on the absence of the authority of ordination. "I am
only a poet," Kierkegaard writes. ". . . I have continually
repeated that they are not sermons or have pointed to 'the
sermon' as something higher."[15] Furthermore, according to
Johannes Climacus, the discourses are distinguishable by their
use of the "ethical categories of immanence, not the doubly
reflected religious categories in the paradox."[16] Therefore, the
sermon not only is distinguishable from the upbuilding discourse on the basis of authority and content but is something
higher.

The distinction between "upbuilding" discourses and discourses "for upbuilding" rests first on Kierkegaard's understanding of his writing as his own education. Therefore, he
was also without the authority of a teacher, and the discourses

[13] *On My Work*, with *Point of View*, KW XXII (*SV* XIII 497).
[14] In the Prefaces there are some minor differences in punctuation. See pp.
5, 53, 107, 179, 231, 295.
[15] Supplement, p. 488 (*Pap.* X[6] B 145).
[16] *Concluding Unscientific Postscript* to Philosophical Fragments, KW XII (*SV*
VII 216). See also *JP* I 630, 638 (*Pap.* VI A 147; VIII[1] A 6).

themselves had the same intrinsic relation to him as to any other reader.

From the very beginning, I have stressed and repeated unchanged that I was "without authority." I regard myself rather as a *reader* of the books, not as the *author*.

"Before God," religiously, I call my whole work as an author (when I speak with myself) my own upbringing and development, but not in the sense as if I were now complete or completely finished with respect to needing upbringing and development.[17]

"For upbuilding" pertains to the nature of the content of a work as well as to Kierkegaard's own relation to that content. Therefore the expression is used in the subtitle of *The Sickness unto Death*, a work of the second period. Just as Anti-Climacus, the author of that work, is above Johannes Climacus, the author of *Fragments* and *Postscript*, or before him in rank, so also the content of that work is more rigorous and more authoritatively Christian.

It finally came to bear the inscription:
For upbuilding and awakening.
This "for awakening" actually is the "more" that came out of the year 1848, but it is also the "more" that is so much higher than my own person that I use a pseudonym for it.
I use only the poetic designation: "upbuilding," not even "for upbuilding."[18]

The phrase "for upbuilding" is also used in the title and text of "Thoughts That Wound from Behind," Part Three of *Christian Discourses* (1848). The use of "for upbuilding" in the text bears out Kierkegaard's distinction between levels of content and the presence or absence of authority. "Watch out, therefore, when you go to the Lord's house, because there you

[17] *On My Work*, with *Point of View*, KW XXII (*SV* XIII 501). See Supplement, pp. 488-89 (X⁶ B 145, pp. 217-18).
[18] *JP* VI 6438 (*Pap*. X¹ A 529).

will come to hear the truth—for upbuilding." "What is spoken of, therefore, and truly for upbuilding, is that there is a deliverance for sinners, comfort for the repentant." ". . . for 'all things must serve for good those who love God.' Oh, how often these words are said and repeated again and again, explained and expounded for upbuilding, for comfort, for reassurance." ". . . **but it is blessed—to suffer mockery for a good cause**, in order that for upbuilding we might become aware of the comfort, or rather, the joy, that Christianity proclaims . . . ."[19]

There is an additional distinction not mentioned in the repeated opening preface sentence but worthy of notice here in order to clarify the conception of "upbuilding discourse" and to indicate its relation particularly to *Works of Love* in the second period of writing. In a journal entry from 1847,[20] Kierkegaard points out "The Difference between Upbuilding Discourse and a Deliberation."

A deliberation [*Overveielse*] does not presuppose the definitions as given and understood; therefore, it must not so much move, mollify, reassure, persuade, as *awaken* and provoke men and sharpen thought. The time for deliberation is indeed before action, and its purpose therefore is rightly to set all the elements into motion. A deliberation ought to be a "gadfly"; therefore its tone ought to be quite different from that of an upbuilding [*opbyggelig*] discourse, which rests in mood, but a deliberation ought in the good sense to be impatient, high-spirited in mood. Irony is necessary here and the even more significant ingredient of the comic. One may very well even laugh once in a while, if only to make the thought clear and more striking. An upbuilding discourse about love presupposes that people know essentially what love is and seeks to win them to it, to move them. But this is certainly not the case. Therefore the "deliberation"

---

[19] *Christian Discourses,* KW XVII (*SV* X 163, 174, 176, 191, 223). See Supplement, pp. 472, 476 (*Pap.* VIII¹ A 20, 21, 486).

[20] *JP* I 641 (*Pap.* VIII¹ A 293). See *Works of Love,* KW XVI (*SV* IX 3, 7); *Upbuilding Discourses in Various Spirits,* KW XV (*SV* VIII 385-87).

must first fetch them up out of the cellar, call to them, turn their comfortable way of thinking topsy-turvy with the dialectic of truth.

The most apparent single common element (from the perspective of the reader) among all the works, whether pseudonymous or signed, is that they are addressed to "the single individual [*den Enkelte*]."[21] The centrality of "the single individual," a characterization of Kierkegaard's understanding of it, and a designation of who that one is are compacted in a passage in "The Accounting."

At the very same time that the sensation *Either/Or* created was at its peak, at that very same time appeared *Two Upbuilding Discourses* (1843), which used the formula that later was repeated unchanged: "it seeks that single individual whom I with joy and gratitude call my reader." And precisely at the critical moment when *Concluding Postscript*, which, as stated, poses "the issue," was delivered to the printer so that the printing could commence as soon as possible and the publication presumably quickly follow—at precisely that moment a pseudonym, most appropriately in a newspaper article,[22] made the greatest possible effort to alienate the public,* and after that began the decisively religious productivity. For the second time I religiously affirmed "that single individual," to whom the next substantial book** (after *Concluding Postscript*), *Upbuilding Discourses in Various Spirits*, or the first part of the same book, "Confessional Address," was dedicated. Perhaps nobody paid much attention to the category "that single individual" the first time I used it, nor was much notice paid to its being repeated unchanged in the preface to every volume of upbuilding discourses. When I the second time or in the second potency repeated the message and stood by my first

---

[21] See *JP* II 1964-2086 and pp. 597-98; VII, pp. 49-50.

[22] "The Activity of a Traveling Esthetician and How He Still Happened to Pay for the Dinner," *Fædrelandet*, 2078, Dec. 27, 1845, the article by Frater Taciturnus that precipitated the *Corsair* affair. See *The Corsair Affair and Articles Related to the Writings*, pp. 38-46, *KW* XIII (*SV* XIII 422-31).

message, everything was done that I was able to do to make the whole weight of emphasis fall upon this category. Here again the movement is: *to arrive at* the simple; the movement is: *from* the public *to* "the single individual." In other words, there is in a *religious sense* no public but only individuals;*** because the religious is earnestness, and earnestness is: the single individual; yet that every human being, unconditionally every human being—which one indeed is—can be, yes, is supposed to be, the single individual.

*Just one thing more, the press of literary contemptibility had achieved a frightfully disproportionate coverage. To be honest, I believed that what I did was a public benefaction;[23] it was rewarded by several of those for whose sake I had exposed myself in this way—rewarded, yes, as an act of love is usually rewarded in the world—and by means of this reward it became a truly Christian work of love.

** For the little literary review of the novel *Two Ages* followed *Concluding Postscript* so closely that it is almost concurrent and is, after all, something written by me *qua* critic and not *qua* author; but it does contain in the last section a sketch of the future from the point of view of "the single individual," a sketch of the future that the year 1848[24] did not falsify.

*** And insofar as there is the "congregation" in a religious sense, this is a concept that lies on the other side of "the single individual," and that above all must not be confused with what *politically* can have validity: the public, the crowd, the numerical, etc.[25]

The two phrases "that single individual [*hiin Enkelte*]" and "the single individual [*den Enkelte*]" have distinguishable

---

[23] See, for example, Corsair *Affair*, pp. 197-98 (*Pap.* VII¹ B 69).

[24] In 1848 there was a culmination of political turmoil in Denmark and in most of Europe. On June 5, 1848, Denmark changed from an absolute monarchy to a constitutional monarchy.

[25] *On My Work*, with *Point of View*, KW XXII (*SV* XIII 497-99). See also " 'The Single Individual': Two 'Notes' Concerning My Work as an Author," Appendix, *Point of View*, KW XXII (*SV* XIII 583-612).

meanings that ultimately become indistinguishable. Initially, *hiin Enkelte* denoted a particularization that soon became absorbed in the universal singular of *den Enkelte*, an example of Kierkegaard's practice of transmutating the particulars of experience into the universally human.[26] In a journal entry from a few years after the publication of the discourses of 1843 and 1844, he writes of the universalizing of the hint to Regine[27] contained in *hiin Enkelte*.

> On the whole, the very mark of my genius is that Governance broadens and radicalizes whatever concerns me personally. I remember what a pseudonymous writer[28] said about Socrates: "His whole life was personal preoccupation with himself, and then Governance comes and adds world-historical significance to it." To take another example—I am polemical by nature, and I understood the concept of "that single individual" [*hiin Enkelte*] early. However, when I wrote it for the first time (in *Two Upbuilding Discourses*), I was thinking particularly of *my* reader, because this book contained a little hint to her, and until later it was for me very true personally that I sought only one single reader. Gradually this thought was taken over. But here again Governance's part is so infinite.[29]

In an earlier journal entry, he emphasizes the universality of *den Enkelte*.

> This is how it is used. The subject of the single individual appears in every book by the pseudonymous writers, but the price put upon being a single individual, a single individual in the eminent sense, rises. The subject of the single individual appears in every one of my upbuilding books, but there the single individual is what every human being is. This is precisely the dialectic of "the single individual"

---

[26] See *Two Ages: The Age of Revolution and the Present Age, A Literary Review*, pp. 98-99 and note 72, *KW* XIV (*SV* VIII 91-92).

[27] Regine Olsen, to whom Kierkegaard had been engaged. See *Letters*, p. 516, *KW* XXV; *JP* VII, p. 68.

[28] Johannes Climacus. See *Postscript, KW* XII (*SV* VII 121 fn.).

[29] *JP* VI 6388 (*Pap.* X¹ A 266, p. 177).

[*changed from:* the particular]. The single individual can mean the most unique one of all, and it can mean everyone. . . . The point of departure of the pseudonymous writers is continually in the differences—the point of departure in the upbuilding discourses is in the universally human.[30]

The accent on the single individual in the pseudonymous works is embodied also in the indirect method, the purpose of which is to make the author of the authors[31] irrelevant and to leave the reader alone with the works and the various positions presented. In the upbuilding discourses of the first period,[32] the accent on the single individual is heightened by the mode of reading that is invited and encouraged—reading aloud. In a journal entry on punctuation, Kierkegaard says: "I always have in mind a reader who reads aloud. . . . Above all, I must repeat that I have in mind readers who read aloud."[33] For example, in the eighteen upbuilding discourses, the frequent absence of question marks in long interrogatory sentences with a descending inflection because of the concluding phrases and clauses is in conformity with the way the portion would be read aloud. There is also the explicit invitation to reading aloud in the Preface to *Three Upbuilding Discourses* (1843):

Small as it is, it probably will slip through . . . until it finds what it is seeking, that favorably disposed person who reads aloud to himself what I write in stillness, who with his voice breaks the spell on the letters, with his voice summons forth what the mute letters have on their lips, as it were, but are unable to express without great effort, stammering and stuttering, who in his mood rescues the captive thoughts that long for release—that favorably disposed person whom

[30] Supplement, pp. 475–76 (*Pap.* VIII² B 192).

[31] See *Postscript, KW* XII (*SV* VII [547]).

[32] See, for example, the preface to "An Occasional Discourse," Part One of *Discourses in Various Spirits, KW* XV (*SV* VIII 117); see also the preface to *For Self-Examination*, p. 3, *KW* XXI (*SV* XII 295).

[33] *JP* V 5981 (*Pap.* VIII¹ A 33) *n.d.*, 1847.

I with joy and gratitude call *my* refuge, who by making my thoughts his own does more for me than I do for him.[34]

The invitation is repeated in another form and the purpose of reading aloud is also stated in the preface to the three discourses of 1844. The book seeks only that reader who "gives an opportunity to what is said, brings the cold thoughts into flame again, transforms the discourse into a conversation."[35]

According to the usual ways of reckoning the impact of a book—reviews and sales—the six small volumes of upbuilding discourses were scarcely a smashing success. Jens Himmelstrup[36] lists only one review, little more than an announcement, of *Two Upbuilding Discourses* (1843). Thereafter, Himmelstrup lists no review or announcement other than Bishop Mynster's article *"Kirkelig Polemik"*[37] (1844). The article is Mynster's reply to observations[38] critical of the approach of the Church to the "more educated." In two pages of the eighteen-page article there are only brief approving references to the dedication by Kierkegaard ("with his rich education") of the discourses to his father, whom Mynster knew intimately, and to Kierkegaard's having learned well from his father, as was manifest in the discourse on Job (the first discourse in *Four Upbuilding Discourses* [1843]), which Mynster calls "a sermon."

The sales of the six volumes matched the paucity and brevity of the reviews of the discourses. Frithiof Brandt and Else Rammel state that by January 1, 1845, the sales of editions of two hundred copies ranged from 139 of *Three Upbuilding Discourses* (1843) to 92 of *Three Upbuilding Discourses* (1844).[39]

---

[34] P. 53.

[35] P. 231.

[36] Jens Himmelstrup, *Søren Kierkegaard International Bibliografi* (Copenhagen: Nyt Nordisk Forlag Arnold Busck, 1962), p. 10.

[37] *Intelligensblade*, IV, January 1, 1844, pp. 97-114.

[38] In *Fyenske Fierdingsaarsskrivt for Literatur og Kritik* (Odense), IV, 1843, pp. 384-85.

[39] Frithiof Brandt and Else Rammel, *Søren Kierkegaard og Pengene* (Copenhagen: Munksgaard, 1935), pp. 20, 33.

Kierkegaard, as his own publisher, remaindered the unsold copies to P. G. Philipsen, who then issued the eighteen discourses in one volume with the common title page *Atten opbyggelige Taler*, 1843-1845. Later, when he ran out of the first two discourses, he bound the sixteen discourses in a volume under the common title *Sexten opbyggelige Taler*. Inasmuch as Brandt and Rammel state that 78 copies of the two discourses (1843) and 61 copies of the three discourses (1843) were remaindered,[40] a copy of *Sexten opbyggelige Taler* must be the rarest Kierkegaard book in existence. Perhaps the editions were somewhat larger than two hundred, and perhaps the editions were not all of the same size, but in any event the sales were meager.

Given the scant critical and public reception of the eighteen discourses at the time, they and later discourses were obliged to wait a hundred years for the acclaim given to them by Martin Heidegger, who distinguishes between the two series in Kierkegaard's *Total-Anlæg* and asserts that "there is more to be learned philosophically" from his upbuilding writings "than from his theoretical ones—with the exception of his treatise on the concept of anxiety."[41]

[40] Ibid. Perhaps Philipsen sold some copies of the two discourses (1843) before making the composite volume of eighteen. Otherwise he would have run out of the three discourses (1843) first, according to Brandt and Rammel's figures.

[41] Martin Heidegger, *Being and Time*, tr. John Macquarrie and Edward Robinson (New York: Harper and Row, 1962), p. 494, n. vi.

Two Upbuilding Discourses

1843

TO THE LATE

Michael Pedersen Kierkegaard[1]

FORMERLY A CLOTHING MERCHANT HERE IN THE CITY

MY FATHER

THESE DISCOURSES ARE DEDICATED

Although this little book (which is called "discourses," not sermons, because its author does not have authority to *preach*, "upbuilding[3] discourses," not discourses for upbuilding,[4] because the speaker by no means claims to be a *teacher*[5]) wishes to be only what it is, a superfluity, and desires only to remain in hiding, just as it came into existence in concealment, I nevertheless have not bidden it farewell without an almost fantastic hope. Inasmuch as in being published it is in a figurative sense starting a journey, I let my eyes follow it for a little while. I saw how it wended its way down solitary paths or walked solitary on public roads. After a few little mistakes, through being deceived by a fleeting resemblance, it finally met that single individual [*hiin Enkelte*][6] whom I with joy and gratitude call *my* reader, that single individual it is seeking, to whom, so to speak, it stretches out its arms, that single individual who is favorably enough disposed to allow himself to be found, favorably enough disposed to receive it, whether at the time of the encounter it finds him cheerful and confident or "weary and pensive." —On the other hand, inasmuch as in being published it actually remains quiet without moving from the spot, I let my eyes rest on it for a little while. It stood there like a humble little flower under the cover of the great forest, sought neither for its splendor nor its fragrance nor its food value. But I also saw, or thought I saw, how the bird I call *my* reader suddenly noticed it, flew down to it, picked it, and took it home, and when I had seen this, I saw no more.

Copenhagen, May 5, 1843[7]

S. K.

THE EXPECTANCY OF FAITH
NEW YEAR'S DAY

PRAYER

Once again a year has passed, heavenly Father! We thank you that it was added to the time of grace and that we are not terrified by its also being added to the time of accounting, because we trust in your mercy. The new year faces us with its requirements, and even though we enter it downcast and troubled because we cannot and do not wish to hide from ourselves the thought of the lust of the eye that infatuated, the sweetness of revenge that seduced, the anger that made us unrelenting, the cold heart that fled far from you, we nevertheless do not go into the new year entirely empty-handed, since we shall indeed also take along with us recollections of the fearful doubts that were set at rest, of the lurking concerns that were soothed, of the downcast disposition that was raised up, of the cheerful hope that was not humiliated. Yes, when in mournful moments we want to strengthen and encourage our minds by contemplating those great men, your chosen instruments, who in severe spiritual trials and anxieties of heart kept their minds free, their courage uncrushed, and heaven open, we, too, wish to add our witness to theirs in the assurance that even if our courage compared with theirs is only discouragement, our power powerlessness, you, however, are still the same, the same mighty God who tests spirits in conflict, the same Father without whose will not one sparrow falls to the ground.[8] Amen.

It is on the first day of the year that we are assembled here, devout listeners![9] The festival we celebrate today is not a church festival, and yet to us its celebration is not less welcome, its invitation to quiet reflection not less earnest. It is in the Lord's house that we are assembled, where we are always to speak of the same thing, although in different ways according to the time and occasion. A year has passed, and a new one has begun; nothing has happened in it yet. The past is finished, the present is not; only the future is, which is not. In everyday life, it is customary for us to give one another some good wish. Since we believe ourselves to be familiar with a person's special situation, his thoughts and actions, we accordingly feel competent to wish him a specific good especially appropriate to him and to his life. On this day, we also do not fail to show others our goodwill and sympathy by wishing them this or that good. But since on this day the thought of the future and its unexplored possibility is so very vivid to us, our wish is usually of a more general nature in the hope that its greater compass will more readily embrace the manifoldness of the future, because we feel the difficulty of wishing something definite with respect to what is indefinite and indefinable. But we do not let this difficulty block our wish, we do not give thought the time to disturb the puzzling and vague impulses of the heart; we feel a goodwill that still ought not to be disparaged as light-mindedness, even though it does not deserve to be honored with the name of love. Only for a particular person do we make an exception. We feel more closely attached to him than to others, are more concerned for his welfare. The more this is the case, the more conscious we become of the difficulty. As thought becomes more absorbed in the future, it loses its way in its restless attempt to force or entice an explanation from the riddle. Peering here and there, it rushes from one possibility to another, but in vain, and during all this the well-wishing soul becomes dejected, sits there and waits for thought to come back and inform it about what it dared to ask for in all sincerity. What others do lightly and effortlessly is hard and difficult for this person; what he him- self does easily for others is hard with respect to the one he loves most, and the more he loves, the harder it is. Finally, he becomes perplexed; he is unwilling to have the beloved slip out of his power, is unwilling to surrender him to the control of the future, and yet he must; he wants to escort him with every good wish, and yet he does not have a single one.

III
17

If a person's troubled soul felt itself trapped like a prisoner in this difficulty, he would probably call to mind the testimo- nies he had heard in these sacred places, he perhaps would go there to reflect again and to investigate whether there might not be one wish so certain that he would dare to put his whole soul fervently into it without holding back any part of it for another wish that was also important to the beloved—a wish so certain that he would rather fear not having fervency enough to wish it as it ought to be wished, a wish that he would not need to accompany with new wishes that it might continue, a wish that would not guilefully continue after one had stopped wishing it, a wish that would not pertain to a particular thing so that he would have forgotten another par- ticular thing that could later intrude disturbingly, a wish that would not pertain to the present but would be appropriate for the future, just as this was indeed the reason that he wished. If there were such a wish, then he would be free and happy, happy in his wish, happier that he could wish it for the other.

As a matter of fact, many good things are talked about in these sacred places. There is talk of the good things of the world, of health, happy times, prosperity, power, good for- tune, a glorious fame. And we are warned against them; the person who has them is warned not to rely on them, and the person who does not have them is warned not to set his heart on them. About *faith* there is a different kind of talk. It is said to be the highest good, the most beautiful, the most precious, the most blessed riches of all, not to be compared with any-

thing else, incapable of being replaced. Is it distinguished from
the other good things, then, by being the highest but otherwise of the same kind as they are—transient and capricious,
bestowed only upon the chosen few, rarely for the whole of
life? If this were so, then it certainly would be inexplicable that
in these sacred places it is always faith and faith alone that is
spoken of, that it is eulogized and celebrated again and again.
The person who is supposed to speak of it must, of course,
either possess this good or lack it. If he possessed it, he would
presumably say, "I readily admit that it is the most glorious of
all, but extol it to others—no, that I cannot do, since that
would make it even harder for those who do not have it;
moreover, there is a secret pain involved in this good that
makes me more lonely than the severest sufferings do." And
that would indeed be a kind and noble thought on his part.
But the person who did not possess it certainly could not extol
it. Then what happened would be the opposite of what does
happen; faith would become the only good that is never mentioned in these places, since it would be too great for anyone
to dare to warn against it, too glorious for anyone to dare to
praise it, out of fear that there might be some present who did
not have it and could not attain it. Therefore, faith is qualitatively different. It is not only the highest good, but it is a good
in which all are able to share, and the person who rejoices in
the possession of it also rejoices in the countless human race,
"because what I possess," he says, "every human being has or
can possess." The person who wishes it for another person
wishes it for himself; the person who wishes it for himself
wishes it for every human being, because that by which another person has faith is not that by which he is different from
him but is that by which he is like him; that by which he possesses it is not that by which he is different from others but
that by which he is altogether like all.

It was that kind of wish the perplexed man was seeking, one
he could wish for another person with all his heart, with all
his might, and with his whole soul,[10] a wish he would dare to
go on wishing, ever more fervently, even as his love became
ever more fervent. —That was the wish that he would wish.—

III
18

If one person went to another and said to him, "I have often heard faith extolled as the most glorious good; I feel, though, that I do not have it; the confusion of my life, the distractions of my mind, my many cares, and so much else disturb me, but this I know, that I have but one wish, one single wish, that I might share in this faith"—if the person to whom he went were favorably disposed, he would answer, "That is a beautiful and pious wish that you must not relinquish, for then I daresay it will be fulfilled." These words would seem amiable to him, and would he not gladly listen to them, because all of us like to hear talk about the fulfillment of our wishes. But time went by, and he made no progress. Then he went to another person and confided his concern and his wish also to him. He looked at him earnestly and said, "How can you be so mixed up? Your wish is not merely pious and beautiful; it ought not to be relinquished at any price. You are far closer to it than you yourself believe, since it is your duty—you shall have faith—and if you do not have it, then it is your fault and a sin."

Very likely he would be taken aback by these words and would think: Then this faith is probably not as glorious as it is made out to be, since it is acquired so easily; indeed, it would also be an absurdity. We travel the wide world over for the other goods; they lie concealed in a remote place accessible to human beings only at great risk. Or if this is not the case, their apportionment is like the water in the pool Bethesda, about which we read in Holy Scripture:[11] Once in a while an angel descends and stirs the water, and the one who comes first—ah, yes, the one who comes first—is the fortunate one. With faith, however, with the highest good, should it not be otherwise, that gaining it involves no difficulty? But he probably would think about it more earnestly, and when he had considered it very deeply he perhaps would say, "He was right, after all; that is the way it is. Those were brave words, full of pith and meaning; this is the way a person should be spoken to, for wishes are futile." Probably he would then quietly begin to move in his inner being, and every time his soul would pause at a wish, he would call to it and say: You know

III
19

that you must not wish—and thereupon he went further. When his soul became anxious, he called to it and said: When you are anxious, it is because you are wishing; anxiety is a form of wishing, and you know that you must not wish—then he went further. When he was close to despair, when he said: I cannot; everyone else can—only I cannot. Oh, that I had never heard those words, that with my grief I had been allowed to go my way undisturbed—and with my wish. Then he called to his soul and said: Now you are being crafty, for you say that you are wishing and pretend that it is a question of something external that one can wish, whereas you know that it is something internal that one can only will; you are deluding yourself, for you say: Everyone else can—only I cannot. And yet you know that that by which others are able is that by which they are altogether like you—so if it really were true that you cannot, then neither could the others. So you betray not only your own cause but, insofar as it lies with you, the cause of all people; and in your humbly shutting yourself out from their number, you are slyly destroying their power.

Then he went further. After he had been slowly and for a long time educated under the schoolmaster[12] in this way, he perhaps would have arrived at faith. "Had been educated"—as if it were another person who had done it. But this is not the case; it is only a misunderstanding, only an appearance. One person can do much for another, but he cannot give him faith. We hear all kinds of talk in this world. One person says, "I am self-educated; I do not owe anything to anyone"—and he thinks he dares to pride himself on that. Another says, "That distinguished master was my teacher, and I count it an honor to dare to call myself his pupil"—and he thinks he can take pride in that. We shall not decide how legitimate this kind of talk is, but in order to make sense it can be applied only to the superbly endowed: those who were either originally self-sufficient or at least so gifted that they could become pupils of the distinguished. But we, devout listeners, we who were too insignificant to become pupils, what should we say if a man said, "When people disdained me, I went to God; he became my teacher, and this is my salvation, my joy, my pride"—

would this be less beautiful? And yet every person can say that, may say that, can say that truthfully, and when he does not say that truthfully, then it is not because the thought is untrue but because he distorts it. Every person may say it. Whether his forehead is almost as flat as an animal's or arches more proudly than heaven, whether his arm is stretched out to command kingdoms and countries or to pick up the scanty gifts that fall from the rich man's table,[13] whether thousands obey his beck and call or not one soul pays any attention to him, whether eloquence blossoms on his lips or only unintelligible sound passes over them; whether he is the mighty male who defies the storm or the defenseless female who only seeks shelter from the gale—this has nothing to do with the matter, my listener, absolutely nothing. Every person dares to say it if he possesses faith, because this glory is the very glory of faith. And you know it, my listener;[14] you do not become afraid when it is mentioned, as if it thereby would be taken from you, as if only in the moment of parting you would gain a taste of its blessedness. Or do you not know this? Ah, then you would indeed be most unfortunate. You could not even grieve and say: The giver of good gifts passed by my door. You could not grieve and say: The storms and gales took it from me—because the giver of good gifts did not pass by your door, and the storms and gales did not take it from you, because they are unable to do that.

So, then, there was a wish, just what that perplexed man was looking for; he was no longer in the situation of need. But a new difficulty appeared, because when he wanted to wish it, he saw that that good could not be obtained by a wish; he himself could not acquire it by wishing it, although this was of minor concern to him, but neither could he give it to another by wishing it for him. Only by personally willing it could the other grasp it. So he was again constrained to let go of him, constrained to leave him to himself; his wish was as powerless as before. And yet this was not his intention. He definitely wanted to do everything for him; when I wish something for a person, I do not require that person's cooperation. The perplexed man had had similar thoughts. He almost wanted to say to the person he loved, "Now just be calm and do not worry; you have nothing to do but be cheerful, contented, and happy with all the good things I intend to wish for you. I will wish, I will not become weary of wishing; I will prevail upon the supremely good God who bestows the good gifts, I will move him with my prayers, and you will then have everything." And see, when he wanted to mention the particular good things, they seemed so dubious to him that he did not dare to wish them for the other person; you see, when he finally found what he was looking for, what he could safely wish, it could not be wished!

Again he was perplexed, again troubled, again caught in a difficulty. Is, then, all life only a contradiction; can love not explain it but only make it more difficult? He could not bear this thought; he had to seek a way out. There must be something wrong with his love. Then he perceived that however much he had loved the other person, he had nevertheless loved him in a wrong way, since if it had been possible by his wishing to procure every good thing for him, also the highest good, faith, precisely thereby he would have made him a more imperfect being. Then he discovered that life was beautiful, that it was a new gloriousness of faith that no human being can give it to another, but that every human being has what is highest, noblest, and most sacred in humankind. It is original in him, and every human being has it if he wants to have it— it is precisely the gloriousness of faith that it can be had only on this condition. Therefore, it is the only unfailing good, because it can be had only by constantly being acquired and can be acquired only by continually being generated.

Then the perplexed man was relieved, but perhaps a change had occurred in himself, in the person for whose welfare he was so concerned, in their relation to each other. They had been separated by the installation, so to speak, of the one in his rights and the positioning of the other within his limits. Their lives had become more significant than formerly, and yet they had become like strangers to each other. His heart, which previously was so rich in wishes, had now become poor; his hand, which previously was so willing to help, had now learned to be still, because he knew that it did not help. What he had come to recognize was the truth, but this truth had not made him happy. Life, then, is a contradiction; the truth cannot explain it but only make it more painful, since the more deeply he recognized it, the more separated he felt, the more helpless in his relation to the other. And yet he could not wish that it were an untruth, could not wish that he had remained ignorant of it, even though it had separated them forever and ever in a way that death itself could not have separated them. He was unable to endure this thought; he had to seek an explanation, and then he perceived that his relation to him had just then attained its true meaning.

"If by my wishing or by my gift I could bestow upon him the highest good," he said, "then I could also take it from him, even if he would not have to be afraid of that. Worse yet, if I could do that, then the very moment I gave it to him I would be taking it from him, since by giving him the highest, I would be depriving him of the highest, because the highest was that he could give it to himself. Therefore, I will thank God that this is not the way it is. My love has only lost its worries and won joy, because I know that by making every effort I still would be unable to preserve the good for him as securely as he himself will preserve it, and he must not thank me for it, either, not because I am releasing him but because he owes me nothing at all. Should I then be less happy for him now, less happy that he possesses the most precious of all gifts? Oh no, I shall only be happier, since if he were indebted to me for it, that would disturb our relationship. And if he does not possess it, then I can be very helpful to him, because I will accompany his thought and constrain him to see that it is the highest good. I will prevent it from slipping into any hiding place, so that he does not become vague about whether he is able to grasp it or not. With him, I will penetrate every anomaly until he, if he does not possess it, has but one expression that explains his unhappiness, namely, that he does not *will* it—this he cannot endure, and then he will acquire it. On the other hand, I will praise the gloriousness of faith to him, and in presupposing that he possesses it, I will bring him to will to have it as his own. Therefore, today, on the first day of the year, when thinking of the future tempts us with its manifold possibilities, I will point out to him that in faith he possesses the only power that can conquer the future. I will speak to him of the expectancy of faith."

Should we not do the same, devout listeners, and in accordance with the occasion and opportunity of the festival day speak with one another of

The Expectancy of Faith.

When we speak of the expectancy of faith, we also speak of expectancy in general; when we speak of expectancy, we naturally assume that we are speaking to those who are expecting something. But those who are expecting something are indeed the happy and fortunate ones. Are they, then, the ones we should choose to address in these sacred places rather than the unhappy ones, those who have already drawn up the balance sheet with life and expect nothing? Yes, we certainly should speak to them, if our voice were capable of it. It should be said that it was a very poor wisdom they had found, that it was easy enough to harden one's heart; the pillow of indolence on which they wanted to doze away their lives aimlessly should be snatched from them. It should be said that it was a proud distinction they had attained in life, that while all other people, no matter how happy or how troubled they became in the world, nevertheless were always ready to confess that God could indeed draw up the balance sheet, that while all other people admitted that on judgment day they would be unable to repay one in a thousand[15]—they reserved for themselves the possession of a just claim on life that had not been redeemed, a claim that at one time would have made the accounting difficult, but not for them. This is how they should be spoken to, but we would rather speak to those who are still expecting something.

Just as those who are expecting something have always been the majority in the world, so in turn their expectancy can be of so many kinds that it is very difficult to discuss them all. But all who are expecting do have one thing in common, that they are expecting something in the future, because expectancy and the future are inseparable ideas. The person who is expecting something is occupied with the future. But perhaps it is not right to be occupied with this; the complaint so often heard that people forget the present for the future is perhaps well founded. We shall not deny that this has been the case in the world, even if least often in our age, but neither shall we omit the reminder that this is precisely the greatness of human beings, the demonstration of their divine origin, that they are able to be occupied with this; because if there were no future, there would be no past, either, and if there were neither future nor past, then a human being would be in bondage like an animal, his head bowed to the earth, his soul captive to the service of the moment. In that sense, one could certainly not wish to live for the present, but very likely it was not meant in that sense when it was recommended as something great. But where should we place the limit; how much do we dare to be occupied with the future? The answer is not difficult: only when we have conquered it, only then are we able to return to the present, only then do our lives find meaning in it. But this is indeed impossible. The future is indeed everything, and the present is a part of it—how could we have conquered the whole before even coming to the first part of it? How could we return from this victory to something that preceded it? Is it not so that thought is creating a misplaced difficulty for itself? By no means. The situation is just as is stated here, for we dare not praise every occupation with the future. The life of the person who totally relinquishes it becomes strong in the present only in an unworthy sense; the person who does not conquer it has one more enemy to incapacitate him in the battle with the present. Therefore, only the life of the one who conquers the future becomes strong and sound.

The ability to be occupied with the future is, then, a sign of the nobility of human beings; the struggle with the future is the most ennobling. He who struggles with the present struggles with a particular thing against which he can use his total energy. Therefore, if a person had nothing else with which to struggle, it would be possible for him to go victoriously

III
24

through his whole life without learning to know himself or his power. He who battles with the future has a more dangerous enemy; he cannot remain ignorant of himself, since he is battling with himself. The future is not; it borrows its power from him himself, and when it has tricked him out of that it presents itself externally as the enemy he has to encounter. No matter how strong a person is, no person is stronger than himself. This is why we frequently see people who have been victorious in all the battles in life become helpless and their arms become powerless when they encounter a future enemy. Accustomed, perhaps, to challenge the whole world to combat, they had now found an enemy, a nebulous shape, that was able to terrify them. This may be why frequently the men whom God called to be tried in struggle went from a worse battle into the battle that seemed so terrible to others; they may at times have smiled in the heat of the struggle when they thought of the invisible battle that had preceded this one. They were admired in the world, because it was thought that they had triumphed in the most dangerous battle, and yet for them this was but a game compared with the preceding one that no one saw. It would be natural, of course, for the person stronger than others to win in the struggle with them, but it is also natural that no one is stronger than himself. When a person struggles with the future, he learns that however strong he is otherwise, there is one enemy that is stronger— himself; there is one enemy he cannot conquer by himself, and that is himself.

But why describe this struggle with the future as being so perilous? "Old or young, have not all of us experienced something? The future is not utterly new, because there is nothing new under the sun[16]—the future is the past. Old or young, do we not all have experience? We will attire ourselves in it; we will follow the tracks of conjecture and the guidance of guessing. We will conquer with the power of inferences, and thus armed we boldly face the future." It is certainly good for a person to be armed when he goes into combat, and even better to be appropriately armed for the specific combat. If a man who is going to compete in a race were to don heavy armor, he certainly would be well armed, but his armor would scarcely be of any advantage. Is it not the same with the weapon of one who is to struggle with the future, since experience is a double-tongued friend who says one thing now and something else later, and guessing is a deceitful guide who abandons one when he is needed most, and conjecture is a clouded eye that does not see very far, and inference is a snare that is more likely to snare oneself than someone else. Moreover, those weapons are difficult to use, because, inasmuch as the experiencing soul did not remain untouched during the experience, fear accompanies guessing, anxiety conjecture, and uneasiness inference. So we probably would be well armed if we arrayed ourselves in experience, but not for the impending struggle, the struggle with the future; we would try to change this into something present, something particular; but the future is not a particular, but the whole.

How, then, should we face the future? When the sailor is out on the ocean, when everything is changing all around him, when the waves are born and die, he does not stare down into the waves, because they are changing. He looks up at the stars. Why? Because they are faithful; they have the same location now that they had for our ancestors and will have for generations to come. By what means does he conquer the changeable? By the eternal. By the eternal, one can conquer the future, because the eternal is the ground of the future, and therefore through it the future can be fathomed.

What, then, is the eternal power in a human being? It is faith. What is the expectancy of faith? Victory—or, as Scripture so earnestly and so movingly teaches us, that all things must serve for good those who love God.[17] But an expectancy of the future that expects victory—this has indeed conquered the future. The believer, therefore, is finished with the future before he begins with the present, because what has been conquered can no longer disturb, and this victory can only make someone stronger for the present work.

The expectancy of faith, then, is victory! The cheerful disposition that has not yet tasted life's adversities, that has not been educated in the school of sorrow, has not been formed by the dubious wisdom of experience, approves of this expectancy with its whole heart, since it expects victory in everything, in all battles and spiritual trials—or, more correctly, it expects to be victorious without a struggle. We would not wish to be the austere figure that has to halt the young person on his path. We would rather be prepared to be a comfort to him when he has learned that this expectancy, however beautiful, was not the expectancy of faith; we would rather be the one who will call him to battle when he feels powerless, the one who will have victory beckon him when he thinks all is lost. On the other hand, the troubled person, who has scarcely dried his tears over the present loss, forms the future otherwise, and the future is indeed light and elusive and more pliable than any clay, and consequently everyone forms it entirely as he himself is formed. The troubled person expects no victory; he has all too sadly felt his loss, and even if it belongs to the past, he takes it along, expecting that the future will at least grant him the peace to be quietly occupied with his pain.

The man of experience frowns on the behavior of both of these. If one has almost every good one could wish for, then one ought to be prepared to have the troubles of life visit also the home of the happy; if one has lost everything, then one ought to consider that time reserves many a priceless cure for the sick soul, that the future, like a fond mother, also hides good gifts: in happiness one ought to be prepared to a certain degree for unhappiness, in unhappiness, to a certain degree for happiness. Nor are his words without result, because the happy one who is not superficial and the troubled one who is not in despair will both lend a willing ear to what he says, and both of them will readily organize their lives according to his guidance. The happy one contemplates the good things in his possession. Some of them he thinks he can lose without pain, others in such a way that he can still easily recover from the pain. There is only one particular good he cannot lose without losing his happiness; he cannot lose it to a certain degree without losing it totally, and thereby his happiness. He will be prepared, then, to lose the good things that he has and in this way, according to the experienced man's advice, he is prepared for a certain degree of unhappiness. But the man of experience said: to a certain degree. These words could indeed also apply to that one good that he could not lose without losing his happiness, could not lose to a certain degree without losing it totally. The man of experience will not interpret his words; he repeats them unchanged, inflexible. He leaves the explanation and the application up to the person whom they are supposed to guide. Then the happy one becomes no less perplexed than the troubled one. This phrase, "to a certain degree," which is supposed to be the watchword, becomes the binding force that ensnares them, and the phrase resounds, has no sympathy, is not concerned about their efforts to understand it, disregards their pleas for an explanation. Experience, which was supposed to guide them, engendered doubt; the words of the man of experience were dubious words.

The believer, however, says: I expect victory. These words are not without result, either, since the happy one who was not superficial and the troubled one who was not in despair both lend a willing ear to his words. Happiness returns again to the happy disposition; its expectancy is of victory, victory in all strife, in all spiritual trials, because experience had taught that there could be battle. But with the help of faith, it expects victory in all of them. Only for a moment does it pause. "It is too much," it says. "It is impossible; life cannot be that glorious; no matter how golden youth was in its supreme happiness, this surely surpasses the most joyous hope of youth." — Yes, it certainly does surpass even youth's most joyous hope, and yet it is so, even if not exactly as you suppose. You speak of many victories, but faith expects only one, or, more correctly, it expects victory. Suppose someone had heard of a teaching that was able to give everyone what is needed, and he then were to say, "But that is impossible—all that a human being such as I needs, all the many things that for me are necessities." Then the person who directed him to Holy Scripture would rightly dare to testify of it that there he would find what he needed, and yet the seeker would discover that it was not quite as he had thought. Scripture says: One thing is need-

III
28

ful.[18] So also with faith: when you talk about many victories, you are like the person who talks about the many necessities. Only one thing is needful, and faith expects victory.

But victory it does expect, and therefore it is joyful and un-daunted—and why not, since it expects victory! But I detect a voice, one you probably know also, my listener. It says, "This is good to hear; these are big words and euphonious turns of speech, but in truth the earnestness of life teaches something else." What, then, did the earnestness of life teach you, you who speak this way? Is it not true that it taught you that your wishes would not be fulfilled, that your desires would not be gratified, your appetites would not be heeded, your cravings would not be satisfied? This it taught you, all this, which we shall not discuss, and it also taught you to come to people's aid with deceitful words, to suck faith and trust out of their hearts, and to do this in the sacred name of earnestness. Why did it teach you this? Could it not have taught you something else? When two people learn different things from life, it can be because they experience different things, but it can also be because they themselves were different. For example, if two children were brought up together and always shared the same things in such a way that when one was singled out for dis-tinction, the other was also, when one was reprimanded, the other was also, when one was punished, the other was also, they could still learn altogether different things. The one could learn not to be proud every time he was singled out for distinction, to humble himself under admonition every time he was reprimanded, to let himself be healed by suffering every time he was punished; the other could learn to be haughty every time he was singled out for distinction, to be indignant every time he was reprimanded, to store up secret anger every time he was punished. So also with you. If you had loved people, then the earnestness of life might have taught you not to be strident but to become silent, and when you were in distress at sea and did not see land, then at least not to involve others in it; it might have taught you to smile at least as long as you believed anyone sought in your face an explanation, a witness. Then life might have given you the somber joy of seeing others succeed where you did not, the comfort that you had contributed your part by stifling within you the scream of anguish that would disturb them. Why did you not learn this? Since you did not learn this, we are unable to heed your words. We do not judge you for doubting, because doubt is a crafty passion, and it can certainly be difficult to tear oneself out of its snares. What we require of the doubter is that he be silent. He surely perceived that doubt did not make him happy—why then confide to others what will make them just as unhappy? And what does he win by this communication? He loses himself and makes others unhappy. He loses himself, instead of perhaps finding rest in silence by preferring to bear his solitary pain quietly rather than to become strident, to become important in people's eyes by courting the honor and distinction that so many crave—to doubt, or at least to have doubted. Doubt is a deep and crafty passion, but he whose soul is not gripped by it so inwardly that he becomes speechless is only shamming this passion; therefore what he says is not only false in itself but above all on his lips. This is why we pay no attention to him.

The expectancy of faith, then, is victory. The doubt that comes from the outside does not disturb it, since it disgraces itself by speaking. Yet doubt is guileful, on secret paths it sneaks around a person, and when faith is expecting victory, doubt whispers that this expectancy is a deception. "An expectancy without a specified time and place is nothing but a deception; in that way one may always go on waiting; such an expectancy is a circle into which the soul is bewitched and from which it cannot escape." In the expectancy of faith, the soul is indeed prevented from falling out of itself, as it were, into multiplicity; it remains in itself, but it would be the worst evil that could befall a person if it escaped from this cycle. By no means, however, can it be inferred from this that faith's expectancy is a deception. True, the person who expects something particular can be deceived in his expectancy, but this does not happen to the believer. When the world commences its drastic ordeal, when the storms of life crush youth's exuberant expectancy, when existence, which seemed so affectionate and gentle, changes into a pitiless proprietor who demands everything back, everything that it gave in such a way that it can take it back—then the believer most likely looks at himself and his life with sadness and pain, but he still says, "There is an expectancy that the whole world cannot take from me; it is the expectancy of faith, and this is victory. I am not deceived, since I did not believe that the world would keep the promise it seemed to be making to me; my expectancy was not in the world but in God. This expectancy is not deceived; even now I sense its victory more gloriously and more joyfully than I sense all the pain of loss. If I were to lose this expectancy, then all would be lost. Even now I have been victorious, victorious in my expectancy, and my expectancy is victory."

Was it not this way in life? If there was someone to whom you felt drawn so strongly that you dared to say, "I have faith in him"—is it not true that when everything went according to your wish, or if not entirely according to your wish at least in such a way that you could easily bring it into conformity with your conceptions, then you had faith in him the way others also had faith in him? But when the inexplicable happened, the inconceivable, then the others fell away, or, more correctly (let us not confuse the language), they showed that they never did have faith in him. Not so with you. You perceived that it was not on the circumstance that you had based your faith, that you could explain what happened, since in that case your faith would have been based on your insight and, far from being a devotedness, would instead have been a confidence in yourself. You thought it would be a disgrace for you to relinquish it, because just as you supposed that the words, "I have faith in him" in your mouth had a meaning different from what they had when the others said them, so you felt that the change could not possibly make you do the same as the others, unless your faith originally had not meant more. So you continued to have faith. Yet you may have been wrong in doing so—not in having faith, not in having faith in this way, but in having faith in a human being in this way. Perhaps the inexplicable was easily explained; perhaps there was a sorrowful certainty that witnessed so powerfully that your faith simply became a beautiful fantasy that you ought to have given up. We do not know. But this we do know—that if in this faith you forgot that there is a higher faith, then, despite its beauty, this faith would only be to your ruination. But if you had faith in God, how then would your faith ever be changed into a beautiful fantasy you had better give up? Would he then be able to be changed, he in whom there is no change or shadow of variation?[19] Would he not be faithful,[20] he through whom every human being who is faithful is faithful; would he not be without guile, he through whom you yourself had faith? Would there ever be an explanation that could explain otherwise than that he is truthful and keeps his promises? And yet we see that people forget this.

III
31

When all their efforts are crowned with success, when their days are pleasant, when in a singular way they feel in harmony with everything around them, then they have faith, then in their happiness they most likely do not always forget to thank God, because everyone will usually be thankful for the good he receives, but everyone's heart is also indulgent enough to want to decide for itself what is the good. When everything changes, when grief supersedes joy, then they fall away, then they lose faith, or, more correctly—let us not confuse the language—then they show that they have never had it.

But you did not do this, my listener. When you caught yourself being changed by all the changes occurring around you, you said, "I confess, now I see that what I called my faith was only something I imagined. I arrogantly fancied that I was doing the utmost one person can do in his relation to another, to have faith in him, and doing what is even much more exalted and beautiful, more blessed than language can describe, to have faith in God. To all my other joys, I also added this one, and yet my faith, as I now see, was only a fleeting emotion, a mirroring of my earthly happiness. But I am not going to build myself up [opbygge] through presumptuousness and meaningless talk; I will not say that I have lost faith; I will not push the blame onto the world or onto others or perhaps even accuse God." This is how you tried to stop yourself, my listener, when you were about to go astray in grief. You did not harden your heart; you were not so foolish as to fancy that if this particular thing had not happened you would have kept your faith, or so contemptible as to want to seek fellowship with this wisdom. This is why you regained, even if slowly, the expectancy of faith. Then when everything went wrong for you, when everything you had slowly built up vanished instantly into thin air and you laboriously had to begin all over again, when your arm was weak and your walk unsteady, then you still held fast to the expectancy of faith—which is victory. Even if you did not tell others, lest they mock you because in all your misery you still expected victory, you nevertheless hid your expectancy in your innermost heart. "The happy days are surely able to embellish my faith," you said; "I adorn it with the wreaths of joy—but they cannot demonstrate my faith; the hard times can surely bring tears to my eyes and grief to my mind, but they still cannot rob me of my faith." And even if adversity did not stop, your soul remained gentle. "It is really beautiful," you said, "that God does not want to appear to me in visible things; we are parted only to meet again. I could not wish to remain a child who demands demonstrations, signs, and wondrous acts every day. If I went on being a child, I could not love with all my strength and with my whole soul.[21] Now we are separated; we do not see each other every day, but we meet secretly in the victorious moment of faithful expectancy."

The expectancy of faith, then, is victory, and this expectancy cannot be disappointed, unless a person deceives himself by depriving himself of expectancy, as the person does who foolishly supposes that he has lost his faith, or foolishly supposes that something in particular has taken it from him, or tries to delude himself with the idea that there is something in particular that is capable of robbing a person of his faith, and finds satisfaction in the conceited thought that this is precisely what has befallen him, finds joy in alarming others with the assertion that there is something like that, something that mocks what is noblest in a person, something that authorizes one who has experience with it to mock others.

Yet someone may say: These words are certainly coherent and internally consistent, but since one does not go further with their help, they are foolish and futile. —One does not go further. If a person wished to go further than to be victorious, then might he indeed lose the victory? Would it be so foolish and empty for a person to become really aware of whether he has faith or not? But when I say, "I have faith," it can all too often be obscure to me what I mean by that. Perhaps I am wrong; maybe I am just creating my own notion of the future; perhaps I am wishing, hoping, longing for something, craving, coveting; perhaps I am sure of the future, and since I do this, it may seem to me that I have faith, although I still do not. But when I ask myself the question: Do you expect victory?—then every obscurity becomes more difficult, then I perceive that not only the person who expects absolutely nothing does not have faith, but also the person who expects something particular or who bases his expectancy on something particular. And should this not be important, inasmuch as no one can be wholly and indivisibly in the present before he is finished with the future? But one is finished with the future only by conquering it, but this is precisely what faith does, since its expectancy is victory. Every time I catch my soul not expecting victory, I know that I do not have faith. When I know that, I also know what I must do, because although it is no easy matter to have faith, the first condition, nevertheless, for my arriving at faith is that I become aware of whether I have it or not. The reason we so often go astray is that we seek assurance of our expectancy instead of faith's assurance that we have faith. The person of faith demands no substantiation of his expectancy. He says, "If I were to presume something to be a substantiation, then in substantiating my expectancy it would also refute it. My soul is not insensitive to the joy or the pain of the particular, but, God be praised, it is not the case that the particular can substantiate or refute the expectancy of faith." God be praised! Time can neither substantiate nor refute it, because faith expects an eternity. And today, on the first day of the year, when the thought of the future presses in upon me, I will not enervate my soul

III
33

with multifarious expectancy, will not break it up into all sorts of notions; I will integrate it sound and happy and, if possible, face the future. Let it bring what it will and must bring. Many an expectancy will be disappointed, many fulfilled—so it will be; experience has taught me this. But there is one expectancy that will not be disappointed—experience has not taught me this, but neither has it ever had the authority to deny it—this is the expectancy of faith, and this is victory.

There is a little phrase that is familiar enough to congregations, even though not always heeded by them. Little and insignificant as it seems, it nevertheless is pregnant with meaning; it is quiet and yet so stirring, calm and yet so full of longing. It is the phrase "at last,"[22] for in this way end many of the sacred collects that are read in the churches: "and then at last obtain eternal salvation." The older person among us, who is almost within reach of the goal, gazes back in thought over the road he has traveled. He recollects the course of events, and the faded figures become vivid again. He is overwhelmed by the abundant content of his experience; he is weary and says: and then at last obtain eternal salvation. The younger person, who still stands at the beginning of the road, gazes in thought out over the long course, experiences in thought what is to come: the painful privations, the secret troubles, the sad longings, the fearful spiritual trials. He is weary of mind and says: and then at last obtain eternal salvation. Yes, it would indeed be a great gift if a person could rightly use this phrase; yet no person learns this from another, but each one individually learns it only from and through God. Therefore we want to commit our minds and our thoughts to you, Father in heaven, so that our souls might never be captivated in such a way by the joys of life or by its afflictions that it would forget this liberating phrase and so that it might not too frequently be impatience and inner disquiet that bring this phrase to our lips, so that our souls in our final hour—when this phrase like a faithful friend has accompanied us in life's many circumstances, has adapted itself to us yet without being untrue to itself, has been our comfort, our hope, our joy, our exultation, has sounded loud and exciting to us, soft and lulling, has spoken to us admonishingly and reprovingly, encouragingly and persuasively—will then be carried away from the world, as it were, on this phrase to that place where we shall comprehend its full meaning, just as it is the same God who, after having led us by his hand through the world, draws back his hand and opens his arms to receive in them the yearning soul.[23] Amen!

EVERY GOOD AND EVERY PERFECT GIFT
IS FROM ABOVE [24]

PRAYER

From your hand, O God, we are willing to receive everything. You reach it out, your mighty hand, and catch the wise
in their foolishness.[25] You open it, your gentle hand, and satisfy with blessing everything that lives.[26] And even if it seems
that your arm is shortened, increase our faith[27] and our trust
so that we might still hold fast to you. And if at times it seems
that you draw your hand away from us, oh, then we know it
is only because you close it, that you close it only to save the
more abundant blessing in it, that you close it only to open it
again and satisfy with blessing everything that lives. Amen.

Every good gift and every perfect gift is from above and comes down from the Father of lights, with whom there is no change or shadow of variation. According to his own counsel, he brought us forth by the word of truth, that we should be a first fruit of his creation. Therefore, my beloved brethren, let every man be quick to hear, slow to speak, slow to anger, because a man's anger does not work what is righteous before God. Therefore put away all filthiness and all remnants of wickedness and receive with meekness the word that is implanted in you and that is powerful for making your souls blessed.

III
38

Every good gift and every perfect gift is from above and comes down from the Father of lights, with whom there is no change or shadow of variation. These words are so beautiful, so appealing, so moving, that it surely would not be the fault of the words if they found no access in the listener's ears, no resonance in his heart. They are by one of the Lord's apostles, and if we ourselves have not deeply perceived their meaning, we nevertheless dare to trust that they are not casual and idle words, a flowery expression of a flimsy thought, but that they are faithful and unfailing, tried and tested, as was the life of the apostle who wrote them. They are not spoken incidentally but with special emphasis, not in passing but accompanied by an urgent admonition: Do not go astray, my beloved brethren (v. 16). We dare, then, to have the confidence that they have not only the power to lift up the soul but also the strength to carry it, these words that carried an apostle through a turbulent life. They are not spoken without any bearing on other words; it is to warn against the terribly mistaken belief that God would tempt [*friste*] a person, to warn against the heart's delusion that wants to tempt God, that the apostle says: Do not go astray, my beloved brethren. We dare, then, to be assured that the words are also mighty to expose delusion and mighty to halt errant thinking.

Every good and every perfect gift is from above and comes down from the Father of lights, with whom there is no change or shadow of variation. These words have been repeated again and again in the world, and yet many people go on living as if they had never heard them, and if they had heard them, the effect on them would perhaps have been disturbing. Free from care, they go their way; a friendly fate makes everything easy for them. Every wish is fulfilled; their every enterprise prospers. Without understanding how, they are in the midst of the movement of life, a link in the chain that binds a past to a later time; unconcerned about how it happens, they are carried along on the wave of the present. Reposing in the law of nature that lets a human life grow up in the world as it spreads a carpet of flowers over the earth, they go on living happy and contented amid the changes of life, at no moment desire to tear themselves free from them and honestly give everyone his due: thankfulness to the one to whom they attribute the good gifts, help to the one they think requires it and in the way that they think will be best for him. That there are good and perfect gifts they undoubtedly know, and they also know where they come from, because the earth gives its yield and heaven provides rain early and late,[28] and their relatives and friends intend the best for them, and their plans, wise and sensible, prosper, which is natural, since they are wise and sensible. For them, life has no riddle, and yet their life is a riddle, a dream, and the apostle's earnest admonition, "Do not go astray," does not halt them. They have no time to pay attention to it or to the words—after all, what does the wave care about whence it comes or whither it goes?[29] Or if certain ones among them, deliberating on higher things, paid attention to the apostle's words, they would soon be finished with them.

III
39

They would let their thought be occupied with them for a moment and then would say, "Now we have understood them; now bring on new thoughts that we have not understood." Nor would they be wrong, since the apostle's words are not difficult, and yet by wishing to abandon them after having understood them, they would demonstrate that they had not understood them.

Every good and every perfect gift is from above and comes down from the Father of lights, with whom there is no change or shadow of variation. These words are very soothing and alleviating, and yet how many were they who really knew how to absorb the rich nourishment of comfort from them, rightly knew how to assimilate it! The troubled ones, those whom life did not allow to age and who die as children, whom it did not suckle with the milk of success but weaned early; the grieving, whose thought endeavored to penetrate through the changing to the lasting—these people were sensitive to the apostle's words and heeded them. The more they were capable of sinking their souls into them, of forgetting everything because of them, the more they felt themselves strengthened and filled with confidence. But it was soon apparent that this strength was a deception. However much confidence they won, they still did not win the power to penetrate life; at times the troubled mind and the confused thought turned again to that rich comfort, at times they perceived the contradiction again. Finally, it may have seemed to them that these words were almost dangerous to their peace. They awakened in them a confidence that was continually disappointed; they gave them wings that admittedly could lift them up to God but were of no help to them in their walk through life. They did not deny the inexhaustible comfort in the words, but they almost feared it even though they eulogized it. If someone owned a magnificent piece of jewelry and there was never a time when he would deny that it was magnificent, he presumably would take it out once in a while, delight in it, but soon he would say, "I cannot wear this for everyday, and it is futile to wait for the festive occasion that would really be adequate for it." He no doubt would put the piece of jewelry away and think sadly that he possessed such a piece of jewelry and that life did not provide him with the occasion to take it out with unqualified joy.

So they sat there in quiet sorrow and did not harden themselves against the comfort in those words. They were humble enough to admit that life is a dark saying,[30] and just as they in their thoughts were swift to listen for a clarifying word, so were they also slow to speak, slow to anger. They did not have the audacity to throw the words away, if only the opportune hour would come. Once it came, they would be saved, so they believed, and you, my listener, said it was bound to happen. Or is there only one spirit who witnesses in heaven and no spirit who witnesses on earth![31] Do only heaven and the spirit that flees the earth know that God is good; does life on earth know nothing of it! Is there no harmony between what happens in heaven and what happens on earth! Is there joy in heaven, only sorrow on earth, or only the news that there is joy in heaven! Does God in heaven bring out the good gifts and lay them away for us in heaven so that we can receive them sometime in the hereafter! This is the way you may have talked in your heart's bewilderment. You did not demand that on your behalf there should be signs and miraculous acts. You did not childishly demand that every one of your wishes should be fulfilled; you only asked for a witness, be it early or late, because your troubled soul concealed a wish. If this were granted, then everything would be fine, then you would give thanks and praise forevermore, then the festive occasion would have come, then you would wholeheartedly witness to the words that all good and all perfect gifts come from above.

But see, this was denied you, and your soul became agitated, tossed about by the passion of the wish; it did not become defiant and wild, you did not impatiently throw off the leash of humility, you had not forgotten that you are on earth and God is in heaven. With humble prayers, with burning zeal, you tried, as it were, to tempt God: This wish is so important to me; everything depends on it—my joy, my peace, my future; for me it is so very important; for God it is so easy, since he, after all, is almighty. But it was not granted. You tried in vain to calm down; in your fruitless restlessness, you tried everything; you climbed the dizzy peaks of presentiment to see whether you could spy any possibility. If you thought you spied one, you were right there with your prayers, so that with their help you could turn the apparent into actuality. But it was a mirage. You climbed down again and abandoned yourself to the anesthetizing dullness of sorrow—surely it would come in time—and morning came, and then night, but the day you desired did not break. And yet you certainly did everything; you prayed early and late, more and more fervently, more and more temptingly. Alas, and still it did not happen.

Then you renounced it; you wanted to charge your soul to be patient;[32] you wanted to wait in quiet longing if only you could win a certitude that eternity would bring you your wish, bring you the delight of your eye and the craving of your heart. Alas, but this certitude, too, was denied you. But then when the busy thoughts had worked themselves weary, when your fruitless wishes had exhausted your soul, perhaps then your being grew more calm, perhaps then your mind, secretly and imperceptibly, developed in itself the meekness that is receptive to the word that was implanted within you and that was capable of blessing your soul, the word that all good and all perfect gifts come from above. Then no doubt you confessed in all humility that God surely did not deceive you when he accepted your earthly wishes and foolish desires, exchanged them for you and instead gave you divine comfort and holy thoughts; that he did not treat you unfairly when he denied you a wish but in compensation created this faith in your heart, when instead of a wish, which, even if it would bring everything, at most was able to give you the whole world, he gave you a faith by which you won God and overcame the whole world.[33] Then you acknowledged with humble joy that God was still the almighty Creator of heaven and earth, who not only created the world from nothing but did something even more marvelous—from your impatient and inconstant heart he created the imperishable substance of a quiet spirit.[34] Then you confessed with shame that it was

good, so very good for you that God did not let himself be
tempted; then you comprehended the apostle's admonition
and why it is linked to the fallacy of wanting to tempt God.
Then you perceived how foolish your behavior was. You
wanted God's ideas about what was best for you to coincide
with your ideas, but you also wanted him to be the almighty
Creator of heaven and earth so that he could properly fulfill
your wish. And yet, if he were to share your ideas, he would
cease to be the almighty Father. In your childish impatience,
you wanted, so to speak, to distort God's eternal nature, and
you were blinded enough to delude yourself, as if you would
be benefited if God in heaven did not know better than you
yourself what was beneficial for you, as if you would not
some day discover to your horror that you had wished what
no human being would be able to endure if it happened.

III
42

Let us for a moment speak foolishly and in a human way.[35]
Suppose there was someone whom you really trusted because
you believed he had your welfare at heart; but you had one
idea of what was beneficial for you, and he had another. Then
would you not try to persuade him? You would perhaps plead
with him and implore him to grant your wish. But when he
persisted in his refusal, you would stop imploring him and
you would say: If by my pleas I moved him to do what he did
not consider to be right, then something even more terrible
would happen. I would have been weak enough to make him
just as weak; then I would have lost him and my trust in him,
although in the moment of intoxication I would have called
his weakness love.

Or perhaps this was not the case with you; perhaps you
were too old to nourish childish ideas about God, too mature
to think humanly about him; you perhaps wished to move
him by your defiance. You probably admitted that life was a
dark saying, but you were not, in keeping with the apostle's
admonition, swift to hear a clarifying word; contrary to his
admonition, you were swift to anger. If life is a dark saying,
then so be it; you would not trouble yourself about the explanation—and your heart grew hard. Externally you may have
been calm, perhaps friendly, your conversation even benevo-

lent, but internally, in the secret workshop of your thoughts, you said—no, you did not say it, but there you heard a voice say: God does tempt a person. And the chill of despair froze your spirit, and its death brooded over your heart. If at times life stirred again in your inner being, savage voices raged there, voices that were not your own but nevertheless came from your inner being. Why was your complaint so vehement, your scream so penetrating; why was even your prayer so aggressive? Was it not because you believed that your sufferings were so great, your griefs so crushing, and consequently your complaint so legitimate, your voice so powerful that it was bound to resound through the heavens and call God out of his hidden depths, where it seemed to you he sat calm and indifferent and ignored the world and its vicissitudes? But heaven shuts itself off to such presumptuous talk, and it is also written that God is not tempted by anyone.[36] Your words were powerless, as powerless as your thought, as powerless as your arm, and heaven did not hear your prayer; but when you then humbled yourself under God's mighty hand[37] and, crushed in spirit, sighed: My God, my God, great is my sin, too great to be forgiven—then heaven opened again, then God, as a prophet[38] writes, looked down[39] from his window at you and said: Yet a little while;[40] yet a little while and I shall renew the countenance of the earth[41]—and see, your countenance was renewed, and God's compassionate grace had loved forth [*fremelsket*][42] in your barren mind the meekness that is receptive to the words. Then you humbly confessed before God that God tempts no one, but that everyone is tempted when he is beguiled and drawn by his own cravings,[43] just as you were tempted by proud, presumptuous, and defiant thoughts. Then you were horrified by your aberration, that the idea that God tempts a person is supposed to explain life, because then to you life would have become a dark saying, then you would have listened to this explanation that, as you would have to admit, simply made everything inexplicable. Then, humbled and shamed, you confessed that it was good that God did not allow himself to be tempted, that he was the almighty God who can crush every arrogant thought, that in your despair you had not found an explanation of life's dark saying that no one could maintain.

Every good and every perfect gift is from above and comes down from the Father of lights, with whom there is no change or shadow of variation. These words are so comprehensible, so simple, and yet how many were they who really understood them, really understood that they were a commemorative coin more magnificent than all the world's treasure, but also a small coin that is usable in the daily affairs of life. III 44

"Every good and every perfect gift is from God." The apostle uses two phrases. "Every good gift," he says, and thereby signifies the inner nature of the gift, that it is sound and blessed fruit with no concealed unwholesome or harmful additive. "Every perfect gift," says the apostle, and thereby signifies the more intimate relation into which, by the help of God, the good gift enters with the individual who receives it, so that the good in and by itself does not become harmful and ruinous to him. Two other phrases correspond to these. "The gift is from above and comes down from the Father of lights." "It is from above," says the apostle, and thereby turns the believer's thoughts up toward heaven, where every good has its home, the blessing that satisfies the mouth and the blessing that satisfies the heart; up toward heaven, from which the good spirits come to rescue people;[44] up toward heaven, from which good intentions return as divine gifts. "From the Father of lights," says the apostle, and thereby signifies that God penetrates everything with his eternal clarity, that he understands people's thoughts from afar[45] and is very familiar with all their paths, that his eternal love hurries ahead and prepares everything[46] and in this way makes "the good gift" into a "perfect gift." God in heaven is not like a person who, if he had a good gift to give, yet gave it away in the dark, with uncertainty—glad, of course, that it was a good gift and he a cheerful giver,[47] but also sad because he did not really know whether it would really be of benefit to the other.

"Every good and every perfect gift," says the apostle. "Every"—what does that mean? Does the apostle mean thereby that the firmament of heaven is a vast storeroom and that nevertheless all that heaven contains is good gifts? Does he mean that God takes from this rich store and now and then, according to the time and the occasion, sends now to this one, now to that one, to one more, to the other less, to one nothing at all, but what he sends is good and perfect? Let us look at the next words: "with whom there is no change or shadow of variation." If that is what the apostle had wanted to convey, he presumably would have replaced these words with "from the God of love, the God of compassion and comfort, the giver of good gifts," or however else he would have expressed it, better and more pithily than we are able to do it. He presumably would have exhorted the believers especially to gratitude according to the time and the occasion, in proportion to the good gifts apportioned to them. This he does not do. What he admonishes against is the aberration of thinking that God would tempt a person, the aberration of thinking that God would let himself be tempted. What he drives home is that God is the constant who remains the same, whereas everything else changes. What he exhorts us to is to love God in such a way that our nature might become like his, that we might gain God in constancy and rescue our soul in patience.[48] He says nothing in these words about the character of the specific gifts, but he speaks of the eternal relation of God to the believer. When joy transfigures life and everything is bright and clear, he warns against this transfiguration and advises that it be referred to the Father of lights, with whom there is no shadow of variation. When sorrow throws its shadow over our lives, when discouragement fogs our eyes, when the cloud of concern takes him away from our eyes,[49] then comes the apostle's admonition that with God there is no shadow of variation. What the apostle warns against is intrusion upon the blessed nature of God through the agitation of temptation, as if his heart had become either cold or weak. What he drives home is that just as God's almighty hand made everything good,[50] so he, the Father of lights, ever constant, at every moment makes everything good, makes everything a good and perfect gift for everyone who has enough heart to be humble, enough heart to be trustful.

But doubt is sly and guileful, not at all loudmouthed and defiant, as it is sometimes proclaimed to be; it is unassuming and crafty, not brash and presumptuous, and the more unassuming it is, the more dangerous it is. It does not deny that these words are beautiful, that they are comforting; if it did that, the heart would rebel against it; it merely says that the words are difficult, almost enigmatic. It wants to help the troubled mind to understand the apostolic saying that every good and every perfect gift is from God. "What does this mean? What else but that everything that comes from God is a good and a perfect gift, and that everything that is a good and a perfect gift is from God." This explanation certainly is simple and natural, and yet doubt has craftily concealed itself in it. Consequently, it goes on: "Therefore, if a person is to be able to find peace in these words in his lifetime, he must be able to decide either what it is that comes from God or what may legitimately and truly be termed a good and a perfect gift. But how is this possible? Is every human life, then, a continuous chain of miracles? Or is it possible for a human being's understanding to make its way through the incalculable series of secondary causes and effects, to penetrate everything in between, and in that way to find God? Or is it possible for a human being's understanding to decide with certainty what is a good and a perfect gift for him? Does it not run aground on this again and again? How often has humankind, how often has every single person, had the painful experience that wanting to venture something that was denied to one is a folly that does not go unpunished?" With that, doubt was all through with its explanation of the words—and also all through with the words. It had changed the apostolic, authoritative saying into empty talk that passed without pith and meaning from mouth to mouth. It was sufficiently humble not to insist that the words should be blotted out and consigned to eternal forgetfulness; it wrested them from the heart and handed them over to the lips.

Was this the way it was, my listener? Are these words per-

III
46

haps not to be attributed to an apostle of the Lord? Are they
perhaps to be attributed to that subheavenly spiritual host?[51]
Did a curse rest upon them so that they would be homeless in
the world and find no abode in a human heart; was it their
destiny to confuse people? Is it not possible to halt that alarming movement in which thinking exhausts itself and yet goes
no further? Was it perhaps nevertheless true that God does
tempt a person, even if in no other way than by proclaiming a
word that only confuses his thinking?

The Apostle Paul says, "Everything created by God is good
if it is received with thankfulness."[52] It is mainly to admonish
against an earthly shrewdness that would enslave believers in
ceremonies that the apostle says these words. Yet what does
the apostle do? He raises the believer's mind above earthly and
finite cares, above worldly shrewdness and doubt, by means
of a devout observation that we always ought to thank God,
since the thankfulness[53] of which the apostle speaks cannot be
a thankfulness that one person ought to show another, and
those false teachers also believed that by contravening the ceremony the believer sinned against God. Should not the same
hold for every person's relation to God, that every gift is a
good and a perfect gift when it is received with thankfulness?

Is it not true, my listener, that you interpreted those apostolic words in this way and that you were not baffled about
what was a good and a perfect gift or about what came from
God, because every gift, you said, is good if it is received with
thankfulness from the hand of God, and from God comes
every good and every perfect gift. You did not anxiously
question what it is that comes from God; you happily and
boldly said: This, for which I thank God. You did not trouble
your mind with deliberating over what was a good and a perfect gift, because you confidently said: I know that this for
which I am thanking God is that, and therefore I thank him
for it. You interpreted the apostolic words in the expanding of
your heart. You did not insist on learning much from life; you
wished to learn but one thing: always to thank God, and
thereby to learn to understand one thing: that all things serve
for good those who love God.[54]

Are, then, the apostolic words that every good and every perfect gift is from above and comes down from the Father of lights a dark and difficult saying? And if you think that you cannot understand it, do you dare to maintain that you have wanted to understand it? When you had doubts about what came from God or about what was a good and a perfect gift, did you risk the venture? And when the light sparkle of joy beckoned you, did you thank God for it? And when you were so strong that you felt you needed no help, did you then thank God? And when your allotted portion was little [*liden*], did you thank God? And when your allotted portion was sufferings [*Lidelser*], did you thank God? And when your wish was denied, did you thank God? And when you yourself had to deny your wish, did you thank God? And when people wronged you and insulted you, did you thank God? We are not saying that their wrong thereby ceased to be wrong— what would be the use of such pernicious and foolish talk! It is up to you to decide whether it was wrong; but have you taken the wrong and insult to God and by your thanksgiving received it from his hand as a good and a perfect gift? Did you do that? Well, then you have worthily interpreted the apostolic words to the honor of God and to your own salvation. It is beautiful that a person prays, and many a promise is given to the one who prays without ceasing,[55] but it is more blessed always to give thanks. Then you have worthily interpreted those apostolic words more gloriously than if all the angels spoke in flaming tongues.[56]

But who had courage like that, a faith like that; who loved God in such a way? Who was the joyous and staunchly devout warrior who stood at his post in life so perseveringly that he never dozed off? And if you did that, my listener, did you not conceal it from yourself? Did you say to yourself, "I do understand the apostolic words, all right, but I also understand that I am too cowardly, or too proud, or too lazy to want to understand them properly"? Did you admonish yourself? Even if this seems to be a hard saying, did you consider that also the timid person has a faithless heart and is no honest lover? Did you bear in mind that there is a judgment also upon all other love, for in repentance it is God who loves you. In repentance, you receive everything from God, even the thanksgiving that you bring to him, so that even this is what the child's gift is to the eyes of the parents, a jest,[62] a receiving of something that one has oneself given. Was it not so, my listener? You wanted to give thanks to God at all times, but even this was very imperfect. Then you understood that God is the one who does everything in you and who then grants you the childlike joy of regarding your thanksgiving as a gift from you. This joy he gives you when you have not feared the pain of repentance and the deep grief in which a person becomes as happy as a child in God, when you have not feared to understand that this is love, not that we love God but that God loves us.[63]

And you, my listener, you who in a simpler and humbler way understood the profound meaning of the thought that you were not like other people, was it so easy not to misinterpret the apostolic words? You fully comprehended that every good and every perfect gift comes from God, but, alas, you could not comprehend that in you it could become anything but something harmful? The dew and the rain are certainly a good gift from above, but if the noxious plant understood itself and could speak, it would perhaps say, "Stop! Go back to heaven again so that I may perish of drought; do not refresh my root lest I thrive and grow and become even more noxious!" And you did not understand yourself, did not understand the apostolic words, since in that case it would not be true that every perfect gift comes from God, because then God would not be greater than a person's anxious heart,[64] and how then could every good and every perfect gift come from him?

Perhaps there was something in your life that you wished undone; if this were possible, then you would take every perfect gift from God's hand with joyful thanksgiving. Your joy at the mere thought of it was so great that it seemed as if it would tempt God to undo what had been done. But God is tempted by no one. Perhaps you tried to forget it so that your thanksgiving would not be feeble and like a smoking wick.[65] Ah, but if you could forget it, how then would it be possible for you to understand the apostolic words? If it were possible for you to forget it, then every good and every perfect gift would indeed not come from God; you would have shut yourself out from the blessing not by what you had done but by your poor and selfish and arbitrary understanding of the words, just as the person whose wish was denied would shut himself out from the blessing by wanting to think that the wish denied was not also a good and a perfect gift, even though it was harder for you to dare to understand it than for him.

III
51

Perhaps you understood the apostolic words in another way, thought that punishment from God is also a good and a perfect gift. The wrath within you wanted, as it were, to come to the aid of divine wrath so that the punishment might consume you, and yet the punishment you suffered was different from what you had supposed it would be. Perhaps it involved more than you, and yet you were the guilty one; perhaps its scope was rather extensive, and yet you were the only one who should be its object. Even if you secretly acknowledged that divine Governance knows how to strike a person, knows how to make itself understandable to him, even if no one else understood this, the apostolic words remained obscure to you, and it seemed as if the punishment itself became a new temptation. What was punishment and what was incident became ambiguous to you; if it was only incident, then your soul demanded punishment; if the whole thing was punishment, then you could not make it your own. You were willing to renounce everything, every wish, every desire; you were willing to give up any idea that the best you had done in your soul's utmost exertion, in the assurance that it was good, was anything but foolishness and sin; you were willing to suffer any punishment—but this *more* that was attached to it, this you could not bear—was this, too, a good and a perfect gift? Then your soul grew dark; you could not understand the words? But what did you do then? Did you reject the words? Oh no! You held fast to them in all your distress. And when all the devils stood ready to rescue your soul from the insanity of despair by the explanation that God is not love, is it not true

TO THE LATE

Michael Pedersen Kierkegaard[69]

FORMERLY A CLOTHING MERCHANT HERE IN THE CITY

MY FATHER

THESE DISCOURSES ARE DEDICATED

[71]Although this little book [72](which is called "discourses," not sermons, because its author does not have authority to *preach*, "upbuilding discourses," not discourses for upbuilding, because the speaker by no means claims to be a *teacher*) knows quite well what its author knows even better—that it is a trifle that could easily be trampled underfoot or killed as it ventures out into the great world or snatched up by a bird of prey and never reach its destination—I nevertheless cheerfully, without fear, without anxious agitation, shut my door at the time of its departure. Small as it is, it probably will slip through, since it shifts for itself and goes its way and tends to its errand and discerns its own enigmatic path—until it finds that single individual [*hiin Enkelte*][73] whom I with joy and gratitude call *my* reader—until it finds what it is seeking, that favorably disposed person who reads aloud to himself [74] what I write in stillness, who with his voice breaks the spell on the letters, with his voice summons forth what the mute letters have on their lips, as it were, but are unable to express without great effort, stammering and stuttering, who in his mood rescues the captive thoughts that long for release—that favorably disposed person whom I with joy and gratitude call *my* refuge, who by making my thoughts his own does more for me than I do for him. And if it does not find him, or not in this way, my joy still remains: to send it forth, because just as "the cold of snow in the time of harvest is a faithful messenger to the one who sends him, he refreshes the soul of his master" (Proverbs 25:13).

S. K.[75]

THE EPISTLE: I PETER 4:7-12[77]

What is it that makes a person great, admired by creation, well pleasing in the eyes of God? What is it that makes a person strong, stronger than the whole world; what is it that makes him weak, weaker than a child? What is it that makes a person unwavering, more unwavering than a rock; what is it that makes him soft, softer than wax? —It is love![78] What is it that is older than everything? It is love. What is it that outlives everything? It is love. What is it that cannot be taken but itself takes all? It is love. What is it that cannot be given but itself gives all? It is love. What is it that perseveres when everything falls away? It is love. What is it that comforts when all comfort fails? It is love. What is it that endures when everything is changed? It is love. What is it that remains when the imperfect is abolished? It is love. What is it that witnesses when prophecy is silent? It is love. What is it that does not cease when the vision ends? It is love. What is it that sheds light when the dark saying ends? It is love. What is it that gives blessing to the abundance of the gift? It is love. What is it that gives pith to the angel's words? It is love. What is it that makes the widow's gift[79] an abundance? It is love. What is it that turns the words of the simple person into wisdom? It is love. What is it that is never changed even though everything is changed? It is love; and that alone is love, that which never becomes something else.

III
274

The pagan, too, extolled love, its beauty and its power; but his love could turn into something else that he extolled almost more. Love was beautiful, more beautiful than everything; but revenge was sweet, sweeter than everything. So inferior was the pagan's thinking about love and about the heavenly, so selfish was everything both in heaven and on earth, that the power who benevolently gave human beings the joy of love en-

viously reserved revenge for himself because it was the sweet-
est. No wonder, then, that revenge concealed itself in all the
pagan's love, that anxiety was not driven out even if it was
forgotten. No wonder that the enemy worked quietly even
when love slept most securely, that anger secretly lay in am-
bush and watched for its chance. No wonder that it suddenly
rushed out in all its wildness; no wonder that it filled the pagan's soul, which imbibed its forbidden sweetness and thereby
assured itself of its kinship with the heavenly! No wonder that
no love was happy, just as no one in paganism was happy before the last hour had come,[80] which in turn could only bit-
terly mock a person with the idea that he *had* been happy! No
wonder that sorrow infiltrated all joy, that the next moment,
even in the moment of joy, incessantly walked by as alarming
as the figure of death! How could a pagan succeed in overcoming the world; but if he did not succeed in that, how then
would he be able to gain the world!

What is it that is never changed even though everything is
changed? It is love, and that alone is love, that which never
becomes something else. The devout Jew also gave witness for
love, but his love was the child of changeableness and variation, and he knew how to hate his enemy. Even though he left
revenge to the Lord, because it belongs to him,[81] his soul still
was not unfamiliar with its sweetness. This consciousness is
also sweet, that the Lord's revenge is more terrible than any
human revenge, that a person curses his enemy, but the Lord
curses the ungodly one and the ungodly one's family through
many generations.[82] No wonder, then, that anxiety continually kept one eye open even when love was most free from
care; no wonder that anger, even when love least dreamed of
it, sat quietly and reckoned everything given and received,
reckoned what was yours and what was mine! No wonder
that no love was happy until its final hour, because not until
then was love's *uncertain* claim perfectly met.

What is it that is never changed even though everything is
changed? It is love. And only that which never becomes something else is love, that which gives away *everything* and *for that
reason* demands nothing, that which demands nothing and

III
275

therefore has nothing to lose, that which blesses and blesses when it is cursed, that which loves its neighbor but whose enemy is also its neighbor,[83] that which leaves revenge to the Lord because it takes comfort in the thought that he is even more merciful.

It is of this love that Peter speaks in the text just read, and just as this love many times and in many ways[84] received an apostolic witness, so he witnesses here again to its power when he says: Love will hide a multitude of sins.

It is these words, this witness, that we shall look at more closely as we deliberate on *how love hides a multitude of sins.*

But how should we speak of this? Should we speak in such a way that we do not give ourselves time to dwell on the words, because the mere sound contains a silent reproach that evokes a sorrowful longing for them and produces a striving toward them, toward the goal that is set for every human being to strive toward? Should we speak in such a way that if possible even in this hour the single individual might resolve to take the opportune moment, that if possible the words might move someone they encountered standing still and doing nothing to begin the race, someone they encountered on the track to speed up the race, someone they encountered running the race to run faster and hurry after the perfect.[85] Should we speak that way—as if we were speaking to the imperfect! Should we call to mind how rarely, indeed, is found even someone who either never knew or has utterly forgotten "the world's childhood learning" [86]—that revenge is sweet. Should we call to mind that every human being, if he is honest, only all too often catches himself in being able, protractedly, penetratingly, and expertly, to interpret the sad truth that revenge is sweet. Should we call to mind how rare indeed is even the person who left revenge to the Lord, trusting that he had a still more lenient explanation of the guilt, a still more merciful judgment against it, that he is greater than a human heart.[87] How often, on the other hand, every honest human being must confess to himself that he did not exactly renounce revenge by leaving it to the Lord. Should I call to mind how even more rare is the person who forgave in such a way that the contrite enemy actually was his neighbor, the person who in his forgiveness actually abolished the partition wall and was aware of no difference between them, was unaware that he himself was called in the early morning and his enemy in the eleventh hour,[88] was unaware that he himself was fifty pennies in debt, his enemy five hundred.[89] Should I call to mind how rare is even the person who loved in such a way that when his enemy prospered his ear heard no whisper of envy because his heart did not know envy, loved in such a way that his "eye did not begrudge the gift"[90] when good fortune favored his enemy, the person who loved in such a way that when things went badly for his enemy he forgot that it was his enemy. Should we warn against a certain ingenious common sense that in human eyes is less culpable, that cunningly knows how to discover people's faults, that admittedly does not misuse its knowledge to condemn but nevertheless by its curiosity does not so much violate the neighbor as hinder itself. Should we admonish everyone to aspire to that Christian love because everyone so often needs forgiveness himself. Should we admonish everyone to judge himself and in so doing forget to judge others, warn against judging and denouncing because no person can quite see through another, because it has sometimes happened that the wrath of heaven did not consume the one on whom it was called down but the Lord in secret graciously and benignly found him well pleasing; should we admonish everyone against zealously calling down wrath upon another, lest by his irreconcilability he focus a more dreadful wrath upon himself on the day of judgment.[91]

Is this the way we should speak? Indeed, it certainly would often be beneficial for us to be spoken to that way, but it is very difficult to do it so that in his discourse the one who is speaking does not himself act contrary to the discourse and come to judge others. Indeed, even to judge oneself in the discourse is very difficult, lest the one speaking be entangled in a new misunderstanding and thereby play havoc with others. This is why we choose the easier task; we shall dwell on the words themselves, and just as every other love has been eulogized in the world, we shall discuss and eulogize the love that has the power to perform the wondrous feat of hiding a multitude of sins. We shall speak as to those who are perfect. If, then, there is someone who does not feel himself to be perfect, the discourse would still make no distinction. We shall let our soul rest in the apostolic words, which are not a deceitful, poetic locution, not a daring outburst, but a faithful thought, a valid witness, which in order to be understood must be taken literally.

III
277

Love will hide a multitude of sins. Love is blind, declares an old proverb, and it does not thereby suggest an imperfection in the lover or an original condition in him, since only when love had won a place in his soul, only then did he become blind and then became more and more blind as love became victorious within him. Or did love become more imperfect when, having first deceived itself by refusing to see what it nevertheless saw, it finally did not even see it anymore? Or who concealed better—he who knew that he had hidden something or he who had forgotten even that? To the pure, all things are pure,[92] declares an old saying, and does not thereby suggest an imperfection in the one who is pure that should gradually disappear; on the contrary, the purer he becomes, the purer everything becomes for him. Or was it an imperfection in the one who is pure that he, having first kept himself unspotted by the impurity by refusing to know what he nevertheless knew, finally did not even know anything more about it?

It does not depend, then, merely upon what one sees, but what one sees depends upon how one sees; all observation is not just a receiving, a discovering, but also a bringing forth, and insofar as it is that, how the observer himself is constituted is indeed decisive. When one person sees one thing and another sees something else in the same thing, then the one discovers what the other conceals. Insofar as the object viewed belongs to the external world, then how the observer is constituted is probably less important, or, more correctly, then

what is necessary for the observation is something irrelevant
to his deeper nature. But the more the object of observation
belongs to the world of spirit, the more important is the way
he himself is constituted in his innermost nature, because
everything spiritual is appropriated only in freedom; but what
is appropriated in freedom is also brought forth. The difference, then, is not in the external but in the internal, and everything that makes a person impure and his observation impure
comes from within. The external eye does not matter, but "an
evil eye comes from within."[93] But an evil eye discovers much
that love does not see, since an evil eye even sees that the Lord
acts unjustly when he is good.[94] When evil lives in the heart,
the eye sees offense, but when purity lives in the heart, the eye
sees the finger of God. The pure always see God,[95] but "he
who does evil does not see God" (III John 11).

A person's inner being, then, determines what he discovers
and what he hides. When an appetite for sin lives in the heart,
the eye discovers the multiplicity of sin and makes it even
more multiple, because the eye is the lamp of the body, but if
the lamp that is in a person is dark, then how great is the darkness![96] When the anxiety of sin lives in the heart, the ear discovers the multiplicity of sin and makes it even more multiple,
and it would do no good for such a person to be blind, because
a rascal looks down and listens with his rascal's ear (Sirach
19:26-27). When love lives in the heart, the eye is shut and
does not discover the open act of sin, to say nothing of the
concealed act, "for the one who winks his eye has evil in
mind" (Proverbs),[97] but the one who understands the wink of
the eye is not pure. When love lives in the heart, the ear is shut
and does not hear what the world says, does not hear the bitterness of blasphemy, because he who says "you fool" to his
brother is guilty before the council,[98] but he who hears it
when it is said to him is not perfect in love. When rashness
lives in the heart, a person is quick to discover the multiplicity
of sin, then he understands splendidly a fragmentary utter-
ance, hastily comprehends at a distance something scarcely
enunciated. When love lives in the heart, a person understands
slowly and does not hear at all words said in haste and does

not understand them when repeated because he assigns them a good position and a good meaning; he does not understand the long angry or insulting verbal assault, because he is waiting for one more word that will give it meaning. When fear lives in the heart, a person easily discovers the multiplicity of sin, discovers deceit and delusion and disloyalty and scheming, discovers that

> Every heart is a net,
> Every rogue like a child,
> Every promise like a shadow.[99]

III
2/9

But the love that hides a multitude of sins is never deceived. When stinginess lives in the heart, when one gives with one eye and looks with seven to see what one obtains in return (Sirach 20:14), one readily discovers the multiplicity of sin. But when love lives in the heart, then the eye is never deceived, because when love gives, it does not watch the gift but keeps its eye on the Lord. When envy lives in the heart, the eye has the power to elicit the impure even from the pure; but when love lives in the heart, the eye has the power to love forth [*elske op*[100]] the good in the impure, but this eye sees not the impure but the pure, which it loves and loves forth by loving it. Yes, there is a power of this world that in its language translates good into evil, but there is a power from above that translates evil into good—it is the love that hides a multitude of sins. When hate lives in the heart, sin is right there at the door of a human being,[101] and the multitude of its cravings is present to him; but when love lives in the heart, then sin flees far away and he does not even catch a glimpse of it. When quarreling, malice, anger, litigation, discord, factionalism live in the heart, does one then need to go far to discover the multiplicity of sin, or does one need to live long to bring it forth all around one? But when joy, peace, patience, gentleness, faithfulness, kindness, meekness, continence[102] live in the heart, no wonder then that a person, even if he stood in the middle of the multiplicity of sin, would become a stranger, a foreigner, who would understand only very little of the customs of the country; if an explanation were required of him, what a covering of a multitude of sins this would be!

Or if this is not so, should we shrewdly say: The multiplicity of sin in the world is and remains just as great whether love discovers it or not? Should the apostolic words and the love they describe be left in abeyance as a euphuistic mode of speech that cannot meet the test of investigation? But then would that common sense actually understand love as well as it understood the multiplicity of sin! Or would it admit the opposite, that the multiplicity of sin remained just as great whether the understanding discovered it or not; would it not rather congratulate itself on its own ingenuity in discovering and tracking down sin's hiddenness? But then it would be equally true that the understanding discovered the multiplicity of sin and that love hid it, but the one would not be more true than the other. Or was there yet a third way, whereby a person came to know it without intellectually knowing it or lovingly not knowing it—would not such knowledge be an inhuman knowledge? It is not, then, just a rhetorical expression to say that love hides a multitude of sins, but it is truly so, and this is the power of Christian love, which, unlike other love, is not great because of spectacular achievement but is greater in its quiet wondrousness.

Happy the person who saw the world in all its perfection when everything was still very good; happy the person who with God was witness to the glory of creation. More blessed the soul that was God's co-worker in love; blessed the love that hides a multitude of sins.

Love will hide a multitude of sins. A *multitude* of sins—that is a terrible phrase and readily brings to mind another connection in which it is used frequently, the multiplicity of creation, prompting us to think of the countless hosts of generations, the innumerable swarms of living creatures that cannot be numbered because no number is large enough, and because there is no moment when one can begin to count, since countless numbers are born every moment. Is it not just the same

with the multiplicity of sin, for just as it is said that to him
who has, it shall be given, and he shall have in abundance,[103]
so also is sin very prolific, and one sin gives birth to many,
and it multiplies more and more. But love hides the multiplicity of sin. If the eye of love were not shut, if in its own observation it did not hide the multiplicity, how then could it venture to want to halt the power of sin! So it is precisely by
having covered the multiplicity of sin in advance that love covers it.

A wise man of old has said: Refrain from disputes, and you   III
will reduce sins (Sirach 28:8). But the person who reduces sins   281
surely hides a multitude of sins, and hides it doubly by not
sinning himself and by keeping another from it. And yet the
person who refrains from disputes keeps a person from sinning only momentarily; perhaps the same person may look
for disputes in another direction, but the one who turns a sinner from the error of his ways—of him the Apostle James says:
He hides a multitude of sins.[104]

But is it possible to relate properly how love hides a multitude of sins, or is it not even more multiple than the multiplicity of sin? When love sees the bruised reed, then it knows
how to hide a multitude of sins so that the reed is not crushed
under the burden. When it sees the smoking wick,[105] then it
knows how to hide a multitude of sins so that the flame is not
put out. When it has been victorious over a multitude of sins,
then it knows how to cover the multitude again, then it makes
everything festive for the reception, just as the prodigal son's
father[106] did, then it stands with open arms and waits for the
delinquent, has forgotten everything and brings the delinquent himself to forget everything as it again hides a multitude
of sins. Love does not weep over the multitude of sins; if that
were the case, then it would indeed see the multitude itself,
but it covers the multitude. And when sin resists it, then love
becomes even more multifarious, never wearies of faithfully
pulling in unequal yoke with it,[107] does not weary of believing
all things, hoping all things, enduring all things.[108] When sin
hardens itself against love and wishes to be rid of it, when it

returns abuse and scorn and ridicule for kindness, then love does not repay abusive language with abusive language;[109] then it blesses and does not curse.[110] When sin enviously hates love, when in its malice it wants to bring love itself to sin, then it finds not guile in love's mouth but prayer and admonition. But when prayers and admonition only incite sin and become a new occasion for the multiplicity of sin, then love is mute but no less faithful—faithful as a woman, it rescues as a woman does: "without a word" (I Peter 3:1). Sin thought that it had managed so that their ways would soon be parted, but see, love stayed with it. And sin wants to thrust love away; it forces love to walk one mile, but see, love walked two miles; it struck love's right cheek, but see, love turned the other cheek; it took love's coat, but see, love gave also its cloak.[111] Already sin feels its powerlessness; it cannot withstand love any longer; it wants to tear itself away; then it insults love as painfully as possible, because it thinks that even love cannot forgive more than seven times. But see! Love could forgive seventy times seven times,[112] and sin grew weary of occasioning forgiveness more quickly than love grew weary of forgiving. Indeed, just as there is a power in sin that has the perseverance to consume every better feeling a person has, so there is a heavenly power that starves the multiplicity of sin out of a person—this power is the love that hides a multitude of sins.

Or is it not so? Should we prefer to praise a sagacity that knows how to describe the multitude of sins even more shockingly? Or should we rather ask this sagacity where it obtained such knowledge? Indeed, if it could convince love that this is the way it is, then love presumably would never begin and would achieve nothing. But this is why love begins by hiding a multitude of sins, and this is why it ends where it began— by hiding a multitude of sins.

Blessed is the man whose sins are covered;[113] more blessed is the love that hides a multitude of sins.

Love will hide a multitude of sins. If love had been victorious in the world—well, then the multiplicity of sin would indeed

III
282

be covered and everything would be perfected in love. If love's legions were numerous in the world, if they were numerically equal to the enemy's, so that it could struggle hand to hand— indeed, how then could love not be victorious, inasmuch as it is the stronger! If, however, the servants of love are but a little band, if each individual is a solitary person, will love then actually be capable of hiding a multitude of sins? Or are not the apostolic words—insofar as by them we think of something other than love's pious ignorance, its zeal within its boundaries—in that case, are not the apostolic words a beautiful yet futile speech? Should we regard the apostolic words as inspired foolishness and praise instead the sagacity that declares: The course of life follows definite laws; in the time of extremity let love live next door to ungodliness—it is of no benefit to ungodliness. Would the understanding then be just as ready to say the opposite, that it makes no difference if ungodliness lives with love? Will the understanding deny that in life the innocent must frequently suffer with the guilty? Let us ask the understanding.

III
283

An elderly pagan, named and acclaimed in paganism as a sage,[114] was sailing with an ungodly man on the same ship. When the ship was in distress at sea, the ungodly man lifted up his voice to pray, but the sage said to him, "Be quiet, dear fellow. If heaven discovers that you are on board, the ship will capsize." Is it not true, then, that the guilty can cause the destruction of the innocent? But then is not the opposite just as true? Perhaps the understanding merely lacked the courage to believe this, and whereas it had enough of the bleak sagacity that discovers the wretchedness of life, it did not have enough heart to comprehend the power of love. Is not this the way it is—the understanding, after all, always makes a person only despondent and fainthearted, but love gives unbounded courage, and this is why all the apostles spoke with bold confidence. What if instead of an ungodly man there had been on board that same ship a devout man, an apostle! Did that not happen? A pagan ship sailed from Crete bound for Rome, and there was a storm at sea; for many days they saw neither sun nor stars. On board this ship there was an apostle, and Paul

stepped forward and said to his companions on the ship,
"Men, I bid you take heart, for not one of you will perish."[115]
Or would ungodliness actually have greater power than love;
would the presence of an ungodly person on board have the
power to alter the circumstances for the others, but an apostle
would have no such power? Or does not the Lord himself declare that for the sake of the elect the days of tribulation will
be shortened?[116]

III
284

Is it an unworthy conception of God to think that love hides
a multitude of sins in this way? In our deliberating and speaking, do we perhaps forget that God in heaven is not halted by
any deception, that his thought is vivid and present, that it
penetrates everything and judges the counsels of the heart?[117]
Would someone be right in reminding us to stick to the truth
when we praise love and to say that it is beautiful and lovely
of love to be so eager to hide a multitude of sins and avert
wrath rather than to exaggerate grossly by saying that love
hides a multitude of sins? Has not the person who speaks this
way forgotten what we do not forget, that love prays for the
sins of others; has he not forgotten that the prayer of a righteous person avails much?[118]

When Abraham spoke urgently to the Lord and pleaded for
Sodom and Gomorrah,[119] was he not covering a multitude of
sins? Or is it perhaps commendable perspicacity on someone's
part to say that his pleading was just as much a recollection of
the multitude of sins and hastened the judgment, just as his
own life was already a judgment, which if capable of consti-
tuting a condition would inevitably make the judgment even
more terrible? How did Abraham pray? Let us speak of it in
human terms! Did he not, as it were, sweep the Lord along in
his line of thinking, did he not bring the Lord to forget the
multitude of sinners in order to count the number of the righteous—if there were 50, 45, 40, 30, 20, yes, even only 10 guilt-
less persons? Was not Abraham covering a multitude of sins;
does the destruction of the cities prove the opposite, or does it
prove anything other than that there were not even ten guilt-
less persons in Sodom? And yet what was Abraham himself

compared with an apostle? What was his bold confidence
compared with an apostle's?

How great is a human being, that his life, if it is righteous,   III
will judge even angels;[120] more blessed is the love that hides a   285
multitude of sins.

We have praised the power of love to hide a multitude of
sins; we have spoken as to those who are perfect. If there is
someone who does not feel himself to be perfect, the discourse
would make no distinction. Let us dwell once again on this
love in order to observe the image of it that clearly presents
itself to the soul. If anyone by observing himself in this mirror
became convinced of his unlikeness, if everyone felt this way,
the discourse would make no distinction.

[121]When the scribes and the Pharisees had seized a woman in
open sin,[122] they placed her in the middle of the temple, face
to face with the Savior; but Jesus stooped down and wrote
with his finger on the ground. He who knew all things surely
knew also what the Pharisees and the scribes knew before they
told it to him. The scribes and the Pharisees quickly discovered her guilt; it was indeed easy, since her sin was open. They
also discovered another sin, one of which they made themselves guilty as they craftily laid snares for the Lord. But Jesus
stooped down and wrote with his finger on the ground. Why,
do you suppose, did he stoop down; why, do you suppose,
did he write with his finger on the ground? Did he sit there
like a judge attending carefully to the prosecutors' speech, listening and stooping down to note the complaint so as not to
forget it, so as to judge scrupulously; was this woman's guilt
the only thing the Lord put in writing? Or is he who is writing
with his finger on the ground instead writing in order to erase
and forget? There the sinner stood, surrounded by those who
were perhaps even more guilty, who loudly accused her, but
love stooped down and did not hear the accusation, which
vanished into thin air; it wrote with its finger in order to erase
what it itself knew, because sin discovers a multitude of sins,

III
286

but love hides a multitude of sins. Yes, even before the eyes of sin, love hides a multitude of sins, because with one word from the Lord the Pharisees and the scribes were silenced, and there was no accuser anymore, there was no one who condemned her. But Jesus said to her: Neither do I condemn you; go and sin no more—for the punishment of sin breeds new sin, but love hides a multitude of sins.

LOVE WILL HIDE A MULTITUDE OF SINS[123]

Just as apostolic speech is essentially different in content from all human speech, so it is also in many ways different in form. For example, in order to draw an individual forward, it does not halt the listener and invite him to rest; it does not halt the speaker and allow that he himself forgets to work.[125] Apostolic speech is concerned, ardent, burning, inflamed, everywhere and always stirred by the forces of the new life, calling, shouting, beckoning, explosive in its outbursts, brief, disjointed, harrowing, itself violently shaken as much by fear and trembling as by longing and blessed expectancy, everywhere witnessing to the powerful unrest of the spirit and the profound impatience of the heart. How could anyone have time for a long speech when he himself is running;[126] then he himself would have to stand still! How could anyone have time for prolix pondering when he is trying to be all things to all people;[127] then he would be unable to change the weapons of the spirit fast enough! How could anyone have much time for human minutiae when he is heading, under the full sail of hope, toward the perfect? But if apostolic speech is always as impatient as that of a woman in labor, then two considerations in particular are likely to stir it up even more—on the one hand, the idea that the night is over and day has broken,[128] that the night has lasted long enough and the point is to use the day; on the other hand, the idea that the time is coming when one can no longer work,[129] that the days are numbered, the end is near,[130] that the end of all things is approaching.

The text just read also witnesses to this apostolic ardor and begins with a "therefore," to which the immediately preceding words in the apostle's letter correspond: "but the end of all things is at hand," words that explain not only this "therefore" but also something in the text that perhaps, humanly speaking, could require an explanation, which also demon-strates how very different apostolic impatience is from the rashness of an excited person. Does it not seem odd that right after the beautiful admonition: "Above all, have a heartfelt love for one another,"[131] right after the significant words of comfort joined to that: "Love will hide a multitude of sins," comes such a seemingly casual admonition as this: "Gladly lend your house to one another without grumbling!" And yet this admonition illustrates precisely apostolic authority and wisdom. Indeed, what excited person, after having said, "The end of all things is at hand," would have added an admonition like that? Does it not go without saying that it would be su-perfluous? Would he not, if possible, by his speech bring about the evacuation of the houses, so that there would be scarcely anyone who would want to borrow a house, and if there was such a one, he would not need to be in a predicament? But an apostle is not impatient in this way, and his restlessness is su-perior to any human levelheadedness. The apostle loves his congregation too much to suppress spinelessly the shocking news that the end of all things is near, but on the other hand he knows how to call the congregation promptly to order again, as if the shock were forgotten, as if there were peace and security, a desirable opportunity to demonstrate its love to the neighbor even in life's unimportant circumstances. Therefore, the words "the end of all things is near" are not an arid storm cloud that passes over and throws everything into disorder but an anxiety that clears the air and makes everyone gentler and more deeply inward, more loving and swifter to buy the opportune time, but also strong enough not to be ex-hausted by the thought that the hour of opportunity is past. The apostle who is speaking is not drunk on dreams but sober in his thinking and in his speech.

"But the end of all things is near." These are shocking words even in the mouth of a rash and reckless person, to say nothing of an apostle's. For this very reason, Peter adds words of com-fort strong enough to overcome anxiety: "Love will hide a multitude of sins." Or are they perhaps not needed? Is every-thing past with the end of all things? Is any other cover needed

than the one granted to everyone, the righteous and the unrighteous? Is not the person lying in the bosom of the earth
covered and well put away? Would there be someone who did
not understand the apostle because he did not expressly state
the day when there will be a question about such a love? Or
have the words of terror and also the words of comfort lost
their meaning, inasmuch as the end of all things did not come
as had been predicted? Is an apostle an ineffectual man to
whom it is important only to predict the end of all things in
general, but without any bearing on himself and others except
insofar as it could satisfy their curiosity? Or was it not his primary concern that with the end of all things his days and the
days of the congregation were numbered? But this did actually
pertain to the apostle and the congregation; this continually
repeats itself in each generation; and the next thing repeats itself also, because every person must die[132] and thereupon
come to judgment.

But armor is also needed for the day of judgment. It is this
and its perfection that the apostle describes.[133] This armor is
love; it is the only thing that will not be abolished, the only
thing that remains with a person in life and remains with him
in death and that will be victorious in the judgment.[134] Love is
not like a deceitful friend who first inveigles a person and then
remains with him in order to mock. No, love remains with a
person, and when everything becomes confused for him,
when his thoughts rise up accusingly, when anxieties con-
demningly rear their heads, then love intimidates them and
says to him: Just have patience; I will remain with you and
witness with you, and my witness will overcome the confusion. Indeed, even if love has led a person astray, even if it
cannot acquit him later, it will nevertheless say: Would I abandon you in the hour of need? Even if you were abandoned by
everything, even if you were abandoned by yourself, I am still
with you, I who led you astray but who also have this comfort
for you, that it was I who did it. What if this were not so!
What power is able to bring a person to risk the terror in this
way as love does! How horrible, then, if it did not also know

how to interpret itself to itself, make itself understandable to the single individual even if not another soul understood it.

Let us, then, consider the apostolic words more closely. The apostle speaks to imperfect beings; how could one who is perfect have a multitude of sins that would need to be hidden! But the imperfect, the brokenhearted—them he also comforts with the thought that love will hide a multitude of sins. We shall not light-mindedly tamper with the apostolic words; we shall not sagaciously deceive ourselves and cheat the words by thinking that the person who has love is perfect. These words do not apply to the person who does not find within himself a multitude of sins that need to be hidden; but they are of no use to the person who refuses their comfort, because the comfort is precisely this—that love is able to live in the same heart in which there is a multitude of sins and that this love has the power to hide the multitude.

Therefore, we shall now look for the comfort offered in the apostle's words by considering: *how love will hide a multitude of sins.*

But how is this possible; love does indeed discover precisely in a person himself a multitude of sins. Has not many a person in this world gone on living lightly and carefreely in the happy mentality of youth, without being arrogant about his own perfection but also without feeling humbled or halted by an oppressive conscience—until love gripped him and the past no longer pleased him, because love in so many ways had discovered imperfection and weakness? Did things go better for the sensible person? He frowned on the light-mindedness of youth, he kept watch on himself, he strove to rid himself of his faults, but in this striving he also gained a self-satisfaction that did not fear the test of the understanding, that accepted honor from people,[135] that challenged the world to a struggle—then love took aim at him, and see—he who had carried his head high, he who had dominated people by his glance, he now dropped his eyes, because he had discovered a multitude of sins. And he who could stand before the rigorous judgment of the understanding could not endure the mild judgment of love! But such things did not happen to the righteous person. He was rigorous with himself and did not wish to be like others; he knew that anyone who wanted to preserve himself had to work and to renounce much, but he also knew what he gained in this battle, knew that *he* gained an understanding of the wisdom that there is justice in heaven, because he considered himself just and righteous.[136] Then heaven's love looked down at him, and see—he who had been confident of being able to give everyone his due, to man what belongs to man, to God what belongs to God,[137] he who already in his lifetime had looked forward to undergoing an accounting on judgment day, he had now discovered the multitude of sins to the point where he could not repay one in a thousand.[138] Indeed, it was not only that love instantly discovered what was hidden—no, it was as if love increased the multitude of sins in the future. What he in his proud self-confidence had easily overcome now seemed difficult to him because in love his soul was concerned. Where previously he had suspected no temptation, he now saw it luring him, and he sensed a fear and trembling he had never known. And it was really true; he easily convinced himself of that, for if he would surrender himself into the hands of his own righteousness, the temptation vanished.

III
291

But then is it possible that the same power that discovers a multitude of sins, the same power that almost multiplies the multitude as it infuses the human heart with love's concern, is it possible that the same power can hide it in the same person? And yet would it be good if this were not so? What, then, is love? Is it a dream in the night that one has merely by sleeping? Is it a stupor in which everything is forgotten? Shall we hold love in such disdain that it is in this sense that it covers a multitude of sins? Then it would be better to retain the light mentality of youth, or the adult's self-examination, or the individual's own self-righteousness. Must wisdom be bought, understanding be bought, peace of mind be bought, the blessedness of heaven be bought, must life be bought in the pain of birth, but love is not supposed to know any birth pains? Love is no dream. If we were to call it that, then it

would be best to say: This, its first pang, is a troubled and
anxious dream that ends with a blessed awakening in the love
that covers a multitude of sins. Love takes everything. It takes
a person's perfection, and if he wants to clutch it, then love is
severe with him; but it also takes his imperfection, his sin, his
distress. It takes away his strength, but also his suffering—or
what terrible sufferings would love not hide as if they did not
exist, but only love's joy over rescuing another? But when
love takes it from him, then love indeed hides it; when it takes
everything, it hides everything; when, in proportion to what
it takes from him, it gives him something else instead, then it
hides beyond all understanding.

People have often thought that there were other means that
could take away and thereby hide what they might wish hidden. But an ancient pagan has already said: It does not help a
person to ride away from care; it is sitting behind him on the
horse.[139] These words of his have often been repeated as words
that manifest a profound insight into the human heart. And
yet—if that old pagan who rode through life on his horse with
care behind him, if he did not have to look back—but love
does not do that. How would the eye [Øie] that loves find time
for a backward look, since the moment [Øieblik, glance of the
eye] it did so it would have to let its object go! How would the
ear that loves find time to listen to the accusation, since the
moment it did so it would have to stop listening to the voice
of love! And if the eye strays after it, if the ear eavesdrops, then
the heart is petty, and this is not the fault of love—indeed, this
angers love. The person who thinks of his own perfection
does not love, and he who takes his own imperfections into
account does not love. Indeed, if he thought himself so imperfect that he was disqualified from love because of this, he
would show that he did not love, since he would take his imperfection into account and include it in his accounting as if
this were a perfection. But love takes everything. And the person who excludes himself either wants to be happy about himself and not to be happy about love or wants to be sad about
himself and not to be happy about love.

But in order to love a person in this way, one must have the

courage to will to love; the secret of earthly love is that it bears
the mark of God's love, without which it would become sil-
liness or insipid philandering, as if a person in comparison
with another were so perfect that he could arouse this anxiety
or truly be able to take everything. To love God in this way
requires a humble bold confidence; in every human heart
God's love awakens crying like a newborn baby, not smiling
like the child that knows its mother. But now when God's
love wants to hold fast to the Lord, the enemy rises against
one in all its terror, and the power of sin is so strong that it
strikes with anxiety. But love does not shut its eyes in the hour
of danger; it volunteers itself, as a venerable hymn writer says,
to press

> Through the arrows of sin
> Into the repose of paradise.[140]

III
293

And the further away it sights the multitude of arrows, the
more terrible they seem, but the closer it presses forward, the
less it sees the arrows, and when it has intercepted all the arrows in its heart and is wounded by them, it no longer sees
them but sees only love and the blessedness of paradise.

When Jesus sat at dinner one day in a Pharisee's house, a
woman entered. No woman had been invited as a guest, this
one least of all, because the Pharisees knew that she was a sinner.[141] If nothing else had been able to terrify and stop her, the
Pharisees' proud contempt, their silent disapproval, their
sanctimonious anger would probably have frightened her
away; "but she stood behind Jesus at his feet, weeping, and
began to wet his feet with her tears and wipe them with the
hair of her head and to kiss his feet and anoint them with the
ointment." There was a moment of anxiety; what she had suffered in solitude, her grief, the accusations of her own heart,
became even more terrible, because her heart was well aware
that its charges had endorsement in the faces of the Pharisees.
But she went on, and in beating the enemy she beat herself to
calmness, and when she had found rest at Jesus' feet, she forgot herself in her work of love. As she wept, she finally forgot
what she had wept over at the beginning; the tears of repen-

tance became tears of adoration. She was forgiven her many sins, because she loved much. There were those in the world who, after wasting their lives in the service of desire, finally lost themselves and scarcely recognized themselves anymore. This is desire's shameful and appalling fraud—that it defrauds a person out of himself and lets him keep only a superficial, passing intimation of authentic being [*Tilvær*], that it arrogantly wants to defraud God out of his co-knowledge in creation. This woman was granted the grace to weep herself out of herself, as it were, and to weep herself into the peacefulness of love. The person who loves much is forgiven much, and this is love's blessed deception, "that the person who is forgiven much loves much"—so that to need much forgiveness becomes an expression of love's perfection.

Yet even if love was capable of removing from the accused's sight a multitude of sins so that, lost in love, he saw them no more, because love hid them—is he thereby saved forever? Will nothing halt him on his way and suddenly make him recollect what love has hidden; is no judgment pronounced on a person from without? Does love have the same power here also, so that not even the judge discovers a multitude of sins because love hides them? Can a judge be deceived; does he not penetrate every veil and disclose everything? Can a judge be bribed; does he not uncompromisingly require what is the judgment's requirement? Can the world's judgment be deceived? Offer it your love, and you will continue to be a debtor; bring it your heart's best emotion, and you will continue to be a debtor; offer it tears of repentance, and the judgment requires its own justice. Can love's judgment, then, be bribed? Offer it gold, and it will despise you; offer it power and dominion, and it will disdain you; offer it the glories of the world, and it will condemn you for loving the glories of the world; trumpet your wonderful deeds, and it will condemn you for not being in love. The judgment requires what is the judgment's requirement, and the world's judgment requires what belongs to the world, and this conceals from the world whatever is lacking; but love's judgment requires what belongs to love, because the person who judges makes requirements, but the person who makes requirements seeks, and the person "who hides a multitude of sins seeks love" (Proverbs 17:9); but the person who finds love hides a multitude of sins; the person who finds what he sought indeed conceals what he did not seek.

So, then, are not the apostolic words a comfort that gives bold confidence in the face of judgment; are they not a comfort precisely as is needed; is it not beyond all understanding! To remember everything is a great thing to the understanding; that love hides a multitude of sins is foolishness to it. Or should we deprive ourselves of this comfort by sensibly wanting to measure out love, so to speak, by wanting to portion it out as compensation for particular sins and in this way continue in the sins? Should we shut ourselves out from love; if we continue in love, who is it, then, who accuses? Or is not the love in a person that hid a multitude of sins from himself the same love that out of love hides a multitude of sins?[142] Indeed, even if love had not entirely triumphed in a person, even if anxiety discovered what love did not have the strength to cover in him, yet on the day of judgment love will come to the aid of love in him, drive out fear, and hide a multitude of sins.

[143]When Jesus sat at dinner one day in a Pharisee's home, a woman entered that house; she was downhearted; she was carrying a multitude of sins. The judgment of the world was legible on the faces of the Pharisees; it could not be deceived; her sorrow and her tears concealed nothing but disclosed everything, and there was nothing to discover but a multitude of sins. She was not seeking the world's judgment, however, "but she stood behind Jesus at his feet and wept." Then *love* discovered what the world concealed—the love in her; and since it had not been victorious in her, the Savior's love came to her assistance so that the one "who was released from a debt of five hundred pennies might love more,"[144] and he made the love in her even more powerful to hide a multitude of sins, the love that was already there, because "her many sins were forgiven her, because she loved much."[145]

III
295

Blessed the person whose heart witnesses with him that he loved much; blessed the person when God's spirit, which knows all, witnesses that he loved much; for him there is comfort both here and hereafter, because love hides a multitude of sins.

PRAYER

[146]Father in heaven! You hold all the good gifts in your gentle hand. Your abundance is richer than can be grasped by human understanding. You are very willing to give, and your goodness is beyond the understanding of a human heart, because you fulfill every prayer and give what we pray for or what is far better than what we pray for. Give everyone his allotted share as it is well pleasing to you, but also give everyone the assurance that everything comes from you, so that joy will not tear us away from you in the forgetfulness of pleasure, so that sorrow will not separate you from us, but in joy we may go to you and in sorrow remain with you, so that when our days are numbered and the outer being is wasting away,[147] death may not come in its own name, cold and terrible, but gentle and friendly, with greetings and news, with witness from you, our Father who is in heaven! Amen.

[148]In the world's capital, in proud Rome, where all the splendor and glory of the world were concentrated, where everything was procured whereby human sagacity and rapaciousness tempt the moment in the anxiety of despair, everything to astonish the sensate person, where every day witnessed something extraordinary, something horrible, and the next day had forgotten it upon seeing something even more extraordinary—in far-famed Rome, where everyone who in any way believed himself able to capture public attention hastened as to his rightful stage, prepared everything in advance for his reception so that he, although intoxicated with self-confidence, might shrewdly avail himself of the scantily allotted and begrudged propitious moment—there lived the Apostle Paul as a prisoner, there he wrote the epistle from which our text is taken. He was brought here as a prisoner, a stranger to all, and yet he brought with him a teaching, of which he witnessed that it was divine truth, communicated to him by a special revelation, [149] and the unshakable conviction that this teaching would be victorious over the whole world. If he had been an insurgent who agitated the people and made the tyrant tremble, if he had been taken to Rome as a captive so that the ruler could satisfy his desire for vengeance with Paul's suffering, could have him martyred with the choicest tortures— yes, then probably for a short time his fate would have shaken everyone in whose breast human feelings were not yet dead, by its horror would have incited the lustful and inquisitive mob for a moment—indeed, the tyrant's throne might have been overthrown! But Paul was not treated in this way. He was too insignificant for Rome to fear him; his foolishness was too naive for the powers to arm themselves against him. Who was he, then? A man who belonged to a despised people, a man who did not even belong to them any longer but had been cast out from them as an offense—a Jew who had become a Chris-

tian, the most lonely, the most abandoned, the most harmless man in all Rome. He was treated as such. His imprisonment was not strict, but he was a prisoner, and he who brought with him that conquering conviction was now assigned the solitude of imprisonment as his sphere of action and the soldier who was ordered to guard him every day.

In the capital city of the world, in tumultuous Rome, where nothing could withstand the unbridled power of time, which swallowed everything as quickly as it made its appearance, which consigned everything to forgetfulness without leaving a trace—there lived the Apostle Paul, an insignificant man, in solitary confinement, quiet and unobtrusive, not consigned to being forgotten, since there was no one in the enormous city who knew or cared about his existence. But while everything around him was rushing on in futility, more swiftly than a shadow, for him the conviction stood firm that the teaching he professed would be victorious over the whole world—over the whole world, from which he at present was separated, and the only person he saw was the soldier who guarded him.

III
298

When a person who is guilty suffers and bears his punishment patiently, he is not commended for it; but if he is innocent and suffers patiently, then he is commended.[150] This is beautiful to contemplate, pleasing to hear, fine to profess—but it is hard to do. Yet by the help of God the person who at heart is devout and fears God will prepare his soul in humility until it rejoices in God again and is calm in the Lord. Then he will rescue himself in patience, even though it would be extremely hard for him to have his expectancy vanish as a dream, to see himself, who wanted to win the whole world, end up by being a prisoner, not even succumbing in the struggle but fading away like a mirage. If there were any who had placed their faith in him and hoped for him, he will remember them, and his soul will not be unacquainted with the painful concern whether they also will abandon him. From his prison he will perhaps write to them, "Do not forsake me now when I am forsaken by all; keep your confidence in me, as you did formerly; do not forget me now when I am forgotten by all."[151] Perhaps he would move their hearts; perhaps some in-

dividual would come to him and, if allowed, visit the imprisoned man, grieve with him, comfort him, and be built up by
him. It is beautiful to talk about this; the very thought moves
the heart of every better person.

But Paul was an apostle. Even though distressed, he nevertheless was always happy; even though he was poor, he always
made many rich; even though he had nothing, he nevertheless
possessed everything.[152] From his captivity, he writes to the
distant congregation, "Therefore I ask you not to lose heart
over the hardships I am suffering for you, which are your
glory."[153] He who himself might seem to need comfort is
quickly, as it were, on good terms with God, happy in hardship, undaunted in danger, not occupied with his own suffering but concerned for the congregation, and he thinks about
his own hardship only insofar as it might cause the congregation to lose heart.

III
299

If someone had found peace and tranquillity in his adversity,
then the sorrow that others might lose their bold confidence
and faith over his misfortunes would perhaps awaken in him
new disquietude. Yet the fear of God within him will prevail,
and he will trustingly commit those he loves to God's hand. It
is touching to speak of this; every better person certainly feels
that this quiet submission is worthy of aspiration. But Paul
was an apostle, and he writes from his captivity, "The hardships I am suffering for you are your glory."

He who has a teaching to commend to people and who
strives to win them surely has a witness to which he unhesi-
tatingly directs the single individual. But when this witness
fails, then he no doubt perceives that power has been taken
from him, and although it is very hard, he nevertheless becomes reconciled with God in his heart. He may sorrow as one
abandoned by the bridegroom and by joy,[154] but also as one
who did not run aimlessly,[155] who does not forget that higher
than saving others is saving one's own soul, subjugating the
unruly mind to the obedience of faith, keeping the straying
thoughts in the bonds of love by the power of conviction. It is
beneficial to speak of this, and any honest person certainly
confesses that it is blessed to put one's own house in order this

way when one has served one's time with the great work and has been assigned the lesser.

But now Paul! Did he live in the favor of the mighty so that it could commend his teaching? No, he was a prisoner! Did the wise hail his teaching so that their reputation could guarantee its truth? No, to them it was foolishness.[156] Was his teaching capable of quickly supplying the individual with a supranatural power, did it offer itself for sale to people through legerdemain? No, it had to be acquired slowly, appropriated in the ordeal that began with the renunciation of everything. Did Paul, then, have any witness? Yes, indeed—he had every human witness against him, and in addition he had the concern that the congregation would lose heart or, worse yet, be offended at him, because offense surely is never closer than when truth is oppressed, when innocence suffers, when injustice is sure of its victory, when violence is on the increase, when ignorance does not even need to use power against the good but, careless and unconcerned, remains ignorant of its existence. But does Paul, forsaken by the witness, despair? By no means. Since he had no other witness to appeal to, he appeals to his hardships. Is this not like a miracle? If Paul had not otherwise effectively demonstrated that he had the power of miracle, is this not a demonstration? To transform hardships into a witness for the truth of a teaching, to transform disgrace into glory for oneself and for the believing congregation, to transform the lost cause into a matter of honor that has all the inspiring force of a witness—is this not like making the cripples walk and the mute speak!

What gave Paul the power for this? He himself had a witness; he was no doubter who in his innermost being retracted the strong thoughts. He had a witness superior to anything in the world,[157] a witness that witnessed all the more powerfully the more the world went against him. Was he a weak man, then? No, he was powerful. Was he wavering? No, he was steadfast; he was mightily strengthened by God's spirit in his inner being.[158]

Therefore what the apostle desires for every individual in the congregation is what he himself was, what his whole life demonstrates. Even if the situation in his day was different, even if struggle and conflict made it more necessary but also perhaps more difficult to attain this strengthening in the inner being, nevertheless for all ages and in all circumstances it remains the one thing needful for a person, to save his soul in this inner strengthening. After all, every person in all ages does indeed have his struggle and his spiritual trial, his distress, his solitude in which he is tempted, his anxiety and powerlessness when the witness slips away. So let us ponder more closely:

Strengthening in the Inner Being.

Only a thoughtless soul can let everything around it change, give itself up as a willing prey to life's fickle, capricious changes, without being alarmed by such a world, without being concerned for itself. How unworthy and nauseating such a life is, how far such a life is from witnessing to the human being's high destiny—to be the ruler of creation. [159]If the human being is to rule, then there must be an order in the world; otherwise it would be mockery of him to assign him to control brute forces that obey no law. And if he is to rule, then there must be a law within him also; otherwise he would be incapable of ruling; either he would disturbingly interfere, or it would be left to chance whether he ruled wisely or not. If this were the case, then the human being would be so far from being the ruler of creation that creation might wish instead that he did not exist at all. Therefore, just as soon as a person collects himself in a more understanding consideration of life, he seeks to assure himself of a coherence in everything, and as the ruler of creation he approaches it, as it were, with a question, extorts an explanation from it, demands a testimony.

Only the person who has abandoned his soul to worldly appetites, who has chosen the glittering bondage of pleasure and has not managed to extricate himself from its light-minded or heavy-spirited anxiety, only he is satisfied to let the creation bear its witness so that he can shrewdly and prudently use it in the service of the moment. And since the human being is the ruler of creation, it obeys even the unworthy authority. How doleful is such a perdition that does not even think it is living thoughtlessly but instead thinks that it understands everything and in its heart's aberration thinks it is turning everything to its advantage. When he sees the red sunset in the evening, he says, "Tomorrow will be a beautiful day." But when he sees the early morning sky red and darkening, he says, "Today there will be a storm," for he knows how to judge the sky, the weather, and the wind.[160] Therefore, he says, "Today or tomorrow I will go to this or that city and stay there a year and bargain and reap profits."[161] When he cultivates his soil intelligently, he counts on a rich yield. His eyes gleam at the sight of the rich crops, at what he may have thoughtlessly called the blessed fruit. He hastily builds his barns larger, since it is easy to predict that the old ones cannot hold this abundance. Then he is secure and happy, praises existence, and goes to bed, but then the text reads: This night I will require your soul from you.[162] —His soul from him; is that not asking too much? I wonder if he would understand it. Nothing is said of the rich crops or of the newly erected barns, but what is mentioned is perhaps something he forgot in all this—that he has a soul. —But the person who reflects on life with any earnestness at all readily perceives that he is not the lord in such a way that he is not also a servant, that it is not his superior intelligence alone that distinguishes man from the animals.

Only the person who cravenly runs away from every more profound explanation, who does not have the courage to assume the responsibility of the master by submitting to the obligation of a servant, who does not have the humility to be willing to obey in order to learn how to rule and at all times is willing to rule only insofar as he himself obeys—only he fills time with perpetual deliberations that take him nowhere but only serve as a dissipation in which his soul, his capacity for comprehending and willing, vanishes like mist[163] and is extinguished like a flame. How doleful is such a self-consuming, how far from witnessing by his life, from giving expression in his life, to a human being's exalted destiny—to be God's co-worker.[164]

[165]Through every deeper reflection that makes him *older* than the moment and lets him grasp the eternal, a person assures himself that he has an actual relation to a world, and that consequently this relation cannot be mere knowledge about this world and about himself as a part of it, since such knowledge is no relation, simply because in this knowledge he himself is indifferent toward this world and this world is indifferent through his knowledge of it. Not until the moment when there awakens in his soul a concern about what meaning the world has for him and he for the world, about what meaning everything within him by which he himself belongs to the world has for him and he therein for the world—only then does the inner being announce its presence in this *concern*.

This concern is not calmed by a more detailed or a more comprehensive knowledge [*Viden*]; it craves another kind of knowledge, a knowledge that does not remain as knowledge for a single moment but is transformed into an action the moment it is possessed, since otherwise it is not possessed. This concern also craves an explanation, a witness [*Vidnesbyrd*], but of another kind. If in his knowledge a person could know everything but knew nothing of the relation of this knowledge to himself, then, in his effort to assure himself of the relation of his knowledge to the object, he probably would have demanded a witness, but he would not have comprehended that a completely different witness is required, and then the concern would still not have awakened in his soul. As soon as this awakens, his knowledge will prove to be comfortless, because all knowledge in which a person vanishes from himself, just as [166]any explanation provided by knowledge of this kind is equivocal, explains now this and now that, and can mean the opposite, just as any witness of this kind, precisely when it witnesses, is full of deceit and riddles and only engenders anxiety.[167] [168]How, indeed, would a person through this knowledge be sure that his prosperity is God's grace, so that he dares to rejoice in it and safely devote himself to it, or that it is God's wrath and is only deceitfully hiding the abyss of perdition from him so that his downfall might be all the more terrible? How would a person through this knowledge be sure that adversity is heaven's punishment, so that he can allow himself to become crushed by it, or that it is God's love, which loves him in the ordeal, so that he, dauntless and confident in the distress of temptation, may reflect upon love? How would a person through such knowledge be sure that he was placed high in the world and entrusted with much because in him God loved his chosen instrument, or that it was because he was supposed to become a proverb to people, a warning, a terror to others? His knowledge can certainly assure him that everything is going well for him, that everything accommodates itself to him, that everything happens as he wishes, that everything he points to is given to him, that everything goes wrong for him, that everything fails, that every horror he is apprehensive about comes upon him the very next moment, that he is more highly trusted than anyone else—but more this knowledge cannot teach him. And this explanation is extremely equivocal, and this knowledge is extremely comfortless.

¹⁶⁹In this concern, the inner being announces itself and craves an explanation, a witness that explains the meaning of everything for it and its own meaning by explaining it in the God who holds everything together in his eternal wisdom and who assigned man to be lord of creation by his becoming God's servant and explained himself to him by making him his co-worker, and through every explanation that he gives a person, he strengthens and confirms him in the inner being. In this concern, the inner being announces itself—the inner being that is concerned not about the whole world but only about God and about itself, about the explanation that makes the relation understandable to it, and about the witness that confirms it in the relation. At no moment does this concern cease; the knowledge gained is not an indifferent knowledge. For example, if a person were to have in mind deciding this matter once and for all and then being finished with it, so to speak, the inner being would only be stillborn and would vanish again. But if he is truly concerned, then through God everything would serve for strengthening in the inner being,

III
303

because God is faithful and does not leave himself without witness.[170] But God is spirit[171] and therefore can give a witness only in the spirit; it is in the inner being. Any external witness from God, if such a thing could be thought of, can just as well be a deception.

[172]*Then prosperity will serve such a person for strengthening in the inner being.* We frequently hear people say that life is very deceitful, and however different individuals' hopes and desires may be, a good many agree that the beautiful demand of the expectations is never fulfilled, even though all too many first deceived themselves by seeking consolation in the fancy that once upon a time they did in truth nourish great expectations. Then they complain about the world, that it is a land of wretchedness; about time, that it is hard toil and futile inconvenience that bring a person no closer to his goal but take him further and further away; about people, that they are faithless, or at least lazy, lukewarm, and selfish; about themselves, that they, like everything else in life, do not turn out to be what they once thought they were; about the whole order of things here on earth, that every empty and external affair prospers, that the deed that is mighty in verbiage is crowned, the sentiment whose potency consists in platitudes is praised, the distress that proves itself by screaming finds sympathy, but that the honest effort wins nothing but ingratitude and lack of appreciation, that quiet, inward feeling meets nothing but misunderstanding, and deep, solitary grief meets nothing but abuse. Seldom is heard a more earnest voice that enjoins everyone to be open to life's schooling and to allow oneself to be brought up in the school of adversity, a tested discourse that with all emphasis asks, "Is it the rich who are to be saved,[173] is it the mighty who walk the narrow way,[174] is it the happy who deny themselves, is it the learned and wise who accept the scorned truth?" [175]This discourse, however, is ignored, but the complaint continues to sound—not only that the single individual has adversity in his life, but that all life is nothing but adversity, and that this makes all existence a dark saying that no one can understand.

But prosperity, it is easy to understand. And yet—Job was

an old man and had grown old in the fear of God; he offered a burnt offering for each of his children whenever they went to a banquet.[176] —"But prosperity is easy to understand"—and yet even the *fortunate person* cannot understand it himself. [177]Look at him, that lucky one whom good fortune delighted to indulge in everything. He does not work, and yet he is a Solomon in magnificence; his life is a dance, his thought is intoxicated with wishful dreaming, and every dream is fulfilled; his eyes are satiated more swiftly than they crave, his heart conceals no secret desire, his hankering has learned to recognize no boundary. But if you were to ask him where it all comes from, he would probably answer light-mindedly, "I myself do not know." Being light-minded, he probably would even be amused by his answer as a joke quite in keeping with everything else, but he would not comprehend or even suspect what he actually said and how he passed judgment on himself. The civil authorities see to it that everyone keeps what legitimately belongs to him. When they find a person whose abundance and wealth astonish everyone, they demand from him an explanation of the source. But if he cannot explain it, he is suspected of not having obtained it by honest means, of not being in legitimate possession of it, of perhaps being a thief. Human justice is only a very imperfect semblance of divine justice. It keeps a watchful eye on every human being. If a person, in reply to its question as to the source of it all, has no other answer than that he himself does not know, then it judges him, then it turns out to cast suspicion on him that he is not in *legitimate* possession of it. This suspicion is not a servant of justice but is justice itself; it is this that accuses and judges and pronounces the sentence on him and guards his soul in prison so that it does not escape.

What, then, is required of the fortunate person? What else but a strengthening in the inner being? But he had no concern, no inner being; if it had ever existed, it had vanished and was blotted out. But the person in whose soul the inner being announces itself in that concern does not become happy when good fortune indulges him in everything. He is invaded by a secret horror of the power that is bent on capriciously squan-

III
305

dering everything in this way; it makes him anxious about being involved with it. It seems as if in return it demanded of him something so terrible that he scarcely has a name for the anxiety over it. He would receive with thankfulness a much smaller portion if he might only know from whom it comes. But this is what the concern within him craves, this explanation, this witness. If he were placed on the top of a mountain to gaze out over all the kingdoms and countries of the world and were told, "This is all yours,"[178] he would first want to know who had put him there, whom he was to thank. But if good fortune nevertheless goes on persecuting him, as he might say, his concern becomes greater and greater; but as the concern grows, his soul gains strengthening in the inner being. In this way, prosperity would become for him an occasion for concern to increase, and in this way prosperity would serve him for strengthening in the inner being because he who possesses the whole world and thanks God is strengthened in the inner being. [179]Then he will rejoice in quite another way than that fortunate person does, because he who has the whole world and is as one who does not have it[180] has the whole world—otherwise he is possessed by the world. Then he rejoices in all the good gifts, but he rejoices even more in God and with God, who gave them. Then he feasts his eyes on the splendor of the earth, rejoices that the storerooms are full; then he enlarges his barns.[181] Then he goes to sleep secure, and when he hears, "This night I will require your soul from you," he understands this demand, is ready at once, and is better informed about his soul, which he will take along with him, than about all the magnificence he possessed and is now abandoning, all the magnificence he delighted in, and which day by day became for him a strengthening in the inner being through his thanksgiving.

"But prosperity is so easy to understand," and yet not even the *favored* can properly understand it. Just look at the favored one whom nature equipped with all magnificence, to whom it gave power and sagacity and strength of mind and dauntlessness of heart and perseverance of will. Look at him! [182]Why does he sometimes quake inwardly, he who made the whole world quake? Why does he sometimes blanch inwardly, he who dominated everything by his sagacity? Why does he sometimes feel powerless in his innermost being, he who intrepidly faced everything? Or is it not something to make one shudder in a period of quiet, to make one feel faint in an odd moment—to have power and not know *for what purpose* one has it! Civil justice keeps watch so that everyone stays within his bounds, so that each individual may serve the whole. When it discovers a man whose power is attracting everyone's attention, it demands that he explain for what purpose he uses it, and if he is unable to do so, he is suspected of not being a good citizen but perhaps a thug. Human justice is only a semblance of divine justice, which also directs itself to the single individual and its scrutiny is more rigorous. If it meets a person who, on being asked for what purpose he has this power, can give no other answer than that he himself does not really know, then justice turns out to cast suspicion on him. Perhaps it does not take the power from him, since he may not have misused it yet, but the suspicion becomes an anxiety in his soul that awakens when he least expects it. What does such a person lack? What else but strengthening in the inner being?

But the person in whose soul the inner being announces itself in that concern does not rejoice when he discovers that he has power. He becomes uneasy, almost afraid for himself. With anxiety he ascertains how much he is able to do. But when he nevertheless cannot get rid of the power, his concern and the anxiety in his heart increase—until this concern engenders strengthening in the inner being. Then he knows not only that he has power, but he also knows what that favored one did not know—to whom the honor is due and to whom it legitimately belongs. Then he rejoices every time his efforts are crowned with success, then he longs to reach the goal of his striving, but he rejoices even more in God, longs even more for the moment when he, with his God, will rejoice that they succeeded. Then his soul embraces the whole world, and his plans are far-reaching, but when in the stillness of the night he hears, "Make an accounting of your stewardship,"[183] he

III
307

knows what this summons means, he knows where he has the balance sheet, and even if there are deficiencies in it, he cheerfully leaves the world of thoughts and achievements in which he nevertheless did not have his soul, leaves the elaborately complicated and far-reaching work that from day to day had been the occasion for strengthening in the inner being.

"But prosperity is so easy to understand"—and yet at times it is not understood even by the person who is intimate with adversity. Just look at him! He had learned that there is distress in life; in cruel misfortunes, he had confessed to himself how weak and powerless a person is in his own strength. Yet he did not give up courage, he did not become despondent, he kept on working. Whether he achieved anything thereby, whether he progressed or retrogressed, whether he moved or stood still he did not know, because a great darkness had spread around him and it was like a continual night. Yet he exerted himself to the utmost of his strength. See! Then the sun of prosperity rose again, illuminated everything, explained everything, assured him that he had come a long, long way, that he had attained what he had been working for. Then he cried out in his joy, "It just had to happen this way, since a person's efforts are not fruitless and meaningless toil." [184]With that he had spoiled everything and had received no strengthening in the inner being. He had forgotten his confession in the period of distress, forgotten that fulfillment is not more certain because it has come than it was when he had confessed that he could not count on attaining it through his own strength. Adversity he had understood, but prosperity he could not understand. Then the inner being went out, as it were, in his soul. Or if justice visited him and asked him for an explanation, would it be satisfied with his answer? He

III
308 could better have understood the Lord in the pillar of fire that once shone in the night, but when daylight came, he could not see the pillar of cloud. [185] —But, on the other hand, the person in whose soul the inner being announces itself in that concern won a complete strengthening in the inner being when the day of joy triumphed over darkness, since to accept the joy without this concern about the witness would indeed be an aban-

donment of oneself in a delusion. But he accepted the witness with joyful thankfulness, because it came to one whom it did not find sleeping. And the inner being increased day by day in favor with God. And when in time the Lord called the servant away, he knew the way and left everything, and he took along only the witnesses, in which he had had his blessedness.

"But prosperity is so easy to understand," and yet frequently the unfortunate person does not understand it, either, or really know of what he speaks. One may speak cheerfully to a fortunate person; if what is said does not appeal to him, he can, of course, rejoice in his own good fortune and disregard the speaker. With the unfortunate person, it is another matter, lest what is said become a new torment if it does not appeal to him, lest he become more impatient if he thinks that the one speaking has himself experienced nothing, and feel it as a new indignity that someone who is unfamiliar with his suffering wants to comfort him. But whoever said it, it nevertheless remains true that the unfortunate person often does not understand what prosperity is. And yet in another sense, who understands it better than the unfortunate? Who would know how to speak about the delights of riches better than the one who lives on crumbs, who would describe power and might more glowingly than the person who sighs in bondage, who would portray the beauty of human society more ravishingly than the person who lives in solitude? But the one who would know how to describe it may not always have understood himself; but if he did not understand himself, how could he understand in a deeper sense what is outside him? But if, on the other hand, he understood himself or tried to understand himself, if he truly was concerned about understanding himself, if the inner being announced itself within him in that concern, then he will understand prosperity, then he will understand the significance of its being denied him, then he will not occupy himself with flights of fancy and fortify himself with dreams but in his adversity will be concerned about himself.

[186] *Then adversity will serve such a person for strengthening in the inner being.* And how would it not be so? The inner being does indeed announce itself in that concern, and adversity does in-

deed allow precisely the external, the visible, and the tangible to vanish and to be confused, but does it therefore always call the inner being into existence? Hardship does indeed make everyone concerned, but does it always make one concerned about God? Has not life more frequently affirmed the truth of those earnest words that are spoken by the same one who warned against prosperity and that therefore have the ring of profound meaning: "that hardships, too, are temptations." Look at him, the *concerned one*! Look more closely at him— you hardly recognize him from the time he walked out into life very joyful, strong, and confident. His destiny in life was to him so clear and so desirable; his mind knew his ambition, and his heart was in it; his strength worked trustingly—and hope promised him success. There is a hope that is heaven's fatherly gift to the child, a hope that grows with the child, a hope with which the young person goes out into life. This hope guarantees everything for him. Indeed, who but the Lord God in heaven gave him this hope? Should it not, then, be valid out in the wide world, in all the kingdoms and countries that belong to the heavenly king, who gave it to him! But this was not the case, and soon hardships had wrested from the stronger or tricked from the weaker his beautiful hope. Then everything became confused for him. No longer was there a sovereign in heaven; the wide world was a playground for the wild pandemonium of life; there was no ear that brought the confusion together in harmony, no guiding hand that intervened. No matter how a person could find consolation in life, hope was lost, so he thought, and hope remained lost. Then his soul grew concerned. And the more he stared down at the anarchy into which everything seemed to have disintegrated, the more power it gained over him, until it completely bewitched him; his mind reeled, and he himself plunged down into it and lost himself in despair. Or even though concern did not acquire such a seductive power over him, his soul nevertheless became aloof and alien to everything. He saw what others saw, but his eyes continually read an invisible handwriting in everything, that it was emptiness and illusion. Or he withdrew from people and murderously

wore out his soul in cares, in gloomy thoughts, in the barren
service of turbulent moods. What did such a person lack, what
did he fail to win when he lost everything—what else but
strengthening in the inner being?

[187]But the person who had this concern in his soul before
the arrival of the concern that comes from the outside, the
person whose soul was never satisfied by joy in such a way
that it lost concern about the witness but was not overwhelmed by the external concern in such a way that the possibility of joy vanished so long as he was still concerned about
the witness—for him, the concern that came from the outside
little by little became a friend. It joined the concern within
him; it prevented him from being mistaken about life; it
helped him to allow his soul to sink deeper and deeper into
concern until it discovered the witness. Then little by little he
became lighter and lighter; he gradually threw overboard the
worldly weight of earthly desires and rested with the witness
in God, blessed by the hope that he had won. So there is, then,
a hope that Scripture declares is gained through experience.[188]
What experience might Scripture mean? Might it be the experience in which a person makes sure that he obtains everything for which he hopes? Scripture says that this experience
is the fruit of spiritual trial. But the world cannot take away
such hope, because it is acquired in tribulation and becomes
strong through tribulation. Adversity helped him to gain
strengthening in the inner being. The person who learned
what he learned from what he suffered,[189] and learned the
good from what he suffered, gained not only the best learning
but what is much more—the best instructor—and the person
who learns from God is strengthened in the inner being. Then
even if he lost everything, he would still gain everything, and
Abraham possessed nothing but a burial place in Canaan,[190]
and yet he was God's chosen one.

[191]Consider him, the *person who was wronged*. He complains
not about life but about the people who corrupt everything
and embitter what God made good. Consider him a bit more
closely. You hardly recognize him from the time when, young
and confident, he went forth into life full of expectancy, his

countenance so open, his heart so warm, his soul in such a
hurry to meet everyone; for him there was only delight and
glory. But it did not remain that way. People's deceit, as he
thought, had soon tricked him out of his faith; people's cunning had ridiculed his openness; people's coldness and selfishness had vitiated his enthusiasm, people's envy had plunged
down his courage, his energy, his fervor, his proud striving,
and his glorious achievement into the same wretchedness in
which they themselves live. However one bears life, he
thought, people are lost. Then everything became confused
for him: there was no God who intended everything for good,
but everything was left up to human beings who intended
everything for evil. But the more his soul stared down into
the abyss of dark passions that arose in him, the greater was
the power that the anxiety of temptation gained over him, until he himself plunged down into it and lost himself in despair.
Or even though the pain did not sweep him off his feet in this
way, he stood case-hardened among his fellow human beings;
he saw the same thing that had happened to him repeat itself
in others, but he felt no sympathy. Indeed, what good would
it have done anyway, since he had no comfort to offer. Or he
hid from people in order in solitude of soul to immerse himself in his bleak wisdom, to fathom the thought of despair in
all its horror. Or he became bent like a reed, languishing in a
slowly consuming sadness, an anxiety to himself and to everyone who witnessed how he was being snuffed out.

But the person in whose soul the inner being announced
itself in that concern of which we speak, the person whose
soul no human being's love filled in such a way that the witness departed from his thoughts, that person probably never
found people to be as that wronged person found them, and
yet he perhaps found them to be different from what he had
hoped and wished them to be. But even though the terrible
thing happened, even though people rose up against him as
assailants or deserted him as deceivers, even though the enemy
persecuted him, even though the friend betrayed him, even
though envy laid snares for his feet, what were they able to do
to him? They could increase his concern; they could help him

to drive from his soul every feeling through which he belonged to creation in such a way that he did not also belong to the Creator. But they could not prevent the concern about God that was present in his soul from seeking its object more deeply and inwardly. And one who seeks God always finds, and he who constrains a person to seek helps him to find. Then his soul in its concern sought more and more inwardly until he found the witness. The person who loves God is strengthened in the inner being, and the person who loved people, and only through this love learned, as it were, to love God, has had only an imperfect upbringing; but the person who loved God and in this love learned to love people was strengthened in the inner being. If someone denied him his love, then that person helped him to find God's love, which is more blessed than anything that arose in a human heart;[192] if some friend denied him comfort, then he helped him to find God's comfort, which is beyond measure; if the world denied him its approval, then it helped him to seek God's, which passes all understanding.

III
312

[193]Consider him, the person who was *tried*, who was tested in the distress of spiritual trial. Perhaps you did not see him very often, because spiritual trial does not always come with visible signs. He was not tested in what we actually call adversity; people did not forsake him. On the contrary, externally, everything was beautiful and friendly. Yet his soul was in distress, and since this was not due to the external world, he could not seek people's comfort either. Outwardly everything was going well, and yet his soul was in anxiety, devoid of trust and bold confidence. He did not seek peace and tranquillity in externals, and yet his heart continued to be troubled. Then the inner being within him drooped; it seemed to him as if his outward success were only for the purpose of preserving his inner suffering so that he would not find relief even in the tribulations of the world; it seemed to him as if it were God himself who laid his powerful hand on him, as if he were a child of wrath,[194] and yet he could not come any closer to understanding or explaining how this could be. Then his innermost being rebelled within him, then he did what is related in an

old devotional book: "he boasted that he was lost,"[195] and that it was God himself who had plunged him down into damnation. Then the inner being within him froze.

But the person in whose soul the inner being announced itself in that concern of which we speak did not relinquish the concern. Even if he did not find the explanation, he nevertheless did find the explanation: that he should wait for the explanation. He nevertheless did find the explanation, that God was testing him; he nevertheless did find the comfort, that when God tests the time of testing can certainly become very long, but that God can make up for everything because to him one day is as a thousand years.[196] Then he became more calm in his distress. He did not flee the pain of spiritual trial; it became for him a confidant, a friend in disguise, even though he did not comprehend how, even though he strained his thought in vain to explain his riddle. But his calmness and humility increased in proportion to his concern, so that, however much he suffered, he always chose to remain with his spiritual trial rather than to be any other place in the world. Then at last the witness dawned in the full assurance of faith, because he who believes God contrary to the understanding is strengthened in the inner being. For him the spiritual trial served as a strengthening in the inner being; he learned the most beautiful thing of all, the most blessed—that God loved him, because the one God tests he loves.[197]

For such a person, then, prosperity and adversity serve for strengthening in the inner being. But nobody can provide this strengthening for himself; indeed, the one who receives a witness is not the one who gives it. Paul also reminds us of this in our text,[198] *because the witness itself is a gift from God*, from whom comes every good and perfect gift,[199] the most glorious gift of all, a gift from the Father in heaven, from whom all fatherliness in heaven and on earth derives its name. These are the apostle's words, and he ascribes the strengthening in the inner being to this fatherliness of God and ascribes it to him in such a way that God's love shows itself as fatherly love in this very expression, the strengthening in the inner being. We call God "Father"; we rest happily and confidently in this name as the most beautiful, the most uplifting, but also the truest and most expressive of names, and yet this expression is a metaphorical expression drawn from earthly life, even though from the most beautiful of earthly relations. But if the expression is figurative, metaphorical, does it actually reach up to heaven to describe what it is supposed to describe, or does it not dwindle away the higher it ascends, like an earthly longing, which always speaks only obscurely. [200]Yes, to one who looks at the external, the expression remains figurative and unreal; if he thinks that God gives the good gifts as a father gives them, but yet in such a way that it is the gifts that demonstrate, so to speak, that God is our Father, then he is judging externally, and for him truth itself becomes figurative. But the inner being looks not at the gifts but at the giver. For the inner being, the human distinction between what might be called gift and what language is not inclined to designate as gift vanishes in the essential, in the giver; for the inner being, joy and sorrow, good and bad fortune, distress and victory are gifts; for it, the giver is primary. Then the inner being understands and is convinced that God is a Father in heaven[201] and that this expression is not metaphorical, imperfect, but the truest and most literal expression, because God gives not only the gifts but himself with them in a way beyond the capability of any human being, who [202]can be present in the gift only in a feeling or in a mood, not essentially, cannot penetrate infinitesimally the total content of the gift, cannot be completely present in the whole gift, even less completely present in the least part of it. Therefore, if it ever seemed to you, my listener, as your thoughts emigrated from the paternal home, lost their way out in the world in order to rise to the conception of him, the almighty God, Creator of heaven and earth as the common Father of all, that you nevertheless lost something thereby, namely, some of the preferential love that was yours in the paternal home, because you were but a child and he was your earthly father, *your* father alone, then we shall not deny that the metaphor might not seem to you to be entirely appropriate. [203]But when you came to him, your earthly father, happy beyond measure because you had gained the whole world, and you surely found him happy (how could he not rejoice with the happy one, [204] especially with the happy one who was dearer to him than all else), but still, precisely because he loved you, he was happy only on the chance that what you had gained would not become your ruin—and, on the other hand, happy because you had gained the whole world, you came to your heavenly Father, and he shared your joy completely, precisely because your rejoicing with him was an unfailing guarantee that what you had gained would serve you for good—or when in sadness and tears you came to your earthly father and you surely found him weeping (how could he not weep with the one who weeps, [205] especially with the weeping one he loved more than all else), but still you could not really make yourself understandable to him, and so he grieved more because you were grieving than over that which grieved you—and, on the other hand, in sadness and with troubled soul, you came to your heavenly Father, who is the only one who has ears to hear what is said in secret and the fatherliness rightly to understand it—or when you, troubled and depressed, came to your earthly father and found him weak and wavering, without comfort for you, and his sorrow only increased your pain—and, on the other hand, crushed and shattered, you came to your heavenly Father and found him strong, and all the stronger the weaker you were, willing to help, and all the more willing the greater the distress . . . . . then, my listener, the metaphor is not entirely appropriate either. Then you perceived that it is not because you have a father or because human beings have fathers, that it is not for this reason that God is called Father in heaven, but it is as the apostle says—from him all fatherliness in heaven and on earth derives its name. Therefore, even though you had the most loving father given among men, he would still be, despite all his best intentions, but a stepfather, a shadow, a reflection, a simile, an image, a dark saying about the fatherliness from which all fatherliness in heaven and on earth derives its name. Oh, my listener, have you grasped this blessedness, or, rather, has my discourse reminded you of what you possess better and more inwardly and more fully and more blessedly than I

can describe it; or, rather, has my discourse disturbed for you III
nothing of what you did possess, for what is more blessed   315
than this thought, which no good fortune, no favor, no concern, no insult, no spiritual trial, neither things present nor
things to come[206] can wrench from a person but only serve to
confirm and to strengthen.

[207]The very first, so they say, is the most beautiful, and the
heart is attached to it: to the first person who welcomed him
in the hour he was counted among the living, the first sky that
arched over the place of his birth, to the first language that is
called his mother tongue, to the first people who are called his
ancestors, to the first teaching that expanded his soul, to the
first peers who understood him, to the first idea that inspired
him, to the first love that made him happy—blessed is the person who could truthfully say: God in heaven was my first love;
blessed is the person whose life was a beneficent strengthening
of this love; blessed is the person who, even though in his life
he made the mistake of taking the outer instead of the inner,
even though his soul in many ways was ensnared by the
world, yet was again renewed in the inner being by turning
back to his God, strengthened in the inner being.

Four Upbuilding Discourses

1843

TO THE LATE

Michael Pedersen Kierkegaard[208]

FORMERLY A CLOTHING MERCHANT HERE IN THE CITY

MY FATHER

THESE DISCOURSES ARE DEDICATED

PREFACE

Although this little book (which is called "discourses," not sermons, because its author does not have authority to *preach*, "upbuilding[209] discourses," not discourses for upbuilding,[210] because the speaker by no means claims to be a *teacher*[211]) is not unaware of the two that preceded it, it nevertheless is not confident that they have prepared the way so that with certainty it dares to count on being included with them or with certainty dares to promise this to the one who sends it out— and who at the same time stands far off by himself. It differs from the earlier ones only in that it goes out somewhat later. What is not found in the second and third hours may be found in the fourth, or what was found there may again be found in the fourth: that which it seeks, that single individual whom I with joy and gratitude call *my* reader, that favorably disposed person who receives the book and gives it a good home, that favorably disposed person who in receiving it does for it by himself and by his acceptance what the temple box by itself did for the widow's mite:[212] sanctifies the gift, gives it meaning, and transforms it into much.

S. K.

JOB 1:20-21

Then Job arose, and tore his robe, and shaved his head, and fell upon the ground, and worshiped, saying: Naked I came from my mother's womb, and naked shall I return; the Lord gave, and the Lord took away; blessed be the name of the Lord.

Not only do we call someone a teacher of humankind who by a special stroke of fortune discovered some truth or fathomed it by unflagging toil and thoroughgoing persistence and then left his attainment as learning that subsequent generations strive to understand and in this understanding to appropriate to themselves; but we also call someone—perhaps in an even stricter sense—a teacher of humankind who had no teaching to hand over to others but left humankind only himself as a prototype, his life as a guide for everyone, his name as security for many, his work as an encouragement for those who are being tried.

Such a teacher and guide of humankind is Job,[214] whose significance by no means consists in what he said but in what he did. He did indeed leave a statement that by its brevity and beauty has become a proverb preserved from generation to generation, and no one has presumptuously added anything to it or taken anything from it; but the statement itself is not the guide, and Job's significance consists not in his having said it but in his having acted upon it. The saying itself is certainly beautiful and worth pondering, but if someone else had said it, or if Job had been someone else, or if he had said it on another occasion, the saying itself would also have become something different—meaningful, if it had any meaning at all, as spoken, but not meaningful because he acted by asserting it, because the asserting was itself an action. If Job had applied his whole life to an inculcation of this saying, if he had regarded it as the sum and substance of what a person ought to let life teach him, if he had merely kept on *teaching* it but had never attempted it himself, had himself never acted in his asserting it, then Job would have been someone different and his significance would have been different. Then Job's name would have been forgotten, or at least it would not have mattered whether anyone knew it—the important point would be the contents of the words, the richness of the thought that lay in them. If humankind had received this saying, then it would have been this that one generation passed on to the next, whereas now it is Job himself who accompanies the generation. When one generation has finished its service, completed its work, fought through its struggle, Job has accompanied it; when the new generation with its incalculable ranks, each individual in his place, stands ready to begin the pilgrimage, Job is there again, takes his place, which is the outpost of humanity. If the generation sees nothing but happy days in prosperous times, then Job faithfully accompanies it; but if the single individual experiences the terror in thought, is anguished over the thought of what horror and distress life can have in store, over the thought that no one knows when the hour of despair may strike for him, then his troubled thought seeks out Job, rests in him, is calmed by him, for Job faithfully accompanies him and comforts him, not, to be sure, as if he had suffered once and for all what would never be suffered again, but comforts as someone who witnesses that the horror has been suffered, the horror has been experienced, the battle of despair has been fought to the glory of God, for his own rescue, for the benefit and joy of others. In happy days, in prosperous times, Job walks along at the generation's side and safeguards its happiness, grapples with the anxious dream that some sudden unspeakable horror will assail a person and have the power to murder his soul as its certain prey. Only a light-minded person could wish that Job were not along, that his revered name did not remind him of what he is trying to forget, that life also has terror and anxiety; only a selfish person could

wish that Job did not exist so that the idea of his suffering   IV
would not disturb his flimsy happiness with its rigorous ear-   11
nestness and scare him out of a sense of security drunk with
callousness and damnation. In tempestuous times, when the
foundation of existence is tottering, when the moment shivers
in anxious expectancy of what may come, when every explanation falls silent at the spectacle of the wild tumult, when a
person's innermost being groans in despair and "in bitterness
of soul"[215] cries to heaven, then Job still walks along at the
generation's side and guarantees that there is a victory, guarantees that even if the single individual loses in the struggle,
there is still a God who, just as he proportions every temptation humanly, even though a person did not withstand the
temptation, will still make its outcome so that we are able to
bear it[216]—yes, even more gloriously than any human expectancy. Only the defiant person could wish that Job did not exist, that he could completely divest his soul of the last love still
present in the wail of despair, that he could whine about life,
indeed, curse life in such a way that there would not be even
an echo of faith and trust and humility in his words, that in his
defiance he could stifle the scream in order not to create the
impression that there was anyone whom it provoked. Only a
soft person could wish that Job did not exist, that he could
instead leave off thinking, the sooner the better, could give up
all movement in the most disgusting powerlessness, could
blot himself out in the most wretched and miserable forgetfulness.

The saying that reminds us of Job as soon as it is spoken,
the saying that leaps vividly to everyone's mind as soon as
Job's name is mentioned, is a plain and simple saying and
hides no secret wisdom[217] that has to be investigated by the
profound. When a child learns this saying, when it is entrusted
to him as an endowment, he does not understand how he shall
use it; then he understands the saying, understands thereby essentially the same as do the very wise. Yet the child does not
understand it, or rather he does not understand Job, since
what he does not grasp is all the distress and misery in which
Job was tested. Of this the child can have but a faint presenti-

ment, and yet how fortunate the child who understood the saying and received the impression of what he did not grasp, that it was the most terrible of all, who, before sorrow and adversity made his mind subtle, possessed the childishly lively conviction that the saying really was the most terrible of all. When the youth turns his thought to these words, he understands them and understands thereby essentially the same as do the child and the very wise. Yet he may not understand them, or rather he does not understand Job, does not understand the source of all the distress and wretchedness in which Job was tried; and yet how fortunate the youth who understood the saying and humbly bowed under what he did not understand before distress made his thought obstinate, as if he were discovering what no one before had known. When the adult deliberates on this saying, he understands it and understands thereby essentially the same as do the child and the very wise. He also understands the distress and affliction in which Job was tested, and yet he may not understand Job, because he cannot understand how Job was able to say it—and yet how fortunate the adult who understood the saying and admiringly held fast to what he did not understand before affliction and distress made him suspicious also of Job. When the tested person who fought the good fight[218] by being mindful of the saying mentions it, he understands the saying and understands thereby essentially the same as do the child and the very wise, he understands Job's wretchedness, he understands how Job could say it. —He understands the saying, he interprets it, even if he never talked about it, more gloriously than the person who spent his whole life explaining just this one saying.

Only the person who has been tried and who tested the saying in being tested himself, only he rightly interprets the saying; Job desires only that kind of pupil, only that kind of interpreter; he alone learns from him what there is to learn, the most beautiful and the most blessed, compared with which all other art or wisdom is very inessential. Therefore, we quite properly call Job a teacher of humankind and not of individuals, because he presents himself to everyone as his prototype, beckons to everyone with his glorious example, calls everyone

IV
12

in his beautiful saying. Although at times the simpler person, the less gifted, or the less favored by time and circumstances probably wished, if not in envy then in troubled despondency, that he had the capacity and the opportunity to be able to grasp what the wise and learned in various periods have fathomed and to become absorbed in it, and felt in his soul the desire of also being able himself to teach others and not always only to be receiving instruction—Job does not tempt him in that way. What good would human wisdom be here? Would it perhaps try to make more understandable what the simplest person and the child readily understood and understood just as well as the very wise! What good would eloquence and the power of words be here? Would they be able to produce in the speaker or any other person what the simplest person is able to do just as well as the very wise—action! Would not human wisdom rather make everything more difficult! Would not eloquence, which despite all its gloriousness never once manages to articulate simultaneously the variety that simultaneously dwells in a person's heart, rather anesthetize the energy of the act and let it fall asleep in protracted deliberation! But even if all this is true and as a result the single individual tries to avoid saying anything that would disturbingly intervene between the struggling one and the beautiful prototype, who is equally close to every human being, lest by increasing his wisdom he also increase his grief,²¹⁹ takes care not to become trapped himself in the fine words of human persuasion, which are exceedingly sterile—it by no means follows that deliberation and elaboration would not have their importance. If the person deliberating were previously unacquainted with the saying, then it would indeed always be beneficial for him to learn to know it; if he did know the saying but had not had occasion to test it in his life, then it would indeed be beneficial for him to learn to understand what he would perhaps apply at some time; if he had tested the saying but betrayed it, even though he thought that it was the saying that had betrayed him, then it would indeed be beneficial for him if he deliberated on it once again before he again took to his heels and ran away from the saying in the excitement of the struggle and the

IV
13

flurry of the battle. Perhaps the deliberation would at some time have its importance for him; perhaps it would happen that the deliberation would become vivid and present in his soul just when he needed it in order to penetrate the confused thoughts of his disquieted heart; perhaps it would happen that what deliberation understood in pieces[220] would suddenly come together reborn in the moment of decision, that what deliberation sowed in corruption would rise up on the day of distress in the incorruptible life of action.[221]

We shall, then, endeavor to understand Job more clearly in his beautiful words: *The Lord gave, and the Lord took away; blessed be the name of the Lord!*

In a country to the east lived a man whose name was Job; he possessed the blessings of the land, abundant herds and rich pastures. "His words upheld the stumbling and braced the trembling knees."[222] His tent was as blessed to dwell in as the bosom of heaven, and in this tent he lived with seven sons and three daughters, and with him in this tent "lived the friendship of the Lord."[223] Job was an old man; his joy in life was his children's joy, over which he watched lest it become their ruin. One day, while his children were celebrating together at the house of the firstborn son, Job sat alone by his hearth. When he had offered a burnt sacrifice for each of them, his heart was disposed to rejoice in the thought of his children's joy. As he sat there in the quiet security of joy, there came a messenger, and before he had finished speaking, there came another, and while this one was still speaking, there came a third messenger, but the fourth emissary came from his sons and daughters, with word that the house had collapsed and had buried them all. "Then Job arose, and tore his robe, and shaved his head, and cast himself upon the ground, and worshiped."[224] His sorrow did not make use of many words, or rather he did not say a single one; his appearance alone gave witness that his heart was shattered. Could you want it any other way! Or does not the person who takes pride in not being able to sorrow on the day of sorrow have the shame of

IV
14

not being able to rejoice on the day of joy, either? Or is the sight of such immutability not unpleasant and stultifying, indeed, shocking, even though it is heartwrenching to see the venerable old man, who with his fatherly countenance was just now resting in the joy of the Lord, now cast upon the ground with his robe torn and his hair shaved! Having surrendered to sorrow, not in despair but with human emotions, he was quick to judge between God and himself, and these are the words of judgment: "Naked I came from my mother's womb, and naked shall I return."[225] With those words, the dispute was settled, and in his soul every demand was silenced that would claim from the Lord something he was unwilling to give or would desire to keep something as if it had not been given. Then comes the confession from the man whom not sorrow alone but also worship had cast to the ground: "The Lord gave, and the Lord took away; blessed be the name of the Lord!"

The Lord gave, and the Lord took away. The first thing here that halts deliberation is that Job said, "The Lord gave." Are these words not irrelevant to the occasion; do they not contain something extraneous to the event itself? If at one moment a man has lost everything he treasured and has lost the greatest treasure of all, perhaps the loss will overwhelm him in such a way that he does not even dare to say it, even though in his innermost being he is conscious before God that he has lost everything. Or he will not let the crushing weight of the loss rest on his soul, but he will, as it were, detach himself from it and with deep emotion say: The Lord took away. To submit to the Lord in silence and humility in this way is indeed also deserving of praise and emulation, and such a person would also save his soul in the struggle even if he lost all joy.

    But Job! The moment the Lord took everything away, he did not first say, "The Lord took away," but first of all he said, "The Lord gave." The statement is brief, but in its brevity it effectually points out what it is supposed to point out, that Job's soul was not squeezed into silent subjection to the sorrow, but that his heart first expanded in thankfulness, that the

IV
15

first thing the loss of everything did was to make him thankful to the Lord that he had given him all the blessings that he now took away from him. With him it was not as Joseph prophesied[226]—that the seven years of abundance would be totally forgotten in the seven lean years. His thankfulness no doubt was not the same as in those days that already seemed so far away, when he received every good and every perfect gift[227] from God's hand with thankfulness. But his thankfulness was nevertheless honest, just as honest as the idea of God's goodness that was now so vivid in his soul. Now he recalled everything the Lord had given, some particular thing with perhaps even more thankfulness than when he had received it; it had not become less beautiful because it had been taken away, nor more beautiful, but was just as beautiful as before, beautiful because the Lord had given it, and what might seem more beautiful to him now was not the gift but God's goodness. He recalled his prosperity; his eye rested again upon the rich pastures and followed the abundant herds. He recalled the joy of having seven sons and three daughters; now there was no need to make any offering for them but the offering of thankfulness for having had them. He recalled those who perhaps still recollected him with thanksgiving, the many he had instructed, "whose weary hands he had strengthened, whose trembling knees he had braced."[228] He recalled his days of glory, when he was powerful and highly regarded among the people, "when the young withdrew out of respect for him, when the old rose and remained standing."[229] He recalled with thankfulness that he had not turned from the path of righteousness, that he had rescued the poor who lamented and the fatherless who had no helper, and therefore even now at this moment "the blessing of the abandoned was upon him"[230] as before. The Lord gave—this is a short statement, but for Job it said a great deal, because Job's memory was not short and his thankfulness was not forgetful. With thankfulness resting in his soul in quiet sadness, he said a gentle and friendly farewell to everything all together, and in this farewell everything vanished like a beautiful recollection—indeed, it was as if it were not the Lord who took it away but Job who gave it back to him. Therefore, when Job had said, "The Lord gave," his mind was well prepared to please God also with the next words, "The Lord took away."

Perhaps there was someone who on the day of sorrow also recalled that he had known happy days; then his soul became even more impatient. "If he had never known happiness, then the pain would not have overwhelmed him, for what is pain but an idea that the person who knows nothing else does not have, but now it is precisely joy that has educated and developed him to perceive pain." Then his joy became his own ruin; it was never lost but only lacking, and in its lack it tempted him more than ever before. What had been his eyes' delight, his eyes craved to see again, and his ingratitude punished him by inducing him to believe it to be more beautiful than it had ever been. What his soul had delighted in, it now thirsted for, and ingratitude punished him by picturing it to him as more delightful than it had ever been. What he once had been able to do, he now wanted to be able to do again, and ingratitude punished him with fantasies that had never had any truth. Then he condemned his soul, living, to be starved out in the insatiable craving of the lack. —Or there awakened in his soul a consuming passion that he had not even enjoyed the happy days in the right way, had not sucked out all the sweetness of their voluptuous abundance. If only he might be granted one brief hour, if only he might recover his former glory for a short time so that he might satiate himself with happiness and thereby gain indifference to the pain. Then he abandoned his soul to a burning restlessness. He would not admit to himself whether the enjoyment he craved was worthy of a man, whether he might not rather thank God that his soul had not been so frantic in the time of joy as it had now become; he refused to be dismayed by the thought that his craving was the occasion for his perdition; he refused to be concerned that the worm[231] of craving that would not die in his soul was more wretched than all his wretchedness.

Perhaps there was someone who in the moment of loss also recalled what he had possessed, but he presumptuously wanted to prevent the loss from becoming comprehensible to

IV
17

him. Even though it was lost, his defiant will was nevertheless able to retain it as if it had not been lost. Instead of trying to bear the loss, he chose to waste his energies in impotent defiance, in losing himself in a demented possession of what had been lost. Or in the same moment he cravenly avoided any humble striving to reconcile himself to the loss. Then forgetfulness opened its abyss, not so much for the loss as for him, and he did not so much evade the loss in forgetfulness as he threw himself away. Or he mendaciously tried to defraud the good once bestowed on him—as if it had never been splendid, had never made him happy; he thought he could strengthen his soul by wretched self-deceit, as if there were strength in falsehood. —Or his soul became utterly wanton, and he convinced himself that life was not as hard as it was imagined to be, that its terribleness was not as described and was not very difficult to bear if one, please note, began, as he had done, with not finding it terrible to become a person like that. Indeed, who would ever finish if he were going to talk about what happens often enough and probably will be repeated often enough in this world; would he not grow weary much sooner than would the passion for changing, with ever new ingenuity, what has been explained and understood into new illusion with which it would deceive itself!

Let us, therefore, rather return to Job. On the day of sorrow, when everything was lost, he first of all thanked God, who gave it, deceived neither God nor himself, and even though everything had been shaken and overthrown, he remained what he was from the beginning, "honest and upright before God."[232] He confessed that the Lord's blessing had rested mercifully upon him; he gave thanks for it; therefore, it did not remain with him as a nagging memory. He confessed that the Lord had richly blessed his work beyond all measure; he gave thanks; therefore, the memory did not remain as a consuming restlessness. He did not conceal from himself that everything had been taken away from him; therefore, the Lord, who had taken it away, remained in his upright soul. He did not evade the thought that it was lost; therefore, his soul remained quiet until the Lord's explanation again came to him

and found his mind, like good earth, well cultivated in patience.[233]

The Lord took away. Did Job not say something here that
differed from what was the truth? Did he not use a remote
expression for something that could be designated with a
more immediate expression? The statement is short and des-
ignates the loss of everything. It is natural now for us to repeat
it after him, inasmuch as the saying itself has become a sacred
proverb; but is it always just as natural for us to associate Job's
thinking with it? Or was it not the Sabeans who raided his
peaceful herds and cut down his servants;[234] did the messenger
who brought the news speak of something else? Or was it not
the lightning that consumed the sheep and their shepherds; did
the messenger who brought the news speak of something else,
even though he called the lightning the fire of God?[235] Was it
not a storm from the desert yonder that blew down the house
and buried his children; did the messenger mention any other
perpetrator, or did he mention anyone who had sent the
stormy weather? Yet Job said, "The Lord took away," and at
the very moment he received the message he understood that
it was the Lord who had taken away everything. Who informed Job of this, or was it a mark of his piety that he shifted
everything over to the Lord in this way; or who authorized
him to do this, and are we not more devout, we who sometimes hesitate for a long time before speaking this way?

Perhaps there was someone in the world who lost everything. Then he sat down to consider how it had happened. But
the whole thing remained inexplicable and obscure to him.
His joy vanished as if it were a dream, and the trouble remained with him like a dream, but how he had been ejected
from the gloriousness of the one into the wretchedness of the
other he never did learn—it was not the Lord who had taken
it away; it was an accident. Or he convinced himself that it was
the deceit and cunning of people or their open aggression that
had wrested it from him, just as the Sabeans had cut down
Job's herds and their keepers. Then his soul revolted against
people; he thought that he was doing justice to God by not

upbraiding him for it. He understood perfectly well how it had happened, and the more immediate explanation he had was that these people had done it, and the more remote explanation was that the people were evil and their hearts corrupt. He understood that those closest are a detriment to him; perhaps he would have understood it in a similar way if they had benefited him; but that the Lord, who dwells far off in heaven, could be closer to him than the person closest to him, whether this person did good or evil to him—from this conception his thought was very remote. Or he understood perfectly well how it had happened and knew how to describe it with the eloquence of horror. How would he not understand that when the sea is raging wildly, when it heaves itself toward heaven, people and their fragile buildings are then flung about as in a game; that when the storm rages in its fury, human projects are but child's play; that when the earth quakes in the anguish of the elements and when the mountains sigh, men and their glorious works then sink as a nothingness into the abyss. And this explanation was sufficient for him, and above all sufficient to make his soul indifferent to everything. It is true that whatever is built upon sand[236] does not even need a storm to topple it, but was it therefore also true that a person cannot build and live somewhere else and be saved! Or he understood that he himself was to blame, that he had not been prudent; if he had reckoned everything in a timely way, it would not have happened. And this explanation explained everything, after first having explained that he had distorted himself and had made it impossible for himself to learn anything from life and especially impossible to learn anything from God.

But who would ever finish if he were to tell what has happened and what probably will be repeated often enough in life? Would he not grow weary much sooner than the sensate person would grow weary of beguiling himself with specious and disappointing and deceptive explanations? Let us, therefore, leave that from which nothing is to be learned—except what was not unfamiliar to us before—so that we might reject this worldly learning and turn to him from whom we can learn the truth, to Job and to his devout words "the Lord took away." Job traced everything back to God; he did not detain his soul and quench his spirit with deliberation or explanations that only feed and foster doubt, even though the person suspended in them does not even notice that. The very moment everything was taken away from him, he knew it was the Lord who had taken it away, and therefore in his loss he remained on good terms with the Lord, in his loss maintained intimacy with the Lord; he saw the Lord, and therefore he did not see despair. Or does he alone see God's hand who sees that he gives, or does not also the one see God's hand who sees that he takes away? Or does he alone see God who sees God turn his face toward him, or does not also he see God who sees him turn his back, just as Moses continually saw nothing but the Lord's back?[237] But the one who sees God has overcome the world, and therefore Job in his devout words had overcome the world, in those devout words was greater and stronger and more powerful than the whole world, which here certainly did not want to lead him into temptation but to overcome him by its power and bring him to his knees before its boundless might. Indeed, how weak, almost childishly so, is the blustering of the storm when it wants to make a person tremble before it by tearing everything away from him, but he answers: It is not you who are doing it; it is the Lord who takes away! How powerless is the assailant's arm, how worthless the schemer's cleverness; how almost pitiable is all human power when it wants to plunge the weak person into despairing submission by wrenching everything from him and in his faith he says: It is not you, you can do nothing; it is the Lord who takes away.

Blessed be the name of the Lord! So Job not only overcame the world, but he did what Paul desires his struggling congregation to do: he held his ground after having overcome everything (Ephesians 6:13). Alas, perhaps there was someone in the world who overcame everything but fell the moment he won the victory. Blessed be the name of the Lord! So the Lord remained the same,[238] and should he not therefore be praised as always? Or had the Lord actually changed? Or did the Lord not remain truly the same, just as Job did? Blessed be the name of the Lord! So the Lord did not take everything away, for he did not take praise away from him, and he did not take away peace in the heart, the bold confidence in faith from which it proceeded, but intimacy with the Lord was still his as before, perhaps more inward than before, for now there was nothing at all in any way capable of drawing his thoughts away from it. The Lord took everything away; then Job collected all his sorrow, as it were, and "cast it upon the Lord,"[239] and then the Lord took that away from him also, and only praise was left and in it his heart's incorruptible joy.

If any house is a house of sorrow, Job's house is, but where these words are heard, "Blessed be the name of the Lord," there joy also has its home. And Job indeed stands before us with the image of sorrow expressed in his countenance and in his posture, but he who says these words still witnesses to joy, as does Job, even if his witness is addressed not to the happy but to the troubled and still speaks understandably to the many who have ears to hear.[240] The ears of the troubled are formed in a special way, and just as the lover's ears may well hear many voices but nevertheless really only one, namely, the voice of the beloved, so the ears of the troubled may well hear many voices, but they pass by and do not penetrate his heart. Just as faith and hope without love are but sounding brass and a tinkling cymbal,[241] so all the joy proclaimed in the world in which sorrow is not heard along with it is but sounding brass and a tinkling cymbal that tickle the ears but are repulsive to the soul. But this voice of comfort, this voice that trembles in pain and yet proclaims joy, this is heard by the ears of the troubled one; his heart treasures it, and it strengthens and guides him to find joy even in the depths of sorrow. —My listener, you have understood Job's praise, have you not—at least it has seemed so beautiful to you in the quiet thought of contemplation that you have forgotten whatever you do not wish me to remind you of, what certainly is sometimes heard in the world in the day of distress instead of praise and *benediction*. So let it be forgotten; you will not cause, any more than I will, the memory of it to be kept alive.

IV
21

We have spoken about Job and sought to understand him in his devout words; the discourse, however, has not wanted to impose itself on anyone. But does that mean that it should be utterly devoid of meaning or devoid of application and not pertain to anyone? If you yourself, my listener, were tried as Job was and stood the ordeal as he did, then it would indeed apply precisely to you if what we have said about Job is otherwise correct. If up until now you have not been tried in life, then it indeed applies to you. Are you perhaps thinking that these words are applicable only to the kind of extraordinary situation in which Job was placed? If something similar were to befall you, do you perhaps expect that the terror itself would give you this strength and develop in you this humble courage? Did Job not have a wife—what do we read about her?[242] Perhaps you are thinking that the horror itself cannot acquire the same power over a person as the daily bondage to much lesser hardships. Then watch out that you do not become a slave to some hardship any more than to some person, and above all learn from Job to become honest with yourself so that you do not deceive yourself with imagined power, with which you experience imagined victory in imagined struggle.

IV
22

Perhaps you say: If the Lord had taken it away from me—but nothing was given to me. Perhaps you think that this is by no means as terrible as Job's suffering but that it is far more exhausting and consequently an even more difficult struggle. We shall not dispute with you, for even if your struggle were that, dispute over it would be useless and would be an intensification of the difficulty. But you do agree with us that you can learn from Job, and if you are honest with yourself and love people, then you cannot wish to avoid Job in order to venture out into new and unfamiliar distress and keep the rest of us unsettled until we learn from your witness that in this difficulty, too, a victory is possible. So, then, learn from Job to say: Blessed be the name of the Lord. This does indeed apply to you, even though the above was less applicable.

Or are you perhaps thinking that something like this could not happen to you? Who taught you this wisdom, or on what do you base this conviction? Are you wise and sensible, and is this your comfort? Job was the teacher of many people. Are you young, and is youth your security? Job, too, was once young. Are you old, on the edge of the grave? Job was an old man when sorrow caught up with him. Are you powerful, and is this the proof of your exemption? Job was highly regarded by the people. Is wealth your security? Job possessed the blessings of the land. Are friends your security? Job was loved by all. Do you trust in God? Job was an intimate of the Lord. Have you really pondered these thoughts, or do you rather avoid them lest they force a confession from you, which you now perhaps call a depressed mood? And yet there is no hiding place in the whole wide world where trouble will not find you, and no one has ever lived who could say more than you can say, that you do not know when sorrow will visit your house. So, then, be earnest with yourself; fix your eyes upon Job. Even if he terrifies you, it is not this that he wants if you yourself do not want it. When you scan your whole life and think of it as finished, you certainly would not wish to have to make this confession: I was a fortunate one who was not like other people, who never suffered anything in the world, and who let every day take care of itself or, rather, let it bring me new joys. You would never wish to make such a confession, even if it were true. Indeed, it would contain your own shame, for even if you were protected more than everyone else, you would still say: It is true that I myself have not been tried, but still my mind has often become grave at the thought of Job and the idea that no one knows the time and the hour when the messages will come to him, the one more terrible than the other.

IV
23

EVERY GOOD GIFT AND EVERY PERFECT GIFT IS FROM ABOVE[243]

JAMES 1:17-22

Every good gift and every perfect gift is from above and comes down from the Father of lights, with whom there is no change or shadow of variation. According to his own counsel, he brought us forth by the word of truth, that we should be a first 'fruit of his creation. Therefore, my beloved brethren, let every person be quick to hear, slow to speak, slow to anger, because a man's anger does not work what is righteous before God. Therefore put away all filthiness and all remnants of wickedness and receive with meekness the word that is implanted in you and that is powerful for making your souls blessed.

Only of the tree of the knowledge of good and evil was man not allowed to eat[244]—lest the knowledge should enter the world and bring grief along with it:[245] the pain of want and the dubious happiness of possession, the terror of separation and the difficulty of separation, the disquietude of deliberation and the worry of deliberation, the distress of choice and the decision of choice, the judgment of the law and the condemnation of the law, the possibility of perdition and the anxiety of perdition, the suffering of death and the expectation of death. If this had happened, if the command had not been transgressed, then everything would have remained as it was, so very good, and this witness that God gave creation[246] would have resounded from humankind as an unceasing, blessed repetition. Then the security of peace would have prevailed in everything; then the quiet celebration of beauty would have smiled solemnly; then the blessedness of heaven would have enveloped everything; then heaven would not even have been mirrored in earthly life, lest presentiment should rise from the depths of innocence; then no echo would have summoned longing from its secret hiding place, for heaven would be earth and everything would be fulfilled. Then man would have awakened from the deep sleep in which Eve came into existence[247] in order once again to become absorbed in joy and glory; then the image of God would have been stamped upon everything in a reflection of glory that would lull everything into the spell of the perfection that moved everything, itself unmoved.[248] Then the lamb would have lain down to rest beside the wolf,[249] and the dove would have built its nest next to the bird of prey; the poisonous herb would have been harmless; then everything would have been very good. There would have been truth in everything, for Adam did indeed give the proper name[250] to everything as it truly is; there would have been trustworthiness in everything, for everything would be what it seemed to be; justice would have sprung up out of the earth.[251] And yet there would not have been the distinction between good and evil, because this separation was indeed the very fruit of the fruit of the knowledge. And yet no one would have asked *where* everything came *from*. Nor would the voice of the Lord have wandered in the Garden of Eden and asked for Adam.[252] Adam would not have hidden himself in the garden and in his inner being, but everything would have been open, and the Lord was the only one who would have hidden himself, even though he was imperceptibly present in everything. Adam would not have had time to ask where it came from, because it offered itself at the moment, and the gift itself offered itself in such a way that receiving it did not arouse questions about the giver.

Then the man broke the peace by plucking the forbidden fruit of the knowledge of good and evil. He went astray, and by means of the knowledge he went astray again, because the serpent deceived Eve (Genesis 3:13), and thus by way of a deception the knowledge came into the world as a deception. The fruit of the knowledge, which the man relished, planted the tree of the knowledge in his inner being, which bore its fruits, which now probably did not seem delectable to him, for the fruit of the knowledge always seems delectable and is delectable to look at,[253] but when one has savored it, it fosters trouble, compels the man to work in the sweat of his brow, and sows thorns and thistles for him.[254] What happened at the beginning of days, that the fruit of the knowledge was delectable to look at, is continually repeated in every generation and in the individual.[255] If the Lord's warning was unable to save the first human being from this deception, how would a human voice be able to do anything but make that fruit even more delectable for the individual to look at.

The Garden of Eden was closed; everything was changed, the man became afraid of himself, afraid of the world around him. Troubled, he asked: What is the good, where is the perfect to be found? If it exists, where is its source? But the doubt that had come along with the knowledge coiled itself alarmingly around his heart, and the serpent that had seduced him with the delectable now squeezed him in its coils. Would he find out what the good and perfect is without learning where it came from, would he be able to recognize the eternal source without knowing what the good and perfect is? Doubt would explain to him first one thing, then another, and in the explanation itself it would lie in wait for him in order to disquiet him still more. What happened at the beginning of days is repeated in every generation and in the individual; the consequences of the fruit of the knowledge could not be halted. With the knowledge, doubt became more inward, and the knowledge, which should have guided man, fettered him in distress and contradiction. At times the knowledge was to him something unattainable for which he sighed; at times it seemed to him a blissfulness that his soul was continually losing; at times it was a knowing that made his heart ashamed; at times a realization that only made him tremble; at times a consciousness of himself, at times a consciousness of the whole world; at times it stimulated every one of his capacities, and at times it enervated his whole being; at times it overwhelmed

him with its abundance, and at times it starved him with its
emptiness.

Is doubt, then, the stronger? Is the one who will success-
fully invade the house of the strong[256] a new doubt? Does one
take away his weapons by using the same weapons against him
that he himself uses, or would not one thereby just strengthen
him; and is it not doubt's stratagem to make a person believe
that he by himself can overcome himself, as if he were able to
perform the marvel unheard of in heaven or on earth or under
the earth[257]—that something that is in conflict with itself can
in this conflict be stronger than itself! Or how does the unclean
spirit behave when by itself it drives itself out of a person; does
it not return with seven others so that the last is worse than
the first (Matthew 12:45)? Or what happens to a person who,
in conflict with himself, does not confess that even if he were
able to overcome everything he still would not have the power
to overcome himself by himself? Does not this victorious self
change into something far worse than the corrupted self that
it vanquished; and does it not go on living securely within him
because there is no stronger self in him—except this self that
is even worse? No, therefore one first of all binds the strong
person or hands him over to be bound, and not until then does
one force one's way into his house to take his weapons away
from him (Matthew 12:29). That this is the way it is, anyone
will surely admit who has honestly wanted to undergo this
experience and has not preferred—instead of a humble, even
if in another sense an elevating, truth—a brilliant deception by
which he managed to fool himself and above all became capable of arousing the admiration of people and satisfying their
fraudulent claim that demanded a deception. If, however, one
prefers to have little with blessing,[258] to have truth with concern, to suffer instead of exulting over imagined victories,
then one presumably will not be disposed to praise the knowledge, as if what it bestows were at all proportionate to the
trouble it causes, although one would not therefore deny that
through its pain it educates a person, if he is honest enough to
want to be educated [*opdrages*] rather than to be deceived [*be-*
drages], out of the multiplicity to seek the one, out of the abun-

dance to seek the one thing needful,[259] as this is plainly and simply offered precisely according to the need for it.

So let us deliberate in more detail and do our part to understand and in our deliberation be captured for freedom, as it were, by the beautiful apostolic words that explain both the what and the whence in: *that every good gift and every perfect gift is from above.*

"If you, who are evil, know how to give good gifts to your children, how much more will your heavenly Father give good things to those who ask him?" (Matthew 7:11; Luke 11:13). These words bend down so sympathetically to the troubled one, speak with such concern to the concerned one, that they raise him up and strengthen him in the bold confidence of full conviction. If, that is, a person is not like the doubter, indifferent about himself and occupied only with the great sorrows of life and existence, but is like the concerned person, primarily concerned about his own task, his minor role, what better words could be addressed to him than these words, which are so childlike, which he himself to a degree always is, reminiscent of life's first unforgettable impression, reminiscent of a father's love for his child, his solicitude about giving it good gifts! If it holds true that just as a father has compassion on children, God has compassion on the one who calls upon him,[260] that just as a father gives his child good gifts, God gives good gifts to those who pray to him for them—if this is firmly set, then the comfort offered is the most reliable of all. So it was that he once understood the words, rejoiced in them, rejoiced in what they reminded him of, rejoiced in what they promised, rejoiced that they prompted him to think again about his father's solicitude for him by explaining the words to him, rejoiced that his father's love consummated all his goodness to him by explaining to him God's love; but it did not occur to him that these words, like all sacred words, at various times can be milk for children and strong food for adults,[261] even though the words remain the same. It did not dawn on him that the words could have another interpretation whereby they became even more glorious, that the metaphorical language could become even more comforting when actuality also began to explain to him the metaphors of earthly life, that the conclusion of the words could become even more firmly set when reversed—something his soul would need when life had reversed everything for him.

Then he had grown older; everything was changed, was shaken by a terrible upheaval; God pronounced another judgment, that even the human being, who nevertheless was the most perfect creation, that even he was evil. This was pronounced not in a judgment of wrath in order to inspire fear but in a metaphorical saying that tried to find an expression for the divine in the most beautiful relation in earthly existence. The words said: You, who are evil—not as if this were the theme of what was said but as a truth decided once and for all and merely mentioned. But the very fact that it was presupposed in this way disturbed the effect of the metaphorical saying, disturbed him also because he persisted in thinking that life had truly taught him that even the most sincere human love, when it wanted to do the very best thing, had sometimes only harmed another person, that he himself, when his impulse was pure—indeed, when he was willing to make every sacrifice, even when he wanted to do everything for another— had only caused him pain. "If," he then said, "God's love does not know how to give good gifts any better than a father's love, then there certainly is small comfort in these words." In this way the words became for him what fatherly love was for him—a beautiful, hallowed, wistful recollection, an uplifting mood that quickened in his soul the conception of the best in the human being but also of the human being's weakness, quickened the soul's most blessed longing but also retracted it again in order to subordinate it to the sadness of concern. Then he thought that he had outgrown the words and did not grasp their upbringing solicitude, did not grasp that the words remained unchanged, that they had always spoken doubtfully of fatherly love's power to give good gifts but had witnessed all the more powerfully to God's heart and will.

Then he immersed himself in the words; he refused to allow the words to draw him up to themselves, to forget the metaphorical for the actual, but the words of comfort and the words of power became for him the seed of doubt. If the human being, who is the most perfect of all, is evil, then all earthly life lies in evil. Or if whatever earthly life possesses becomes evil only through the human being, then it is a matter of indifference from the start, is neither good nor evil, but the fact that it is only an appearance, is not something essential, is again a qualification of evil. What, then, is the good, what is the perfect? In that metaphorical saying it is stated that a father, although he is evil, nevertheless gives his child the good gift he asks for and does not give him a stone when he asks for bread, or a snake when he asks for a fish, and then come the words of application: If you, who are evil, know how to give good gifts, would not your heavenly Father give them? But were the bread and the fish in themselves a good gift, or were they that only insofar as they were needed, and yet in turn is not the need itself an imperfection in human life? And even if a person did have the need, might it not nevertheless be more beneficial for him if this were denied to him? In a higher sense, may he not have that need, just as when the prodigal son asked for bread and he was given beechnuts and acorns so that he might come to himself and repent the error of his ways?[262] Consequently, a person may know how to give good gifts, but he cannot know whether he is giving a good gift, just as, conversely, the evil person may know how to give an evil gift but cannot know whether he is giving an evil gift. The one who knew how to sow good clean seed in his field certainly knew how to sow it, but he did not know whether he did it, he did not know what might happen while he slept[263] and what he might be shocked to see when he woke up;[264] yes, even if he had not slept, he still would not have known the even greater shock in store for him. He may know what seems to be beneficial, whether he bases his opinion on his own thinking and experience or on someone else's report; he may know how to give it, but whether he does give it he does not know. He may know what is good in its intrinsic perfection, but whether he is giving it, he cannot know, as soon as he wants to know it in a kind of knowledge other than that which

IV
30

is indifferent to every person—that he knows how to give it
and that he has given it—whereas the question arising out of
concern, whether he actually did give it, remains unanswered.
And if his soul does not know this concern, then he has no
right to be called father, because a father is distinguishable
from any other man by having concern, is distinguishable
from his best friend by having a higher degree of concern than
he has. So there is nothing good and perfect in the world, for
either the good exists only in such a way that by coming into
existence it becomes a dubious good, but a dubious good is
not a good, and the good that can be only in such a way that
it cannot come into existence is not the good, or it exists in
such a way that it is conditioned by a presupposition that must
be present and that is not itself the good.

So, then, doubt became the stronger. What he himself had
discerned, what he himself had experienced, what he with
sympathetic concern and to his own grief had become convinced of—that earthly life is vanity, that even people's good
gifts are weak-willed and only fill him with disquiet—this he
now found to be confirmed in Scripture also. Thus it was now
plain and clear to him that this was what the words meant,
and that far from supporting the most beautiful in life and letting it continue, they on the contrary tacitly condemned it and
allowed it to disappear. He thought that he might manage
with this explanation, although he admitted that it was capable of helping neither him nor anyone else. How did it help
you to have your eyes shut so that the world's glamour no
longer diverted them, how did it help you to have your ears
shut so that the world's empty babble did not work its way in
through them, how did it help you that your heart grew cold
and everything became alien and indifferent for you, how did
it help you to know that people do not give good gifts, how
did it help you to know the deepest anguish of human life—
that not even your love was capable of giving good gifts—ah,
how did it help you if your eyes were not open again to see a
heavenly glory *from above*, if your ears were not open to perceive the ineffable speech sounding *from above*, if your heart
was not deeply moved, your hand not stretched out to grasp

every good and every perfect gift, which comes *from above*, if your left hand was not ignorant of what your right hand was doing!²⁶⁵

But how do you read this? Are not the words still the same; have they ever said anything other than what you now think you have discerned, because of which you forget what they add? Have the words ever concealed that human beings are not capable of giving good gifts? If they could, then no person would need God's gifts. Or would the words have been, or would life have been, more perfect and richer in comfort if they had said: Just as a father gives good gifts, so God gives good gifts? Or was not this what you yourself had discovered, was not this what the words said but you refused to understand, said as something evanescent, said in order to arouse the pain that makes the soul more receptive to what it has to add. Because the whole world is evil, is God therefore not good? Would you be better served if he were good only as the whole world is good? Is this not the one thing needful and the one blessed thing both in time and in eternity, in distress and in joy—that God is the only good, that no one is good except God?²⁶⁶ Is this not the only salvation, the only guidance, whether you walk the smiling paths of joy or the narrow way of sorrow, "that the spirit of God is good and leads you on a level path" (Psalm 143:10)?

Read further, then: "So your heavenly Father gives good gifts." It does not say, "So your heavenly Father knows how to give good gifts," but it says, "So he gives good gifts," for his knowing is not something other than his giving, his knowing does not take leave of the gift and abandon it to itself but is at all times a co-knowledge with the gift and thus also in the moment it is received, and this accounts for the similarity in the metaphorical saying that a father's love has a similarity to, is a reflection of, God's love, even though a father's love is still never the same as God's, never so strong, so inward, and therefore is not capable of doing what God's love is capable of doing, which in the power of its love is almighty.

When the words are understood in this way, the metaphor, which made it easy to understand for the child but also difficult for the adult, vanishes; then the words say what the apostle says—that every good gift and every perfect gift is from above. What earthly life does not have, what no man has, God alone has, and it is not a perfection on God's part that he alone has it, but a perfection on the part of the good that a human being, insofar as he participates in the good, does so through God. What, then, is the good? It is that which is from above. What is the perfect? It is that which is from above. Where does it come from? From above. What is the good? It is God. Who is the one who gives it? It is God. Why is the good a gift and this expression not a metaphor but the only real and true expression? Because the good is from God; if it were bestowed on the single individual by the person himself or by some other person, then it would not be the good, nor would it be a gift, but only seemingly so, because God is the only one who gives in such a way that he gives the condition along with the gift,[267] the only one who in giving already has given. God gives both to will and to bring to completion;[268] he begins and completes the good work in a person.[269]

Would you deny, my listener, that no doubt can invalidate this precisely because it remains outside all doubt and abides in God? If you, then, do not want to abide in it, it is because you do not want to abide in God, in whom you nevertheless live, move, and have your being[270]—and why do you not want this? Even though doubt cannot understand it, it does not therefore become untrue, since, on the contrary, it would become doubtful if doubt could understand it. Even though it cannot and will not become involved with doubt, it does not therefore become untrue, since, on the contrary, by wanting to become involved with doubt it would not become any more true than the doubt. It remains true precisely because it cuts short doubt, because it disarms doubt. If it did not do this, it would have no power over doubt but would itself be in the service of doubt, and its conflict with doubt would be only an apparent conflict, inasmuch as it would be a friend of doubt, and its victory over doubt would be a deception, since it would indeed be doubt that was victorious. Human thought knows the way to much in the world, penetrates even where darkness and the shadow of death are, into the bowels of the mountain, knows the way into it that no bird knows, and its eye sees every precious thing (Job 28:1-11), but the way to the good, to the secret hiding place of the good, this it does not know, since there is no way to it, but every good and every perfect gift comes *down* from above.

Perhaps you will say: Who would want to deny that every good gift and every perfect gift is from above? But not wanting to deny it is still a very long way from wanting to understand it, and wanting to understand it is still a very long way from wanting to believe it and from believing it. But he who is not for is always against.[271] Does the fruit of the knowledge here again seem so delectable that instead of making a spiritual judgment you demand an identifying sign from the good and the perfect, a proof that it actually did come from above? How should such an identifying sign be constituted? Should it be more perfect than the perfect, better than the good, since it is assumed to demonstrate, and it pretends to demonstrate, that the perfect is the perfect? Should it be a sign, a wonder? Is not a wonder the archenemy of doubt, with which it is never combined? Should it be an experience? Is not doubt the very unrest that makes the life of experience unstable so that it never finds peace or takes a rest, is never finished with observing, and even if it ever did that would never find rest? Should it be confirmation in flesh and blood? Are not flesh and blood the confidants of doubt, with whom it continually consults?[272]

But if the demonstration cannot be made, then can doubt not be halted? That is not the case. If the demonstration could be made in the way that doubt demands, then doubt could not be halted any more than sickness can be arrested by the remedy the sickness itself requests. If, however, you want to be convinced, then in what follows the apostle shows you the more perfect way[273] along which you die to doubt as the perfect comes to you, because the word of faith certainly would not fight doubt with its own weapons, and first of all one binds the strong one and then takes his weapons away from him.

First of all, the apostle pulls away the veil of darkness, removes the shadows of variation, breaks through the shifting of change, and turns the believer's eyes up toward heaven so that he may set his eyes on that which is above (Colossians 3:1-2), for that which is above certainly must appear in all its eternal glory as raised above all doubt, the Father of lights, whose clarity no shadow changes, no shifting varies, no envy eclipses, no cloud snatches away from the believer's eyes.[274] If this is not firmly set, if in this regard you want to put your trust in doubt's false friendship, then very soon doubt will repeatedly change everything for you with its shadows, confuse it with its variations, obscure it with the fogs of night, take everything away from you as if it had not been. This is why the apostle declares: Every good gift and every perfect gift is from above and comes down from the Father of lights, with whom there is no change or shadow of variation.

Then the apostle turns to the single individual in order to explain the condition that makes it possible for him to receive the good and perfect gift. This condition God himself has given, since otherwise the good would not be a gift. This condition is in turn itself a perfection, since otherwise the good would not be a perfect gift. Earthly need is no perfection but rather an imperfection. Therefore, even though a person's gift were able to satisfy it completely, the gift would still be an imperfect gift because the need was imperfect. But to need the good and perfect gift from God is a perfection; therefore the gift, which is intrinsically perfect, is also a perfect gift because the need is perfect. Before this need awakens in a person, there must first be a great upheaval. All of doubt's busy deliberation was mankind's first attempt to find it. However long this continues, it is never finished, and yet it must be finished, ended, that is, broken off, before the single individual can be what the apostle calls a first fruit of creation. That this signifies a new order of things is easy to see, because in the beginning man was so far from being a first fruit of creation that he was created last. There is, then, a new beginning that is not attained by the continued influx of doubt, for then there would really never be a beginning that would begin with something other than doubt. Therefore, whereas in the old order of things man came last and it was doubt's task, as it were, to fathom everything that had gone before, now man is the first, has no intermediary between God and himself, but has the condition he cannot give himself, inasmuch as it is God's gift. This is why the apostle declares that God, according to his own counsel, brought us forth by the word of truth. He did it by himself and according to his own counsel, or had he made some pact with a human being that he would consult with him?[275] But one who is born by the word of truth is born to the word of truth. The condition is a gift of God and a perfection that makes it possible to receive the good and perfect gift. —The apostle says, "According to his own counsel, he brought us forth by the word of truth, that we should be a first fruit of his creation." If here again you want to call upon doubt for help, then doubt will surely—as it always does—rob you as it gives. It will not let the condition be a gift and will thereby defraud you of the perfection and the possibility of receiving the perfect gift; is it not an imperfection on your part that you do not absolutely need God[276] and as a result do not absolutely need his good and perfect gift, either?

But just as the condition itself is a perfection, so it is essential that it be kept as such, that it not be divided and fragmented so that it has only a half meaning, and also that it not be garbled. While the eyes of faith, then, steadfastly continue to be set on that which is above, quietly see heaven open,[277] the apostle would now allow, indeed encourage, the single individual to use doubt in the right way, not to doubt what stands firm and will stand firm forever in its eternal clarity, but to doubt that which in itself is transitory, which will more and more vanish, to doubt himself, his own capacity and competence, so that it becomes an incapacity that is discarded more and more. False doubt doubts everything except itself; with the help of faith, the doubt that saves doubts only itself.

The apostle then gives the admonitions that are to serve for strengthening and maintaining the single individual as a first fruit of creation. "Therefore let every man be quick to hear." What do you suppose he is to be quick to hear? Do you suppose it is the tedious discourses of doubt, or the opinions of

IV
35

men, or the inventions of his own heart? Oh, he who is quick
to listen to such things—whatever he achieved in the world,
whatever he became—he would scarcely become what the
apostle next admonishes every person to become, slow to
speak; haste to pay attention to such things fosters this very
haste to speak. But the person who is quick to listen to the
divine Word—which sounds now, as formerly, when one is
silent, when the Pharisees and the scribes have gone away or
are silenced,[278] when the crowd has dispersed and gone—he
also becomes slow to speak, because what he hears is indescribably satisfying and makes him even quicker to hear and
even slower to speak. Indeed, what is there for him to say?
Ultimately he will not even say with David: Hasten, O Lord,
to speak![279] but will say to his own soul: Hasten, oh, hasten to
listen!

And when he is quick to hear in this way, he will also be
quick to listen to the admonition, "Let every man be slow to
anger, for a man's anger does not work what is righteous before God."[280] The primary effect of anger that is not righteous
before God is that a person is made hard of hearing in attending to the admonition. But even if a person were slower to
anger, even if his anger, humanly speaking, had no effect because it, humanly speaking, was overcome, yet it can remain
in one's inner being and there work what is not righteous before God, since in anger there emerges the very thing that a
person by the help of faith should die to, and when anger has
gained control of him, even if he in his anger triumphed over
the whole world, he has lost himself and damaged his soul.[281]
But the person who is quick to pay attention to what does not
incite an answer or rash words is also slow to anger; he will
not let the sun go down on his anger,[282] and he will fear an
even more alarming eclipse, that he might never more be able
to see the Father of lights, who is hidden by the shadows of
wrath that changed the unchanging.

"Therefore put away all filthiness and all remnants of wickedness," for man does indeed carry the perfect in frail ves-
sels, which makes it difficult for him to carry it, but it does

not let itself be carried in the service of selfish advantage or in the burning of desire or in the fellowship of impurity;[283] and on the remnants of wickedness there rests a curse that very easily, in a tragic way, makes of them—just as the blessing on the blessing's remnants[284]—an overabundance.

"And receive with meekness the Word," because he who is quick to hear so that he thereby becomes slow to speak does not take himself by surprise in his haste and does not take God's kingdom by force[285] but comprehends the things of heaven, for "meekness discovers hidden things" (Sirach).[286] He knows that no one can take what is not given to him and cannot have what is given if he does not take it as given and that the good is a gift for which meekness waits. But meekness is also assured that God gives every good and every perfect gift and in that assurance "it watches with thanksgiving" (Colossians 4:1).[287]

Then he receives "what is implanted there," consequently that which was there before he received it, that which when received "is powerful for making his soul blessed." This he receives, the good and the perfect gift by which the need that was itself a perfection is satisfied. This is why the words in that metaphorical saying with which we began read as follows: "If you, then, who are evil, know how to give good gifts to your children, how much more will the heavenly Father give the Holy Spirit to those who ask him?"[288]—because to need the Holy Spirit is a perfection in a human being, and his earthly need is so far from illuminating it by analogy that it darkens it instead. The need itself is a good and a perfect gift from God, and the prayer about it is a good and a perfect gift through God, and the communication of it is a good and a perfect gift from above, which comes down from the Father of lights, with whom there is no change or shadow of variation.

IV
37

EVERY GOOD GIFT AND EVERY PERFECT GIFT IS FROM ABOVE[289]

THE EPISTLE: JAMES 1:17-22

The same apostle from whose epistle the above text is taken warns in the very next passage against the worldly endeavors that sought to penetrate also the congregation in order to establish difference and distinction in the service of vanity, to emancipate it from the bond of perfection that knits its members together in equality before God, and to make it a slave in subjection to the law that rules the world and presumably has always ruled it: "to flatter people for the sake of advantage" (Jude 16). The idea so frequently stressed in Holy Scripture for the purpose of elevating the lowly and humbling the mighty, the idea that God does not respect the status of persons, this idea the apostle wants to bring to life in the single individual for application in his life. And this is perfectly true; if a person always keeps his soul sober and alert in this idea, he will never go astray in his outlook on life and people or "combine respect for the status of persons with his faith."[290] Then he will direct his thoughts toward God, and his eye will not make the mistake of looking for differences in the world instead of likeness with God. If a man comes to an assembly of the congregation with a gold ring on his finger and wearing fine clothes, he will not stare at the fine clothes, will not let his sensate eye be entertained by this splendor, will not let his sensate mind make him a slave to a human being, a slave who does not know how to rise above the concern occasioned by the lack of all this show. If a poor man comes in wearing shabby clothes, his eyes will not banish him to the most inferior place by his footstool.[291] And even if he sometimes forgets about equality again and loses himself, distracted by life's confusing distinctions, nevertheless his mind, every time he goes to the hallowed place, will be preserved in equality before God during that time and will be educated to preserve increasingly

this equality in the clamor of the world and with it to penetrate the confusion. In the world, the differences work franti-
cally to embellish and to embitter life, as beckoning goals, as
rewards of victory, as oppressive burdens, as attendants of
loss; in the world, external life takes arrogant pride in differences—or cravenly and worriedly sighs under them. But in
the hallowed place, the voice of the ruler is heard no more than
in the grave; there is no difference between man and woman,
no more than in the resurrection;[292] the presumptuous demands of wisdom are not heard there, the pomp and glory of
the world are not seen there, for it is seen as something that is
not seen. There even the teacher is the servant, and the greatest
is the lowliest, and the most powerful person in the world is
the one who needs intercessory prayer more than anyone else;
there every externality is discarded as imperfect, and equality
is true for all, redeeming and equally redeeming. When the
person who possesses the world is like one who does not possess it,[293] and the person who does not possess the world is
like one who does not crave it, "or when the lowly boasts in
his exaltation, and the rich in his lowliness" (1:10,11),[294] or
when the woman seized in open sin here finds forgiveness,[295]
and the man who merely looks at a woman with lust is
condemned[296]—is not equality then present in its truth, is not
the thralldom of the world abolished, its law gone like a
shadow and forgotten like something learned as a child and
everything made perfect under equality's "divine law to love
one's neighbor as oneself"[297] in such a way that no person is
so exalted in rank that he is not your neighbor in exactly the
same sense as no person is so inferior in rank or so wretched
that he is not your neighbor, and the equality is incontrovertibly demonstrated by your loving him as you love yourself!
Indeed, woe to the person so arrogant that even here he could
not forget the difference, but woe, too, to the person so base
that even here he could not forget the difference.

   But just as equality, figuratively speaking, stands guard at
the entrance to the hallowed place and keeps watch so that no
one enters without having discarded that which belongs to the
world, the power and the squalor, so that the intercessory

prayer can be prayed equally truly and interchangeably for the ruler and the powers that be and for those who are sick and sorrowful, for the person who leans on his scepter and for the overburdened person who has to be contented that God is his rod and his staff[298]—in the same way every upbuilding view of life first finds its resting place or first becomes upbuilding by and in the divine equality that opens the soul to the perfect and blinds the sensate eye to the difference, the divine equality that like a fire burns ever more intensely in the difference without, however, humanly speaking, consuming it.[299]

In the hallowed places, in every upbuilding view of life, the thought arises in a person's soul that helps him to fight the good fight with flesh and blood, with principalities and powers,[300] and in the fight to free himself for equality before God, whether this battle is more a war of aggression against the differences that want to encumber him with worldly favoritism or a defensive war against the differences that want to make him anxious in worldly perdition. Only in this way is equality the divine law, only in this way is the struggle the truth, only in this way does the victory have validity—only when the single individual fights for himself with himself within himself and does not unseasonably presume to help the whole world to obtain external equality, which is of very little benefit, all the less so because it never existed, if for no other reason than that everyone would come to thank him and become unequal before him. Such a rash and worldly haste, which presumably even thinks that some external condition or other is the genuine equality to which anything that stands higher must be brought down, to which anything that stands lower must be lifted up, produces nothing but confusion and self-contradiction, as if true equality could be expressed in any externality as such, although it can be victorious and be preserved in any externality whatever, as if a painted surface were the true equality that brings life and truth and peace and harmony to everything, when on the contrary it seeks to kill everything in a spirit-consuming uniformity.

IV
41

The differences, however, are so numerous and so variable,

inasmuch as what seems a bagatelle to one person grows to be
something enormous to another, that it is difficult to speak of
them or to find a characteristic and conclusive term for the
particular. Yet, when we consider the apostle's words that
every good and perfect gift is from above, the fact of difference in life that comes to everyone's mind first, either as an
experientially derived and set-aside recollection or as a present
experience, has found a more specific expression that has been
acknowledged as describing a rather common contrast in life.
To be able to *give* or to be obliged to *receive*, this difference
encompasses the great multiplicity of human beings, even
though within its own compass it characterizes a large number
of more closely defined forms. This being able to *give* or being
obliged to *receive* divides people into two great classes, and at
the mere mention of this brief phrase everyone understands it
more extensively, associates with it many happy or many sad
recollections, many confident hopes or painful expectancies.
How much deliberation this little phrase has evoked! How
much the veteran in the toilsome service of this difference
could tell! How very much has the youth discerned when
for the first time he was startled by this inscription over life's
door and, before he had clad himself in the difference, became
immersed in pondering: whether it would be happier to give,
and how happy it would be; whether it would be harder to be
obliged to receive, and how hard it might be; what would be
more desirable; what he would choose if he had the choice;
whether what he had heard was true, that the most glorious
thing to do was to have nothing to do with the world, to be
able to say: I came into the world naked, I possessed nothing,
I was a stranger in it, and I leave it again naked;[301] whether it
would be very hard and irksome to possess the treasures of the
world; whether being able to communicate to others would
be so difficult a work and involve so much responsibility. Yet
any such deliberation, which flirts with the circumstances and
premises of life as a game for the power of the imagination,
serves only to halt freedom's power to act and to grieve the
spirit[302] in romantic hankering and pain. Even with regard to
a more profound contrast, Paul suggests in a brief statement

that there is no time for prolonged deliberation: "Were you a
slave when called? Then do not let this bother you. If you can
be free, then rather choose that."[303] Even though no one is as
capable of being potent in brevity as an apostle, we shall still
not add to the deliberations but summon the soul from distractions into the equality that manifests itself when we pierce
through differences by means of the apostle's words. Let us,
then, try to make a pilgrimage, as it were, with the text into
differences as we continually let the words remind us *that every
good gift and every perfect gift is from above.* If that stands firm,
then the difference is indeed canceled, because a difference in
imperfection, which is indigenous in people's gifts, can only
be transient, then at last the words of the apostle are continually heard as a divine refrain that is able to perfect every difference in equality before God.

The words of the apostle require, then, that the person able
to give must humble himself and his gift under the words. If
he is not disposed to want to give, these words have no meaning for him. If he sits and broods like a dragon on his earthly
treasures, or if he has at his disposal the hypocritical explanation that whatever help he could give is already given, "is a
gift,"[304] if he hoards, like a miser, the good things of the spirit,
jealous of them—well, of what benefit is it to him that the
words wanted to teach him to bestow them in the right way?
After all, he needed no such guidance. The words cannot help
him, these words that were able to help the most wretched of
all.

But when you are willing to give, then the words check to
see whether your willingness means that you are a joyful
giver, who is well pleasing to God.[305] But if your willingness
does not signify joyfulness, then just pour out your rich gifts,
throw away the wealth that bored and wearied your soul,
whose value is but a plague to you; change the state of the
earth, if that were possible, relieve every need until you are
the only one who begs—ah, every good and every perfect gift
still comes down from above, and thus providence does not
need specifically your treasure and your goods, since it always
has twelve legions of angels[306] ready to serve humankind, and

if it needed specifically your possessions, then it certainly could take them away from you, just as it gave them to you. But you learned another kind of wisdom, that there is no good gift either up there or down here, and you could just as well keep everything or give everything away; you still would not achieve or produce equality before God. —Or if it was illicit goods and your hands were defiled, what would the gift be then but a blasphemy against God, how would you be able to grasp that the good gift is from above, you who did not even know how to give to each one his own.

When you are willing to give, then the words are on the alert so that you are not inclined to take back, so that equality before God is brought about, not the equality that is achieved when birds of a feather flock together and the rich man gives a banquet[307] for the rich man, so that he must invite him in return, and the powerful support the powerful. You were willing to give and to assist someone in need who had nothing to give in return, and yet you demanded something from him: his respect, his admiration, his subservience—his soul. How much, really, is the little you possess, even if you were the richest of men, even if your name were to supersede the name of that man who for centuries was called the richest man and after whom the richest were named![308] How high, really, was that mountain one could climb without seeing anything that did not belong to you? Have you forgotten that there was one who could climb the highest mountain, the peak of which pierced the clouds, could scan the kingdoms and lands of the earth and say to the one who was famished from fasting, "All this I will give you if you will fall down and worship me."[309] Have you forgotten that this was the tempter? Would you actually do another person a good turn that would do him harm; would you want to be his benefactor in such a way that you became his soul's enemy? How much does a person really need for living, since his life does not consist in food and drink?[310] You who want to make the needy one anxious in subservience, are you not afraid that with one single word he may strip the glamour from all your glory and turn your silver and gold into counterfeit coin that no one will take? Would you betray your neighbor with a kiss[311] in this way, murder his soul as you saved his body?[312] Oh, every good and every perfect gift is indeed from above, and earthly treasures as such have no promises, no preeminent right to be called that. If, then, you are able to give, for your own sake and for the sake of the other never forget that it is from above, lest you, who want to be and could be his benefactor, may need him instead, need him to decline to receive, need him to make you learn that you two are incompatible, that he is not as down and out as you are high and mighty, that you are not able to corrupt his soul even though you can make his body suffer. Do not be a profiteer with your goods, do not do as the person who knows how to make his gift yield even more after he has given it away; do not bring about the even more dreadful thing, which you and the whole world cannot make good again— that he suffers injury to his own soul.[313] Give your gift, keep an eye on it, and even though you yourself are not to blame for it, if you see that the needy one is being led into temptation, then come with the admonition, direct him to God, or preferably abstain entirely from giving to him; in all the prolixity of philanthropy that enables you to rejoice in your wealth, do not forget that it is better and more blessed and infinitely more important to save a soul. When this idea comes alive in your soul, it will humble you and your gift in fear and trembling[314] under the apostolic words so that your gift becomes sufficiently insignificant in your own eyes, and *you yourself even more insignificant than the gift.*

IV
44

Or you are really willing to give, but you need a long time to deliberate so that the gift may prove to be rightly and wisely considered in keeping with your sagacity. Ah, there is much deliberation that certainly makes a person more sagacious and demonstrates his sagacity but does not make him better or more pleasing to God. All the scruples that the left hand discovers when the right hand consults with it[315] are not of the good and are sufficiently well known, and even if you discovered a new one, it would be a very dubious honor. And why does the deliberation that follows such philanthropy generally last so long again, unless it is because its reward is missing[316] and therefore it must be satisfied with the deliberation? But when you consider that every good gift is from above, then the right hand you stretched out to give will quickly hide itself, and the left hand will never find out anything; then you will rejoice in secret, as a benefactor may, rejoice in the same way as he who received the gift, and both of you rejoice over the same thing, that the gift came from above, since there really was an invisible hand that gave it—it was your hand; and you are convinced that there is an invisible hand that will truly make it a good gift—it is God's hand.

Or you are willing to give; you put the gift aside, so to speak, for the needy one, but you let him wait for it. My friend! "An expectancy that is protracted for a long time makes the heart sick, but the desire fulfilled is a tree of life" (Proverbs 13:12). What indeed would you give the other person to understand by your conduct except that it was for you that he had to wait? Would this be such a glorious piece of information that you would like him to understand it; would not such an understanding easily be harmful to him in the matter of his salvation? And how would it benefit you— would it make you more perfect? God in heaven surely knows best what is the highest that a person can aspire to and complete. But Scripture declares that no more is required of a person than that he be trustworthy as a steward.[317] But a steward is more insignificant than the house and goods he administers. You, however, wanted to be the lord and master; consequently, you did not want to be perfect. By your delaying, you wanted the needy one to understand that you had other things to take care of, that he had to allow time, that he, the nobody, had to wait. Ah, God in heaven does not let one sparrow keep waiting for him. Therefore, do not let the needy one implore at length; otherwise it becomes obvious that you are not giving for the sake of God but perhaps to buy your freedom from his pleas. Was it not unjust of the judge to do justice only to free himself from the widow's pleas;[318] was he not an unjust man even when he did justice; was it not an injustice to the widow that she later thanked him for doing his duty as if it were a great benefaction? The longer you let the needy one plead, the deeper he is mired in his earthly need, until he may not be able to lift his soul up out of it even with the help of your gift. And what you have to give either is not a good and a perfect gift or, if it is that through you, is that because you are only the steward and consequently *more insignificant than the gift*.

Or you were willing to give, but your gift was so insignificant that you hesitated to give. Oh, but every good and every perfect gift is from above, and therefore your insignificant gift can be the good gift just as well as the greatest gift may be. And the one who gives in the right way shuts his eyes; then you do not see the gift, how small it is, before you plainly see what God made it into, and once again you confess that you are *more insignificant than the gift*, which is always the case with the giver when he gives a good gift or does his part so that it can become that.

Yet it is not only by means of external and earthly goods that one person can help another; he may also help him by means of guidance and advice, consolation and admonition and sympathy, and here, of course, the giver apparently becomes more important. Perhaps you purchased your experience at a high price; the admonition you have to offer you acquired on the day of affliction and extorted from life's hardships with much toil, and so you are unwilling to squander it, trifle with it, since what you acquired the hard way you will also hold high in value. Ah, but the one from whom you bought it was in fact life, and at the time you bought it, life, as you say, was not good to you—do you now want to be for someone else what life was for you, so that someday he, too, will say: I bought it at a high price and had to pay for it the hard way? If you have an admonition to offer, then is it not a gift if you are unable to dissociate it from yourself and yourself from it? Or would your admonition be of less value if the one who received it saw that you, who presumably needed it less now, submitted to it, that it influenced you first and foremost as if you needed it most of all, saw that in repetition it became as fresh and vivid in your soul as it was in the moment of acquisition, so that you yourself *were more insignificant than*

IV
46

your admonition. If, then, you do have an admonition to give, do not lift your head high in censure, do not open your eyes to probe, but bow your head and your eyes under the admonition so that it may sound from above just as meaningfully for you as for the other. Every good and every perfect gift is indeed from above, and even if your admonition were the very best, you still do not know whether it will incite the soul of another to rebelliousness or preserve it in humility, whether it will be unto salvation for him or unto damnation.

Or it is your sympathy you have to bestow, and you are willing to do this if someone really needs it, but this requires that he be weaker than you, show less strength in distress and less intrepidity in tribulation than you are capable of, and if that is the case, then your sympathy rushes to strengthen the exhausted and raise the fallen. Ah, but every good and every perfect gift is from above, and the person who offers his gift, let him first see to it that he does not have anything against his brother,³¹⁹ so that the sympathy is bestowed on a condition, which eliminates the reward by reimbursing itself. What is it that he needs—it is sympathy, not you—so be yourself *more insignificant than your sympathy* so that it may be from above, higher than yourself, so that it may be sympathy and not a violation, so that it may not originate in your own heart but be there from above.

Or you are gifted with intellectual power that is rare for a human being. You know how to penetrate truth with your thought, you know how to capture men for it as you see it so that they gladly remain in this indissoluble association, but you could not set yourself aside so that they could know the truth through you and remain in it without you. Were you such a person? We do not presume to address you any more than to address the least distinguished; we merely bear in mind what happens and what could happen. Ah, but every good and every perfect gift is from above, and even the wisest thing a person has grasped nevertheless always becomes dubious in someone else, or he must himself acquire it in the very same way. What would people really gain if you allowed them to entrust themselves to you in this way; indeed, what would you gain if you won the satisfaction you were seeking? Alas, a person can encumber his soul not only with meat and drink but also with the world's honor and people's admiration. And what is the world's honor, which is prinked up to look so fair,[320] and where is the sanctuary in which it dedicates itself so that its honor might be truly worthy of desire! And what is people's admiration, which is wasted on the unrighteous and the dissolute just as much as it is offered to the righteous! Yes, even though it falls upon those entitled to it, how injudicious and foolish this admiration often is. They seem unwilling to be concerned about themselves but concern themselves only with admiring and thereby cause new sorrow for the person admired—if he otherwise was more concerned for their welfare than itching for their admiration. Therefore, if you have any truth to offer mankind, reduce the impact of yourself, nullify yourself, sacrifice yourself when offering your gift, lest people take you instead of the gift, lest their lives be ruined in an illusion by possessing truth without, however, possessing it. Since you are the strong one, you know best how this can be done. Then you are indeed the giver, but nevertheless *more insignificant than the gift*, and every good and perfect gift is from above, even though it came through you.

Or you were such a simple person that you for that reason remained quiet, and it never entered your mind that some word from you would be able to guide or help another person. Ah, but a simple word from a simple person has accomplished marvelous things in the world, has imprinted itself on the memory of the wise one who in all his wisdom had forgotten these words, has made the mighty pause, has disarmed the violent, has shaken the shrewd, has saved the desperate. And why not, for your gift was indeed a good gift and *you yourself more insignificant than your gift*.

The apostolic words are directed to the one whose humble lot it was to be obliged to receive and, like every sacred word, are a gospel for the poor,[321] a heavenly voice that calls to him, that inspires the courage to prevail in the terrible struggle in which one contends, so to speak, with one's friend or in which it is at least very difficult to tell friend from foe, inspires the bold confidence to lift his heart in thanks to God every time his soul is in danger of being imprisoned in the world by becoming a debtor to another person. Or is this perhaps ingratitude that we are recommending? Are the words of the apostle unable to effect equality before God, or do they teach an unfair equality when they say that every good and perfect gift is from above and that consequently every human being, whether he gives or receives, essentially has to thank God, since it is proper to thank only for the good and the good indeed comes only from God? No, the words certainly will not abolish thankfulness, because just as it is a disgrace for the person who gives that he himself knows it, that he does not at least try to make himself invisible in every sense, or nevertheless knows how to make himself invisible in a higher sense even though he is visibly present, just so is it a disgrace for the one who receives that he does not know and does not do his utmost to find out from whom he received. But in this effort of the one to find out what the other is hiding, both will be united in finding God, and when God is found, the disgrace is removed from both of them, the disgrace of being discovered from the one who wished to hide himself, the disgrace of not having discovered him from the one who should discover. In other words, if the person who receives the benefaction does not go out in his thankfulness to find his benefactor, he will never find God; it is in this search that he finds God: by not finding his benefactor, by finding him as he ought to be and then in turn with his assistance finding God, by finding him as he ought not to be and then in turn finding God in his thanksgiving's search. If a person with his thanks romantically seeks to discover God and loses sight of earthly thankfulness, he had better watch out for himself, because if he is not willing to thank the benefactor he sees, how would he truly thank God, whom he does not see?[322] Let a Pharisee propound the truth in order to make bad use of it; the truth still remains that one shall give God the honor for what one owes to a sinful human being, that no one may exalt himself over another so that he makes it impossible for the other to thank God because he stands in his way, that no one may be so base,

so cowardly, so cozy and comfortable, so soft, so engrossed
in earthly things that he is content to thank a human being for
giving him what he craved—but that is still no basis for denying that to repudiate his benefactor openly and to accept his
gifts secretly are as detestable to both God and men as being
ashamed of one's parents, an abomination that tries to make
the giver of the gifts into the only injured party in life. We
praise that blind man in the Gospel[323] because the first use he
made of his sight was to look around to see whether he could
find his benefactor; we praise him because the judgment of the
world did not bring him to repudiate his benefactor, as it prevailed upon Peter to do;[324] we praise him because he preferred
remaining with his benefactor and being held in contempt to
being honored and perhaps serving as a tool in the hands of
the powerful. But suppose he had been unwilling to do more,
suppose his benefactor had been like one of us, a sinful mortal,
by whose benefaction they were bound together in indissoluble friendship instead of being united by their mutual thanks
to God, to whom they gave the honor—then would not the
end have spoiled what was begun so beautifully? Even though
Christ accepted the blind man's adoring worship, this nevertheless was not primarily a response to the benefaction but
was worship in faith, and the situation here was most likely of
such a nature that it could not possibly tempt any sinful man
to a similar request. Christ made the benefaction itself as co-
vert as possible, because when he had made it possible for him
to recover his sight, he sent him away and said: Go, wash in
the pool of Siloam. Here he received his sight, but the Lord
was not standing with him there, and in this way he who was
his benefactor knew how to make himself invisible to him,
even though his benefaction consisted in giving him his sight.

How diverse are the ways in which one person can become
indebted to another we have already seen in the discussion of
those whose happy lot it was to be able to do good. When you
are willing to give thanks, the words watch over you so that
you do not do injury to your soul by being obliged to receive
and by wanting to thank people. Perhaps you were a nobody
in the world, and your place at the rich man's door and your

life were a confirmation of the experience that one can also live on scraps[325] and of the experience that sometimes they are thrown to a human being as if he were a dog. You accepted the gift thrown to you; it was hard to need it—alas, but you could not do without it; it helped you only for a moment, and then you would again feel just as oppressively as before how hard it is to be obliged to receive. Before you had lifted your bowed head again, he, your benefactor, had vanished, not just because he wanted to be anonymous and hurried away to hide himself, but because he had something entirely different to take care of. You sent your expression of thanks after him, but it did not catch up with him, not just because he felt shamefully inferior to his gift, but because his ears were not attentive, since the whole affair was trifling and meaningless to him. And if your thanks had reached him, he presumably would have said: It is hardly worth thanking for, and that would have been his honest opinion, and also that your expression of thanks had no value. Oh, but every good and every perfect gift comes down from above. The powerful man must be content that the lowly man serves him, but the lowly man is served by the powerful, and in your thanksgiving you lifted your heart up to God for having used that powerful man as an instrument to help you.

Or your situation was more favorable; you had your modest subsistence, you lived in frugal contentment in your humble quarters at the bottom of the rich man's palace. But you owed it to him; you owed everything to him, and you yourself felt that the service you could do for him was only a poor repayment—but you were all the more willing to thank him. At times you invited him home, but the way he looked at you easily convinced you of how little your thanks meant to him and that he did not know how to let himself be paid in that coin but knew how to be repaid in another way. Then you could wish that you were a sparrow of the air that had only God to thank for its subsistence,[326] a lily in the field that had only God to thank for being dressed so gloriously,[327] that you had only God to thank, whom it is an immeasurable joy to thank again and again. Oh, but every good and every perfect gift is from above. If your benefactor disregards your thanks, then lift up your heart to God, from whom his gift came, but do not fail to thank him; do for him what you can, which is not little; allow him to have bought, with his dubious mammon, a friend who can receive him in the heavenly mansions.[328]

Or you were unacquainted with this kind of distress, you did not need to thank some human being for earthly gold and goods, for they were your possession; but your soul had been tossed about in the confusion of life, you had been unable to rescue yourself from the difficulty in which you were situated, one that overwhelmed your mind and paralyzed your will. Then you had sought advice and support from another person, whose clear discernment soon penetrated the darkness around you. Now you were happy and contented, your life flowed on quietly and calmly, but you confessed in your heart and with your mouth that you owed it to him. But he refused to accept your thanks. When you spoke to him about it, you readily perceived that your life and its complications had perhaps once occupied his mind, but you had not occupied him, and therefore he could not let himself be thanked. Yes, the person to whom you owed all this may even have been your enemy, who for that very reason refused to accept thanks. Oh, but every good and every perfect gift is from above. If a human being wants to stop being human, if he wants to be just a force of nature, then you certainly cannot thank him any more than the sailor can thank the wind when it fills his sail and he uses it properly, or any more than the archer can thank the string when it propels the arrow and he hits the mark. So do not fall prey to earthly care but lift yourself up to God with thanksgiving. But do not therefore fail to thank your benefactor; your thanks still belong to him. Guard it as property entrusted to your care, as one conserves the property of someone who has died or of someone who has gone to a far country, so that he can receive it, honestly administered, if at any time he desires it.

Or you owed another person something you could not forget any more than he could—your insight, your education, your firmness of thought, your power of speech. He regarded your soul as his debtor, would permit no day of atonement that would give you back to yourself as your own possession.[329] He would probably accept your thanks, but not as that which absolved your life of its debt to him. Ah, but no man can give what he himself has not been given, and of course the greatest gift one human being can give another is life, and even for this the father teaches the child to thank God, who gave it and who in turn is the one who takes it. Every good and every perfect gift is from above, and the pupil certainly is not above the teacher,[330] but if the teacher loves him, then he wishes that the pupil might be as he himself is.

"It is more blessed to give than to receive."[331] The words express the difference that prevails in earthly existence—without mirroring human passions or borrowing its expression from them—that it is better, happier, more glorious, more desirable to be able to give than to be obliged to receive. But the words indicate the difference as it is in the loving heart. Therefore the person who says that it is better or happier or more glorious or more desirable does not say what use he is going to make of this power that is granted to him; neither does he witness to what he has understood in using it properly. But the person who knows that it is more blessed to give than to receive has grasped the fact of difference in life, but as far as he is concerned, he has also reconciled it by giving joyfully and by having his blessedness in giving. Yet the difference remains if the person who has to receive does not perceive a similar blessedness. Should he not? Should not the person who was tried in a more difficult struggle have a similar reward, and yet it is in truth greater to receive than to give— that is, if both are done in the right way.

So let us now consider the apostle's words to see whether they do not express the equality. The one who gives admits that *he is more insignificant than the gift*; after all, it was this confession that the apostle's words gladly accepted from the individual as willingly given or extorted from him against his will. The person who receives confesses that *he is more insig-*

nificant than the gift, because it was this admission that the words gave as the condition in order to exalt him, and indeed this admission in all its humility is often heard in the world. But if the person who gives is more insignificant than the gift and the person who receives is more insignificant than the gift, then equality has indeed been effected—that is, equality in insignificance, equality in insignificance in relation to the gift, because the gift is from above and therefore actually belongs to neither or belongs equally to both—that is, it belongs to God. The imperfection, then, was not that the needy one received the gift but that the rich one possessed it, an imperfection he removed by giving away the gift. Equality was effected not by the needy one's possessing the gift but by the rich man's not having it any longer as a possession, because he had given it to the one in need; and neither did it belong to the needy one as a possession, because he had received it as a gift. When the rich man thanks God for the gift and for being granted the opportunity of bestowing it in a good way, he does indeed thank for the gift and for the poor man; when the poor man thanks the giver for the gift and God for the giver, he does indeed also thank God for the gift. Consequently, equality prevails in the giving of thanks to God, equality vis-à-vis the gift in the giving of thanks. This is devoid of difficulty and easy to understand. Insofar as difficulty does at times tempt a person, it is because the earthly gifts, which regrettably come to mind first when we think about the difference between being able to give and being obliged to receive, are in themselves very imperfect and therefore have this power of imperfection to make distinctions. The more perfect the gift, however, the more clearly and incontrovertibly the equality promptly manifests itself. But it is, of course, the good and perfect gift of which we say that it is from above, but the only good and perfect gift a human being can give is love, and all human beings in all ages have confessed that love has its home in heaven and comes down from above.[332] If a person does not want to accept love as a gift, he inspects what he gets, but if he receives it as a gift, the giver and the receiver are inseparable in the gift, and both are made essentially and

IV
53

entirely equal vis-à-vis the gift in such a way that only earthly understanding in its imperfection can make duplicitous [*tvetyde*] that which signifies [*betyde*] one and the same. And the more a person weans his soul from understanding the imperfect to grasping the perfect, the more he will appropriate the explanation of life that comforts while it is day and remains with him when night comes,[333] when he lies forgotten in his grave and has himself forgotten what moth and rust have consumed[334] and human sagacity has found out, and yet he will have a thought that can fill out the long interval for him, that will know nothing of the difference that troubled him but is aware only of the equality that is from above, the equality in love, which lasts and is the only thing that lasts, the equality that does not allow any human being to be another's debtor, except, as Paul says, in the one debt, the debt of loving one another.[335]

LUKE 21:19

In your patience you will gain your souls.[336]

The rich bird comes swishing, comes flaunting; the poor bird[337]—and patience is a poor bird, which does not come parading and posturing but comes like a soft breeze and the incorruptible essence of a quiet spirit.[338] Patience is a poor art, and yet it is very long.[339] Who learned it properly from life—who had the patience for that? Who taught it to another person in the right way—ah, perhaps there was someone who taught another patience very well by being very impatient himself! Who spoke fittingly about it, so that he did not rush into impatience of expression and hastiness of phrase? Who listened to the discourse about it in the right way, so that he did not understand it and then impatiently demanded a new discourse and thus certainly comprehended patience and the discourse about it but did not comprehend that it was not to be understood in that way!

To gain one's soul in patience—are not these words, which no doubt have always come inopportunely, capable of simultaneously killing every bold expectancy that longs for renowned deeds, for inspired achievements, for strife and conflict in which the reward is admittedly uncertain but also glorious? Are not these words to the adult what a father's voice is to the child when he calls him from his noisy play, in which he was king and emperor, to the quiet task of patience? Yes, are they not even more alarming since they want to embrace all life and thus do not let themselves be made a laughing matter, as if they were only a sometime earnestness? But if the one who said these words knew what is beneficial for a person, if he said them while at the same time he brought to mind, which is indeed the case, that the abomination of desolation[340] would convulse life radically and totally and consequently provide occasion for great deeds and renowned exploits, then let us at least have the patience to believe (if we are convinced that the words do not benefit but rather hamper the soul) that the fault is in our not properly understanding the words and that it is our own fault that the effect of the words seems so narrow that, instead of giving every human being his soul and the whole world in exchange for its aspiring and striving, it takes away from him the whole world and its glory as something he will never grasp—indeed, even takes his soul away from him in order to let him gain it in patience.

Then let us at least have the patience to believe the words, the patience not to postpone the deliberation until a more opportune time and, lacking this quality ourselves, the patience not to beg the words to have patience, the patience to separate what is inseparably joined in order to put it together again.

"*To gain one's soul.*" Does, then, a person not possess his soul, and can this be the true direction to blessedness, one that instead of teaching a person to gain the whole world[341] by means of his soul teaches him to use his life to gain his soul? A human being is born naked[342] and brings nothing with him into the world,[343] and whether the conditions of life are like friendly forms with everything in readiness or he himself must laboriously find them, everyone must nevertheless acquire the conditions of his life in one way or another. Even if this observation makes an individual impatient and thereby totally incompetent, yet the better people know how to comprehend this and how to conform to the idea that life must be gained and that it must be gained in patience, to which they admonish themselves and others, because patience is a soul-strength that everyone needs to attain what he desires in life. That the hiker en route to his distant destination does not make undue haste at the beginning but at dusk each day patiently relaxes and rests so that he can continue his walking tour the next day—that someone carrying a heavy burden does not overstrain at the beginning but at times sets his burden down and sits down alongside it until he has new strength

to carry it—that someone who patiently cultivates his ground
patiently waits for rain early and late until harvest time
comes[344]—that someone who earns his living by trading sits
by his wares and waits patiently until a buyer comes and until
he comes with the payment—that someone who stretches his
net for birds waits through the day until evening and sits patiently near his net without moving until the birds come—that
someone who obtains his sustenance from the sea sits patiently all day long with his lines—that the mother who wants
to have the joy of her child does not wish it to grow up in a
hurry but waits patiently through sleepless nights and troubled days—that someone who wants to win favor with people
works early and late and does not spoil everything by impatience—that someone who wants to speak to people about
what seems unimportant to them does not rush at the beginning and then cease but continues to speak and waits patiently—this people do understand. They understand that for
better or for worse this is the way it is, and they submit to it;
they understand that it is good and beneficial that it is this
way, and they let themselves be formed by it, and in their view
of life they give to this behavior preference over the wild, un-
disciplined outbursts that achieve nothing but only give rise
to confusion and harm. The condition of which they speak is
outside the individual, and the condition for attaining what is
desired is patience—therefore he is not really gaining patience
but gaining what is coveted. Thus there are very many and
very different conditions, but is the soul, then, such a condition? Then is it saying too little to say that a person comes
naked into the world and possesses nothing in the world if he
does not even possess his own soul? If the preceding observation was able to make an individual impatient and unfit for
living, well, why should not this observation also make everyone basically impatient? What is there to live for if a person
has to spend his whole life gaining the presupposition that on
the deepest level is life's presupposition—yes, what does that
mean?

Patience has helped us to the point where the words that in
their brevity seemed so forbidding, so insignificant, hardly

worth paying attention to, now in their brevity prove to be so
significant that they tempt us instead in another way, as if they
were unfathomable. And is it not alarming to tread this path
where one immediately and at every moment admittedly sees
the goal but never reaches it, unlike the hiker who indeed arrives at his goal, unlike the burden-bearer who arrives at his
destination; where one almost never moves from the spot, unlike the hiker who now sees one setting, now another, unlike
the burden-bearer who loses sight of one view, now another;
where one sees no change, unlike the trader who sees now one
person, now another, unlike the bird and fish catcher who
catches now one, now another—but one continually sees only
oneself. [Is it not alarming to tread this path] where, unlike
the person who, out to win favor with people, at times hears
cheering and at times booing, sometimes many voices, sometimes single voices, one hears just one lone voice, speaking
truth that almost makes one shudder, because it seems that if
a person has once heard it he can never escape from it either in
time or in eternity; where one almost never gains anything:
not the attainment of the goal, not the laying down of the burden, not the rich harvest, not wealth, not a wonderful catch,
not the happiness of a child, not people's favor, has not benefited others but gains only himself, a reward so small that even
the little infant that dies at birth apparently possesses the same
thing. [Is it not alarming to tread this path] where one wins
nothing that can invite people to happy participation, because
one wins only oneself—that is, is deceived, just like the merchant if no one came into his shop the whole day and we
would tell him, "Now you have learned patience," or just like
the fisherman who had fished all day and caught nothing.[345]
Or would not such an overturning of thought and speech be
even more strange than the oddity that a man's life can so
change that the tangible things, which to him were the most
certain of all, become dubious and the things of the spirit,
which disappointed him because of their remoteness, become
the most certain of all, infinitely more certain than the tangible
things?

But if a person possesses his soul, he certainly does not need to gain it, and if he does not possess it, how then can he gain it, since the soul itself is the ultimate condition that is presupposed in every acquiring, consequently also in gaining the soul. Could there be a possession of that sort, which signifies precisely the condition for being able to gain the same possession? In the external sense, there is no such possession. The person who possesses the external does not need to gain it—in fact, he is even unable to do that. He can give away what he possesses and then see whether he can gain the same thing again; he can use what he possesses to gain something new, but he cannot simultaneously possess and gain the very same thing.

If there is any question of such a possession, then it must be found in the internal. If it is not to be found in the external as such, then it is not to be found in the temporal as such either, since, more closely defined, it was actually temporality that made it impossible to possess and to gain the external simultaneously, because that which is in the moment either is or is not, and if it is, then it is not gained, and if it is gained, then it is not. A self-contradiction—which enunciation of both these statements would be—temporality does not understand this either as a riddle or as the solution of the riddle. In the eternal, there is no such self-contradiction, but not because it, like the temporal, either is or is not, but because it is. The eternal is not either a something possessed or a something gained but is only a something possessed that cannot be gained any more than it can be lost. Then this self-contradiction must be sought, if anywhere, in the internal, but the internal is, after all, in its most universal expression, the soul.

It is in the soul, then, that we must seek what we set out to find in connection with these words: to gain one's soul. The soul is the contradiction of the temporal and the eternal, and here, therefore, the same thing can be possessed and the same thing gained and at the same time. Indeed, what is more, if the soul is this contradiction, it can be possessed only in such a way that it is gained and gained in such a way that it is possessed. The same contradiction can also be expressed in another way. One who comes naked into the world possesses nothing, but the one who comes into the world in the nakedness of his soul does nevertheless possess his soul, that is, as something that is to be gained, does not have it outside himself as something new that is to be possessed. If this were not the case, if the seemingly empty thought or this expression for emptiness—nakedness of soul—were not still the soul, then it could not be possessed and could not be gained except as the external is possessed and gained, both of which in the deeper sense are an illusion, for that which is gained can be lost because it was not possessed and that which is possessed can be lost because it was not gained. However, that which safeguards the possession of the soul from being an illusion is precisely the gaining of it, and that which guarantees that the gaining of it is not an illusion is precisely that it is possessed beforehand.

Insofar, then, as a person is to gain his soul, he does not possess it. Who, then, is the one who possesses it? Insofar as it exists, as it certainly does, since it is to be gained, it must certainly belong to someone, although in such a way that it can be gained, not as the external is gained but in such a way that one who gains it gains his possession. One who is to gain the world is, of course, assumed to possess his soul—should not the reverse also be so, that one who is to gain his soul possesses the whole world; and just as one who wants to gain the world gradually gives away his soul in exchange for the world, so one who gains his soul must have something to give instead, and what else can this be but the world? What people aspire to—to possess the world—a person was closest to it in the first moment of life, because his soul was lost in it and possessed the world in itself, just as the undulation of the waves possesses in itself the restlessness of the sea and its depths and knows no other heartbeat than this, the infinite heartbeat of the sea. Admittedly people think that what they speak of as the possession of the world is something entirely different. But this is just a deception. The world can be possessed only by its possessing me, and this in turn is the way it possesses the person who has won the world, since one who possesses the world in any other way possesses it as the accidental, as something that can be diminished, increased, lost, won, without his possession being essentially changed. If, however, he possesses the world in such a way that the loss of it can diminish his possession, then he is possessed by the world. Or does this seem to be quibbling? May it not rather be that the person who could not or would not understand this became a hair-splitter in the service of the world? May it not be the world's stratagem to lead a person to think that if he possesses the world this does not mean that he is possessed by it? Would the world be less shrewd than he, would it offer itself to a person, as it indeed does, without knowing that it would win most when a person won it? The imperfect cannot be possessed by a person as his sole possession without his coming to be possessed by it, for when a person only wants to be external, secular, temporal, then are the world and temporality unconditionally more powerful than he? Therefore, a person can truly possess the imperfect only by surrendering it, which, of course, signifies that he does not possess it even though he possesses it. A person is able to possess the perfect when he also possesses himself, but his possessing it does not mean surrendering, since on the contrary it is a deepening in it.

In the first moment, then, a person is in a position that people later crave as something glorious; he is lost in the life of the world; he possesses the world, that is, he is possessed by it. But in the same moment he is different from the whole world, and he senses a resistance that does not follow the movements of the world's life. If he now wants to gain the world, he must overcome this disquiet until once again, like the undulation of the waves, he vanishes in the life of the world—then he has won the world. However, if he wants to gain his soul, he must let this resistance become more and more pronounced and in so doing gain his soul, for his soul was this very difference: it was the infinity in the life of the world in its difference from itself.[346]

Insofar as he then gains his soul, the world possesses it. But the world possesses it unjustly, since it is his possession. In its deceitfulness, the world expresses this contradiction thus, that he possesses the world. His gain, then, is a legitimate gain, insofar as he gains his possession. But whose possession, then, is his soul? It is not the world's, since illegitimate possession is no possession; it is not his, for he of course must gain it. Consequently, there must still be a possessor. This possessor must possess his soul as legitimate property but nevertheless must not possess it in such a way that the person himself cannot gain it as his legitimate possession. Therefore, this possessor can be none other than the eternal being, than God himself. Here emerges the same self-contradiction as the one between possessing and gaining the same thing in the same moment. This cannot be done with the temporal and the external. For example, no external and temporal thing can be fully possessed by several people at the same time but is always possessed by only one. If it is said that the world possesses it, then no one else possesses it; if a person thinks that he possesses it, he is possessed by it; if he really does possess it, he possesses it as something surrendered and consequently does not possess it, and yet the world does not possess it either; therefore the external and temporal becomes what it is supposed to be only when no one at all possesses it or when it has become a matter of indifference. The eternal cannot be possessed by several people, either; it can be possessed only by one for the same reason that it cannot be both possessed and gained.

What people foolishly and impatiently crave as the highest without really knowing what they want, what is horrifying to see when someone succeeds in doing it—namely, to win the world and to have won it—this is what a person begins with, and it is so far from being the goal that it is the very thing he should abandon. His soul is a self-contradiction between the external and the internal, the temporal and the eternal.[347] It is a self-contradiction, because wanting to express the contradiction within itself is precisely what makes it what it is. Therefore, his soul is in contradiction and is self-contradiction. If it were not in contradiction, it would be lost in the life of the world; if it were not self-contradiction, movement would be impossible. It is to be possessed and gained at the same time;

it belongs to the world as its illegitimate possession; it belongs
to God as his legitimate possession; it belongs to the person
himself as his possession, that is, as a possession that is to be
gained. Consequently he gains—if he actually does gain—*his
soul from God, away from the world, through himself.*

Therefore, it was foolishness and impatience to want to gain
the world, a striving to become the imperfect that one already
was, a desperate aspiration to secure what one already was, in
such a way that it became more and more difficult ever to be
rescued from it. Therefore, to gain his soul was a task that
announced a struggle with the whole world, since it began
with letting a person be at the goal of that earthly craving,
possessing the whole world in order to give it away. This was
a struggle that brought a person into the most intimate relation with God, a struggle that promised him himself in eternal
understanding with God, promised him the gain not of the
external, which cannot be possessed essentially by anyone and
which because of and in spite of this imperfection in one way
or another makes a debtor of anyone who actually comes to
possess it. This struggle, however, promised him the gain of
that which can be possessed essentially, which does not belong
to any other soul in the world, which by being gained does
not make him a debtor to fortune or fate or chance or people
or friends or enemies or the world, since on the contrary
through this gain he extricates himself from debt to the world
by giving to the world what is the world's[348] and becomes a
debtor only to God, which is not to be a debtor, since God is
the only good and himself gives the possibility of becoming
his debtor. Can there be anyone impatient enough to refuse to
comprehend this gloriousness, even though he did not have
the patience to gain it?

"*In patience.*" The words do not say "through" or "by
means of" patience, but "in" patience, and thereby suggest
that the condition stands in a special relation to the conditioned. Of course, the merchant also needed patience, as did
the fisherman, but in addition needed various other things—
needed insight and experience, tools and merchandise. If,
without these or without knowing about them, he sits in pa-

tience and waits, if he thinks that knowing about patience is adequate for gaining his living and his catch, then he will soon find himself deceived. But if the person who wants to gain his soul does not want to understand that when he has won patience he has won what he needed, what was of more value than any other winning, then he will never gain it. It is already obvious here how secure this gain is, since in a profound sense it is so cunning that the more the world deceives, the more patience wins. In this gain, the very condition is also the object and is independent of anything external. The condition, therefore, after it has served the gaining, remains as that which is gained; this is different from what happens when the merchant has sold his merchandise and the fisherman has caught his fish—they lay aside patience and also their tools so that they may enjoy what has been gained.

In the external, patience is some third element that must be added, and, humanly speaking, it would be better if it were not needed; some days it is needed more, some days less, all according to fortune, whose debtor a person becomes, even though he gained ever so little, because only when he wants to gain patience does he become no one's debtor. Therefore, even though patience is praised in external life, it nevertheless is and remains a burden. For example, the hiker carries a walking stick. He does not deny that it has weight and that to that extent he has to carry more than he would otherwise, but he reckons that the walking stick will aid him so much in his hiking that the gain will be greater and his walking made less burdensome. If he could be convinced that this was not so, he would not take along a walking stick, just as he now lays it aside upon reaching his goal. If the likelihood that the condition would drop away from the conditioned prevailed also for the person who wants to gain his soul, then no one would be so deceived as he, because the condition that made possible the gaining of the soul was precisely the possession of the soul. Consequently, if it were possible that when he had gained his soul he could lose the condition, then he would also have lost what had been gained.

In the external, patience is a condition that is praised, since the world is as it is and since experience has taught that accordingly patience is necessary. But it cannot be endorsed with full certainty as the one thing needful[349] in the external; perhaps at times impatience would be more profitable and would hasten the gain of what is coveted. In other words, since the external is a dubious good, any condition for gaining it can also be only a dubious good, and the ultimate consequence of imperfection is that there is no certainty that can assure it with full certainty. The perfect, however, can be gained with full certainty, because it can be gained only by coming into existence within its own presupposition. Perhaps there was a merchant who through his impatient plans quickly became rich, whereas another patiently waited in vain, for the bad seed also grows in impatience, but the good seed grows only in patience.[350] But this certainty that no doubt or experience can attain also grows in patience. "It grows in patience." In these words, the condition and the conditioned are again inseparable, and the words themselves suggest duplexity and unity. The person who grows in patience does indeed grow and develop. What is it that grows in him? It is patience. Consequently, patience grows in him, and how does it grow? Through patience. If the person who gains himself will just be patient, he will surely grow in patience. In the one case, the word means that in which a person grows, as if one were to say he grows in favor, in wealth; in the other case, it means that whereby he grows, as if one were to say through sagacity, through the counsel and help of friends.

"*To gain his soul in patience.*" When we put the words together and consider how a person will be able to comply with them, the first requirement is that he have the patience to understand that he does not possess himself, that he have the patience to understand that a gaining of his own soul in patience is a work of patience, and that he therefore ought not to pay attention to the passion that rightly thinks that it can grow only in impatience. The words inculcate this in a twofold way by containing in their brevity a redoubling [*fordoblende*][351] repetition.[352] They admonish one to gain one's soul "in patience," and they admonish one to "gain" it. This word alone contains an admonition to patience. It does not say, "Seize your soul," as if it were a matter of a moment, as if the soul rushed by and it were a matter of seizing the moment and the soul, but thereby all would also be either lost or won. Nor does it say, "Save your soul," a phrase that Scripture in other respects frequently uses[353] with its devout earnestness. And it is indeed also certain that the person who gains his soul also saves it. But the phrase "to save one's soul" does not focus the mind on patience in the same way and could easily suggest a precipitousness with which everything would have to be decided. "To gain one's soul," however, immediately turns the mind to quiet but unflagging activity. This manifests itself even more clearly and by the contrast even more earnestly when we consider that these words are said in connection with and in the process of describing in shocking imagery the horror that would befall Jerusalem, as if it were the destruction of the entire world, when there would be signs in sun and moon and stars, and the sea and the waves would roar, and the powers of heaven would be in tumult[354]—then, if ever, would be the moment to admonish everyone to save his soul. Yet the words used are: "gain your soul in patience." Can a more sublime contrast be imagined, or is this not the hour in which the admonition is transfigured in heavenly glory? The elements disintegrate,[355] the sky is rolled up like a garment,[356] the abyss of annihilation opens its throat and roars for its prey, the shriek of despair sounds from every direction, even inanimate nature groans in anxiety—yet the believer does not press forward battling in order to find rescue, but while nothing has continuance, while even the mountain, tottering, abandons the site where it has stood without moving for thousands of years, he remains quiet and gains his soul in patience, while people are about to die of fright and the expectation of things to come.[357]

The emphasis that is already given by the phrase "to gain" is inculcated even more penetratingly by the added phrase "in patience"; indeed, the words in their entirety are a kind of picture of the whole process of gaining, that it takes place much as the words proceed with their communication—that is, it is all a repetition. It is a question not of making a conquest, of hunting and seizing something, but of becoming more and more quiet, because that which is to be gained is there within a person, and the trouble is that one is outside oneself, because that which is to be gained is in the patience, is not concealed in it so that the person who patiently stripped off its leaves, so to speak, would finally find it deep inside but is in it so that it is patience itself in which the soul in patience inclosingly spins itself and thereby gains patience and itself.

If a person wants to embark upon this gaining, he is required to have the patience to begin in such a way that he truthfully confesses to himself that it is a work of patience. If he does not begin in such a way, he will never gain, since this gaining is not like an earthly gaining that may for some time seem to net no gain, but on the contrary it is a loss, at least apparently, and therefore it takes patience to want to begin it, since the very thing that is inflammatory and provocative to impatience nevertheless declares itself to be a gaining. What is all this winning of which we speak? It is to acquire one's soul as it is, but it does indeed seem that one has it from the start. Here it is a question not of adding something to the soul but of subtracting something from it, that is to say, something it apparently possessed.

But is there, then, no other way in which a person can grasp his soul? Can he not wrest it away from the power that illegitimately possessed it? With what is the soul to do this except itself? But since it wants to grasp itself, it does not possess itself. Moreover, is not that power stronger than he, since it has been able to take possession of his soul? What is always the weapon of the weaker? It is patience. But then must he not possess his soul in order to have the patience in which he gains his soul? Not at all, for patience comes into existence during the gaining, and in this gaining he does not become stronger and stronger, which must be assumed if he were to use force, but he seemingly becomes weaker and weaker. Precisely because the world possessed his soul illegitimately, the ultimate consequence of this, also because the world actually is the stronger, is that he becomes weaker and weaker in regard to the life of the world. If the soul were not heterogeneous to the life of the world, it could never be gained, but since it still belongs to the world, the gaining can have no other presupposition than this insignificant "patience," and this again in such a way that it is not, but becomes.

In patience, the soul comes to terms with all its possessors, with the life of the world in that it sufferingly gains itself from it, with God in that it sufferingly accepts itself from him, with itself in that it itself retains what it simultaneously gives to both without anyone's being able to deprive the soul of it— patience. The soul can obtain nothing through power; it is in the hands of an alien power. If the soul were free in some other way, it would not be the self-contradiction in the contradiction between the external and the internal, the temporal and the eternal. This self-contradiction is again expressed in the soul's being stronger than the world through its weakness, in its being weaker than God through its strength, in its inability to gain anything but itself unless it wants to be deceived, and in its being able to gain itself only by losing itself.

"But what, then, is a human soul?" If you impatiently ask someone else this question, you will scarcely find the answer, nor are you, as it seems, on the right road. Or is it not a manifestation of impatience that one person hurries forward to explain to everyone else what the soul is and that a second person waits impatiently for him to explain it, that the hearer impatiently expedites the speaker's explanation and then in turn becomes impatient because he finds it inadequate? Or was it with this that he ought to be impatient, or was it not as it should be, and a stroke of good luck that it was as it should be, that what the speaker said did not bar him from gaining his soul in patience? Or should he not rather have become impatient with his having been so impatient and then do his best, as a fruit of impatience, to learn to be willing to begin with patience?

To know what a human soul is, what this means, is still a long way from beginning to gain one's soul in patience, and it is a knowledge that exhibits its difference from that gaining inasmuch as it does indeed grow in impatience. And even though this knowledge may have its significance, it often deceived a person the very same way the world does, in that he thought that he possessed it, whereas it was his knowledge that possessed him.

"But if a person is to gain his own soul, then he certainly must know it before he begins." This, of course, is true, precisely because the person who knows his soul has still not therefore gained it, but it is precisely therefore also true that if he does not begin to gain it, he does not know it. Even if he could know it completely before he gained it in patience, this knowing would still be only a possessing just like that first possessing—the condition for his being able to gain his soul in patience. This is why all knowing that is unrelated to a gaining is incomplete and deficient, inasmuch as a person still does not know how he becomes, since he becomes through the gaining, and even in association with the gaining he remains deficient, for "we still do not know what we shall become."³⁵⁸

The person who knows his soul sees himself in a mirror, but he can forget what he looks like, as the Apostle James says, and therefore what he goes on to say is pertinent here: "that the one who hears the Word properly is the one who does it."³⁵⁹ As long as he merely hears the Word, he is outside it, and when the proclaimer is silent, he hears nothing; but when he does the Word, he continually hears what he himself is proclaiming to himself. And any mere hearing of the Word is infinitely more imperfect than the doing, not only because the doing is superior but because in comparison with the exactitude of the doing any oral communication is very imperfect, both in its brevity and in its prolixity. Therefore knowledge of one's own soul, if one wants to regard it as a gaining, is a self-deception, because even in its greatest completeness it still is but a hint of what manifests itself in its definiteness during the gaining.

Therefore a person certainly must know his soul in order to gain it, but this knowing is not the gaining, inasmuch as in this knowing he ascertains that he is in the hands of an alien power and that consequently he does not possess himself or, to define it more closely, he has not gained himself. When the devil believes and yet trembles,³⁶⁰ there is a self-knowing in

IV
66

this believing, and the more perfect it is, the more he will tremble, precisely because he does not will to gain himself.

A person knows his soul, then, if he truly knows it as something that he may even be able to describe accurately but that is in the possession of another and that he probably desires to possess, but knowledge as such does not help him in this. Even though patience is required for this knowing, as for any other, this nevertheless is not what the words speak about, as is shown by this—that in knowledge patience is not simultaneously the condition and the conditioned. The knower is again deceived, just as the merchant would be if instead of winning knowledge he won patience. The knower does just what the hiker does—he puts aside his patience when he has won knowledge. The person who wants to be patient only in order to know his soul will not gain his soul in patience.

The person who wants to gain his soul in patience knows that his soul does not belong to him, that there is a power from which he must gain it, a power by whom he must gain it, and that he must gain it himself. He never abandons patience, not when he has gained it, since it was indeed patience that he gained, and as soon as he gives up patience, he gives up the acquisition again; neither does he abandon patience when it seems that his efforts are frustrated, because insofar as that is the case, he knows that it must be because of a wrong kind of patience or because of impatience. Therefore, whether he gains patience in the terrible moment of decision or gains it slowly, he gains his soul in patience, whether he is immediately transferred into eternity or from that moment on he is transferring himself at every moment into eternity.

When the impatience of feelings dangles the gain before him, he knows that it is deceiving him, for it wants to render patience superfluous to him, and the gain is only in patience. When the impatience of knowledge wants to safeguard the gain for him, indeed, the gain in all its multiplicity, he knows that it deceives, for it wants to dismiss patience, and the gain is only in patience, and patience is not the multifarious but the single and the simple. When the intention wants to take the gain by force,[361] he knows that it is deceiving him, because it also takes patience by force. When the past wants to shock him with its horrors, the future with its anxious expectancy, when the whole world threatens him with its atrocities, when time enters the world's service to prolong the pain and the agony inordinately, or when time does not threaten in this way but cunningly lets him understand that it never shuts its eyes while he is sleeping—then he knows that all this is a deception—not its threats, not whether it has the power to carry them out, but that it is a deception that this will render patience superfluous to him and, if he ever did begin on it, make him regret it as one who was not able to endure, that this will separate for him the patience from the gain that remains in patience when everyone has taken his own down to the last penny.

IV
68

Should we now ask, "Who described this conflict properly?" As if the proclamation were not always imperfect, and as if the proclamation were not always something other than the gain? As if the description would not tempt the speaker to impatience in the expression of passion and the listener to impatience in listening and to impatience in demanding a new discourse, whether he found the one heard to be too elaborate (and then the speaker should praise him if it did not mean that his soul was utterly thoughtless) or too simple, which certainly should not be praised (for the person who thinks that multiplicity and multitudinousness assist him in the gain is like the person who believes that simplicity stops him), since only the simple is an assistance. Or was not the description itself something that the world and time were capable of taking away without taking away the patience and the gain that is in patience, which even in the moment of death gains a person his soul for the eternal if he dies in patience!

Two Upbuilding Discourses

1844

Although this little book (which is called "discourses," not sermons, because its author does not have authority to *preach*; "upbuilding discourses," not discourses for upbuilding, because the speaker by no means claims to be a *teacher*) has left out something, it nevertheless has forgotten nothing; although it is not without hope in the world, it nevertheless totally renounces all hope in the uncertain or of the uncertain. Tempted, perhaps, as the earlier ones were not, it takes no delight in "going to the house of feasting,"[2] desires as little as they "that its visit might be in vain" (I Thessalonians 2:1); even though a person was not without education insofar as he learned from what he suffered, it still would never be very pleasant if he needed to suffer much in order to learn little. Its desire is to give thanks if on the word of authority it were to win the tacit permission of the multitude to dare to go its way unnoticed in order to find what it seeks: that single individual [*hiin Enkelte*] whom I with joy and gratitude call *my* reader, who with the right hand accepts what is offered with the right hand; that single individual who at the opportune time takes out what he received and hides what he took out until he takes it out again and thus by his good will, his wisdom, invests the humble gift to the benefit and joy of one who continually desires only to be as one absent on a journey.

S. K.

LUKE 21:19

How someone in the hour of danger and in the moment of terror displayed a strength of soul that might truly be called wondrous has often been witnessed with amazement and told with admiration. How swiftly and how resolutely the understanding surveyed everything and the horrifying situation, how quickly presence of mind assuredly chose the right thing as if it were the fruit of the most mature reflection, how the will, even the eyes, defied the threatening terrors, how the body did not even feel the exertion, the agonizing suffering, how the arms lightly carried the burden that far exceeded human strength, how the feet stood firm where others did not dare to look down because they saw the abyss!

If you have never seen this, my listener, you have nevertheless heard about it. You may have heard how someone who had thoughtlessly frittered away his life and never understood anything but wasted the power of his soul in vanities, how he lay on his sick bed and the frightfulness of disease encompassed him and the singularly fearful battle began, how he then for the first time in his life understood something, understood that it was death he struggled with, and how he then pulled himself together in a purpose that was powerful enough to move a world, how he attained a marvelous collectedness for wrenching himself out of the sufferings in order to use the last moment to catch up on some of what he had neglected, to bring order to some of the chaos he had caused during a long life, to contrive something for those he would leave behind. You may have heard it from those who were there with him, who with sadness, but also deeply moved, had to confess that in those few hours he had lived more than in all the rest of his life, more than is lived in years and days as people ordinarily live.

Let us praise what is truly praiseworthy, the glory of human nature; let us give thanks that it was granted also to us to be human beings; let us pray that we might be granted the grace to perfect this glory gloriously in a more beautiful and more unambiguous way. But we could not praise in this way the single individual of whom we spoke, for a consideration of him makes the soul double-minded, and thought does not give its unqualified approval. Or does not even a mentally handicapped person frequently demonstrate how strong a human being is, and yet we do not praise the mentally handicapped, even though he puts many to shame. Let us then praise what there is to praise and see whether this could lead us to find the place where truth and complete devotion are the yes and amen in praise. No wonder that terror, when it comes externally and with all its horrors, torments the last strength out of a person, that in a way it gives him strength, as it gives even to the animal, but more gloriously, because the essence [*Væsen*] of man is the most glorious. The lesson we could derive from this is very dubious, and the conclusion we could draw is very ambiguous, since probably no one has seen a human being fight this way in mortal danger or with death without having to admit that the outcome at any time could be just the opposite and that moreover such a battle would not decide anything about or for the rest of the combatant's life. However, if a person discovered the danger while all speak of peace and security,[3] if he discerned the horror and after having used the healthiest power of his soul to make himself fully aware of it, again with the horror before his eyes, now developed and preserved the same strength of soul as the one who fought in peril of his life, the same inwardness as the one who fought with death—yes, then we shall praise him. It was already praiseworthy that he discovered the danger. The power required for this is far greater than the power people admire in a crucial moment, because the idea that there is peace and security and people's assurances of it are like a magic spell that readily bewitches with its powerful stupefaction and requires the soul's total power if it is to be broken. But this energy that discovers is not to be praised unconditionally. If like an adventurer someone dared to go out into the remotest regions where men had rarely set foot, if he gazed down and spotted something hidden, discovered something frightful, and then, gripped by anxiety, struck with fear, fell back from the horrors he himself had exposed, tried in vain to escape them, tried in vain to find a hiding place in the throng of people because the horrors pursued him everywhere; and if a person with troubled imagination conjured up anxieties he was unable to surmount, while he still could not leave off staring at them, evoking them ever more alarmingly, pondering them ever more fearfully, then we shall not praise him, even though we praise the wonderful glory of human nature. But if he brought out the horror and detected the mortal danger, without any thought of providing people, by pointless talk, with subject matter for pointless pondering, but grasped that the danger had to do with himself—if, then, with this in mind, he won the strength of soul that horror gives, this would in truth be praiseworthy, would in truth be wondrously wonderful. Who, indeed, would understand it, since no one saw the danger and consequently no one could grasp what otherwise is easy to understand—that the man known to have had a shocking experience became mature in earnestness.

Although all such talk that danger and terror give a person power is fraudulent talk, which people are all too willing to hear because they are all too willing to be deceived, it nevertheless is always beneficial to consider that it also takes power, indeed, literal power, to discover the danger, beneficial to understand the truth that there is always danger because a person "walks in danger wherever he walks"[4] and because a person is never saved except by "working in fear and trembling."[5]

Yet the dangers can be very diverse. People are prone to pay attention to earthly dangers. Even though the terrors of war do not rage destructively and disruptively with violence and lawlessness, but there is peace and justice in the land, even though the destroying angel of pestilence[6] does not proceed from house to house in the cities and kingdoms, but there is health and happiness everywhere—yet there is danger, as we all know, danger to life and land, to health, honor, to welfare and property. People therefore seriously think about preserving and safeguarding what they possess; they therefore distrust each other and life; this mistrust is therefore so common among people that no one finds it offensive, not even one's best friend. Ah, anyone who has just come of age, as it is called, in the world understands very well what I mean. Even though it was your best friend who appealed to you, one whom you trusted more than gold, even though you would not offend him for anything in the world, when you have most kindly complied with his wish, you say these brief words to him, or he himself says, "since life is uncertain,"[7] and you understand each other; it does not offend him to hand you these words in writing, "since life is uncertain" . . . . . so, since life is uncertain. Thus, if a young man who left his parental home and up to now had not had much to do with the world were to hear the words "since life is uncertain," do you suppose he would guess what usually follows this beginning? Do you suppose that an experienced man of the world, a go-getter, if these words were said to him, would make any other connection with this beginning than the one with which he was sufficiently familiar? In such a curious way, life is earnest. That earnest expression goes from mouth to mouth, is heard in the streets and alleys, is heard especially in the noise where busyness seems to have the least understanding of the idea of the shortness of life and the certainty of death.

So, since life is uncertain, there is something one desires to *preserve*, desires to keep safeguarded for oneself. So, there is a means by which a person can achieve his goal, a means that has been tested from generation to generation, for the written word stands fast, and when it has been drawn up under the apprehensive supervision of earthly caution, it does not deceive; then one can safely bargain and trade, exchange and divide, then one discovers with anticipating ingenuity or with belated dismay the hazards of life, but one thinks up shrewd expedients against them—and so life goes on in a very serious dream until death comes and puts an end to the account and the account reckoner.

But the soul of anyone who was suddenly aroused by that

expression was gripped by its curious mysteriousness, gripped by new anxiety, since again and again he heard it used light-mindedly, casually dropped as a remark that concerned every-one but was of no particular concern to anyone; least of all was anyone concerned, since life is uncertain, to find out what, since life is uncertain, is truly worth preserving. It could not be something temporal, inasmuch as for life's sake it probably would be desirable to preserve it, but how could one wish to preserve it for death's sake, since it is precisely that which one abandons in death, which without envy and without prefer-ence makes everyone equal, equally poor, equally powerless, equally miserable, the one who possessed a world and the one who had nothing to lose, the one who left behind a claim upon a world and the one who was in debt for a world, the one whom thousands obeyed and the one whom no one knew ex-cept death, the one whose loveliness was the object of people's admiration and the poor wretch who sought only a grave in order to hide from people. It would have to be something eternal, then, that the discourse was about or, more accu-rately, what it could truly be about, and, in a single word, what else could that be but a person's soul? And it was an important matter, of utmost importance, not to postpone de-liberation about it until tomorrow, for just as the expression abruptly connects life and death, so do life and death alternate abruptly down here, and the next moment could perhaps be too late. It is already bad enough that death can come to a person like a thief in the night[8] before he has learned what is worth preserving, and if that was his soul and consequently he had not preserved it and death could demand it of him or steal it from him, then his loss would be irreparable. There-fore, to lose one's soul—that is the danger; that is the terrible thing, and what one does not preserve one can indeed lose.

Thought itself scarcely comprehends this horror. Language is unable to articulate it clearly. Only the soul's anxiety has a presentiment of what the obscure talk is about. But the anxi-ety awakens to new terror; at the same moment the danger becomes more multifarious, because the soul desires to be possessed and preserved in a different way than earthly goods

IV
79

are and the terror stretches its snare in a different way. If a person who wanted to keep his earthly goods had found a place, an out-of-the-way place in the world where no thieving hand would reach it, where no one would look for it, he could safely deposit his treasure there, certain of preserving it without needing to check on it frequently. But if a person wanted to preserve his soul in that way, he would indeed have lost it. But would it not be terrible if the rich man never dared to put away his treasure, since that would be most risky of all, but carried it around with him night and day and in this way ran the risk of losing it at every moment! If a man did lose his earthly treasure, he presumably would seek to console himself for the loss; he would avoid any reminder of past glory, which would now only cause him pain, and in this way he probably would win peace of mind again. But if someone by being lost himself had lost his soul, then he could not avoid recollection in this way, because the loss would continually be with him through time and eternity in perdition. But such perdition is truly horrible. If someone lost his earthly treasure, it still would be lost only for this life, perhaps not permanently, but even if this did happen, death would still reconcile him to the loss and remove it from him when in the moment of death he became like one who previously had not lost anything. But if he lost his soul, it would be lost for all time and for eternity; if he lost it for a single moment, it would be lost permanently, and death would be unable to help him, but precisely for death's sake he is bound to wish to have preserved it and to preserve it. —Indeed, the more he thought about it, the more anxious he became. Finally he scarcely dared to think about it, because it seemed as if he had already lost it, and yet he dared not stop, for then how would he avoid losing it!

How should we judge someone like that? Should we say that the soul is the only certainty and that, although people can take away everything else, they still allow a person to keep his soul? Or should we not commend him for discovering the danger, that it was something different from what it was generally thought to be, and for being anxious about preserving his soul? The deliberation, however, was too disquieting;

therefore, he would not succeed in understanding the thought. Just as there is only one means for preserving it, so is this means necessary even in order to understand that it must be preserved, and if this were not the case, the means would not be the only means. This means is patience. A person does not first gain his soul and then have the need for patience to preserve it, but he gains it in no other way than by preserving it, and therefore patience is the first and patience is the last, precisely because patience is just as active [*handlende*] as it is passive [*lidende*] and just as passive as it is active. The issue is not as terrible as anxiety thought it was, but on the other hand it is earnest, earnest in the deepest sense as patience understands it.

To Preserve One's Soul in Patience.

To preserve one's soul in patience—that is, through patience to ascertain what it is that one has to preserve. If a person does not use the help of patience, he may, with all his efforts and diligence, come to preserve something else and thereby to have lost his soul. Not only did he lose his soul who was infatuated with temporality and worldly desires, but also the one who, indeed moved in spiritual concern, nevertheless energetically created only an illusion. Not only did he lose his soul who gave it up to love the world and to serve it alone, but also the one who looked at himself in a mirror[9] but did not see properly and continued in the illusion. Not only did he lose his soul who callously seized the certainty of the moment, but also the one who ran aimlessly [*paa det Uvisse*] because he began with the uncertainty [*det Uvisse*] and shadowboxed in the air,[10] since he himself was a fleeting wind. Not only did he lose his soul who danced the dance of pleasure until the end, but also the one who slaved in worry's deliberations and in despair wrung his hands night and day.

When we speak about it in this way, everyone readily perceives how necessary deliberation is for a person, and how necessary patience is for deliberation, and in reflection one sees the terrifying difference between the latter and the former, although they are essentially the same, and the terror nowhere

IV
81

intrudes in a decisive way but arises because the latter is actually no different from the former. But in life this is not obvious, inasmuch as there time lies divisively between the former and the latter, and one must be farsighted to discern it immediately, quick of hearing to understand its witness, because time has a rare persuasiveness, continually talks in between them, and is always saying, "As long as I am, there is always time." Neither does the patient task of deliberation seem necessary in life, since one can very well live and associate with others and represent oneself to others just as one is without rightly understanding oneself. Every day has its trouble[11] but also its pleasure, its goal but also its reward—so why, then, deliberation, which does not make one richer, more powerful? One accomplishes nothing by it, achieves nothing; one does not amount to anything by it but simply and solely finds out what one is—which is indeed a very poor and meager observation.

For example, in the external sense a person can even engage, as we say, in big business; he gives every man his due, designs new plans every day, his enterprise expands more and more, but he never has time to square the accounts[12]—which, of course, would be needless delay. Then perhaps life submitted to him an unexpected claim that he could not pay, and he discovered to his horror that he possessed nothing. Spiritually, deliberation is a difficult and rather unrewarding labor. One dares leave nothing out in the fog, leave no little secret lying there in concealment. Perhaps one discovers that the tower cannot be as high as desired.[13] Perhaps one had never seriously made a beginning on it and therefore did not really find out that one was incapable of doing it; but then one nevertheless had kept this dream in one's soul, this seductive fantasy with which one could at times entertain oneself—why destroy it, since it neither injures nor benefits? One discovers a little defect in one's work—well, the building could last for all that, just as well as all the others, because, after all, one does not build for an eternity—so why make difficulties for oneself? Suppose one discovered no irregularity at all, then why all this deliberation?

No human being is entirely lacking in deliberation; every age has its rights. There sits youth, pensive in the evening hours, and by its side there sits a captivating figure. One hardly dares to call this impatience, since it is only full of longing, and all it talks about is wishes, and no one knows better how to speak for itself or how to speak suitably to youth. So one wishes, and it is indeed blissful that the wish is fulfilled, but it is delicious and beautiful just to hear someone speak who is speaking about the wish. The individual who wishes cannot understand another, even less be of any benefit to him, because there is no limit to the wish. He to whom much was given wishes for more, and he to whom little was given wishes for a little more; the one is astonished at the other's moderation or at his greediness, without a legitimizing of the complaint, however, since they are both wishing. But who dares to speak against it, who dares to interrupt, who has the heart to disturb this whispering in the gloaming; so ingratiating is impatience that it captivates even someone not involved. Yet patience dares to do it, since the profundity of it is that it discovers the danger; and the soundness of patience is that it does not make a great noise but earnestly and quietly helps a person, since it is the only one that truly wishes a person well. Youth does not perceive this immediately; as long as it has ears only for impatience, which very obsequiously ingratiates the wish, this is futile, but when youth becomes a bit troubled, then patience stands by. Even if its words are not the speech of flattery, what it says is still indescribably comforting. "No man can add a cubit to his stature[14] even if he were concerned about it; no man can take what has not been given to him." Is this not persuasive for all time and against all doubt; can these words not remain with one in joy and sorrow; are they not strong enough to preserve a person's soul? And even though the saying seems to want to weed out the luxuriance of the wishes, is it in order to kill the soul, or is it not rather to preserve it, so that through patience it may become what it is and be confident of becoming what it is. Does patience jeeringly tell a person that no one can add a cubit to his stature, as if it wanted to make him feel how small he is and how powerless.

IV
83

Not at all; far be it from patience, which even knows how to make the reproach very gentle; "even if he were concerned about it," it says, by which it also says as mildly as possible that he really should not be concerned about it.

Patience discovers the danger, and the danger would be right there if a person was able to obtain something by wishing in this way, because then it would be impossible to save him; and the danger is precisely that it is supposed to be better to become great in this way, because then life would be without meaning and without truth. Does patience perhaps say with the cold calculation of the understanding that wishing is useless and that therefore one must stop wishing? Not at all; it does not speak about the fulfillment and the nonfulfillment of the wish, for it says: Even if the wish were fulfilled, it would be to a person's loss; he would lose the best, the holiest, to be what God has intended him to be, neither more nor less. Therefore, let us not disturb with thoughts of how mockery or sagacity or discouragement would warn against the wish, but let us be built up by the warning from patience, which truly thinks of everything for the best. It sees the danger in the way impatience infatuates the young person; it sees that impatience could take on a new form and sit grieving with the young person and wish that it had been possible, if only it had been possible. This is why patience speaks earnestly, breaks off all connection with the wish, but then it also strengthens the heart with the strong nourishment of truth,[15] so that to be even the most insignificant and inferior of human beings and to be true to oneself is much more than to become the greatest and most powerful by means of the shabby partiality of the wish. Or do we not scorn the person who sneaks his way ahead by unworthy means to power and might, the person who gathers gold and goods by gambling—if so, should we not also scorn a person if he became what he is by means of a wish? Youth is certainly commended for manifesting its boldness by its bold wishing, but this in truth would be the only wish worthy of praise: if the youth's soul had the depth to wish that no wish might disturb his struggle in life with its humbling obligingness.

Yet no human being is entirely lacking in resolution; youth
also has its rights. At its side in the morning hours there stands
a triumphant figure, its look so confident, its expectancy so
high; it wants to be on the move, on the move to come and to
see and to conquer.[16] The young person standing beside this
figure becomes full of confidence himself, and no boon com-
panion is as pleasing to him, no one fills him with such zeal—
as *purpose* [*Forsæt*]. Who would say a word against it—who
would dare! Yes, purpose is indeed to be praised—the soul's
first thought, the will's first love. Who would dare to call it
impatience? Even one who is not involved is carried away by
it. Yet patience dares just that. Indeed, as long as youth confidently turns up its nose and arrogantly touches the heavens
with its proud head,[17] it will not listen to anything. But when
it becomes earnest enough in deliberation to want to tear itself
away from the impatience that is promising so much and even
now is changing its form, when care makes the young person's knees tremble and his arm weak, who, then, is the loving figure in whom he finds rest? It is patience.

Patience has discovered the danger and the terror, but it also
comforts: Today we shall do this, tomorrow that, God willing.[18] Are these words not indescribably comforting; do they
not take all the premature hardships away from the purpose?
And yet the purpose is not thereby destroyed; does it not become truly glorious only in this way! For God in heaven
swears by himself,[19] as Scripture says, because he has nothing
higher by which to swear, but human purpose swears by God,
and if it swears by itself, it swears by something inferior. Patience discovered the danger, but the danger was not that the
purpose would fall short but that the purpose merely as such
would supposedly have the power to be victorious and that
everything would be decided by the bold purpose of youth; in
that case a person's essence would be perverted, and the most
sacred power in him, the will, would become a wish. Even
though a person won everything by such a purpose, he still
would have lost infinitely in comparison with the one who, in
accordance with God's will and with his help, walked the little
distance to the grave, attained the seemingly lowly station

given to him as his task. Patience does not keep company with despair's mockery, which smiles at purpose as at a childish prank, does not keep company with the miserableness of the understanding that makes purpose petty, since the purpose that makes up its mind to act with the help of God is certainly not petty! Even if the task was lowly, to will to fulfill it with God makes the purpose greater than anything that arose in the natural man's heart. It is not distrust of life that patience teaches, not in distrust that it discovers that the purpose never attains its goal, inasmuch as it always attains its goal, because the goal is God, and in this sense patience teaches trust in life, and probably its purpose is poor in attire, but inwardly it is glorious, faithful, and unswerving at all times.

So it was, then, that the young person went out into life. Fortunate the young person who did that! He went with the help of patience, not rich in wishes, not intoxicated with purpose, but in faith's covenant with the eternal, in hope's covenant with the future, and love's covenant with God and human beings. And patience blessed the covenant and promised not to forsake him. Even though he lost the wish and the youthful purpose, he still would not lose his soul; if a person does not believingly aspire to the eternal, is not hopefully tranquil about the future, is not lovingly in peace and unity with God and human beings, then he has lost his soul. However lowly he is, however small in stature, however poor in talents, whatever his soul is more specifically, in itself and in its difference from everyone else's, his soul nevertheless is preserved in whatever he lost and whatever he was denied.

In deliberation, he understood this with the help of patience, and without patience he would not have understood it.

To preserve one's soul in patience—that is, to keep the soul bound together in patience so that it does not go outside this and thereby become lost when he must begin the long battle with an indefatigable enemy, time, and with a multifarious enemy, the world.

So, then, the young person went out into the world. My listener, whether this discourse seems like an old story that wants to anticipate what you are just about to do, or whether

it comes afterward like an old story about what you left behind long ago, this is how it is, this is how the young person
goes out into the world. But the next part, yes, it is very different, and the single individual—well, if the discourse were
to address all individuals, then each one might shake his head
and say, "No, it did not happen that way with me; my experience was very different from what you are talking about."
Perhaps so; the discourse certainly desires no praise. But
would not this emphasis on the different, if it becomes a staring at heterogeneity, have a certain similarity to the wish, and
impatience, which once was the ingratiating friend, become
the ingenious confidant? Try to break with it sometime, and
then you will see how this thought becomes violent and vehemently complains about patience, as if it wants to make life
sheer boredom, wants to make everyone a poor repetition of
the same. And yet if unity does not lie at the base of diversity,
similarity at the base of dissimilarity, then everything has disintegrated. If, then, no one else dares to say a well-intentioned
word against the diversity that will enrich life to the point of
disorder, patience does. It has seen the danger and the terror,
that if every person were capable of essentially effectuating diversity, then life would be disordered, his own life also; it sees
very well that the danger is not that life forbids it, but that the
danger would exist if life permitted it. Is, then, patience yoked
with the thin-lipped sagacity that thinks life merely grinds
down the variegated character of primitivity, or with the defiance that thinks that only a favored few are capable of asserting diversity? Not at all! Patience speaks very doubtfully
about that kind of favored status. Patience wants to preserve
only the soul; it has the courage to give up everything else;
and when the soul does not believingly aspire to the eternal,
does not hopefully hurry toward the future, is not lovingly in
understanding with God and human beings, then the soul is
lost; but if, on the contrary, it announces itself in this powerful
presence, then the single individual has indeed saved his soul,
however diverse the meanings the words may have for different people.

So the young person went out into life. Yet the path that

IV
86

stretches before him is long, and the world will probably be difficult for him at times. If he does not enlist the help of patience now, then all his strife and struggling will be of little benefit to him; ultimately he will be fighting in a foreign service for something else and will have lost what he should preserve. Not only did he who looked improperly into the mirror lose his soul, but also the one who immediately went away and forgot what he looked like; and not only did he who remained standing all day in the marketplace lose his soul,[20] but also the one who, although called in the first hour, soon left the work and once again stood in the marketplace; and not only did he who never began the race lose his soul, but also the one who, although he began, nevertheless fell short of the goal;[21] and not only did he who never came to the light lose his soul,[22] but also the one who, although enlightened after having once tasted the heavenly gift,[23] nevertheless fell away.

When one speaks about it in this way, it is easy to see the danger, the terror, because one sees it as decisive and because one consults only with patience. In life, diversity has a scattering effect, and when one person perseveres in something longer than another, he holds it up as evidence, and he does not understand the one who failed and is of no help to him, thinks he has succeeded because he persevered a little longer, something that he cannot even know definitely. In various ways they contend with each other over who is going to sit at the head or at the foot, a futile battle since they will all be shut out.[24] So they end up sitting together in the council of the mockers and in the assembly of the discontented, who are unable to dig and are too proud to beg.[25]

Then the young person went on his way, and patience repeated its promise not to abandon him if he would keep to it. His path was delightful, his walking was easy, and not at all as his fatherly friend patience had taught him it would be. The young people joined him enthusiastically; the elderly turned and looked wistfully after him. So quickly did he go that he even left expectancy behind him without missing it, because fortune followed his steps, advancement his deeds, success his plans. His gold procured everything for him, even the service of envy; his favor was the price that bought everything, even the applause of his rivals. His plans became bolder and bolder; even fortune became so happy about them that in order to contend with him it became bolder and bolder. Patience called to him in vain; when at every moment there is a world to win—something patience, in fact, had never spoken of—then patience can very well wait until tomorrow. Then he stood on the pinnacle[26]—proudly he gazed downward. He was nauseated by all of it, by the glitter of gold, by the vanity of pleasure, by the cowardliness of men—everything, in fact, was for sale, everything. Was it fortune that had made him impatient? It certainly had indulged him in everything; it would still indulge him, and nevertheless he languished in the cold heat of impatience.

So, then, the young person went on his way; upon his departure, patience repeated its promise. And the path was narrow, his walking was laborious, and yet it seemed as if he did not move from the spot, so swiftly did the others hurry by, and every time this happened, a shudder went through his soul. The powerful insulted him, the prosperous misunderstood him, the person he had trusted disappointed him. No one stayed with him for fear of being held back; only discouragement stayed behind and wound itself around his soul more tightly than a woman around her love. In vain did patience tell where the danger was—was there, then, not danger enough? At the same moment someone else passed him so swiftly that he grew faint and dizzy comparing his puny hope with the other's fortune. He sank down; he could not go on.

What indeed is this existence, where the only certainty is the only one about which nothing can be known with certainty, and that is death! What is hope?[27] An importunate pest one cannot get rid of, a cunning deceiver who holds out even longer than integrity, a cantankerous friend who always retains his rights even when the emperor has lost his. What is recollection?[28] A troublesome comforter, a cowardly knave who wounds from behind, a shadow one cannot get rid of, even if someone would buy it.[29] What is bliss? A wish one gives away to whoever wants to have it! What is friendship?[30]

IV
88

A figment of the imagination, a superfluity, an added plague! What is all this, what is all this . . . . . and what is this? Who does not know—it is impatience. That old hypocrite who even more hypocritically than those Pharisees[31] binds on heavy burdens that it itself does not touch with one finger! That liar who, case-hardened in lying, finally believes his own fiction! That adored idol who makes everything into nothing! That everlasting windbag who still wants us to listen to him patiently!

Impatience can take many forms this way. In the beginning, one scarcely recognizes it—it is so gentle, so indulgent, so inviting, so encouraging, so wistful, so sympathetic—and when it has exhausted all its arts, it finally becomes loudmouthed, defiant, and wants to explain everything although it never understood a thing.

Should we hesitate to call all of that impatience, even though impatience cunningly refuses to admit it but admits only to being close to it (which nevertheless has little attractiveness), although that is what it worked at night and day, early and late, tempting with good fortune and tempting with bad fortune equally ingeniously, even though the one tempted does not understand the latter. It worked at that in order to establish itself in all its agonizing emptiness, not as impatience about one thing or another, but as that cold fire that consumes the soul, even though it seems to be powerfully present in its passionate expressions! Or may impatience be in the wrong; is everyone perhaps willing to find that it is in the wrong but that the individual who yielded to it is in the right?

Is not patience itself bound to be shocked by this! Admittedly there is no one who perseveres this way in the world and perseveres this way in being concerned about human beings, but patience still refuses to let itself be mocked. It refuses to stand as a liar, and if there is a suffering or distress that cannot be endured, then patience, which wants to overcome everything, lies. Oh, let us not seek escapes, let us not praise it with our lips in such a way that we treacherously assassinate it in the heart, let us not slander it in our eulogy, as if it were capable of very much but the individual dared to reserve for himself one instance in which it was not able to be victorious. No, it shall be victorious; it must be victorious. It is in truth as patience itself says: it abandons no one, does not abandon anyone in any distress, even when one defiantly pushes it away; it still waits for him, and woe to him if he never reconciled himself with it, because it still waits for him, and it will judge him sometime when it is gloriously manifest that patience was capable of overcoming everything, is capable of forcing this admission out of impatience itself.

Or is patience perhaps a phantom figure that beckons in the clouds, that has itself experienced nothing, attempted nothing in life? Patience? This spiritual adviser that knows every distress and every suffering and has persevered and perseveres with it until it will not go on—no, until it cannot—because finally impatience itself is unwilling! Is patience perhaps unsympathetic because its righteous wrath is terrible, or is it not always merciful? Oh, it is in truth that good Samaritan;[32] and no matter how deep the wound is, how old, even how malignant, if only the sufferer utters even a faint wish, patience comes; it knows how to bind up the wound, how to pour oil on it. It always has a little cordial for the sick one, always has a little fund for traveling expenses, just enough for the next moment. It is only a little, not because patience is unwilling to give more, but it does not have much at its disposal and must be sparing with the little it has;[33] patience is always just as active [*handlende*] as it is passive [*lidende*] and just as passive as it is active. Patience comforts the sick one so that he is capable of this little, it tells him the truth: In relation to the condition in which I found you, it is already much that you are capable of doing this little, and if you were really grateful, it would seem marvelous to you.[34] This kind of talk is difficult, because one is loath to hear those words "in relation to" and would very much like to forget what they bring to mind . . . . . if one could immediately begin again as if nothing had happened or if one could still be helped for a little longer. Alas, we are all in debt to patience; patience can justly say to all of us "in relation to," and yet, mercifully, it does not say it often.

Here, too, patience knows very well where the danger and the terror are, that they do not arise because one does not manage to carry through one's plans, does not recover one's earthly losses, does not gain something temporal, does not find some new pleasure to keep one from being nauseated by life. Patience does not fear such things, and it still has a good hope in reserve against those dangers. But patience discovers that the danger was whether the old condition could continue and make the sickness even more dreadful, if that were possible, before the sick one learned once again where the danger really was.

Does patience, then, have something in common with that miserable commonsensicality that comprehends that desire nevertheless ends sometime and ends in nausea, that hardship sometimes ends in despair, and therefore thinks that the sagacious thing to do is to take care to be neither cold nor hot[35]—as if this were not the most despairing condition of all? Or does not patience perceive that the greatest danger is that the elucidating understanding's fears prove not to be the case, for then not even patience could comfort anymore? Now it can, if only the sick one so desires, since the danger is whether the sick one is to be allowed to emancipate himself from the eternal, to wither away in commonsensicality, to expire in callousness, to be desouled in spiritlessness. And against this danger there is still a resource. He who, believing, continues to aspire to the eternal never becomes satiated in such a way that he does not continue blessedly to hunger; he who hopefully looks to the future can never be petrified at some moment by the past, because he always turns his back to it;[36] he who loves God and human beings still continually has enough to do, even when need is the greatest and despair is most imminent. Before he lies down to die, he asks once again: Do I love God just as much as before, and do I love the common concerns of human beings? If he dares to answer in the affirmative, then he does not die or he dies saved; if he dares not, then he certainly has enough to do. Then in love and for the sake of his love he must deliberate whether it is not possible to see, to glimpse, to presage the joy and comfort that still must hide in the sadness, since this must still truly serve him for good.[37] And even if he finds nothing, this deliberation will serve him for good, this deliberation that the impatient person, who is so teeming with ideas and so inventive in turns of phrase, would be able to do even more beautifully if he wanted to.

Shall we now say: Happy the unfortunate one who lay on the road between Jericho and Jerusalem, because patience passed by him as the good Samaritan? Shall we begin from the beginning? Or shall we not say that it passes by everyone, and happy the person who himself was not to blame that it passed by him without helping. Indeed, this is why we call God the God of patience[38]—because he himself is patience and is nowhere far away from us.

To preserve one's soul in patience—that is, to hold it in the power of patience so that it does not slip away when the terrible struggle is with the eternal, with God, and with oneself, because this struggle is such that the person who loses the eternal loses God and himself, and the person who loses God loses the eternal and himself, and the person who loses himself loses the eternal and God. This is indeed the way it is, as the simple person easily understands—and the educated person could only demand that it be made somewhat more difficult so that he might better understand it.

Whether with the help of patience in life's distress a person accepted the comfort that the danger was different from what he had thought it was or a person himself discovered the danger and the terror and in good time was cured of fearing what corrupts the body,[39] the struggle itself can still be terrible. At the same moment when the soul perceives this, it promptly needs patience lest it retreat and prefer to fight the futile struggle with the world. If patience has helped until now, then it is appropriate to use its assistance again in order to understand in all quietness that the most crucial issues are decided slowly, little by little, not in haste and all at once; in this struggle patience is the sole sovereign, is not to be confused with anything else—it prescribes the laws and it awards the symbol of victory.

But this is not learned immediately, and the soul must fight many a hard battle and many a time must begin from the beginning. Then impatience, which has its spies everywhere, sneaks in there also. It has assumed a new form, designed specifically for the struggler's condition. It is not ingratiating, not defiant and stubborn; it is anxious. Let no one venture to spy inquisitively on the soul when it is struggling in extreme anxiety; it is a danger that can end with terror. The struggle begins most terribly when eternity transforms itself into a moment, and this moment will nevertheless be decisive for all eternity. Then impatience sighs its last anxious sigh: It is too late.

Is there no danger, then? Impatience itself screams that there is. But patience has discovered the danger, that the danger is not that it is too late but that impatience itself is wasting the last moment. What human being was ever as mean as impatience! Is it not friendship of sorts to sit with the unfortunate one and wring one's hands and wail with him[40]—and make him forget that there was time.

If, then, patience does have a resource here, it certainly has nothing in common with a miserable commonsensicality, because that never speaks of such distress, scarcely knows that it exists. And even if the understanding has a word that seems to be appropriate, it is only a deception. There was once a king[41] well known among the people; even in this generation he rambles around capriciously in anecdotes just as he did in life. He had a saying: Tomorrow there is another day [*atter en Dag*]. This essentially comforting phrase he understood very light-mindedly, but for that reason (this is what the legend seems to want to teach us) he also had a wish, the fulfillment of which would compensate him for the blessedness of heaven[42]—in case it had always been true, also in eternity: Tomorrow is another day.

Patience has another phrase, a powerful phrase, just what the anxious one needs: This very day,[43] says the Lord. Let us not rashly venture to fathom deeply the mystery here; let us not become too engrossed in this phrase; but let us not forget, either, that it is there. Let us regard it as an angel of deliverance

IV
92

who stands there with his flaming sword, and every time the soul is about to rush out to the outermost boundary of despair it must pass by him; he judges the soul but also strengthens it. The phrase is like a mighty warrior who stands at his post on the outermost boundary of the kingdom, always engaged in that terrible border dispute. When people in the interior of the country have an intimation of the terror and the women and children rush out—he stands there, he soberly turns them back and says: Take courage; I am standing here, I never doze off; go home again, prepare your souls in patience and quiet alertness.

Thus the phrase gives comfort to a person and will comfort him and will also come to meet and comfort him before he goes very far.

My listener, surely you also have struggled in this conflict in which one does not struggle with the world and does not struggle with the aid of cunning or power, because all one's cunning has been seen through and all external power is powerless. What your struggle was we do not know—whether you struggled with the repercussions of a dissolute life; whether it was your thoughts that had plotted against you and stood up like the Pharisees to tempt you with crafty talk,[44] so that the next moment they brought upon you every horror you dreaded—indeed, you did not even dare to give thanks that any one of them was omitted, since it seemed as if it would immediately follow upon this invitation; whether it was offense you saw, and you could not get rid of the sight of it—we do not know. But probably you did indeed also fight the good fight[45] and did overcome and calm your soul in patience. Oh, but moments also came when you did not overcome the temptation, but the temptation overcame you. Then when everything was lost, when you were all alone with your defeat, when the silence deepened around you, and from afar despair beckoned to you, and its enthusiasm already wanted to intoxicate you—alas, despair, too, is an enthusiasm—then perhaps these words came to mind: God will make the temptation and its outcome such that we are able to bear it.[46] Not only the temptation—that we know, that we confess, and

IV
93

happy is he who needs no other gospel—but also its outcome. And the outcome of the temptation is frequently the most dangerous temptation, whether we were victorious and were tempted to arrogance and thus fell after having been victorious, or we lost so that we were tempted to want to lose everything. The words came to your mind, and your soul became sober again, and patience began its good work again.

So let us not forget the phrase—not the latter phrase, that it is there, and not the earlier phrase that comes to meet us. Praised be the God of patience. This is the end of this discourse.

We have spoken about the power of patience to preserve the soul. We have spoken as if patience were outside a person; we are well aware that this is not so. And nevertheless I ask you, you who know better how to praise it than I, know better how to accomplish the good, how to commend it to people, since you have known it better, more inwardly and for a longer time—was it nevertheless not so at times, when concern and your laboring thoughts piled up deliberations that were of no benefit except to give birth to new deliberations, that then the plain, simple, but nevertheless forgotten words of patience prodded you from another direction, was it not as if patience stood on the outside? We have made it appear as if patience were outside, and we have let it speak, as it were, for itself. Who speaks properly about it? The older person, who was old in years, old in experience, venerable in patience? Yes, it is truly beneficial to hear him; he does a good deed by speaking, since only he has the proper authorization, in comparison with which all other education, all seductive glory of the mind, all the eloquence of the angels are but vanity and jest. But sometimes it is not easy for the older person to speak simply, solely, and purely out of patience and to witness only to that. He saw much, he experienced much, he learned many priceless words, which still are not those of patience but of life experience, with which he can benefit himself, also others, but not always another.

The younger person knows so little; the moment may come

when it is manifest that he exerted his thought and his eloquence for nothing, when it is manifest that his words were a
fraud, not to deceive others, far from it, but a fraud in which
he himself was deceived. Then he will even have done damage, done damage with the view that perhaps could not be
carried through, done damage by making people busy themselves with ridiculing the physician who cannot help himself,[47] ridiculing the one who was strong in patience at a distance and thereby forgetting to pay heed to themselves and to
consider the business that every human being has with himself. This, you see, is why we chose to let patience itself speak!
It does not seek confirmation in someone's experience but, as
it says, will gloriously strengthen every experience; it does not
seek borrowed bombast but, as it says, will stand behind what
it promises. And this every human being ought to be prepared
for—to bind himself by the charter that if patience ever collapses for him and the kingdom of eternity thereby drops out
of his hand, he nevertheless will at least exert his whole soul
for the last time to praise patience, to do it the justice of saying
it was innocent.

Praised be the God of patience. This is the end of this discourse.

PATIENCE IN EXPECTANCY[48]

How changed everything is when the fulfillment has come! When the child is born and joy is complete; when night is over and day has dawned; when the battle is fought out and victory is certain; when the agony is over and the jubilation begins; when the work is finished and the reward beckons; when longing is calmed and the benediction says amen—how forgotten, then, the past is, like yesterday,[49] short as a sigh, brief as a moment. The person who has experienced this marvels at it and scarcely comprehends it. The person who has not experienced it does not understand what the talk was all about or what it says about the pangs of childbirth, the darkness of night, the terror of battle, the anxiety of agony, the toil of work, the eternity of longing. But if it is really the case that in this regard the individual does not understand himself and one person does not understand another, then all talk about expectancy is indeed a delusion, since the person who rejoices in the daylight of the fulfillment does not even catch a glimpse of the gray mists of dawn, and the person who keeps the lamp of expectancy lighted during the night does not even see the dawn, and the person who blew out the lamp does not care about the one or the other—but the speaker must certainly be in one of these situations himself.

It is, however, very beneficial for a person to understand himself and to be able to speak with himself about expectancy, because expectancy does not come just once like birth, or just once like death, but it does not cease, any more than do day and night, seedtime and harvest, summer and winter,[50] and will not cease as long as time separates and divides mortal life. Therefore, if a person thinks that he had expected something only once in his life, whether he now was pleased by the foolish wisdom of the unquestionable fulfillment or consoled himself with the foolish wisdom of the unquestionable disappointment, he will nevertheless, without knowing how it happens, soon take hold of himself in expectancy: in order that the fulfillment may continue, may continue to be what it is, and not secretly conceal what it had never hinted; or in order that the fulfillment may not come and mock his defiant commonsensicality. Every human being is tried this way in the active service of expectancy. Now comes the fulfillment and relieves him, but soon he is again placed on reconnaissance for expectancy; then he is again relieved, but as long as there is any future for him, he has not yet finished his service. And while human life goes on this way in very diverse expectancy, expecting very different things according to different times and occasions and in different frames of mind, all life is again one nightwatch of expectancy, and let no one dare, sagaciously or foolishly, to lose himself and finish out his service in piecemeal expectancy, lest in his security or in his busyness, in his joy or in his discouragement, he forget the eternal, which is waiting every moment and at the end of time, inasmuch as this is one and the same; only the earthly and temporal mind, to its own deprivation, makes duplicitous that which in patience wants to be understood as comforting and alleviating and as rescuing and guiding in earnest.

So let us not fascinate and beguile ourselves, let us not confuse and vex one another by making our petty, transitory expectancies, our momentary states of expectancy, our expressions and moods the rule and the explanation, but let us learn from the past, from what is finished once and for all, where the time of expectancy is not lengthened by our impatience, and where in turn the time of expectancy is not shortened by our impatient joy over the fulfillment. Then even if the discourse and the contemplation are not capable of entirely calming and concealing the laboring thought in the restfulness of the deliberation, it nevertheless will always be beneficial for a person to interrupt the daily worries and the captivating repetition of pleasures, to overcome the misunderstood disconsolateness that wants to listen only to what applies solely to its particular situation, in order to be opened up to something greater, in order to devote himself to the only thing that can become the object of concern in a beautiful and redeeming way. Only when the water in the pool of Bethesda was stirred, only then was it healing to descend into it.[51] This is easier to understand in the spiritual sense, because if a person's soul comes to a standstill in the monotony of self-concern and self-preoccupation, then he is bordering on soul rot unless the contemplation stirs and moves him. Then if he is moved, if he, who lay like a paralytic and invalid, gained the strength in the moment of contemplation to pull himself together but complete healing did not follow immediately, it nevertheless will always be a blessing for him that he was moved and stirred, since only in this is there redemption, sometimes at once, sometimes gradually.

IV
97

But what has ever been the object of such expectancy as the birth of the child who now, according to the Gospel just read, is being brought at the age of forty days to the temple to be presented to the Lord! This expectancy was in the world as early as man learned to understand it;[52] it became more clear and definite as time went on, as the chosen ones of the generations rejoiced in the vision and from afar hailed the future event,[53] the nonappearance of which even made them guests and aliens on the earth.[54] Centuries have rolled by, but they, too, are counted; our impatience neither adds to nor subtracts from the long, long period of expectancy. Indeed, how long is a single human being's life, how many are his days of expectancy if he counts them all together! Then came the fullness of time.[55] The expected one, whom the kings from the East came to worship, was born; even though he was born in an inn and laid in a manger, and even though his mother was only a betrothed virgin and his father a humble man of the people, nevertheless the star in the sky was a witness to his birth, the star whose sign the kings followed until they found the child.[56] Now the child was forty days old and was to be presented to the Lord. Then that poor family, which through all generations has been called the holy family, went to the temple to bring the child and the humble offering specified for the destitute. Should there be no witnesses at this solemn ceremony? Should not something happen comparable to what happened when the star shone over the cradle? From the Gospel we learn that two witnesses were present, a godly man and a devout woman, Simeon and Anna.[57] They were not related to the child by the bonds of family and friendship and were not invited by the parents; they were present in accordance with a higher dispensation and represent something higher. They were both well along in years, tired of living and yet joyous in hope.[58] Consequently, they were not concerned about the fulfillment in the same way as the person who meets its coming with a greeting of welcome, but they were like one who bids the fulfillment farewell. What, then, do these two witnesses represent, what else but expectancy? Just as the voice of the prophets echoed once again in the rigorous words of John the Baptizer, so did the patriarchs' believing expectancy rise up in these two figures in order to stand by in the moment of fulfillment. But they, who were appointed by the Lord himself to represent the expectancy in that hour, certainly were the sort of people who at all times are able to stand their test every time contemplation seeks to understand expectancy and the form of expectancy that is in patience.

IV
98

The Gospel just read mentions Simeon only briefly but dwells all the more solicitously on Anna, as if it first and foremost wanted to make her the object of our attention. Consequently, let us not misunderstand this hint, but with Anna as the occasion and with her in mind let us speak of:

Patience in Expectancy.

From the Gospel, we learn that at the time of this event Anna was well on in years, in her eighty-fourth year. Her earlier life had passed quietly; only one change is mentioned, the one that made her a widow when she had lived with her husband seven years after maidenhood. Consequently, she had been married only seven years, and now her age was seven times twelve. Her life was broken off early; she had nothing left that could be the object of her caring while her thoughts were with the one dead; she had nothing she could love forth [*opelske*][59] as a consolation for herself in time, nothing she could love with her whole heart without thereby dishonoring or disquieting the one who had passed away, nothing she could love in such a way that by her very fervency she would gladden the father [husband] in his grave. She was a widow, her life was finished, her expectancy disappointed—she who had expected to live a long time with her husband and to die remembered by a family and relatives. But she was now indeed free; according to Hebrew conceptions, too, a woman is indeed free when her husband is dead; she was indeed free, and in the resurrection there will be no distinction between man and woman.[60] Let us not upset the venerable woman with our plans; let us not seek to console with the sagacious advice of people who do not know what inconsolableness is. Eighteen centuries and more have passed; she does not need our help now any more than she needed it then. We shall not hinder her in following the inclination of her heart; we shall not be in a hurry to attire her in the victorious armor of despair or in the mourning weeds of slow deterioration. After all, she is the object of our contemplation, and there are things in life into which we should not seek to poetize our thoughts but from which we ourselves should learn; there are things in life over which we should not weep but from which we should learn to weep over ourselves.[61]

Her choice is made. It did not happen yesterday or the day before yesterday so that we should be ready with our assistance to get it changed. Her choice is made, and if she has regretted it, the time of regret has been long. She chose to remain faithful to her late husband, as he had been faithful to her, or to say it in another and more truthful way, even though it might not seem as beautiful to her, she chose to remain true to herself; after all, every external bond was dissolved, and only that love bound her in which she had her freedom and without which she would not have known herself again. In this fidelity, her life became very poor in variety, which some people achieve to the point of repulsiveness, but her life became fruitful for the eternal. And whatever you may think of this, my listener, it is certainly up to each individual to decide

on his own, so that according to circumstances one choice
may be just as commendable in its fervent love as another, but
this much is certain—that the woman who is busy consoling
herself over the loss of her late husband is hardly God's choice
to appear as the witness of expectancy in the hour when the
expectancy of the human race has its fulfillment. She remained
faithful to the departed one, and she considered herself well
taken care of, as she was indeed, since there is nothing that so
forms, ennobles, and sanctifies a person as the memory of one
who is dead[62] hidden in a sincere heart; there is nothing that
next to God himself so uncompromisingly tests and searches
a person's innermost being as does a commemoration of one
who is dead preserved in an always present memory; there is
nothing that maintains a person's soul in this kind of persevering and faithful endurance as does the thought of one who is
dead, which never slumbers. The living can sometimes be
taken by surprise by some frailty or can prompt someone else
to be overhasty, but one who is dead is never overhasty. The
living can at times make a mistake or influence someone else
to make one, but one who is dead is made not of flesh and
blood but of the holiest and best thoughts of a thankful memory, which are never in error, since they are purified in the
anxiety of losing the one who has gone to glory. The living
are quick to appreciate our love, quick to repay in fuller measure and sooner than perhaps was deserved; but the longer the
hour of reward is postponed, the more beautiful it is for the
one who desires it early and late. Only the day laborer demands to be paid every day; only faithful love serves seven
years and seven more for the reward,[63] but the person who
loves one who is dead serves his entire life for his love.

Is Anna, then, not expectant? We are well aware that there were
those in the world whose expectancy was not disappointed.
They learned early to harden their hearts and now perhaps
lifted their heads very proudly in order to look out over those
who were bowed down in sorrow. How could that sort of person ever be deceived! And yet if he suddenly were to be reminded vividly of the time when his heart swelled dauntlessly

and confidently, rich in expectancy, then he might be shocked at himself and at his disappointed expectancy, because he had never expected that he would ever foolishly carry his head high like the barren fig tree[64] that expects nothing. If anyone was disappointed, then certainly it was he, and more incurably than all others. The person who is deceived by the world can still hope that he will not be disappointed some other time under other circumstances, but the person who deceives himself is continually deceived even if he flees to the farthest limits of the world, because he cannot escape himself.

We are well aware that there were those whose expectancies were not disappointed. In busy service they allowed themselves not a moment's quiet; they fragmented their souls in multifarious expectancies, expected now one thing, now another; they won and lost, arose early and walked long roads. Their expectancies were not disappointed—but the expectancy, yes, that was out of the question. Where indeed was the master who was capable of describing this indefatigable emptiness, or where were the memory and the thought that were capable of summing up such confusion, or where the eternity that had the time to remember such things! Were they not disappointed, disappointed in their expectancy that time could not run out, disappointed by the expectancies that in dissipation had let them forget that the earnestness of eternity was bound to forget all their aspirations and them also, something they could have avoided. Not to be forgotten in the course of time was the lot of very few people, but something more glorious, not to be forgotten in eternity, is given to every human being who himself wills it. Were they, then, not disappointed, is not the person who does not even suspect the disappointment before it swallows and annihilates him most terribly disappointed?

But Anna, however . . . . . My listener, let your thoughts dwell on this venerable woman, whose mind is among the graves and now, although well on in years, nevertheless stands as the eternal's young fiancée. This tranquillity in her eyes that nevertheless is expectant, this gentleness that is reconciled to life and nevertheless is expectant, this quiet integrity that is

femininely occupied with recollection and nevertheless is expectant, this humble self-denial that nevertheless is expectant,
this devout heart that covets nothing more and nevertheless is
waiting in suspense; beyond flowering nevertheless still vigorous, forsaken nevertheless not withered, childless nevertheless not barren, bent with years and stooped nevertheless not
broken—a widow, nevertheless betrothed, "she is in silence"⁶⁵
with her expectancy. It is beautiful, you may say; if one were
able to describe it fittingly, one could sit and grow old contemplating this picture, powerless to tear oneself away from
it. But if I were to add, "This is what expectancy looks like,"
and go on to say, "Oh, that it might always look like this!"—
there might be someone who impatiently would turn away
from this same picture. "Is this life's expectancy—I who expect to win everything, to satisfy my inexpressible craving,
who expect that life itself will teach me how much more there
is to expect than I suspect? Is this what happens to expectancy?
Does one keep the divining rod in one's hand until it becomes
a dry stick, and does one hold this in one's hand—as the fulfillment?" Now he probably does not need to fear that he will
suddenly, in the twinkling of an eye, come to be like pious
Anna or that without his being aware of it time will sneakily
remodel him after the picture that is beautiful at a distance but
close at hand is alarming. Anna had not always been a widow
either; she, too, had been young, had also known the expectancy of youth. But the person who does not know life's dangers—his courage is only a scarcely praiseworthy foolhardiness, and the person who does not know life's deceit—his
expectancy is only an intoxication in dreams. As surely as
there is danger, so surely is there also disappointment, and not
until a person tries his hand at it in such a way that he chooses
the better part,⁶⁶ chooses expectancy, not until then can Anna
truly become the object of contemplation. There is something
that every person soon discerns in himself, and accordingly he
will not go far if he does not discern it; but if this is what we
are supposed to learn from Anna, she would scarcely have become unforgettable through the centuries; because life passes

away and the lust of it,[67] and he who knows nothing better, he himself passes away, just as do life and desire.

Is Anna not patient in expectancy? Anyone who wants to harvest before he sows or as soon as he has sown, anyone who wants to be victorious without struggling, anyone who wants something but does not want the means is a fool in people's eyes. Everyone believes that the expectant person needs some patience, and only the person who wants to cast away all patience, he alone is called impatient and childish in his impatience. Some patience! If a person were to go out into the world with this wisdom, he would find scarcely a single impatient person without some patience. Does the Gospel mean to say that all the foolish virgins went to sleep immediately or all at the same time?[68] Why should we not assume that there was a difference? Then the first one went to sleep quickly, even before the oil was burned up; but the fifth—she did not attend the wedding either, because she, too, destroyed her expectancy with impatience, and when the oil was burned up she did not think it worth the trouble to obtain new oil in order to sustain the expectancy. If the bridegroom had come a bit earlier, it would not have been known that she was impatient, since she did nevertheless have some patience, just as even the first one had some patience. When the fulfillment comes immediately or quickly, it is so very easy to understand life because one does not learn to understand oneself; but when it fails to come . . . . . Like those bridesmaids, everyone has an original supply of oil with which to sustain expectancy. Now if the fulfillment comes before this is consumed, then everything goes well, and one goes through life without definitely knowing or definitely establishing whether one belongs among the foolish or the wise bridesmaids. The original natural power of endurance can be different in different individuals, but as soon as the fulfillment fails to come for such a long time that this original power is consumed and exhausted, then and only then will it become manifest whether a person has new oil in readiness, only then will his patience in expectancy become manifest. As long as expectancy holds and carries a person, no wonder that he is expectant, but when the last struggle begins, when one must strain oneself to the utmost to hold on to expectancy, then people fall away. How often it is said that no one is to be considered happy before he is dead,[69] but how seldom is a troubled person heard to say that one should not give up as long as one is living, that there is hope as long as there is life—and consequently there is always hope for the immortal who expects an eternity.

Now if there were a person who in his distress dared truthfully to say, "I have been given nothing; in the great design of things that provides for all, I was even more forgotten than the sparrow, which does not fall to the ground without God's will;[70] so I will simply not endure it any longer; from this moment on, I will give up all expectancy and let myself fall to the ground." —Or suppose he did not say it just this way but in his despair nevertheless truly thought he dared to say, "I certainly lost my way, but I turned back again. Nevertheless it was in vain, my expectancy too late; I stretched out my arm, but my foot just slipped; I shouted, but there was no ear to receive my scream. So, then, at this very moment I will give up every expectancy and let myself sink; God must take the responsibility if help comes in the very next moment, when it is too late." In that case, should we sagaciously think that if we were in such a person's place we with our ingenuity would probably find a way out where he found none; or should we cause him new pain by ordering him to look around in the world, where there surely would be someone who had waited longer than he for help? Certainly not, but we will say to him, "Forget the past once again, quit all this calculating in which you trap yourself, do not stop the prompting of your heart, do not extinguish the spirit[71] in useless quarreling about who waited the longest and suffered the most—once again cast all your sorrow upon the Lord[72] and throw yourself upon his love. Up out of this sea, expectancy rises reborn again and sees heaven open—reborn, no, newborn, for this heavenly expectancy begins precisely when the earthly expectancy sinks down powerless and in despair."

Is this not the way it is? Or would a doubting person [*Tvivler*] and a person in despair [*Fortvivlet*] continue to be in the right? Or would he prove to be in the wrong because he disdains the speech of youthful enthusiasm, since it lacks experience, and disdains the speech of experience, since it lacks enthusiasm and has experienced either only good fortune, which cannot help him, or misfortune, but not in the same way he has! The error of the one doubting [*Tvivlende*] and of the one despairing [*Fortvivlende*] does not lie in cognition, since cognition cannot decide with certainty anything about the next moment, but the error lies in the will, which suddenly no longer wills but on the contrary wants to make the indeterminate into a passionate decision. Even at the last moment there is a possibility, or rather there is no last moment before it is past. Is this perhaps a shrewdly devised expression, "one can always say," an expression that captivates the mind and for a short time also the soul, which, however, soon regrets again, yes, is irate, because it let itself be snared in the sophistic subtlety? No, indeed; it is no subtle turn of expression that circumvents the issue, but an observation, yes, an observation that builds up, for what is it that makes the tribulation short— it is time; but what is it that makes the tribulation "brief" (II Corinthians 4:17) even when it lasts a lifetime—it is the expectancy of the eternal and the patience that expects it. And that one can always say it—is this not the eternal expectancy's victory, indeed, more than victory, over the temporal!

Can Anna be disappointed in her expectancy; can the fulfillment come too late? Certainly the fulfillment can come too late for the expectant one; if a person expected the temporal and the vainglorious, then the fulfillment can disappoint not merely by failing to come but also by coming when it is too late. What good would it be, if it was power and dominion that the powerless one craved, if they were offered to him at the moment when nature orders him to relinquish them! What good would it be if it was pleasure and enjoyment that his soul desired and the goblet of intoxication was handed to the invalid whom every moment reminds that life passes away and the lust of it? What good would it be if, to a person who now could clasp only with shaking hands, all the world's gold was given, something he had thirsted for because in his hands it was sup-

posed to be a key to everything! What good would it be—or
would it not be like mockery of him, and would it not be most
disgusting of all if he did not understand the judging seriousness of the fulfillment, that he still had not renounced the
world and had learned nothing over the years, but the fulfillment tempted him, tempted the old man to become a contemptible fool! But you, my listener, you have not placed
your expectancy in that which is deceitful even when it comes;
your expectancies are not disappointed. You are expecting the
resurrection of the dead, of both the righteous and the unrighteous;[73] you are expecting a blessed reunion with those
whom death took away from you and with those whom life
separated from you; you are expecting that your life will become transparent[74] and clear to you, your estate in blessed understanding with your God and with yourself, undisturbed by
the passion that, troubled, seeks to guess the riddles of provi-
dential dispensation. But of course this expectancy is not disappointed, because the time of its fulfillment has not yet arrived. And when the fulfillment does come, it is never
mocking, never deceitful, because the good never mocks a human being. If it fails to come, then this is the best for him, and
if it comes, it comes with all its eternal blessedness. How
could this come too late—then it would itself have to be temporal. Therefore only impatience knows fear, but patience,
like love, drives out fear.[75] In relation to the temporal and the
vainglorious, impatience in a certain defective sense may be
true and grounded, grounded in the frailty of that which is the
object of expectancy; in relation to the eternal, it is just as
beautiful as it is certain that impatience is always untrue.

There is in the world much brooding and pondering and
investigating and calculating and talking concerning expectancy and its relation to fulfillment, inasmuch as expectancy is
certainly a matter that in many ways pertains to every human
being. But in a single word, a word eternity does not understand and recognize, all the wisdom that wants to be only
worldly-wise about expectancy can be summed up, however
copious this wisdom is from generation to generation. The
word varies according to the one speaking, but the word

nevertheless remains the same. The person in despair surrenders his soul in this word; the troubled person repeats it again and again, finds relief in hearing it kindly and sympathetically spoken by another; the defiant one, who forgets God, thinks he is able with this word to mock everything both in heaven and on earth, both the fortunate and the unfortunate; the clever one drops it laconically and still thinks he has said a lot; in his joy over the word, the light-minded one does not even have time to allow the understanding to make it duplicitous—it is the word "maybe" [*maaskee*]. We do not know whether there has ever been a more serious age that did not know this word but rested in eternity's assurance that *it must happen* [*det maa skee*]. We do not know whether a more impatient generation, by repeating that expression of eternal expectancy more and more quickly, itself created impatience's short, hasty, precipitous, frivolous, arrogant, shrewd, comfortless "maybe." Fortunate the person who, like Anna, when the earthly expectancy disappointed, said with a mind dedicated to God, solemn as eternity's language is, confident as eternity's expectancy is: It must happen. Fortunate the person who, well on in years, in his eighty-fourth year said: It must happen.

From our Gospel read earlier, we learn that Anna never left the temple, serving God night and day with fasting and prayer, that she stepped up the very same hour (when the child was brought to the temple) and praised the Lord and spoke about him to all who expected the deliverance of Jerusalem.[76] She had lived as a lawfully wedded wife ought to live with her wedded husband; now she was "a real widow who has been left all alone and has set her hope on God and continues in supplications and prayers night and day" (I Timothy 5:5). One who is faithful over little is set over much.[77] Anna had not demanded the world's comfort for the one dead; then heaven comforted her and the recollection of her loss formed her heart to envision the expectancy as being not merely for herself but for the whole nation. As the Gospel says, humble Anna was a prophet. She, who had given up her earthly expectancy and bound her soul to the eternal alone, was taught

IV
106

by this pain to expect the fulfillment that all generations had hailed from afar. My listener, however you judge concerning that which is indeed up to each one to decide on his own in such a way that one who makes the opposite choice can be no less praiseworthy, this much is nevertheless certain—the eyes of the woman who speedily recovers from the pain of the loss of her husband are hardly open to the expectancy that is not the fruit of temporality but that awakens only in the person who gave up the temporal in order to gain the eternal and then found the grace to see eternity as an expectancy in time. Although a widow and left alone, she nevertheless is the favored one, singled out by her expectancy as the one who is called a prophet, a name rarely given among the Jews to a woman because in the view of that people women were regarded as more imperfect than men.

Is Anna, then, not expecting? If she is not expecting, then who is? A prophet is occupied with the future in a way different from that of an apostle or an angel, to say nothing of the mass of people. But the future is indeed the very object of expectancy. Yet not everyone who is expectant is on that account truly expectant in the deeper sense of the word, since this depends on the object of his expectancy. Although it is a very beautiful commendation to say of a person that he is expectant, so that the one of whom it is said distinguishes himself by his expectancy, just as the hero does by the feat he performs, the poet by the art he practices, the research scholar by the truth he discovers, the philanthropist by the sacrifice he magnanimously makes—a person can also be censured for being expectant. If someone were to expect, early and late, something that did not pertain to him apart from his curiosity, or if someone were to set aside what is assigned to him, what requires his best talents and his daily attention, in order to swagger around as the chosen instrument of expectancy, or if someone were to expect that which truly pertains to him but which his deadened will had thoughtlessly transformed into an object of expectancy, who would then wish to be expectant in this sense! One who expects in this way is not educated by his expectancy, either—on the contrary, his nature degenerates. He wastes the power of his soul and the content of his life in calculations and the irascible unwholesomeness of probabilities; his proud achievement disintegrates and he is decomposed into empty noise; his energy is deadened in cowardly superstition, which finally becomes plunder to the crafty, an object of ridicule to the sensible, an anxiety to the serious-minded; he expects everything and forgets that, whatever God gives, he "gives not the spirit of cowardliness but the spirit of power and self-control" (II Timothy 1:7).

Just as it is required of the expectant person, if his expectancy is noble and worthy of a human being, that he seek this spirit of power and self-control, and that, just as his expectancy is laudable, he must also be one who is properly expectant, so in turn will the object of expectancy, the more glorious and precious it is, form the expectant person in its own likeness, because a person resembles what he loves with his whole soul.[78] Now, who would be capable of cataloging the countless expectancies that with regard to the individual could all be seemly and worthy; but who would deny that in the eminent sense of the word there was only one expectancy in the world, the expectancy of the fullness of time, and this was precisely the object of Anna's expectancy. If anyone is expecting, it is Anna, and although this expectancy, once fulfillment has come, never repeats itself, it will still be beneficial for a person not only to keep a close watch on himself, lest he be lost in the impatient service of expectancy, but also to pay heed to his expectancy so that he dares own up to it even when his mind dwells on the expectant Anna's one and only expectation. One and only since we extol her because she had only one, and we extol her again because her expectation was truly the one and only. Worthy she stands, then, beside Simeon, who desired to see nothing but what he saw and then to go home in peace. Blessed are the eyes that saw what he saw and saw it in the way he saw it;[79] even though a person became as gray-haired as Simeon and as aged as Anna, yet it is blessed to be the expectant one who expects and sees the expected one, in whose place no other one shall come![80]

Is Anna not patient in her expectancy? Even though in the

world we hear at times of someone who expects nothing at all, even though such a person is sometimes thought to have attained the proper assurance, because he craftily made it impossible for himself to discern the loss, yet it is also admitted that this wisdom is of later origin and that no one has it in early youth. Originally, then, like every other human being, he was expectant. With a smile or with tears, one confesses that expectancy is in the soul originally. As long as it is a strident enthusiasm, an unclarified confidence, an inner effervescence, we extol it as the beautiful or childish advantage of youth, as a birthright one nevertheless gives away in the distress of life for a mess of lentils.[81] As long as the happy mentality of youth jubilates in good fortune and satisfaction, it is admittedly appropriate to want to be joyful and happy; but when the opportune hour of happiness wants to be purchased and at a high price, then a later wisdom comes along, and a person does not even want to be happy, wants to be dejected, wants to be unhappy. When does this happen? It happens in the time of distress, or we could also express it another way— it happens when it becomes apparent that patience and expectancy correspond to each other. Why not abbreviate the difficulty, then, by discarding expectancy? And yet it is so that patience and expectancy correspond to each other, and not until these two have found each other, find and understand each other in a person, not until then is there like for like in the friendship that is to be continued; expectancy in patience is like a good word in the right place, like a golden apple in a silver bowl,[82] and not just a dead magnificence but like a treasure that is invested at interest.[83]

Who is it, then, who judges whether a person is patient? Is it time? Not at all, or only in a certain sense, because someone may be patient and have been patient and still did not see his expectancy fulfilled. In the profoundest sense, it is the expectancy itself, its essence, that determines whether a person is patient. The person whose expectancy is truly expectancy is patient by virtue of it in such a way that, upon becoming aware of his impatience, he must not only judge himself but also test his expectancy to see whether this explains his impatience and to what extent it would be wrong to remain patient; if that was possible, he ought to give up the expectancy. Only the true expectancy, which requires patience, also teaches patience. But true expectancy is such that it pertains to a person essentially and does not leave it up to his own power to bring about the fulfillment. Therefore every truly expectant person is in a relationship with God.

Such an expectant person cannot let his expectancy slip into forgetfulness and then when fulfillment comes think that all this long time he has been patient in expectancy. This deception is possible only through the external, which, itself deceptive, teaches the person to deceive himself. In relation to what truly pertains to a person and consequently in relation to true expectancy, this is impossible, since then the fulfillment will never come, because the possibility of it dies out proportionately as the actuality of the expectancy dies out. IV
109

Such an expectant person cannot feed and satisfy his expectancy with probabilities and calculations, because only in patience does he enter into a relation to expectancy, and this begins precisely when probability is fleeting. Probability, however, is only a deceitful advantage over expectancy, which has none. One seemingly comes close to the fulfillment quickly, indeed, very close; suddenly it withdraws. Patience, however, leaves its expectancy up to God and in this way is always equally close to the fulfillment, however foolish this may seem to the earthly understanding.

Such an expectant person cannot delude himself with apathetic dullness, as if it were patience when he also became accustomed (because he did everything from habit) to occupying himself with his expectation but its concern did not awaken his soul. No, anyone who expects what truly pertains to him cannot thereby become indifferent to it, since then he no longer grasps that it truly pertains to him, and neither does he then expect that which truly pertains to him. He cannot become apathetic in habit, since at all times he is just as close to the fulfillment.

The true expectant person keeps company with his expectancy every day. It arises earlier in the morning than he himself, is up and about sooner, goes to bed later in the evening than he himself; the inner being, to whom expectancy belongs, does not need as much sleep as the outer being. His concern is the same every day, because his innermost life is equally important to him at every moment. Yet he does not consume his soul in impatience, but in patience he offers his expectancy; in patience he sacrifices it by submitting it to God.

If this discourse about patience and expectancy is perhaps obscure, then we shall eulogize Anna and confine ourselves to her; she is not difficult to understand. She was a widow of eighty-four years who did not leave the temple; serving God night and day with fasting and prayer, she preserved her expectancy "in all patience and forbearance with joy" (Colossians 1:11).

She did not leave the temple. Yet she was not in the temple with the fulfillment but only with her expectancy. This the expectant person takes with him when he goes out into the streets and alleys at the fourth hour, and at the eleventh hour, and at cockcrow; or he sits still but lets his thoughts go out, listening for the soft footsteps of the fulfillment, watching for the distant cloud in the desert, for the mist on the moor that changes shape with every breeze and changes the expectant one. But Anna did not leave the temple, not only because she waited to see the fulfillment come to pass in that holy place, since then she probably would have climbed the temple tower or consulted the wise men, those versed in the stars and in the Scriptures, but because her expectancy was in God and she was always equally close to the fulfillment, although no probability came and went, visited her in order to comfort, or brought discouragement along with it.

Serving the Lord, because, as you see, she was indeed the Lord's handmaid, but she was also serving her expectancy, and this service was the same. The expectant person does not willingly serve someone else, and people forgive him if he abruptly stands up, if he does not share in their joy or does not help in time of need; after all, he is serving his expectancy. Through this service, he gains the fulfillment. But Anna served another, in whose hand surely lay the fulfillment, just as the fulfillment of every expectation lies in his hand, but she received no enlightenment, and while the days passed and added years to her age until she was very aged, she nevertheless was always just as close to the fulfillment.

With prayer and fasting, but the person who prays and fasts accomplishes nothing, since prayer is idle talk on earth, even though it "works in heaven,"[84] and fasting consumes earthly energy and gives no strength to endure in expectancy. —Yet impatience is an evil spirit "that can be expelled only by prayer and much fasting."[85]

Night and day. Indeed, this is how the expectant one perseveres, night and day, but does it always in prayer and fasting. The hunger of impatience is not easy to satisfy—how, then, through fasting? The demands of impatience certainly use many words and long speeches, but in prayer it is very sparing of words. Temporal patience has provisions on hand for a long time, doggedly perseveres, seldom rests, never prays, but Anna continued night and day. Even though impatience says that it is no art to pray—oh, just to collect one's mind in prayer at a specified time and to pray inwardly, even though for only a moment, is more difficult than to occupy a city,[86] to say nothing of persevering night and day and preserving in prayer the inwardness of heart and the presence of mind and the quietness of thought and the sanction of the whole soul, without being scattered, without being disturbed, without repenting of one's devotion, without anguishing about its being a prinked-up deception, without becoming sick of all one's praying—but Anna, serving the Lord with prayer and fasting night and day, did not leave the temple.

Was Anna disappointed in her expectancy; did the fulfillment come too late? Her expectancy was for something that was to occur in time. Consequently, the outcome must decide whether the fulfillment came or whether the end was a disappointment. Would Anna at this point actually become just as disconsolate as all the talk that is heard about the outcome, which, just like the outcome, always comes trailing after?

The outcome showed that her expectancy came to fulfillment; consequently, she was not disappointed. But in what sense was she not disappointed? Did she herself perhaps amount to something through her expectancy—for example, like the person who was impoverished and again became rich, the person who was toppled and then elevated again, and in a certain sense was elevated because of his expectancy, insofar as he himself had not given up being his own co-worker—did the widow perhaps marry again? My listener, why are you almost ashamed that I mention this word? After all, the expectancy did not arise in her soul when she began her eighty-fourth year; it goes far back in time to the days when she made the choice she acknowledged in her last hour. Is it I who presumptuously mock the venerable woman, or if this had been her expectancy, would not the fulfillment come to her as the most dreadful mockery? Praised, therefore, be Anna; she stands there venerable and highly exalted. Although ordinary human speech becomes silent at the sight of her, the most profound expression in language must call her in the strictest and noblest sense: the expectant one. And does this not also show that the outcome could not disappoint her by coming too late!

And even if it had failed to come, she still would not have been disappointed. The fulfillment came; at the same moment, just like Simeon, she desires only to depart, that is, not to remain with the fulfillment and yet in another sense to enter into the fulfillment. If the moment of the fulfillment had not come in time, will you then deny, my listener, that she nevertheless entered into eternity with her expectancy and went to meet the fulfillment.

By failing to come, the outcome could not essentially deceive her, and by coming too late it could not disappoint her. Do you not believe also that this was Anna's understanding when the fulfillment came, which certainly could have come long before she was eighty-four and nevertheless could have come as the fulfillment of her expectancy. Do you think that she regretted the many years, do you think that her joy perhaps cast the regret into forgetfulness, or do you not think that her joy was precisely those many years in which she had been faithful night and day to her expectancy! And was not the reward able to compensate her richly and inordinately even if she had become ninety-five, yes, even one hundred, years old! She did not amount to something through her expectancy; the fulfillment did not pertain to her temporally in that way any more than the expectancy had. But inasmuch as the expectancy of the age, of the nation, of the generations, of the human race, of Adam, and of millions came to fulfillment, devout Anna stood alongside Simeon as the witness of the expectancy, and thus they stand unforgettable for all time!

What if Anna had been a mother, what if the one dead had remained with her, what if for the second time she had experienced in a still more beautiful sense being called mother—a person does not desire more than this to be deemed happy, but what if Anna wants more? Well, then, what if Anna, herself aged and with her aged husband, had watched the third generation grow up, what if the child now being presented had been thrice removed, what if her husband had been standing by her side instead of Simeon, what if she herself had expected only this fulfillment, in order then to go to her rest, what if three generations had called her mother and this beautiful name had been spoken again and again in as many ways as possible, what if three generations had never forgotten her? —And now! Anna had experienced the pain of life and had sown with tears,[87] had lost her husband early, since then had remained childless and forsaken; then in her eighty-fourth year she came forth in the temple, concealed the expectancy of all ages in her devout figure, and so she stands, always remembered as the witness of expectancy. —Blessed is the one who became poor and forsaken,[88] blessed is the barren one,[89] blessed is the one who lost the world in such a way that expectancy's desire for it never awakened in his soul, blessed is the one whose expectancy walked through the gate of death into the eternal in order to apprehend his expectation until he saw it with earthly eyes and did not desire to see it anymore in time.

People often lament that life is so impoverished, existence so powerless in all its magnificence, that it seeks in vain to take the soul by surprise or to captivate it in wonder [*Beundring*[90]], IV
113

since to wonder at nothing[91] is the highest wisdom, and to expect nothing is the highest truth. The child is astonished at insignificant things. The adult has laid aside childish things;[92] he has seen the wondrous, but it amazes him no more; there is nothing new under the sun[93] and nothing marvelous in life. If, however, a person knew how to make himself truly what he truly is—nothing—knew how to set the seal of patience on what he had understood—ah, then his life, whether he is the greatest or the lowliest, would even today be a joyful surprise and be filled with blessed wonder and would be that throughout all his days, because there is truly only one eternal object of wonder—that is God—and only one possible hindrance to wonder—and that is a person when he himself wants to be something.

Three Upbuilding Discourses

1844

TO THE LATE

Michael Pedersen Kierkegaard

FORMERLY A CLOTHING MERCHANT HERE IN THE CITY

MY FATHER

THESE DISCOURSES ARE DEDICATED

Even though this little book (which is called "discourses," not sermons, because its author does not have authority to *preach*, "upbuilding discourses," not discourses for upbuilding, because the speaker by no means claims to be a *teacher*) addresses itself to a reader, to that single individual whom I with joy and gratitude call *my* reader, the speaker nevertheless does not forget that to be able to speak is an ambiguous art, and even to be able to speak the truth is a very dubious perfection.[95] In this consciousness, the book goes out into the world; inclosed in itself [*indesluttet i sig selv*], it pays no heed to the weather, does not inquire about the wind, does not look to the clouds, is not mistaken about anything, but seeks and looks for only that favorably disposed person who takes an interest in the seeker, gives an opportunity to what is said, brings the cold thoughts into flame again, transforms the discourse into a conversation, the honest confidentiality of which is not disturbed by any recollection of the one who continually desires only to be forgotten, and this is primarily and preferably the case precisely when the recipient accomplishes the great work of letting the perishability of the discourse arise in imperishability.[96]

There is a truth, the greatness and the grandeur of which we are accustomed to praise by saying admiringly that it is *indifferent* [*ligegyldig*], equally valid [*lige gyldig*],[97] whether anyone accepts it or not; indifferent to the individual's particular condition, whether he is young or old, happy or dejected; indifferent to its relation to him, whether it benefits him or harms him, whether it keeps him from something or assists him to it; equally valid whether he totally subscribes to it or coldly and impassively professes it, whether he gives his life for it or uses it for ill gain; indifferent to whether he has found it himself or merely repeats what has been taught. And the only one whose understanding was sound and whose admiration was justified was the one who grasped the greatness of this indifference and in accord with it let himself be formed into an indifference toward what pertained to him or any other human being as a human being or especially as a human being.

There is another kind of truth or, if this is humbler, another kind of truths that could be called *concerned truths*. They do not live on a lofty plane, for the simple reason that, ashamed, as it were, they are conscious of not applying universally to all occasions but only specifically to particular occasions. They are not indifferent to the single individual's particular condition, whether he is young or old, happy or dejected, because this determines for them whether they are to be truths for him. Neither do they promptly let go of the individual and forsake him, but they continue to be concerned about him until he himself completely breaks away, and even to this they are not indifferent, although he is not able to make these truths doubtful about themselves. Such a truth is not indifferent to how the individual receives it, whether he wholeheartedly appropriates it or it becomes mere words to him. This very difference certainly shows that it is jealous of itself, is not indifferent to whether the truth becomes a blessing or a ruination to him, since this contrary decision witnesses specifically against the equal validity; it is not indifferent to whether he honestly places his confidence in it or whether, himself deceived, he wants to deceive others, since this avenging wrath expressly shows that it is not indifferent. Such a concerned truth is not independent of the one who has propounded it; on the contrary, he remains present in it continually in order in turn to concern himself about the single individual.

Those words we have just read, tested and repeated for centuries, are such a concerned truth. And if you could hear the voice of the one who said it, you would be assured as to how moved he himself was; and if you could see him in person, and you yourself were a young person, you certainly would be gripped by the sympathy with which he concerned himself about you, but more particularly he would awaken you to concern about yourself. Who was this man who spoke these words? We do not know, but if you are young, even if you are heir to the throne and your thoughts are such as the expectancy of dominion could inspire, then it is told that he, too, wore the royal purple,[98] although, despite all this, he was of the opinion that the thought of the Creator is youth's best thought. And if you are young, even if your life is lowly and without any glittering prospect, you have his royal word that, despite this, the thought of the Creator is youth's most beautiful splendor.

Therefore, you see, the story that a king spoke these words is, as it were, a devout wish that wants to reconcile the greatest differences in a simple understanding of the same thing by means of the different ways the words themselves are concerned about the difference. When someone of royal birth who someday will rule kingdoms and countries sees on the wall of a humble cottage a picture, such as this might be in modest circumstances, a picture whose inadequacy almost makes him smile and he steps closer and reads these words inscribed on the picture—then the Preacher speaks to him, but the Preacher was indeed a king. And when the son of poverty stands amazed in the palace, when inexplicable thoughts awaken in his soul, when he stares in astonishment at his royal majesty, then the Preacher speaks to him, and the Preacher was indeed a king—then he returns home, reconciled, to his humble dwelling and to his poor picture on the wall.

Is there not, then, a reconciliation? Or will you assume the appearance of contentment in a clumsy attempt to argue that you do not crave the king's magnificence—but neither can you be content with thinking about your Creator! As if that self-made contentment were not an arbitrary merit of which one does not dare to boast—indeed, worse yet, it is a sign of your miserable state that only witnesses against you! There is really nothing in the wide world that is able (no more than the whole world is able) to compensate a person for the harm he would inflict on his soul[99] if he gave up the thought of God; but the person who demanded the highest, blinded though he was, still let it be understood that in a certain imperfect sense he grasped the significance of what he was abandoning. —Or was it perhaps different with you? Perhaps you were unwilling to agree to the reconciliation simply because it was a king who had spoken the words, and "a king, after all, obtains everything he points at; when he has pursued the beckoning of desire to the outermost boundary of pleasure, no wonder that his view of life suddenly changes."

The words, then, were indeed meaningful, but the admonition was not to be taken, because the words were indeed concerned but not concerned about any particular individual, were indeed words of concern, were indeed reconciled to life insofar as they were tempered in sorrow but were nevertheless only a sigh from the hiding place of sadness, a sigh in the hour when the weary soul bids the earth farewell, but still only a bubble that breaks, however deep the depths from which it rises. There is a kind of wisdom that virtually chooses the concealment of mental disorder and by its strange agitation makes up for everything in people's eyes, but the sigh itself and the outburst and the emotion pertain to no one, no one in the whole world, not even the one from whose heart the sigh sounds. At times a short saying like this is heard in the world, heartbreaking words, a language of the heart, not pithy as is the language of thought, but trembling with mood. It will not be a light on anyone's path, since the sun will light the man's way by day, and the moon will shine for him at night, but the will-o'-the-wisp will not give illumination in the night fog, not even for itself.

When a person's life draws toward evening, when, weary and reflective, he associates with death as his one and only confidant, when his spirit has lost the strength to make an accounting in earnest and death has become the comforter, when his will and purpose no longer desire anything but his thought vaguely fumbles in the past, while forgetfulness like a busy day laborer works early and late in the service of the comforter and now youth flits by the soul like a dream—then such a person, musing on life's most beautiful meaning as this once pertained to him, says to himself: Happy the one who did that! But if alongside him stood a young man still totally challenged by life, he would not talk in this way. Only when he is sitting alone, decrepit as a ruin, lost in sadness, only then does he say it, not to anyone else, not to his own soul, but says it to himself: Happy the one who did that! And just as one knowledgeable about medicine knows that there are lines in the face that are lines of death, so a person knowledgeable about the soul knows that this outburst signifies that the spirit wants to be extinguished. The outburst may very well have its meaning, but it is futile to look for the power of the admonition in it, because faith is not there, faith in having accomplished the good oneself, or faith that anyone else will succeed. And anyone who avidly pays attention to such words most often is himself in a similar state or at least has a sad presentiment that something similar will befall him, and therefore both find solace and relief by swooning in this powerlessness in which the admonition does not disturb them, but in which the blessing of the admonition does not rest upon them, either.

"All is vanity and pernicious toil,"[100] says the Preacher, and light-mindedness regards such words as an ingenious plaything, thoughtlessness as a hopeless riddle, and depression as an opiate that makes the last worse than the first.[101] The Preacher has said many a word that can always be beneficial for having been said if it can help someone to save himself from having the same experience or at least help him renounce the vain hankering to be more and more ingenious. But are the words just read of that kind, and did not the Preacher perhaps say everything prior to this solely for the sake of these and similar words, and would he not perhaps have willingly given up saying everything else if only someone would follow these words? Indeed, the Preacher specifically declares that "childhood and youth are also vanity" (Ecclesiastes 11:10), and for that matter even having done what he calls for, "to let your heart cheer you in the days of your youth, to walk in the ways of your heart and the sight of your eyes" (11:9), is vanity—but has the Preacher ever said that to think of one's Creator in one's youth is pernicious toil or that to have thought of him in one's youth would also eventually prove to be vanity? Has he blended what he says about this with everything else, or is the way in which he says this worlds apart from the way in which he says the other things? Has he not relegated everything to vanity precisely so that the eternal and blessed significance of that thought might become properly manifest, so that it might bind the straying soul in obedience to the admonition? He does not say, as he usually does—*so* rejoice in your youth, *so* put away sorrow[102]—where the very expression, by indifferently tossing out what is said, suggests that what he is speaking about is a matter of indifference. He has omitted this casual little word, and as the discourse on the vanities goes on and seems to want to cast everything into vanity, the Preacher stands up to outbid the confusion so that it does not exceed its boundary,[103] to halt the vanity by the specific expression of the admonition: Think, *therefore*, about your Creator.

He does not speak as if this thought were a thought only for youth, which nevertheless must eventually become a thing of the past; he does not speak of it as if it were something past that once had meaning, something past that most desirably had had meaning once—no, the meaning of youth is precisely

IV
127

Three Upbuilding Discourses

the meaning of this thought, and precisely by means of this thought youth will be secured against being vanity, secured against seeming to be vanity at some time. He speaks not as one who wishes, not as one who longs, not as one who swoons, but he speaks to the young with the power of conviction, with the authority of experience, with the trustworthiness of assured insight, with the joyful trust of bold confidence, with the emphasis of earnestness, with the concern of the admonition. He does not talk indefinitely about youth in general, but just as the single individual probably does not understand in general that he is young, since such an understanding belongs specifically to a later age, but understands it personally, so is it precisely in this way that the Preacher wants the admonition to be understood. This is the main concern of the admonition, that even though it can be repeated again and again and applies to countless numbers of people, it speaks every time to the single individual; then it is as if it spoke to him alone, as if it came into existence solely for his sake, as if it were unconcerned about all the rest of the world but all the more concerned about him—indeed, very concerned, as concerned as if he would be doing a good deed if he accepted it. This is how the words sound, and even if you in lightness of spirit or in heaviness of spirit tried to beguile the Preacher, to trick him out of the admonition, which certainly would be lamentable, you would not succeed; the Preacher is not responsible for any ambiguity.

In this way the Preacher speaks admonishingly, and if you are young, even if you were initiated at an early age into much wisdom, he nevertheless is still speaking to you; and if you are young, even if you are rather simple, you nevertheless will not stand imploringly at the door of that wisdom, because the Preacher's concern is also for you, and he is not just saying that you can think about your Creator, but he admonishes you to do it; and if you are young, whether you are joyful or dejected, whether you are carefree or discouraged, whoever you are, it is nevertheless to you, precisely to you, that he is speaking, you to whom the admonition applies, just as does the basis for the admonition: "before the evil days come and the years draw nigh of which you will say, 'They do not please

me.' "[104] This is why he earlier tried to startle the soul out of
its security into seeing the vanity of life, kept it from "believing light-mindedly" (I Corinthians 15:2), because otherwise
his admonition, no matter how well intentioned, would always become a vanity or, rather, a serious matter that would
always be taken in vain. Youth specifically does not think
about the evil days, and does not understand what is meant by
"the sound of the mill becomes weak, and all the daughters of
song are feeble" (Ecclesiastes 12:4), and keeps itself from
doing what it understands better than any other age. And
when the evil days come and the sound of the mill becomes
weak and the daughters of song are feeble, then one has not
thought about the Creator in one's youth and has lost not only
youth but also the understanding of youth's thought of the
Creator.

In this way the Preacher admonishingly addresses the
young, but anyone who wants to speak of those words just
read will strive not only to make clear in his discourse the
thought contained in the words but also to make the discourse
itself clear, for "if the bugle gives an indistinct sound, who
then will prepare for battle" (I Corinthians 14:8). That the discourse is clear—what else does this signify except that it applies to someone, that it does indeed speak to some human
being for upbuilding. Now it is indeed the case that the admonition's concerned truth addresses itself specifically to the
single individual in a particular circumstance of life; but the
discourse about it nevertheless must take good care lest it
make the upbuilding conditional upon the accidental, take
good care lest, out of envy of the accidental, it come into conflict and into contradiction with what otherwise is upbuilding,
since in that case the upbuilding is untrue and is nothing but
an unhealthy amusement based on a preference or a mistaken
wish that foolishly hankers after this. If one wanted to be built
up by the thought of old age, but in a special way so that youth
could not be built up by the same thought, then the upbuilding itself would be untrue. If one wanted to speak for upbuilding to an old man on the theme that everything is over soon,
he certainly would unsettle the young man with this talk; how
could he avoid becoming discouraged and prematurely tired

IV
129

of a life at the end of which one said that the best is that every-thing is over soon. That kind of upbuilding is a deception, a fraudulent compromise, because there is no advantage in being old and just as little in being young. If a person thinks youth is an advantage, he disdains the upbuilding and wants to hear nothing but the mundane words of the like-minded, indeed, the fellow conspirators, about how thrilling it is to be young. If a person thinks, with regard to thought of the Cre-ator, that youth has a definite opportuneness that can never be had again, who would dare to speak with himself about this subject, who would dare to speak to anyone else about it for fear that it would be too late, for fear that upbuilding thought might change into terrifying thought?

But this is not the case. Therefore, when Holy Scripture makes it the condition for entering the kingdom of heaven that a person become a child again,[105] this discourse is up-building precisely because it is addressed to every human being, whereas if it were understood otherwise it would be the silliest and bleakest talk ever heard in the world, because the child itself, after all, does not know what it is to be a child. What holds for childhood holds for youth also, except that there is the difference that with the passing of youth much can also be lost and wasted. The discourse about youth may very well be a source of concern to the single individual, but if the discourse also makes it impossible for this concern to be con-ducive to his reassurance, to become a sadness over the past that serves for his betterment, then the discourse does not build up but is worldly-minded, contentious, and confused. On the other hand, if the discourse will also influence a single young person to prevent the painful aftereffects of being re-miss, it presumably will enhance the significance of youth for him, even though the discourse, with regard to authority, only borrows its way.

Think about Your Creator in the Days of Your Youth.

Think about your Creator in the days of your youth. One does this best and most naturally in youth, and if anyone kept the thoughts of youth through all the rest of his life—well, then he would have accomplished a good work. Let this be our eulogy of youth, even though it is rarely heard, although youth is nevertheless extolled often enough. Just as it is supposed to be harmful for an infant to be handled by everyone, so all this praise seems to be injurious to the health of young people. When the false or unwise friendship of inconsolableness holds forth, will it not infect youth with its irascible unhealthiness, will it not introduce a throbbing disquiet and craving into youth's carefree security? Because inconsolableness is envious of youth, shall one therefore also make youth envious of itself and bewildered about itself? Do not take too much control of the young, nor of the infant, but do not therefore do the opposite, either; do not make it prematurely old, lest it drink the bitterness of not being allowed to be young when one is young, and for a second time drink the bitterness of not having been allowed to be young when one was young. The Preacher is not like this. When youth is merrily celebrating at a banquet, the Preacher is not a desperate character who wants to carry it away into wild passion and momentary enjoyment, not an alarming specter who wants to forget himself in youthful company, not a fool who, though past his prime, fancies that he is still young, but neither is he a peevish and tiresome man who cannot rejoice with the joyful.[106] He joins in the rejoicing, and when youth has heartily enjoyed itself, has danced itself weary, not for life exactly, since youth ought not to do that, but for the evening, then the Preacher sits in a room within the dance hall and talks more earnestly. But he makes the transition just as naturally as youth, which is able, even with a smile on its lips and with enthusiasm, to listen appropriately to the discussion of lofty and holy matters. So, then, let "youth wear the crown of rosebuds before they wither" (The Wisdom of Solomon 2:8), but let no one teach this to youth, teach it to do this "as in youth" (Wisdom 2:6) and thereby influence, or in any other way influence, youth to "reason unsoundly" (Wisdom 2:1), as if this were the only thing it had to do, because thought of the Creator is still youth's most beautiful glory, is also a rosebud, but it does not wither.

[107]In youth one does it *most naturally*. The person who can think this thought along with everything else he otherwise thinks does indeed think most naturally, and the person who does not need to be changed so as to be able to think it and does not need the thought to be changed so that he can think it does indeed think most naturally, because he finds in this thought the equivalent in childlikeness, which makes play the best. In this way those words of the Preacher are already a demonstration that this thought must be the most natural for youth. If he had not been speaking to youth, he very likely would have made lengthy preparations. He perhaps would have demonstrated that there is a God, and then when he had kept the learner busier than the Jews in the land of Goshen in order under his supervision to have him enslave himself to the truth, he perhaps would have intimated that he could even reach the point where God became the Creator. Yes, so it goes. When one grows older, everything becomes so miserable. God in heaven has to sit and wait for the decision on his fate, whether he exists, and finally he comes into existence with the help of a few demonstrations;[108] human beings have to put up with waiting for the matter to be decided. Suppose that a person died before that time; suppose that when the matter was finally decided he was not in the practice of thinking about God as his Creator and the joy over that was all gone! The Preacher does not speak in that way, but just as a friendly person lays the infant's happy future at the cradle, just so does he offer his words, and youth understands them immediately. Youth understands immediately that there is a God, because for the young person God's house is right next to his father's residence, and it is entirely natural for him to be there. But when one grows older, the way to the church is often very long; when the weather is bad in the winter, it is very cold in the church; when the singing of birds fills the woods in summer, the church is not on the path. For the youth, God lives close by. In the midst of his joy and his sorrow, he hears God's voice calling; if he does not hear it, he misses it immediately, has not learned subterfuges, does not know how to conceal himself[109]—until he hears it again.

When one grows older, it is a long way to heaven, and the noise on earth makes it difficult to hear the voice; and if one does not hear it, the noise on earth makes it easy not to miss it. Youth understands it immediately—how marvelous—but is not the fact that it is marvelous again the explanation! There was a thinker,[110] much admired in memory, who thought that miracle was a characteristic of the Jewish people, that in a characteristic way this people leaped over the intervening causes to reach God. But if we point to a youth who did not grow up in that nation, do you not think, then, that the marvelousness of miracle will be manifest here, too? And do you think, then, that adulthood dares to forget completely that which belongs essentially to youth and which does not belong to a particular nation as something accidental? But when one grows older, then along come the intervening causes; and if someone reaches God by the long road of intervening causes, he can say that he comes from far away—that is, if he does reach God, for many perish along the way. Is this the fault of the intervening causes or of the pilgrim?

IV
132

Youth understands immediately that God is Creator, that he has created "heaven and earth and everything found therein."[111] "Everything found therein"—is this not a vast phrase; is it suitable for youth? What has youth seen—after all, it has only peeked into the world; compared with someone who has circumnavigated the earth, what does youth know about the world? But youth knows about God, and since God is not supposed to be far away, to find him is not a matter of seeking him far away. There was a thinker who became a hero by his death; he said that he could demonstrate the existence of God with a single straw.[112] Let the thinker keep his demonstration; give youth the straw—it cannot demonstrate. But why is demonstration necessary at all when one has the straw and—God! When one grows older, along comes the demonstration, and the demonstration is a prominent traveler whom all look upon with admiration.

Youth understands that God has created the world, and yet that was six thousand years ago. But youth understands it immediately—no wonder, for to the young, what are six thousand years but yesterday?[113] When one grows older, six thousand years are a great many years; then one perceives that it was six thousand years ago that the world was created and also six thousand years since everything was very good.[114]

But just as youth quite naturally thinks that God is Creator, so it likewise naturally thinks that which follows as a consequence; and since it does not need to waste any time on fathoming the former, it can promptly begin the latter. But what does follow as a consequence? Well, when one grows older and very sensible, then very strange things follow as a consequence; then one goes beyond[115] an earlier thinker, calls oneself after a later thinker, or gives others a name, and does other similar things that pertain neither to God nor to oneself but only to public opinion. Youth, however, has already begun the latter with the former, because what follows more closely as a consequence of the former than that which lies so near that it does not even seem to follow as a consequence of it, much less follow in addition as a consequence? What else is the latter except that thanksgiving is quiet in humility, that confidence rests in childlike trust, that pain over the disturbance of the harmony is so deep that peace cannot long be absent, the concern so childlike that youth does not need to go far in order to live once again, to be moved, and to have its being in God.[116]

And in youth it is done *best*, because he indeed thinks a thought best who always has it handy and yet hides it deepest, he who does not have to look for it among a host of things in order to find it, who does not look for it in out-of-the-way places.

Youth does not have many thoughts, but from this it only follows that it can better hide the one it has, even though it always uses it. When a person grows older, he has many thoughts; and if one of them is lost, he does just as that woman did—he lights a candle[117] and goes searching for it and meanwhile lets the ninety-nine others shift for themselves.[118] Or he thinks that a thought is lost, and in searching for it wastes time, since it was an illusion. Such things cannot happen to youth; when one has but a single thought, how could it possibly be lost! Having many thoughts is like having many clothes. Now one wears one thing, now another. But youth has one thought, which is always becoming, and wastes no time in choosing. On the other hand, youth has the same place and scarcely less space than the place where the adult hides his thoughts, but when one has only one thought, that thought can have a very good place and ample space.

Youth does not see many people, but that does not mean that youth cannot cling wholeheartedly to humankind and to the human. There was a pagan wise man who, ridiculed by the crowd, decided to ridicule the others. He walked about by day with a lighted lantern looking for *man*.[119] One should not ridicule him; anyone who as a young person has not found *man* may very well need a lighted lantern. When one grows older, one sees many people, meets and parts, but if from youth onward one does not have *man*, what then does one find; and he who finds it, what does he find but the pastor, the schoolteacher, his equals, and everything else he knows so well from home; and what does he find that replaces the best that he loses little by little? So also with the thought of God. When the adult finds this thought again, what else does he find but what he found in his youth! He thought it in his youth, and the first time he did so it was as if he had already thought it for an eternity. It is more difficult for the years to think with such unforgetfulness. When one is older, this thought commonly has only its allotted time, and so it must be. Other thoughts have their allotted times; everything is parceled out, and even if one otherwise lives in abundance, with regard to this thought one commonly lives scantily enough. But youth is the season of overabundance. When a person grows older, he does not grow anymore, but youth is the time of growth, and it grows along with its one and only thought, just like lovers who grew up together. When a person grows older, he often scrutinizes his thoughts and retards himself. One grows best in concealment, and physically a person never grows as much as during the nine months in the womb; and spiritually he never grows as much as in youth's concealed life, when his growth is a divine growth. The older he becomes, the more complicated the accounting becomes, and yet that thought about the Creator is what the schoolmaster in his childhood talked of so much; it is the number carried [*Mente*], and if the number carried is forgotten somewhere, then the reckoning is incorrect throughout.[120]

Let childhood, then, keep the angels, who always behold the face of God;[121] but bestow on youth, O God, a friendly solicitude that keeps it from losing the best. Woe to him who defrauds widows[122] and orphans, but woe also to him who defrauds youth of this thought, even though he gave it everything else! Woe to him who moves the landmark of the poor;[123] woe to him who moves the landmark of youth!

Think about your Creator in the days of your youth. This thought continually recurs, and sometime later it will help you to think most naturally and best of the Creator, however more specifically the help is to be defined with regard to the single individual.

IV
135
It is hard, people say, to separate those who are inwardly united, but how much harder it is when the Creator and youth's thought about the Creator are separated. Human language says very little of this concern, since not only their talk but virtually language itself is so selfish that it talks only of their own affairs and very little of God's, whose concern this separation is.

But what is it, then, that separates them? My listener, should not you yourself know what it was that separated you, and should not the single individual know what it was that separated him from God, even though that which separated was very different for different people! Perhaps it was age that separated them, that he had grown old although God always remained the same. He certainly is not to be censured for growing older; on the contrary, a person surely deserves praise if in this regard he knows the time and the hour.[124] Indeed, nothing is more loathsome than to see the miserable beggar whose eyes and countenance implore everyone for the flattering falsehood that he still seems young, or to see the poor wretch who despite his advanced age still bolsters himself with the lie that he has youth ahead of him, or to see the weakling who has no other defense against the years than a feeble wish that he were still young. He, however, who knows the time and the hour and the opportunity finds the separation less striking, and he is indeed furthest from having forgotten his youth, which even he has done who day and night wants it back. Whether a person will succeed in growing older in such a way that he at no moment notices the separation that will lay the foundation for another kind of understanding,[125] we do not know, but for most people it probably turns out that just as they are separated from what belonged to youth, leave their father's house and their mother's care, are separated even further from them, so are they also separated from God.

Perhaps he then grew older, and with the years came understanding, and with understanding knowledge, and with knowledge grief,[126] and with increased knowledge increased grief. But as he was developed and educated in this way, the simple became more difficult for him, and since without this guidance he wanted to rule himself, everything became more and more complicated. —Perhaps he chose the guidance of thought, and in order not to owe anyone anything he let this seed sow itself and let one thought evolve out of another, until eventually the infinite manifested itself to him and made him dizzy. The more he stared fixedly at it, the more his eye lost the visual power to find the way back to finitude. —Perhaps desire blinded him, life seemed a joke to him, and he let God grieve in heaven while he chose pleasure and let enthusiasm speak in vain about conflict and struggle, about courage in dangers, patience in tribulations, love in life, victory in death, reward in heaven, while he let every day have its pleasure.[127] —Perhaps a worldly-minded worry about food and clothing scattered his mind so that he did neither the one nor the other.[128] —Perhaps he subjected himself to an inconsolable seriousness that made life here below into slavery, God in heaven into a severe master, his will into a terrible law, and in this way he wandered in a desert without finding any relief. — Perhaps it was sin and perdition that lay divisively between

IV
136

him and youth's thought of God, and the wrath of the separation seemed to make an understanding impossible.

We could probably develop this further, but to what purpose? When the separation is there, it is not so important to
stare fixedly at the reason as to sorrow over the separation,
which can manifest itself in such a different way when the evil
days the Preacher speaks of have come or when the *retreat* is to
begin. Just as the first book in the Old Testament has been
called Genesis, the second, Exodus,[129] so it could very well be
said that in human life there is a third book that is called Retreat. There is evident, then, a necessity to turn back to that
which once was so beautiful but which since then has been
disdained, forgotten, disregarded, defiled, and to which
everyone nevertheless now has recourse with a certain shame.
And it is indeed understandable that he was ashamed that he,
no matter what the error of his way was, first attempted
everything before he decided to return, but was it not a blessing that there was something to return to, was it not fortunate
that the blind man had a child who could lead him! And so
one walks for a brief hour like a blind man led by a child.[130]

We do not conceal that one person's retreat can be very different from another's, that one person's can be a more peaceful return, the other's a flight that terror pursues, but it is the
Preacher who says: Therefore think about your Creator in the
days of your youth, think about this for the sake of the retreat.
Even though the moment it is to begin is ever so terrible, even
though a person in self-hatred has destroyed ever so much of
what lay behind him, just a recollection[131] of this thought will
always be of some help to him. Perhaps there was someone
who, reduced to extremity, sought only to gather his bitterness, his wrath, in a single passionate cry and sought in vain
among the sagacious, who usually know all about life's emptiness and nothingness, until he cried out: Oh, the world
passes away and the lust of it![132] But see, then these words
awakened like a recollection in his soul, and with them awakened a redeeming recollection that still called to him with the
integrity of youth: But God's Word abides forever. In this
way, youth's recollection helped where nothing else would

help, and this is how it helps: it breaks the spell of brooding seriousness so that there is joy again in heaven and on earth; it disperses the fogs of busy care in God-surrendered nonchalance; it dissolves the pernicious toil in quiet astonishment at the dark saying "to hope against hope";[133] through the bold confidence that understands nothing, does not understand the ensnaring assertions of self-accusation but understands only God's mercy, it rescues the one who despairs from seeing the despair. Perhaps there was someone who pondered deeply and pondered long over the divine, although what he found out he himself sometimes understood more simply than when he fathomed it, until at last as he sat there thoughtful and ruminative he smiled at all his pondering by paying heed to youth's recollection that whispered to him the simple words and by their intervention transformed the beautiful earnestness into an even more beautiful jest[134] for him. Perhaps there was someone whose plans always brought him victory and people's admiration, although he himself, in comparing the outcome with the calculations, always discovered a little discrepancy, until at last, as he stood there rigorous and dominating, he was tempered by listening to youth's recollection that hummed the simple words to him and by interweaving themselves transfigured his beautiful earnestness into an even more beautiful jest.

We do not extol the retreat as if this alone were life's meaning, as if recollection were everything in life. We are not so presumptuous as to speak triflingly of the truth that more mature human wisdom fathoms or of the beauty that human art produces; even less do we disparage the honest work of adulthood. We are speaking only of the beautiful meaning of the retreat for human life and of how having thought about the Creator in one's youth is the retreat's rescuing angel.

Let a person's work, then, take from him what belongs to it, his time, his diligence, but in the advancing years, O God, preserve a recollection of youth that preserves youth's thought of the Creator. Woe to him who separates what God has

IV
138

joined together; woe to him who separates adulthood from its youth.

Now if there is anyone whom this meditation only painfully reminded of his lack, then it certainly would be unseemly and unworthy of an upbuilding discourse, indeed, all the worse for itself, if it remained unsympathetic, because in that case it would not be upbuilding, would not have found the universal, but would have been beguiled by the accidental. It is probably rather seldom that a person can truly feel this lack, and at times he may delude himself, push the fault away from himself, cravenly hold the soul apart, deceive it with good intentions, choose the pain of the lack instead of the sorrow of repentance. If that is the case, then the discourse may be at ease. If such a person does not want to understand himself, the discourse at any rate has understood him. If, however, there is some person whose youth no loving solicitude has preserved for him, if he had gone out into life poorer than the son of poverty to whom the parents left their poverty, poorer than the one to whom the father at least left a blessing and the mother an admonition, helpless, forsaken, forsaken by himself because he had had no youth—oh, there is no youth so godforsaken but that the fragments, if collected so carefully that nothing is wasted, would not by the blessing of God[135] become an overabundant compensation, and there certainly was no youth, however short it was, so godforgotten that the recollection or the deep and sorrowful longing for it would not be able to rejuvenate the person who was never young. Spiritually, the fulfillment is always in the wish, the calming of the concern in the concern, just as God is even in the sorrowful longing that is for him.[136] And spiritually he did indeed understand his lack, and spiritually he longed for youth. In another sense, youth is but vanity, and longing for it even more vanity, "for charm is deceptive, and beauty is vain" (Proverbs 31:30), and the fickle mind dashes away with fleeting hope, and the dance ends, and the joke is forgotten, and strength vanishes, and youth is past, and its place knows it no more;[137] but youth's thought of the Creator is a rosebud that does not wither, because it does not know the time of the year or of the years, and it is the child's most beautiful ornament, and the bride's most beautiful jewel, and the dying person's best garment.

II CORINTHIANS 4:17-18

Tell someone who your friends are, and he will know you; confide your wishes to him, and he will understand you; not only is your soul manifest in the wish, but inasmuch as the wish craftily betrays to him your inner state he sees through you in another way also. In other words, as you articulate the wish, he is checking to see whether it may be wished. If this is not the case, then he not only knows your wish, but he also draws a conclusion about a confusion in your inner being. In this sense, it has been said that wishing is an inferior art, and one is readily tempted to compare anyone who wishes in this way to one who out of indolence resorts to the beggar's staff: both live on charity, both are unstable, both have nothing but supplications, both are suspect in the eyes of justice. But wishing can also have a more beautiful side. Who has forgotten the priceless enjoyment of childhood—wishing, which is the same for the poor child and for the rich child! Who has forgotten those beautiful stories from a vanished period in which, just as in childhood, wishing is the meaning of life and a blissful pastime! When a man or woman in those legends was granted the opportunity to delight his or her soul by wishes, it was the custom and practice, a sacred tradition, to wish first of all for heaven's salvation. Once that was assured, one could properly abandon oneself to the hilarity of wishing. Of course, the whole thing was only a jest, but let us never forget that in the midst of life's earnestness there really is and ought to be time to jest, and that this thought, too, is an upbuilding observation. He who is properly thankful and humbly grasps the profundity that all his busyness, divinely speaking, still only betrays the misrelation between that and what he must accept as a given in life, he also has time for innocent and God-pleasing jest—he will also know how to wish. He does not spoil the beauty of the gift or the indubitability of the giving grace by bringing up his own merits; he does not himself bring along his confusion. From the very inordinateness of the gift, he learns the happy calmness that is not intrusive with tireless activity, that is humble even in thankfulness. Just as the pagans make long and redundant prayers about what God already knows (Matthew 7:7[138]), so it is also a pagan defect always to be busy, always enslaved in earnestness.

It may be a merit of our present age that in many ways it has known how to work the wish weary and in that way to wean the soul from wishing; it may be to its advantage if it thereby has developed an honest earnestness that for the good renounces the fraudulence of wishes. We do not reproach the age for having made the idea of the power of the wish into playing with words if it thereby motivates someone to work with his own hands instead of with the borrowed energy of the wish. [139] But the wish for heaven's salvation—is this, too, a play on words, as wishing for heavenly help has become for the frivolous, who think that we ought to depend upon God the way we depend upon people—that is, if you help yourself, then God does the rest. And if the wish for heaven's salvation has become playing with words, has the aim in it been to incite people to work all the harder to gain it? This seems not at all to be the case. Instead, eternal salvation seems to have become what the thought of it has become, a loose and idle phrase, at times virtually forgotten, or arbitrarily left out of the language, or indifferently set aside as an old-fashioned turn of speech no longer used but retained only because it is so quaint. And whereas in the old days one received heaven's salvation by the grace of God, nowadays heaven's salvation often seems to have become like an old, decrepit person who in the house of the mighty sustains his life on the miserable bread of charity.

To whom, then, shall someone turn who wishes to deliberate on what consequences the expectancy of an eternal salvation has for this earthly, troubled life; with whom shall he consult? Everyone in our age knows enough about civic affairs, so let us by speaking of them for a moment clarify the answer for ourselves. If some state official wants one or another issue to be considered and deliberated, he does not call together aliens and foreigners who have no connection with the fate of the country whose welfare they are supposed to consider. But neither does he call together loafers and irresponsible tramps, "who learn to run idly from house to house, but not only idly but with gossip and useless traffic" (I Timothy 5:13), because the recommendations of such people only "give rise to questions" (I Timothy 1:4) instead of providing the answers. Finally, he does not call together robbers and agitators in order to give them the opportunity to discuss at leisure how best they could devour the country. He makes another choice; he assumes that a certain concern is desirable, that having one's own welfare as closely related as possible to the welfare of the country is the best guarantee that the recommendation, just like the inventor of the recommendation, will not turn out to belong nowhere. It is the same with our deliberation on the subject of which we speak.

If anyone thinks that this present life is a life not only of labor but also of reward, a life not only of sowing seed but also of harvesting, then we must let him follow the rules of sagacity that are in harmony with his view of life. But we would not care to ask his advice, since he is, after all, an alien and a foreigner who has no knowledge of, no connection with, that far country about which we are asking. If anyone only light-mindedly and just in passing lets his thoughts wander about, curiously and fitfully occupied with the future, then we must leave him to seek the company and the collaboration of the like-minded, "whose loose talk only eats its way like gangrene" (II Timothy 2:17). Finally, if anyone, no matter for what reason, is living in conflict with that future, so that he is not merely ignorant like the alien and the foreigner, not merely light-minded like that romantic knight of thought, but with all his might wants to have it destroyed, then he certainly would be least suited to sit in a deliberative council. So, then, one chooses otherwise; one assumes that the concern not only does not make a person partisan but in a special way makes him competent to deliberate; one assumes that the very close connection between his welfare and that future makes him especially entitled to do that. Therefore, the person who owns treasure in heaven[140] and whose soul is with this treasure, one who has gained friends here on earth who are able to receive him in the next world,[141] one whose thought has gone ahead and is going ahead to prepare a place for him,[142] one whose concern foresees an explanation that life denies, one whose longing holds the beloved firmly and does not let him go in death, one whose grief continues to follow the dead to the grave, one who would be shocked by the horror of his being canceled out of heaven's salvation, more shocked than the citizen is if the country, whose son he is, were to be wiped off the earth: such a person is a good citizen, a well-intentioned person, from whom the inquirer dares to expect guidance and help, the question an answer.

But perhaps we have been mistaken about this whole matter; perhaps heaven's salvation is something that to such a degree follows of itself that it is foolish to talk about what follows in turn from that. Salvation is a matter of course; nothing follows in turn from it. Therefore, let us not waste time by first making doubtful something that is a matter of course, and then by allaying the doubt that never brings the assurance one has when one lets it come as a matter of course, and finally lose time because of what follows from the concern of doubt. But whether or not it is a matter of course, this point of view still does not deny that heaven's salvation is a good and can disapprove of the wish for it only insofar as the wish already is a kind of unnecessary concern, since salvation is a matter of course whether one wishes it or not. Basically every human being has the wish, except that the individual does not invite attention to the fact that he is wishing; in like manner every human being breathes, but for that very reason it would be foolish for the individual to go into a transport of joy because he is able to breathe.

For a moment, my listener, let us speak foolishly, or rather let us continue for a moment to speak foolishly; presumably you already perceive that in its considerable acumen this discourse borders on foolishness. Let us, then, foolishly assume that God in heaven resembles a weak human being who does not have the heart to deny eternal salvation to anyone, whether one desires it or not—indeed, so weak that he forces it on everyone, as it were, whether one wishes it or not. Such a weak human being is seen occasionally in life. He possesses some kind of goods, and in the little circle that is the object of his solicitude everyone knows that in time he will distribute these goods to everyone. So they all receive of the goods— this constitutes the commonality, but what is the difference? Some of them become callously indifferent, virtually ridicule the weakling in their hearts; unconcerned about him, they look after their own affairs, exempt themselves from any prior concern about whether they are making themselves worthy of it and are not exploiting his goodness, exempt themselves from any subsequent concern about whether their thankfulness is appreciative of the giver and the gift. Others, however, make the reception doubtful to themselves by wishing for it, and even though they do not think they deserve the gift, such nevertheless is their attitude and goodwill toward the person through whose goodness they receive it; and even though they see that the goodness is a weakness, they conceal this from him and from themselves, feel justified and obligated to act this way, because thankfulness is the only expression of their relation to him, since it is a gift, and a gift it remains.

IV
143

If the receiving of heaven's salvation were like this, my listener, how would you wish to receive it? Could you wish to receive it as those first persons received the earthly gift? Even if you thought your salvation was ever so secure, you nevertheless would feel deeply ashamed every time you compared your life with theirs for whom concern about this issue time and again filled many a moment, many an hour, whether it was the wish that occupied them now or the heart that was moved in thankfulness or the disposition that they formed in order to be, according to their best insight and ability, pleasing to the giver, and by which they prepared for the transition. A sudden transition is a terrible hazard. At times one visualizes how terrible it must be for the drunken person to wake up suddenly in confusion of thought; one has pictured the horror that must have gripped the rich man when he awakened in hell.[143] But if with heaven's salvation it were the case that a person awakened to it the moment he breathed his last sigh, it seems to me that a person who has been as remote from it as the abyss is from heaven would have to die again of shame, would have to wish himself elsewhere again, since heaven's salvation and his unworthiness could not correspond; it seems to me that this person would inevitably feel as unhappy as someone who in a strange country wishes only to leave it.

We have spoken foolishly, but even so it has indeed been shown that the thought of heaven's salvation dare not become a matter of indifference to a person. How would salvation become a matter of indifference to him for whom the discourse need not venture out to the outermost boundary of thoughtlessness, but whose soul is well educated to hear the serious words of earnestness "that God is not mocked" (Galatians 6:7), whose soul is prepared by considering what presumably would completely overwhelm the confused, "that no one can serve two masters, since he must hate the one and love the other" (Matthew 6:24), whose soul is fully awakened from sleep to understand what presumably would hurl the sleepwalker into the abyss, "that love of the world is hatred of God!" (James 4:4). Such a person has the spiritual sense to be disgusted at the thought that heaven's salvation, despite its gloriousness, could be nonsense, has the maturity of understanding to grasp that heaven's salvation can no more be taken by force[144] than it can be redeemed like a fine in a game of forfeits. Such a person has the time to consider the one thing needful,[145] the heart to wish for heaven's salvation, the earnestness to reject the flirting of light-minded ideas, the fear and trembling in his soul to be terrified at the thought of breaking with heaven or of taking it in vain. But to him, then, the thought of this salvation will not be wasted, either, the wish will not be futile, the concern not be fruitless trouble, and, like the inactivity of the lily, which does not spin, and the improvidence of the bird, which does not gather into barns,[146] the prayer will not be without blessing; the work will not be without gain even though he does not deserve heaven's salvation but becomes qualified to inherit it only by vigilance in expectancy. And this employment will also become a gain for him in this life, and the consequence of this expectancy will become a blessing for him in time, because the expectancy of an eternal salvation is able (which otherwise seems impossible) to be in two places at the same time: it works in heaven and it works on earth; "it seeks the kingdom of God and his righteousness and gives the rest as an over-measure" (Matthew 6:33). If the expectancy does not do this, then it is fraudulent, the craftiness of a sick soul that wants to sneak out of life, and is not the authentic presence of a healthy soul in the temporal; then it is not the expectancy of the eternal but a superstitious belief in the future; then the person does not rest in the trustworthiness of the eternal but dupes himself with the possibility of the future, which merely engrosses one as does the solving of a riddle. Then the expectancy is an ingratiating hankering that has not consulted with earnestness about the fulfillment's different decision. The more profoundly earnestness comprehends the anxiety of separation—if the latter does not destroy responsibility and force the soul to go bankrupt, as it were—the more genuine is the expectancy.

The consequence of the expectancy, then, is twofold, but for the time being let us confine ourselves to deliberation on the consequence for the present life; in the deliberation, let us continually keep before our eyes the apostolic words just read, while our thoughts dwell on the Apostle Paul, the concerned and powerful witness to the future, and so let us speak about:

> *The Expectancy of an Eternal Salvation with Regard to the*   IV
> *Meaning of this Expectancy for the Present Life.*   145

The expectancy of an eternal salvation will help a person to understand himself in temporality. The tested eye of experience is often justly extolled as being able to help someone in life in quite another way than is the eye of youth, which is in the service of imagination, is misled by mental deception, is clear-sighted at a distance, whereas its deceptive second sight [*andet Syn*] cannot sustain the inspection [*Eftersyn*] of observation. In contrast to youth's precipitousness, it is to the advantage of experience that it is strong in piecemeal observation. For this very reason, it is important as a guide in life, because temporal life is piecemeal and is like a dark saying[147] that is best understood when it is understood little by little. Experience has the advantage of always having a goal [*Maal*] by which it measures [*maale*], a goal toward which it strives, and as it divides up the range of finitude it always knows how to measure out [*udmaale*] the particular, and as it proceeds from the certain it knows how to calculate the uncertain. It knows how to make a rough estimate, to determine the length of the way and of the time; it has a criterion [*Maalestok*] for power and endurance, for resistance, for dangers and difficulties, and, whether life enters in favorably or disturbingly, it knows how to cope with it accordingly; it is not easily caught napping, and if it is, it quickly rallies and measures again. Perhaps many a human life goes on in this way, actively engaged in the service of temporality, but also belonging totally to temporality.

If, however, a person's soul is expecting an eternal salvation, this expectancy will no doubt disturb him momentarily, cause him to disdain experience, since its goal is too low for him, its criterion on too small a scale. But youth's impetuosity and the giant stride of imagination will not help him, either, and yet he cannot be without a goal and a criterion, since a life without them is inconsolable and disordered. Yet one who has only the criterion of temporality perishes with temporality and perhaps does not even hold out with that. Even if one's life proceeds quietly and peacefully, events can still come along that are beyond the scope of experience. If this happens to him, he is prey to despair. On the other hand, even if he manages to slip through life without having any such misfortune challenge his calculations, then, if he has learned nothing higher in life, he is still a child of temporality for whom the eternal does not exist. But if a person sustains that expectancy in his soul, he has a goal [*Maal*] that is always valid, a criterion [*Maalestok*] that is always valid and valid in itself; by means of this goal and this criterion he will always understand himself in temporality. Just as good fortune and prosperity, popular favor, success and gain will not trick him out of his goal and give him the false goal [*falske Maal*] of vanities in its place and wildly teach him to enjoy himself as one who has no hope,[148] so will neither sorrow nor the counterfeit [*Falskmaal*] of suffering teach him to sorrow in despair as one who has no hope.

"For our affliction, which is brief and light, is preparing for us an eternal weight of glory beyond all measure."[149] These are the apostle's words that we read earlier. My listener, if you had never heard Paul's name mentioned, if this name, far from being the revered and saintly name it has become for you from earliest childhood, were unknown to you—suppose this, and then suppose that these words were laid before you with the request that you deduce from them what must have been the lot of the man who could give such a witness to life on earth and salvation beyond. You would probably examine the words, compare them with the witness of others concerning the distress of life and the glory of eternity, and then would probably deduce that this man had lived a fairly quiet and serene life in honorable obscurity, removed from life's great decisions, presumably not entirely unfamiliar with suffering's hidden wisdom that is for the initiates, but nevertheless not tried in the extreme test, in the mortal danger of earthly distress, of spiritual trial. If you were asked to exchange this statement for a similar one, you might take a somewhat familiar line that we cannot use here since it is in a foreign language, but the beautiful meaning of the felicitously chosen words is approximately this: that the earth is beautiful enough as a biding place[150] for the person who expects an eternity, but not sufficiently beautiful to cause someone to forget that one is still only on the way.

This explanation presumably would satisfy you and the others—and now suppose that just then a man came in who said: These words are by the Apostle Paul, and then went on to tell you—which no one, of course, needs to tell you—that this man was halted on the road of offense and consequently was indeed tried in the mortal dangers of the soul, that he was caught up into the third heaven[151] and consequently was indeed tempted to have a distaste for earthly life, that he witnessed with an enthusiasm that made him seem a raving man

IV
147

to his hearers,[152] that for forty years he was knocked about in the world, without a fixed residence, outlawed and abandoned, to the Jews an offense, to the Greeks foolishness,[153] rejected by the world, in mortal danger, in hunger, in nakedness, in prison,[154] and that he finally was executed as a criminal—would you not be startled, would it not make your head swim because your criterion could not produce such a combination!

Let youth try its hand at this! Yes, youth is quick to admire, and its opinions are no less swift; when it comes to a round number, it is quickly at its goal and in a hurry to put two and two together. Even if it is inspired by the thought of Paul, oh, its enthusiasm does not understand him and only deceives itself. Let experience spell it out syllable by syllable, and it probably would say: A life like that is certainly an everlasting affliction and not to be endured—an everlasting affliction—is this the illuminating interpretation of the words of the text, "our affliction, which is brief and light"?

Yet Paul certainly was not without a goal and without a criterion, since eternity was his goal and its salvation his criterion. When the storm clouds of affliction began to gather and to threaten with their terror, when the soul was about to perish of fright and anxious apprehension, then, I think, if we dare to speak this way, he took his criterion, felt his way, and see, the affliction was brief and light. When the congregation went astray, when false teaching and human fickleness jumbled meanings together so that the way of truth became impassable and there was no goal, then heaven was his goal.

When he himself is sitting in prison, when error is growing and thriving while he is unable to do anything, when the goal of his activity is foolishness to experience because it goes backward, then heaven is his goal. When the degree of his suffering unsettles his soul, then, I think, he takes out his criterion, and see, his suffering becomes brief and light, whereas it probably would have been unendurable if he had sought guidance in human grounds of comfort. When life's burdens rest heavily upon him, when thought adds to that the burdens of past days and he almost collapses under the weight, when experience has long ago lost courage and is ready to declare him "the most miserable of men" (I Corinthians 15:19), when even the otherwise God-surrendered person has no other comfort than "the wish that all his calamities might be laid together on the scale in order to be weighed" (Job 6:2), no other alleviation than to know how heavy the burden is—then Paul weighs his, and see, it becomes light, because heaven's salvation is an eternal weight of blessedness beyond all measure, and he was the most miserable of men only when he "hoped only for this life" (I Corinthians 15:19).

Experience, of course, understands weights and measures, but of what is it capable? It is scarcely capable of lifting the apostolic sufferings to place them on the scale, but Paul understands that heaven's salvation has an eternal overweight. Experience certainly knows how to comfort in many ways, but only heaven's salvation knows how to comfort beyond all measure. Experience certainly has long known how to think of some cheer for the troubled, but, as is natural, it does not know a joy that passes all understanding.[155] Experience knows all the many inventions of the human heart, but a rapture that did not arise in any man's heart[156] it does not know. And yet the life that is without a goal and a criterion is inconsolable and disordered, and yet the life whose experience did not end with verifying that experience is inadequate, is only aimless running that becomes lost on the wrong path, is shadowboxing in the air[157] that the wind blows away, writing in the sand that the sea erases. Anyone who has experienced this will no doubt seek a goal that is always valid, a criterion that is always valid. And the expectancy of an eternal salvation is a refuge in distress, a fortress that life cannot take by storm, an assignment that distress and sufferings cannot cancel; and life together with this conception is more nourishing for a person than mother's milk to the nursing child, and he returns from this conception strengthened, strengthened most of all precisely when his striving is not to wean himself from this nourishment but to make it his wont.[158]

When life's demand exceeds experience's understanding, then life is disordered and inconsolable, unless the expectancy

IV
148

of an eternal salvation orders and calms. When the rich young man is required to go and sell all his property and give it to the poor,[159] experience does not know how to help, because a portion of it is not what is required. And if there was someone who was not required to sell everything in order to become perfect, since what he had was of such quality that scarcely anyone would buy, what would experience know then? And the person who does not need to bury the dead first of all[160] because they were buried long ago, but his grief only increased with the years, what compensation does experience have for him if he is not comforted by the thought that there are always more births than deaths? And if there is a solitary pain, which indeed gnaws the deepest, alien experience will not comfort it, since it of course does not hear the scream, and even if it is heard, the dimensions of the pain cannot always be determined by the scream. Personal experience cannot help it, inasmuch as the scream was suppressed because the pain was not understood. And the person whose mouth was bound in a way in which not even the ox's mouth is bound when it threshes out the grain[161] for others, and the person whose soul was troubled even though he gave others joy, and the person "whose lips' front door was closed" (Ecclesiastes 12:10) even though he knew that his words would surround him with the curiosity of the crowd but scarcely win for him the sharing of his pain—how will experience comfort him? But the expectancy of an eternal salvation comforts beyond all measure. There is a covenant of tears with God, and this covenant is not seen, is not heard, except by him who sees in secret[162] and understands from afar, but it is in a covenant with salvation in the God who will wipe away the tears.[163] And there is a fellowship of sufferings with God,[164] the secret of which is the assurance of an eternal salvation in trustful understanding with God. —An eternal salvation in the next world—my listener, do you ask in what it consists and what it will bring? Is it not sufficient for you that here it is already capable of making your affliction brief and light, that it is capable of making a union of your troubled soul with the inwardness of joy, inseparable like everything God has joined together, fruitful like the covenant God himself blesses?[165]

The expectancy of an eternal salvation will reconcile everyone with his neighbor, with his friend, and with his enemy in an understanding of the essential. The child wants to have everything it sees, and youth is not much better, wants everything to conform to it and the whole world to indulge its wishes, but experience knows how to partition and divide; it distinguishes between mine and thine, gives Caesar the things that are Caesar's,[166] the neighbor what is his, the enemy what befits him, and keeps its own. This is why we extol experience for this ordering of life, which in the land of temporality goes on in mere interaction. Perhaps many a human life is tirelessly employed in this way until it finishes with temporality. But if this is the way it goes on, then such a life is only miserable, however much it is prinked up and polished; it is niggling, whether it deals in millions or in pennies, is as pitiable as children's play if it is supposed to be earnestness. If the prospect is that people's lives will go on in this way, then it is even fortunate if distress and danger break into this monotonous security, into which the better and more noble sink in lethargy as if by a spell. When a common danger stands at everyone's door, when a common calamity teaches people to hold together and drums reconciliation into them, then it certainly is seen how they are reconciled in the understanding of the same things and how this reconciliation would benefit them jointly and would benefit the individual. But when the danger is over and the calamity has had its day, then there is all too quickly a relapse into the old way of life, and the reconciliation coerced by the need sometimes carries within itself the seed of a deeper separation than the one that was eliminated. And even if that reconciliation casts an enhancing radiance over a period of the individuals' lives, it nevertheless belongs essentially not to them but to the observation and the observer who inherits it, until the story about it is also forgotten. Even though it is beautiful to envision this, such a life is a life of temporality, is the fruit of temporality, but also the prey of temporality, and the most that can be said of it is that it was a beautiful mo-

IV
150

ment. But compared with eternity, this beautiful moment of temporality is nothing but the silver flash [*Sølvblink*] of imitation metal. But he whose soul is expecting an eternal salvation always has present something that is intrinsically valid and in comparison with which everything petty shows up as petty; he is continually influenced by something that in his aspiring for it does not bring him into conflict with anyone or with anything of this world, something that in being possessed does not shut out anyone else. In other words, he can lose the earthly, and if he loses it in the right way, the loss will make easier the difficulty of a camel's going through the eye of a needle;[167] and if he himself is properly concerned, he will not want to shut anyone out.

"Because we do not esteem the things that are seen but the things that are unseen, for the things that are seen are temporal, but the things that are unseen are eternal."[168] These are the apostle's words that we read earlier, and this may well be our procedure also. While heaven's salvation is usually left in abeyance with regard to what it may eventually be, it might be better to do this with earthly and temporal things, let them go for what they are and not esteem them. One who esteems the temporal will gradually be rendered incapable of being attentive to the eternal, and one in whose eyes the things of this earth remain estimable will gradually lose the capacity to prize the things of heaven. But the visible things are temporal, and the temporal is not only perishable but is at odds with itself and therefore must be dissolved and cannot last.[169] This is why the treasure causes the miser pain while he is collecting it, pain while he possesses it, pain when he must leave it. This is why the spendthrift scatters without joy what the skinflint hoards without joy; this is why the new wine bursts the old wineskins;[170] this is why forgetfulness erases the vainglorious enterprises, yes, even all the toil and care with which a person fancies he is becoming important; this is why time eats away earthly love, indeed, even the hate, powerless as it is, that wants to bully its way into eternity. But the person who turns away from the temporal to the eternal and is concerned about his salvation is reconciled with himself and with everyone

IV
151

else, because the eternal is always in agreement with itself, and its agreement shuts out only that which shuts out itself.

But "concerned about his salvation"—is not this expectancy a new burden one takes upon oneself instead of being the eternal remedy that heals all sickness, even the sickness unto death?[171] It is true that at times people chose another kind of certainty than that of this concern. They specified particular distinctive marks, set up conditions, and by means of these were convinced of salvation just as one is convinced of the existence of something that one holds in the hand. They did not perceive that this temporal assurance was precisely the illusion; they did not perceive that "they suspended eternity in a spider web";[172] they did not perceive that it was a bird in their hand that they had captured, a bird that wanted to fly. But while they were more and more forfeiting heaven's salvation through all this certainty, they were winning—the right to make their stipulations decisive for others, the right to shut out others. Let them keep this right; after all, it would truly be the most tragic misunderstanding if someone in his zeal to shut out others was so lulled to sleep that he did not dream of being shut out himself. No wonder, then, that temporality was again recognized, proclaimed in its prescriptive right, that hate and anger and earthly prejudice and secular considerations again forced their way into eternity in order to set it at odds with itself and divide it against itself! Who is not horrified at such distortion! I for my part have always sought in vain to understand it.

But let us nevertheless seriously consider this matter; heaven's salvation is and still remains the settlement that settles everything. Indeed, even though the concern did not provide a person humble entrance, it is still worth endeavoring to gain it so that there may be an inwardness, a hallowed place in the soul, where the consciousness retreats, lets the world go, incloses itself in itself, becomes reconciled with itself and thereby with the differences in life, an inclosure where thoughts of finitude, insofar as they presumptuously want to force entry, are found every morning to be overthrown, like Dagon's statue at the foot of the Ark of the Covenant,[173] be-

IV
152

fore the sublimity of the concern that is solely concerned about the intrinsically valid, and that is not the expectation that wants to enter heaven triumphantly and wants its festive entrance to be decisive for others.

Insofar as that lamentable misunderstanding "that became a prey of worldly wisdom" (Colossians 2:8) consisted in its binding heaven's salvation to finite conditions, it could perhaps by another misunderstanding seem that the light-mindedness, the careless rashness, that is not inconvenienced by any condition would be preferable. This, however, is far from being the case, and we did agree that anyone who has no concern is once and for all shut out from considering an issue to which only concern gives access for deliberation. That misunderstanding, then, was not that one assumed the conditions but that the concern to determine them was so quickly satisfied that the single individual even gained the time and the opportunity and the disposition to decide the question with regard to others. And yet as soon as the concern ceases, the single individual to whom this happens is shut out from the deliberation. But someone who is truly concerned surely grasps that there must be a condition, but he will never be able to fathom it finitely, since the concern will prevent a finite fathoming. Even when he has thought about it the most, he must still admit that he cannot determine in a finite way what the conditions are, because it is precisely finitude that the concern takes away from him. An uncertainty will always remain in everything he finds out, and this uncertainty nourishes the concern, and the concern nourishes the uncertainty. This uncertainty can be expressed in this way—that he expects eternal salvation by the grace of God. But he does not in turn expect God's grace by virtue of some finite condition, because then it is not grace, and then the concern will also quickly turn into earthly security. Now if he is continually concerned in this way but is also continually saved in grace, if he perceives that it would be a bad sign if the concern ceased, how could he ever have enough conceited certainty to decide this question for another?

But suppose also that there were particular conditions that

could be expressed accurately in words and by means of which observant thought could test the state of the single individual; how then could he, if he were again concerned—and if he is not, then he is surely taking the whole thing in vain—how then could he ever with finite certainty be able to decide whether these conditions were present in him? Now, let these conditions be acts, specific conceptions, moods—who really knows himself so intimately that he would take the responsibility for guaranteeing that these conditions are present in him just as they ought to be and are not illegitimate children of doubtful parentage! Who could do this if he were truly concerned, and who would not have to be truly concerned if he earnestly considered this matter! But if there continually remains an uncertainty in his soul, because of which he resorts to grace, how could it enter his mind to want to decide this for others, inasmuch as before one begins on that, one must first be altogether certain about oneself. But one who is altogether certain through grace—something we indeed wish for the single individual—is, humanly speaking, quite uncertain.

For a moment, let us speak metaphorically and by means of an imperfect metaphor direct our attention to the eternal validity under discussion. An army sometimes has a select little troop called the immortal battalion,[174] and a warrior esteems it a great honor to be accepted into it. Let us suppose that there was a man (we are well aware, of course, that this would be a lamentable aberration that probably never happened, and we trust that any similar aberration might never happen) who was just as concerned about being admitted into that battalion as everyone ought to be concerned about being an heir of heaven's salvation. The conditions were sufficiently known; distinction in battle was required, but also a certain appearance, a specific height, physique, etc. He would then examine himself to see whether he filled all these requirements, not in general, not casually, because he would be too concerned for that, and he knew that if he was deficient in merely the slightest way he would not be accepted. And whether anything was lacking or everything was present in the right proportion the commander would decide in his appraisal. In his appraisal—

because all the conditions could very well be present singly but together would not produce that noble harmony required for admission. I certainly think that this appraisal would create in him the disquietude of concern. But suppose that he felt perfectly secure; yet we do not forget that he was just as concerned about that admission as a person ought to be concerned about heaven's salvation. But one difficulty remained. The admission could not take place immediately; he had to wait a few days. What could not happen in those days? And even though those passed without mishap, at the very moment he entered the commander's palace, he might stumble—do you suppose that such a person would have the time and the opportunity and the disposition to go around observing other men to see whether they were qualified to be admitted into that battalion? Do you suppose that he would not perceive with deep concern that to be quite close to being admitted was still a rejection? Would he not perceive this with deep concern if he was just as concerned about being admitted into that battalion as everyone ought to be concerned about being an heir of heaven's salvation?

Yet even if a person knew the conditions down to every jot and tittle and perceived that without a doubt he qualified (let us suppose this)—then would there be the time and the opportunity and peace of mind for him to decide the question for others? How? Is not heaven's salvation so great a good, then, that it needs no increment by means of some external circumstance? The person who has salvation certainly can neither wish to become more blessed by some irrelevant thought nor wish to be disturbed by any irrelevant thought. If, then, a person who thinks that his salvation is assured nevertheless thinks about something like this, it simply shows that he is not thinking about salvation, and this other thought may very well make him lose salvation, just as the consciousness of the good deed causes one to lose the reward.[175] Then a person who is himself concerned would scarcely wish to shut out anyone, but would he, as we sometimes hear, perhaps be sympathetic enough to wish another to be admitted? Oh, spare your sympathy for a better occasion, and if you can do some-

IV
154

thing for a person, then do it, properly ashamed, for we are all unprofitable servants,[176] and even our good deeds are nothing but human fabrications, fragile and very ambiguous, but every person has heaven's salvation only by the grace and mercy of God, and this is equally close to every human being in the sense that it is a matter between God and him; and let no third person, himself having been restored to grace, forfeit this by unwarranted interference.

If there was a person who embittered my life early and late (something I have not actually experienced) and thought nothing but the worst of me, would his also being saved be able to disturb my salvation, or would I be so conceited as to want to help him to that end by my sympathy! Oh, the concern about an eternal salvation turns the mind from all misplaced considerations! If there was someone who had taken the brunt of the heat and the toil of the day and I was hired at the eleventh hour and our reward was the same,[177] do you suppose this would be able to disturb him if he bore in mind that the reward is an eternal salvation? He would indeed have great sufficiency and overabundance and would receive no more if I were shut out. If he was a righteous man who from his youth had kept the commandments[178] and throughout a long life had expected heaven's salvation (which truly is an unusually glorious posthumous reputation) and I was a robber who "this very day,"[179] consequently in the same moment, came just as far as he, do you suppose this would be able to disturb him? Well, if I thought it was because of my own righteousness, then it certainly would disturb him and disturb heaven itself so that it would push me out again, but if I, observing all the formulations and without any reservation, am now willing to admit that it was grace, do you suppose that that righteous man would continue to be so unreasonable, not toward me, because I, after all, had slipped in—but toward himself by retaining his anger? And if he was not what in a more elevated way is called a simple man, but what in plain, everyday speech is called a real simpleton, and you, my listener, were a wise person who profoundly asked, "What is truth?"[180] and restlessly pondered the question with competence and success—do you

IV
155

suppose it would disturb you if he became just as blessed as you and heaven's infinite salvation made you both equal?

Indeed, when you eventually die, there will be a difference; then it will be said, and justly said, that scholarship goes into mourning and its devotees lament the loss, and your funeral will be different, since it is a beautiful custom that the deceased is dressed in his best suit, but the question still remains whether death does not in turn undress him. And if he was what is called a husband, a man who in modest circumstances had lived happily with his wife and had begotten children with her and had enjoyed the company of other men but had seldom been moved by the thoughts that would have made you forget everything by day and kept you sleepless by night, do you suppose it would disturb you that he became just as blessed as you? Oh, "if God held all truth in his right hand, and in his left eternal striving"[181] . . . . . no, if God held salvation in his right hand and also held in his left hand the concern that had become the content of your life, would you not yourself choose the left although you nevertheless became like someone who chose the right? There must indeed be an equality, and what is more inconsolable than the equality in which people sometimes take refuge, the equality of death that makes everyone equally poor, and what is more blessed than the equality that makes everyone equally blessed?

Is this not the way it is, my listener, and therefore within yourself you presumably said to your God: Father in heaven, when I think about the matter of my salvation, I do not take out the accounting, because I know very well that I cannot pay one in a thousand,[182] and I know very well that Peter stood more securely on the billowing sea[183] than someone who insists on his rights before you. And I will not build my salvation on any work, not on the very best I may have done, since you alone know whether it was a good work; and not on the best I could do, since you alone know whether it will become a good work. Save my soul from the niggling spirit that wants to diminish you and your gift, to diminish me by making me greater than anyone else; save my mind from the pondering that wants to fathom what is not given to be understood; root out of my thought the sophistry that slyly takes the best and gives me the worst. What I did as a child easily and naturally, that I believed without understanding; what I did later (and this I know I have done), that I believed a person contrary to the understanding; what I will continue doing even though being sagacious is deemed greater than believing; what I will apply myself to with all my might, lest the glory of the understanding beguile me and make me harm my soul—should I not be willing to do this in relation to you! Since I am capable of nothing myself, should I not desire the concern and confidence and courage to believe you and in this faith to expect your salvation!

JOHN 3:29-30

This joy of mine is complete. He must increase; I must decrease.

An old saying states that everyone would rather see the rising sun than the setting sun. Why everyone? Do you suppose this includes someone whose sun it is that is setting? But why shouldn't he? The rising sun shines for him just as for all the others—indeed, perhaps shines most brilliantly to his eyes precisely because its luster obscuringly hastens the setting. If a person could ask such a question seriously, he presumably would be so young that he would not understand at all what is being discussed, or so inexperienced that he would deceive himself with an extraordinary and fancied anticipation of the magnanimity with which he would do great deeds in his life; or he might be a man who was trying to toughen his soul the way others toughen their bodies to an ugly and bad toughness; or, finally, a man who used the hardening of the understanding and the cold inflexibility of its conclusions to ridicule people, used against them what he did not use against himself, preached this wisdom to them for their instruction, although he himself nevertheless did not believe it, indeed, even during the preaching kept a back door open through which his secret vanity, like the woman of ill repute (James 2:25), let in the spies of vanity. Everyone else would presumably understand what is being discussed and really understand that self-knowledge is a difficult matter; although it is easy to understand the rest of the world, the understanding suddenly changes very substantially when it pertains to oneself. This should never be forgotten, and just as the child uses a pointer in order not to miss a single letter, so a person should not, if life is to have deeper meaning, become accustomed to understand every-

IV
158

thing in general, should not be in a hurry to understand everything, but should patiently follow the pointer that continually
points to himself. And even though in every other sense it is
just a figurative expression to say that we see the finger of God
in life, a person who is concerned about himself understands
it quite literally, because all deeper and more inward self-
knowledge is under divine guidance and continually sees the
finger of God that points to him. To miss one letter confuses
the whole word, and yet this confusion is nothing compared
with the confusion that occurs when a person, in understanding life in its totality and the history of the human race, skips
over one human being—himself—since the individual human
being is, after all, not like a single letter, in itself a meaningless
part of the word, but is the whole word. And yet this happens
very frequently, and therefore very little is learned from life.
Even one who lives the most secluded and forgotten life is
bound to have a great abundance of examples, admonitions,
warnings, and disciplines if only he does not evade the finger
that is pointing to him, since the most simply constructed
sundial gives the hour accurately if only the sun's rays are permitted to fall on it.

How often that old saying is repeated this way in the world,
is used in the right place by the observer, but how seldom it is
understood in good time, and when understanding finally
dawned and it was too late, how did it sound? Moreover, how
easy it is for the single individual to evade the reference, since
the saying is so general! General discussion of general truths
can certainly give a person much to remember and can develop his understanding, but it is of only very little benefit to
him, as little as it is of benefit to have an arsenal full of weapons that are inappropriate to one when there is use for them.
Above all, generality is not for upbuilding, because one is
never built up [*opbygges*] in general, any more than a house is
erected [*opføres*] in general. Only when the words are said by
the right person in the right situation in the right way, only
then has the saying done everything it can to guide the single
individual to do honestly what one otherwise is quick enough
to do—to refer everything to oneself. And even though divine

and human law forbids coveting what is one's neighbor's, it is never forbidden to covet the neighbor's advice or to use his guidance. Therefore, everything is in order here, because what we have said holds in full measure for the words of John the Baptizer read earlier, and no one need have any scruples about appropriating these words. IV 159

So it was John the Baptizer who said these words. He lived in the Judean desert, far from the vanity that bickers about the place of honor, far from the fickleness that elevates and drags down, celebrates and crucifies, as far as his clothing was from soft raiment and his nature from the pliancy of a reed.[184] He was not the Messiah, not one of the old prophets, not the prophet;[185] he was the voice of one crying in the wilderness,[186] and he cried in the wilderness to prepare the way for the one who was to come after him, the thongs of whose sandals he was not worthy to loosen.[187] Yet he himself was no ordinary man, "the greatest among those born of women."[188] His origin was as marvelous as the origin of the one whose coming he proclaimed, but the difference here again was the same as the difference between the marvel that an aged woman becomes pregnant,[189] which is contrary to the order of nature, and that a pure virgin bears a child by the power of God,[190] which is above the order of nature. Is not this difference already a beautiful intimation of the difference between the setting and the rising! And he cried in the wilderness until the crowd's attention aroused the attention of the council to the point that it sent emissaries to him. But he did not misunderstand himself or his sojourn in solitude or his camel-hair shirt or his food in the desert,[191] as if all this were merely a means for him to pave his own way to honor and esteem among the people. No, he was and he remained the voice crying in the wilderness. This was his task; he himself certainly perceived its significance, but he also knew that its significance was that it would be abolished and forgotten, like the night watchman's cry when it is obvious to all that day has broken. Then rose the sun of him whose morning star aroused the wonder of the wise men; its glory shone, and no one understood better than John that its rising was the setting of his sun. But he re-

278 *Three Upbuilding Discourses* (1844)

joiced over it as deeply as the patriarchs who had longed for the sight,[192] as sincerely as the believers for whom it continued to shine. And yet he knew that the ceremony after which he was named would be abolished, would disappear as a baptism with water in contrast to a baptism with fire and the Holy Spirit.[193] Then the news came to him that this had happened, and his disciples were despondent because the person to whom John had borne witness was baptizing and everyone was coming to him,[194] but John replied: This joy of mine is complete. He must increase; I must decrease.

The same thing that happened to the greatest among those born of women also happens to lesser ones; what happens in the unique decision also happens in the lesser ones, and the words are not profanely used by learning from them to compose oneself in the lesser situation of one's own life. The words are not dragged down to the low level of a worldly wisdom, particularly since one does not wish to forget that just as one has been helped by the words, there are still one concern and one joy left, because everyone does indeed and should participate in the glorious outcome of that unique decision. Therefore, even though the observation does not dwell on that event itself, it and the way the words are applied can nevertheless be upbuilding, just as the concubine's son was not without Abraham's blessing,[195] even though he was not in the distinctive sense the child of promise. And the only one who would not need the lighter food would be the person so lost in joy over the gloriousness of the one who must increase that he did not notice at all, still less was troubled by, the similar thing that happens to himself and to others in the lesser decisions.

Who does not know that things like these have happened and do happen in the world—that someone who once ruled over countries and kingdoms has ceased to rule and is obliged to see a more powerful ruler take his place; that someone who once was hailed with jubilation soon, yes, so soon that the whole thing seems to have been a dream, hears the same jubilation shouting another name; that someone whose commanding figure was familiar to everyone regards himself in the next moment with the anxiety of uncertainty about whether he has lost his mind or the world its memory so that it confuses with him someone else; that the master whose pupil only yesterday sat at his feet must bow his shoulders today under the other's advancement; that the businessman who was kind enough to set his servant on his path now sees that his path means the benefactor's downfall; that the girl who once filled her beloved's thoughts now sits and sees his bold ambition pursuing a higher goal; that the singer whose words were on everyone's lips is forgotten today and his songs have been more than replaced; that the orator whose words echoed everywhere must now seek the solitude of the desert if he wants echo; that the friend from youth who was on an equal basis with his fellows now with amazement perceives the distance;[196] that the lowly cottage where the parents lived, where the humble cradle stood, is now collapsing like a recollection that cannot catch up with the mighty. And yet, how strange—if you let your thoughts dwell on those distinguished people whose memory the generations have preserved, you will find that the way each individual distinguished himself is very different, and you will find in turn that several are distinguished by the same thing. But in that select group you still seem to lack one place, and yet the lack is indeed a contradiction; how would the one whose task it was to be reconciled—to being forgotten—find a place in recollection? But for this very reason it is of importance to consider it by itself, and it is especially beautiful to do this—because no earthly reward is beckoning.

So let us then deliberate in more detail on what frame of mind is the right one and consider, which amounts to the same thing, how John said these words: *He must increase; I must decrease.*

John said them in *humble self-denial*. From the very beginning, he understood this as his mission in the world; therefore in a way he was diminishing from the very beginning, or at least he was familiar with the thought, since otherwise he

IV
161

would have made the way difficult for the one who was to come by too powerfully attracting the attention of the crowd or holding it spellbound too long. To that extent, the Baptizer's life seems to be unique and incapable of providing guidance for others. Nevertheless, similarities to such a mission may be found also in less important situations. Many a person has been born since that day whose destiny was only to pave the way and who early in his life had to realize that this was his work. From the very beginning, such a person is under the necessity of denying himself and must not first have the experience of distinction, which, the longer it lasts, the more easily it comes to beguile self-denial's liberating and loosening power in a spell; but on the other hand every such person has never in his whole life, not in youth's hope, not in adulthood's achievement, experienced the beautiful period in which the sun stops its course, stands still,[197] and still does not set.

We shall not decide which life fights the good fight most easily, but we all agree that every human being ought to fight the good fight,[198] from which no one is shut out, and yet this is so glorious that if it were granted only once to a past generation under exceptional circumstances—yes, what a description envy and discouragement would then know how to give! The difference is about the same as that in connection with the thought of death. As soon as a human being is born, he begins to die. But the difference is that there are some people for whom the thought of death comes into existence with birth and is present to them in the quiet peacefulness of childhood and the buoyancy of youth; whereas others have a period in which this thought is not present to them until, when the years run out, the years of vigor and vitality, the thought of death meets them on their way. Who, now, is going to decide which life was easier, whether it was the life of those who continually lived with a certain reserve because the thought of death was present to them or the life of those who so abandoned themselves to life that they almost forgot the existence of death? And if in this regard even the example of John does not apply to all, for those to whom it does apply it can indeed be instructive, because there are temptations here also. Or was

IV
162

it not a temptation when the council's emissaries[199] almost occasioned him to misunderstand himself? But John stuck to what he had understood about himself, his humble task and his humble relation to the one to come; the council did not disturb him.

It is easy to find partially or totally analogous situations on a small scale in everyday life, and that the situations are smaller, not in any valid sense crucial, not world-historical, not historic, makes no essential difference; an arithmetic problem is the same whether it involves millions or pennies. If parents have the right understanding of themselves, their humble self-denial begins the minute their child is born. This does not mean that the child is to be sovereign without listening and obeying; but, although this subordination to the parents is essential for the child, in the expression of joy that a child is born into the world[200] there is a beautiful harmony with the thought: He must increase; we must decrease. Or would it not be foolish for someone to think that this is valid only for a much later time and for a certain few parents who discovered to their amazement that their child was superior to others? Is not this thought really insulting to parents, inasmuch as it would have brought about a distortion so that they, even though they fought the good fight, would have spoiled it because, forgetting that they were parents, they fought the good fight more as outsiders in relation to an outsider.

And now the many to whom the Baptizer's exalted example is entirely applicable, although in unpretentiousness, the many who at an early age are given to understand humbly that for them the form of a servant[201] is not something assumed, those who at an early age are prompted to bear in mind that for them there is someone who must increase while they decrease! Perhaps to such a one there at times also comes advice from higher places, a misunderstood hint, a false call, but then there presumably was also someone who was not distracted in his humble self-denial, who did not foolishly snatch at phantoms and did not grudgingly and peevishly continue in lowliness. But even if a person (whatever the occasion of his self-denial, since the essential in self-denial is indeed that one deny

IV
163

oneself) does not comprehend from the very beginning that he is decreasing, he nevertheless ought never be entirely ignorant of the thought that he can come to that. Every human being is only an instrument and does not know when the moment will come when he will be put aside. If he himself does not at times evoke this thought, he is a hireling, an unfaithful servant, who is trying to free himself and to cheat the Lord of the uncertainty in which he comprehends his own nothingness. That much in life is empty and worthless, people certainly do know, but how frequently the single individual makes an exception, and even the highest mission in the spiritual world is only an errand, and one who is equipped for it with all spiritual-intellectual gifts is only on an errand—but why is the sending out of angels so beautiful, inasmuch as they return again to God's throne so speedily that they have no time to be tempted by the thought that they are taking care of their own affairs! In the Gospel, it is the master who goes on a journey, and the unfaithful servant thinks that he has gone so far away that he will never return.[202] In life, it is the servant who goes on a journey, and the unfaithful servant deceives himself into thinking that he can go so far away that the master cannot take away what has been entrusted to him. But property and gold can vanish like a dream, and the honor of men is swiftly changed to mockery, and the time of service can soon be over. But the thought of being dismissed liberates the servant to be one of God's co-workers,[203] just as the thought of death liberates a person, saves him from being a bond servant who wants to belong only to the earth, from being a cheat who does not want to belong to God.[204]

In humble self-denial the Baptizer spoke these words. But in another sense does not his situation seem even less able to be a guide and an example for anyone, because the one who came after him truly did do him full justice. Just as the humble self-denial with which John prepared the way for the one who was to come is seldom seen in this world, so there is never seen a peaceful and gentle entry such as the entry of the one who came not to be served but to serve.[205] Frequently, how-

ever, the successor comes in such a way that the sound of his
footsteps in the distance only awakens the predecessor's anxiety and resentment, so that his approach seems to be not to
fulfill but to trample down what has been begun, until "his
feet stand at the door ready to carry him out" (Acts 5:9). This
is certainly true, but it does not follow that one wrong makes
the other wrong right, even though it seems to explain it, indeed, to excuse it; and nevertheless the good ought to be done
and will be done "if the spirit that dwells in us does not arouse
jealousy and envy but gives abundant grace" (James 4:5).
Even though the steps of him who came after John were humble and could not exasperate, even though his appearance
could not tempt the Baptizer, because the one who came after
him "had been before him,"[206] even though he witnessed that
he was the greatest among those born of women, yet he also
declared that the least of his disciples was greater than John.[207]
Indeed, could it be put any more forcefully that all John's
work would simply be discontinued, that his baptism was a
preparation that would be discarded, his preaching a voice in
the desert,[208] his form but a weak shadow, his own life a shutting out? And yet John himself was not responsible, because
of his unbelief, for being shut out, but his work was simply
that which he completed with the utmost zeal.

In humble self-denial John said these words and said them
to his disciples. In their eyes he was still the great one; they
were accustomed to hail him as master. Secretly they perhaps
had nourished the thought that he himself was the one who
was to come; indeed, before them the Baptizer might have
wanted to suppress it. Now he has made his appearance—the
expected one—and the disheartened disciples trusted that the
news they were bringing to the Baptizer would elicit from
him the desired explanation. The expected one had come; the
Baptizer could have let him have the stage, himself stepped
aside, hidden himself in an out-of-the-way place with his disciples, and in their eyes continued to be the master, even
though he himself had not uttered that thought, even less let
it be known in the world, where it would only be a hindrance
to the one whose way he was supposed to prepare. How ben-

IV
165

eficial it is to contemplate what is worthy of veneration! Even what would have been excusable, humanly speaking, yes, almost laudable, we are ashamed to attribute to the Baptizer, not merely because the opposite has been stated; but even if nothing had been stated, who would falsely impute these thoughts to him! He remained true to himself; precisely when his disciples' news seemed to call for a different response, he gave witness to them of that which he had proclaimed in the wilderness before the coming one appeared and had preached to the people. He requested them to witness along with him that this had been his witness from the beginning, and the disciples had to witness along with him that this witness was his conclusion, his yes and his amen.

This was John. If it is true that something similar may be found in life's lesser situations, does what could resemble John actually resemble him? Perhaps there was someone who did not fail to notice that a new day was beginning to dawn; who the successor would be was not yet discernible—then he wanted to know nothing. But daybreak cannot be concealed; nevertheless, who the coming one[209] was could not be determined. Then, like Herod, he ordered that all the children under two years of age should be killed.[210] —Perhaps there was someone whose sun of fortune had begun to descend, and someone else was the favorite. Well, who the fortunate one is going to be is not an issue of truth; so he consulted with spite, and the arrow of revenge that flies in the dark struck the hated one. —Perhaps a new Pharaoh was enthroned who knew not Joseph[211] and the great services he had rendered, but the forgotten one himself brought about the forgetting of his services by the one who knew him and now knew his rancor. —Or he hid himself from people; he was not going to benefit the new by his witness. He took it as a disgrace that his time was over, just as if the disgrace were that his time was over rather than that his soul was unfamiliar with humility and self-denial. — Perhaps there was someone who saw his decline and then abandoned himself to grief and withered away in grieving, as if this decline were death, as if only someone who is planted

by streams of water[212] increased and not also someone who
plants himself in the blessed soil of self-denial.

Yes, how many roads there are in the hour of decision! And
yet there is only one road; the others are wrong roads,
whether they lead to the place where envy concocts its plans,
where grief has its haunts, where the worm of desire does not
die,[213] where disconsolateness stares at its loss, where mockery alarms others with its vile wisdom, or where the tongue
of slander betrays the abundance of the heart[214]—all these
roads lead away, far away, and thought does not even dare to
follow them. But humble self-denial remains true to itself and
continues in harmony with the one who ought to increase,
even though he himself must decrease, as did John, since with
that witness his sun went down, and yet when was he greater
than he was at that moment? But as a result he, too, increased
and was greatest when he went down.

IV
166

With genuine joy John said these words. If you, my listener,
recollect, as you indeed do, the Baptizer's powerful preaching
unto repentance, his prophetic boldness in judging the high
and the low, the holy wrath with which he laid the ax to the
foot of the tree[215]—then you are bound to be deeply moved
when you consider the sad gentleness, the joyous fervency,
with which he speaks of his relation to the coming one. That
under a camel-hair shirt there can also beat a heart so rich in
feeling not only for truth and justice, to which his life was
indeed dedicated! That he has been able to preserve this feeling
out there in the desert! That the soft breeze of self-denying joy
can be sensed in the thunder of the judgment![216] His statement
points out exactly what it was supposed to point out, but the
expression is so celebrative, so festively beautiful, that one is
almost tempted to picture the Baptizer's stern figure dressed
in festive garments as if he were on his way to a banquet,[217] a
friendly man who is bringing happy greetings, yes, as if that
earnest, dark hermit, who mournfully sang to the people even
if they would not weep, as if he, mellowed, joined in the dance
in accordance with the joyful game, as if once again the children in the marketplace would not understand,[218] even though

it involved them—and the Baptizer was the only one who was excluded. Oh, there is an emotion that has an overabundance of beautiful words and is very quick to melt into sentimental moods, but when the man in the camel-hair shirt whom the storms did not affect, when he is mellowed, who is then not moved by his words! His mood is no false feeling; on the contrary, the discriminating judgment of truth is present in the words he speaks, and the zealous judge has judged himself first of all: "No one can receive anything except what is given to him from heaven" (v. 27). These are the words with which he judges himself, distinguishes between himself and the one to come; it is the judge who is speaking, and yet the statement is a eulogy of his having fulfilled it. Now that he has put his house in order, his wedding greeting follows: "He who has the bride is the bridegroom, but the bridegroom's friend, who stands and hears him, rejoices greatly at the bridegroom's voice. Therefore this joy of mine is now full" (v. 29). Then he thinks of himself and of his situation, that he is the alien, indeed, the one shut out, and now this is his farewell: He must increase; I must decrease.

With genuine joy he said these words. Now it is certainly true that his whole life had been designed for the appearance of the one who now appeared, and to that extent it was certainly bound to give him joy. But it still does not follow that his joy was full, just as we must not forget, either, that his having understood his life this way from the beginning was his work of noble self-denial and the triumph of that work is that the joy is full. It is certainly true that he did not see the coming one indifferently shove him aside but saw him advancing as a prince of peace, but still the witness remains the same. Even if no one else comprehended the chasmic abyss between the coming one and the Baptizer, he comprehended it, and yet he gave full expression to it and to his joy that this was precisely the way it was. For him this joy was full, that he was seen in all his lowliness beside the glory of the coming one. If this did not become clear, then for him his joy would not have been full. No wonder the believer was bound to rejoice that the glory of the expected one was the glory of God, since he shared in it and precisely thereby became greater than John; but he was indeed the one who decreased.

With genuine joy he said these words; or do you find some deceit in his mouth, some false feeling that hides the truth, some half-truth that is glossed over with excessive feeling? The expression itself is presumably just as fervent, just as beautiful, as that which it expresses, which is certainly the most beautiful—the genuine joy of self-denial. As for its truth, we are well aware that there is a wisdom that is especially adept at understanding the past with hindsight, in calming the minds of those who are dead and forgotten, in guiding those who have helped themselves, in offering consolation that is irrelevant to anyone. Wisdom of that kind, which never dares to revive the past, lest it become apparent that it knows nothing at the crucial moment but everything too late, wisdom of that kind presumably would at this point explain that John nevertheless always retained a certain vanishing significance as preparation, a certain partial justification as a passageway for the higher. This is not the way John understood it; this is not the way he wanted to be understood. His self-denial was deeper and therefore his joy higher. He who has the bride, he declares, is the bridegroom. He could not have stated more explicitly that he himself was shut out. He understood the difference exceedingly well; no intrusiveness would bring him closer, but this was why for him the joy was full. He was the bridegroom's friend, who stands and hears his voice and rejoices greatly; but the least one in the kingdom of heaven is greater than John, because he does not stand outside listening to the bridegroom's voice.

With genuine joy John said these words and said them to his disciples. And even though his joy was full, he still could have hidden it in his heart, he could have expressed it less explicitly and not in such a way that his own diminishing had to become conspicuous to his disciples, who were scarcely prepared to comprehend his joy. Indeed, he could have done it for the sake of his disciples so that they, who perhaps had set their hopes on him despite his witness, might not all too deeply feel how

IV
168

much they were being diminished along with the master. But no! His joy became full for him the more he was diminished. Just as the joy of the believers in heaven will be great because of the glory, so his joy was full in being diminished.

This was John, and this is how the single individual is to fulfill something similar in lesser situations. If he has first of all learned to deny himself humbly and to master his mind, then joy will also be victorious. But the first must be learned first—later, that which is greater; one is first initiated into the lesser mystery, later into the greater mystery. And no one dares to be totally without this thought. In an earlier time, it was the custom to contemplate one's death frequently, until one was so quietly intimate with this thought that it did not at all disturb one's task in life; indeed, one was so intimate with the thought that one even had time to consider one's apparel and had everything ready. So also with the person who in good time becomes intimate with the death-thought of self-denial; he, too, will have time to contemplate the fullness of the joy that is the incorruptible apparel of self-denial.

IV
169

And yet life seems to provide contrary evidence—not that this cannot happen but that it does not happen. Humanly speaking, it is already something great if a person denies himself and finds that another ought to increase and he ought to decrease and resigns himself to it with the curious inconsolable compliance with which one is reconciled to one's fate. An ancient pagan poet, who was quite famous but now, advanced in years, harbored the thought that his time would soon be over, said to the blond youth who sat beside him watching the contest, "You see, my son, how it goes: the loser is silent, and the crowd jubilates."[219] And so it really is, and the jubilation is not for the loser, but he goes his solitary way and is reconciled to being defeated and bears no grudge against the victor—but that he would be seen in the arena, that he would rejoice over the other's victory—this is asking too much, and that his joy would be full is preposterous. —Perhaps there was someone who also saw another increase, and his heart did not hide his envy, but his congratulations were nevertheless ambiguous and not gratifying to hear. —Or he could not forget himself over the bridegroom's voice, and his participation brought to mind his own special significance, and so his joy was not and did not become full. —Or his joy was of a kind that turned someone or other's mind to him away from the joyful. —Or even in the moment of joy "he grumbled against" (James 5:9) the stronger one, because he himself had to be diminished. —Or he stayed away because his mind was too weak to preserve the joy when he would hear the bridegroom's voice. —Or his heart hid more joy than he admitted even to his intimate friends. —But John's joy was full; he was the bridegroom's friend, and his joy was full; he stood with him, and his joy was full; he heard his voice, and his joy was full.

He must increase—who is this "he"? In the sense in which we have used the word, everyone can identify him with another name; this is how change occurs here on earth: one increases and another decreases, and today it is I and tomorrow you. But one who in humble self-denial and with genuine joy saw another increase—his mind will be turned into a new joy, and this new joy of his will surely be full.

An old saying states that everyone would rather see the rising sun than the setting sun. Why everyone? Do you suppose this includes someone whose sun it is that is setting? Yes, for he, too, ardently desires to rejoice just as the bridegroom's friend does when he stands and hears the bridegroom's voice.

IV
170

Four Upbuilding Discourses[220]

1844

TO THE LATE

Michael Pedersen Kierkegaard

FORMERLY A CLOTHING MERCHANT HERE IN THE CITY

MY FATHER

THESE DISCOURSES ARE DEDICATED

Although this little book (which is called "discourses," not sermons, because its author does not have authority to *preach*, "upbuilding" discourses, not discourses for upbuilding, because the speaker by no means claims to be a *teacher*) is once again going out into the world, it is even less fearful of drawing any impeding attention to itself than it was the first time it started on the journey; it hopes rather that because of the repetition the passersby will scarcely notice it, or if at all only to let it shift for itself. Just as a messenger now and then goes his routine way at set times and soon is a familiar sight, so familiar that the passerby scarcely sees him, does not turn to look after him—in the same way this little book goes out like a messenger, but not like a messenger who comes back again. It seeks that single individual whom I with joy and gratitude call *my* reader, in order to pay him a visit, indeed, to stay with him, because one goes to the person one loves, makes one's home with him,[222] and remains with him if this is allowed. That is, as soon as he has received it, then it has ceased to be; it is nothing for itself and by itself, but all that it is, it is only for him and by him. And although the trail always leads ahead to *my* reader, not back, and although the previous messenger never returns home,[223] and although the one who sends him never discovers anything about his fate, the next messenger nevertheless goes intrepidly through death to life, cheerfully goes its way in order to disappear, happy never to return home again—and this is precisely [224]the joy of him who sends it, who continually comes to his reader only to bid him farewell, and now bids him farewell for the last time.[225]

Copenhagen, August 9, 1844[226]

S. K.

"A person needs only a little in order to live and needs that little only a little while"—this is a high-minded proverb that is worthy of being received and understood as it wants to be understood; it is too earnest to want to be admired as a beautiful expression or an elegant locution. As such it is thoughtlessly used at times: one calls it out to the needy person, perhaps in order to console him in passing, perhaps also just to have something to say; one says it to oneself, even on a lucky day, since the human heart is very deceitful, is all too eager to take high-mindedness in vain and is proud of needing only a little—while using much. One says it to oneself on a day of need, and hurries ahead to welcome oneself admiringly at the goal—when one has accomplished something glorious—but one is as little served thereby as the proverb is.

"One needs it only a little while," but just as it sometimes happens that when the days lengthen, winter also strengthens, [228] so it is always the case that the winter of want and hardship makes the days long even if time and life are short.

How much, then, is the little that a person needs? This question cannot really be answered in general, and even someone who has had the experience—if not of needing little, at least of having to manage with little—even he will not be able to define in general what that little is. Just as time often brings new comfort to the sad, new buoyancy to the crushed, new compensation to the one who lost much, so it is solicitous about the sufferer, even when it continues to take. It seldom takes everything at once, but little by little, and in this way gradually makes him accustomed to doing without, until he himself perceives with amazement that he needs even less than what he once regarded as the least—in fact, so little that he would think with dismay of having to need so little (even though he would not express himself quite clearly, since the dismay really is not due only to needing little) and would al-

most be incensed by the contradictory idea of having to need
it in order to be able to continue to need it, even though he
would not quite understand himself, since the perfection definitely would not consist in coming to need more.

But how much, then, is the little that a person needs? Let
life answer, and let the discourse do what the distress and
hardship of life sometimes do—strip a person in order to see
how little it is that he needs. And you, my listener, join in as
you must or wish to join in according to your particular situation; the discourse will not arouse dismay if it really means
to provide any comfort and does not aim to deceive you, as
when the ice and snow of despair create the deceptive mountain torrent and accordingly the caravan shifts its course, proceeds into the desert, and perishes (Job 6:15-18). It cannot
arouse your dismay if you yourself have experienced it and
found comfort; and if you have not experienced it, then the
discourse about it can dismay you only if your strength is in
the observation that something like this happens only rarely.
But who, then, is more wretched: the one who has experienced it, or the cowardly, weak fool who does not perceive
that his comfort is a fraud, that it is of little benefit when
calamity strikes, that this is the rare instance?

So take it away from him: wealth and power and dominion,
the treacherous obligingness of false friends, the submissive-
ness of desires to the whims of wish, the triumphs of vanity
over idolizing admiration, the flattering attention of the
crowd, and all the envied grandeur of his appearance—he has
lost all this and is content with less. Just as the world is unable
to recognize him because of the drastic change, so he can
scarcely recognize himself—so changed is he that he who
needed so much now needs so much less. It is really far easier
and far more gratifying to understand how this change can
make him unrecognizable to himself than how that other
change can make him unrecognizable to others. Is it not fatuous that clothes are what make a person unrecognizable, so
that one does not know him without his clothes, and is it not
dismal that clothes are the object of admiration, not the man!
But a more devout observation readily sees that he is changing

his clothes and is being dressed in festive apparel, because the
earthly wedding garment and the heavenly are radically different. But few possessions with contentment is already a great
gain[229]—so take that away from him, not the contentment but
his last possession. He does not suffer want, he does not go to
bed hungry; but where he is going to obtain the necessities—
that he does not know, not at night when he drops off to sleep
from worry, not in the morning when he awakens to it, but
he nevertheless obtains them: the little he needs in order to
live. So, then, he is poor, and the word that is so hard to hear
he must hear said of himself. He feels it doubly hard, because
he himself did not choose this condition, as did the one who
threw away his possessions in order to test himself and who is
perhaps more easily reconciled to voluntary poverty but not
therefore always better reconciled if he only renounced vanity
by means of an even greater vanity.

"Needs only a little," the proverb said, but to know that a
person needs only a little without knowing for sure at any moment that he can obtain the little he needs—anyone who can
bear this needs only a little; he does not even need (this does,
after all, amount to something) to know that this little is secure. If, then, it is true that a person needs only a little—in
order to live—then he needs no more, since he will indeed find
a grave, and in the grave every human being needs equally
little. Whether the dead man owns (alas, what a strange contradiction), perhaps for a hundred years, the grave in which
he lies or he has had to elbow his way in among others,[230] has
had to fight his way ahead even in death in order to have a little
place, they own equally much and need equally little and need
that for only a little while. But the first little while that the
proverb speaks about may become long, because even if the
way to the grave was not long, if you perhaps not infrequently
saw him wend his weary way out there in order to conquer
with his eyes the little land he intended to occupy as a dead
man, could not the way become very long in another sense? If
he sometimes became despondent, if he did not always understand that a person needs only a little, did you have nothing
else to say to him than a repetition of that proverb? Or did you

v
83

probably say to him something that came quite naturally, so
naturally that in your heart even you yourself perhaps did not
have confidence in the comfort you were offering to another:
Then be contented with the grace of God.[231]

Pause now a moment, lest everything be confused—
thought, discourse, and language—lest everything be confused in the sense that the relation certainly remains the same
but only by being reversed, so that that man is the one who
has the comfort and you are the one who needs it, so that he
is the rich man and you are the destitute one, although it was
completely turned around until you heard the little magic formula that transformed everything. Perhaps you did not even
notice it yourself; one treats many a word this way, just as the
child treats a momentous word, without discovering the
thought's sting in it that wounds unto death in order to save
life.[232] To be contented with the grace of God! The grace of
God is indeed the most glorious of all. We certainly shall not
dispute about that, since basically this is every human being's
deepest and most blessed conviction. But very seldom does he
think about it and ultimately, if he really wants to be honest,
yet without being quite clear himself about what he is doing,
he applies to this idea that old proverb: Too little and too
much spoil everything. If he were to think the thought in its
eternal validity, it would promptly aim a fatal blow at all his
worldly thinking, aspiring, and pursuing, turn everything up-
side down for him, and this he cannot long endure. Then he
relapses to the low level of the worldly, to his ordinary conversation and way of thinking. In fact, the older a person becomes, the more difficult it is for him to learn a new language,
especially one that is so very different. Once in a while he notices that there is something wrong with the way he uses these
words mixed in with all his worldly conversation; he has a bad
conscience about the words and derives no blessing from
them. Yet the grace of God is indeed the most glorious of all.

But now if a person possessed something that surely is not
so glorious, possessed all the treasures of the earth, and you
then said to him: Be contented with it—he would no doubt
smile at you. If he himself said to you: I shall be contented

with it—you would probably be shocked, since what more could he demand, and what brashness to be willing to be *contented* with the *most!* What one is contented with must be the little, but to be contented with the most glorious of all seems an odd way to talk; and that this comfort is suggested by a person who himself does not comprehend it is still rather odd, as if someone (and not without sympathetic concern) gave the destitute person a penny, admonishing him to be contented with it, although this penny made its receiver the possessor of the whole world. Would it not be odd that the giver himself could think so poorly of the gift he offered that he accompanied it with the admonition to be contented! Or would it not be as if a man, on his way to a banquet to which he had been invited by a powerful personage, met a lowly person to whom he said (in order to offer him a kind of comfort): Be contented with sitting down to dinner in the kingdom of heaven!233 Or if the lowly person himself was articulate and said: Alas, I was not invited by the powerful one and cannot accept his invitation, either, since I am invited elsewhere and must be contented with sitting down to dinner in the kingdom of heaven—would this not be an odd way to speak? The more one thinks about it, the stranger earthly life and human language become. Right in the middle of all the earthly and worldly difference, which is jealous enough of itself, the God-difference is thoughtlessly mixed—indeed, even in such a way that basically it is shut out. To come in the name of the king opens every door for a person, but to come in God's name is the last thing he should try; and the person who must be contented with that must be contented with little. If he came to the door of the mighty one, if the servant did not even understand from whom he brought greetings, if the mighty one himself impatiently came out and saw the lowly person who was supposed to bring greetings from God in heaven—perhaps the door would be shut against him.

Yet the discourse does not want to take you by surprise, my listener, or to produce a sudden effect. When the words say: to be *contented* with the grace of God, the reason must be that the grace of God does not express itself in the way a person

V
85

would like to understand it but speaks in a way that is more difficult to understand. In other words, as soon as the grace of God gives a person what he desires and requests, he not only is contented with grace but is happy over what he receives and in his way of thinking readily understands that God is gracious to him. That this is a misunderstanding (which no one should be in a hurry to denounce) is obvious enough, but one should not for that reason forget to practice at the seasonable time understanding the more difficult and true. If, namely, a person can be assured of the grace of God without needing temporal evidence as a middleman or as the dispensation advantageous to him (in his opinion) as interpreter, then it is indeed obvious to him that the grace of God is the most glorious of all. Then he will strive to be gladdened by it in such a way that he is not merely contented with it, to give thanks for it in such a way that he is not contented with grace: will not grieve over that which was denied, over the language difference between God's eternal trustworthiness and his childish little faith, which, however, no longer exists since now "his heart is strengthened by grace and not by food" (Hebrews 13:9).

If a destitute person dared to enjoy the friendship of a powerful personage, but this powerful man could do nothing for him (that the grace of God allows the absence of earthly evidence corresponds to this), nevertheless, the fact that he had such a friendship was nevertheless already very much.[234] But perhaps the difficulty lies here, because the destitute person could indeed be convinced that the powerful man actually was not able to do anything for him, but how could he be definitively convinced that God cannot—he is, after all, almighty!

V
86

This presumably accounts for the fact that the thought of impatience continually insists, as it were, that God can surely do it, and therefore, because people are so impatient, therefore the language says: to be contented with the grace of God. In the beginning, when impatience is most strident and vociferous, it can scarcely understand that this is a laudable contentment; as it is cooled and calmed down in the quiet incorruptibility of the inner being, it comprehends this better and better until the heart is stirred and sometimes, at least, sees the divine glory that had taken on a lowly form.[235] And if this glory again vanishes for a person so that he is again destitute, as he still was also while he saw the glory, if it again seems to him that contentment still belongs to being contented with the grace of God, then he still at times shamefully admits that the grace of God is in itself worth being contented with—indeed, it alone is worth being desired; indeed, to possess it is the only blessedness.

Then in a beautiful sense the human heart will gradually (the grace of God is never taken by force) become more and more discontented—that is, it will desire more and more ardently, will long more and more intensely, to be assured of grace. See, now everything has become new,[236] everything has been changed. With respect to the earthly, one needs little, and to the degree that one needs less, the more perfect one is. A pagan who knew how to speak only of the earthly has said that the deity is blessed because he needs nothing, and next to him the wise man, because he needs little.[237] In a human being's relationship with God, it is inverted: the more he needs God, the more deeply he comprehends that he is in need of God, and then the more he in his need presses forward to God, the more perfect he is. Therefore, the words "to be contented with the grace of God" will not only comfort a person, and then comfort him again every time earthly want and distress make him, to speak mundanely, needful of comfort, but when he really has become attentive to the words they will call him aside, where he no longer hears the secular mentality's earthly mother tongue, the speech of human beings, the noise of the shopkeepers, but where the words explain themselves to him, confide to him the secret of perfection: that to need God is nothing to be ashamed of but is perfection itself, and that it is the saddest thing of all if a human being goes through life without discovering that he needs God.

Let us, then, clarify for ourselves this upbuilding thought:
V
87

To Need God Is a Human Being's Highest Perfection.

A circumstance that is familiar to all seems to suggest, at least as a fleeting reminder to everyone, that it is true that to need

God is a perfection. In the churches of the various countries, after the sermon a prayer is offered for the king and the royal house. That prayers are offered for the sick and the sorrowful cannot demonstrate that to need God is a perfection, since these people, after all, are the sufferers. But the king, he is the powerful man, indeed, the most powerful, and yet he is prayed for very specifically, but the sick and the sorrowful are prayed for only in general, even though the Church hopes and trusts that God in heaven will understand it very specifically, that whereas the Church does not think about any specific person, he thinks about each specific person in particular. And if it is otherwise with God's understanding, if his cares of governing allow him to be concerned about the single individual only in general—well, then God help us! Alas, but this is the last thing a person says in his misery; even when he cannot endure this last thought, that God would be solicitous about the single individual only in general, even then he says: God help me to endure this thought, and in this way he still brings God to concern himself about him in particular.

But why is a prayer offered for the king in particular? Is it because he has the earthly power and holds the fates of many in his hands; is it because his well-being determines the well-being of countless others; is it because every "shadow of adversity" that passes over the king's house also passes over the whole nation; is it because his illness halts the functioning of the state and his death disturbs its life? A purely secular concern such as that can certainly occupy many people, and not in an unbeautiful way, but it nevertheless will scarcely motivate anyone to pray or to pray in any other way than with the restraint that is required when we pray for earthly goods, since in that case a king becomes a kind of earthly good. In this sense, then, the intercession would become more and more inward as the personal life of the one praying is linked more and more closely to him, until finally the prayer would no longer be an intercessory prayer any more than the wife's prayer for her husband is an intercessory prayer. But precisely because it makes intercession, the Church cannot pray in this way, but it makes this intercession presumably because it is convinced that the higher a person stands, the more he needs God.

Yet even though prayer is offered in all the churches for a king, it does not follow from this that the king for whom prayer is offered himself comprehends that to need God is a human being's highest perfection. And even though the single individual in church silently gives his consent to the intercessory prayer, and, alas, even though the many who do not go to church still have no objection to the intercessory prayer, it does not follow from this that they understand it devoutly, that the higher one ascends in earthly power and dominion, the closer one comes only to intercessory prayer. It is all too easy for the mighty to take it in vain; it is all too easy for the one praying to say it in vain. On the other hand, we do not deny that wanting in all earnestness to understand what a person does not yet understand earnestly enough—if he wants to seek his own way to this consciousness and not leave it to God, who knows best how to alarm all self-confidence out of a person and keep him, when he is about to sink into his own nothingness, from maintaining by himself the diver's connection with the earthly—we do not deny that wanting in all earnestness to understand this makes life difficult. Let us just admit it without thereby becoming so discouraged or cowardly that we want to sleep our way to what others have had to work for; let us not take it in vain when the believer enthusiastically declares that all his suffering is only brief and short,[238] that the yoke of self-denial is so easy to bear. But neither let us doubt that the yoke of self-denial is beneficial, that the cross of sufferings ennobles a person more than anything else, and let us hope to God that someday we shall come so far that we, too, are able to speak enthusiastically. But let us not demand this too early, lest the believer's zealous words discourage us because this does not occur immediately. It frequently happens that a person fixes in his memory some particular powerful words. When suffering comes to his house, he is reminded of the words and thinks he will be victorious immediately in the joy of those words. But not even an apostle uses powerful words at all times; he, too, is sometimes weak;[239] he, too, is alarmed, and he thereby makes us understand that the powerful words are dearly bought and are never possessed in such a way that one does not again have an opportunity to assure oneself of how dearly they were bought.

But even though this understanding makes life more difficult not only for the light-mindedness of the fortunate one and for the many whose hankering is to be like him, but also for the unfortunate, since this understanding still does not act like magic, does not have any decisive external effect, should we therefore praise it dubiously or crave it double-mindedly? And yet it certainly is a precarious matter that what is offered as comfort in life starts out by making life more difficult in order—yes, in order—to make it truly easier; so it is with every one of truth's miracles, just as it was with that miracle at the wedding in Cana:[240] truth serves the poor wine first and keeps the best until last, whereas the deceitful world serves the best wine first. Just because a person became unhappy, "excessively unhappy," as he himself says, it by no means follows from this that the understanding that conditions the comfort, the understanding that he himself is capable of nothing at all, has yet matured in him. If he believes that he lacks only the means, then he still believes in himself; if he thinks that if he were given power or the admiration of men or the attainment of his wish, if he thinks that the complaint contains a legitimate demand for something temporal that becomes more legitimate the more vehement the complaint becomes—then, humanly speaking, he still has a bitter cup to drink before the comfort comes. Therefore it is always a difficult matter for one person to offer another such a comfort, because when the troubled one consults him and he then says, "I certainly do know where comfort is to be found, indescribable comfort; indeed, what is more, it transforms itself little by little in your soul into the highest joy"—then the troubled one will probably listen attentively. But when there is added, "Nevertheless, before this comfort can come, you must understand that you yourself are simply nothing; you must chop down the bridge of probability that wants to connect wish and impatience and desire and expectation with the object wished for, desired, and expected; you must renounce the worldly mentality's association with the future; you must retreat into yourself, not as into a fortress that still defies the world while the self-inclosed person nevertheless has with him in the fortress his most dangerous enemy (indeed, it may even have been the enemy's advice he followed when he closed himself up in this way), but into yourself, sinking down into your own nothingness and surrendering yourself to grace and disgrace"—then the troubled one would very likely go away distressed, like the rich young man who had much property,[241] distressed even though he did not have much property but still resembled the rich young man so much that one could not tell them apart. Or if the troubled one had strayed and become bogged down in deliberation so that he was unable to act, because from both sides an equal case was made, and someone else said to him, "I know a way out, and you will be the victor for sure. Give up wishing; act, act in the conviction that even when the opposite of what you are wishing happens you will still have been victorious," then there probably would be someone who would turn away impatiently because a victory such as that would seem to him a defeat, and because he would consider such a way out even more burdensome than the complex disquietude of his doubting soul.

V
90

But what is a human being? Is he just one more ornament in the series of creation; or has he no power, is he himself capable of nothing? And what is his power, then; what is the utmost he is able to will? What kind of answer should be given to this question when the brashness of youth combines with the strength of adulthood to ask it, when this glorious combination is willing to sacrifice everything to accomplish great things, when burning with zeal it says, "Even if no one in the world has ever achieved it, I will nevertheless achieve it; even if millions degenerated and forgot the task, I will nevertheless keep on striving—but what is the highest?" Well, we do not want to defraud the highest of its price; we do not conceal the fact that it is rarely achieved in this world, because the highest is this: that a person is fully convinced that he himself is capable of nothing, nothing at all. What rare dominion—not rare in the sense that only one individual is born to be king, since everyone is born to it! What rare wisdom—not rare in the sense that it is offered to just a few, since it is offered to all! What wonderful rarity that is not depreciated by being offered to all, by being accessible to all! Indeed, if a person turns outward, it probably seems as if he were capable of doing something more amazing, something that would satisfy him in quite another way, something that would draw enthusiastic admiration, because that rare loftiness is not an appropriate object of admiration, does not tempt the sensate person since, on the contrary, it judges the admirer to be a fool who does not know what he is admiring and orders him to go home or judges him to be a fraudulent soul and orders him to repent. To external observation, man may well be the most glorious creation, but all his glory is still only in the external and for the external: does not the eye aim its arrow outward every time passion and desire tighten the bowstring, does not the hand grasp outward, is not his arm stretched out, and is not his ingenuity all-conquering!

But if he nevertheless is unwilling to be like an instrument of war in the service of inexplicable drives, indeed, in the service of the world, because the world itself, the object of his craving, stimulates the drives; if he nevertheless does not want to be like a stringed instrument in the hands of inexplicable moods or, rather, in the hands of the world, because the movement of his soul is in accord with the way the world plucks its strings; if he does not want to be like a mirror in which he intercepts the world or, rather, the world reflects itself; if he does not want this, [242]if he himself, even before the eye aims at something to make a conquest, wants to capture the eye so that it may belong to him and not he to the eye; if he grasps the hand before it grasps for the external, so that it may belong to him and not he to the hand; if he wants this so earnestly that he is not afraid of tearing out the eye, cutting off the hand,[243] shutting the window of the senses if necessary—well, then everything is changed; the power is taken away from him, and the glory. He struggles not with the world but with himself.[244] Observe him now; his powerful figure is held embraced by another figure, and they hold each other so firmly interlocked and are so equally matched in suppleness and strength that the wrestling cannot even begin, because in that moment that other figure would overwhelm him—but that other figure is he himself. Thus he is capable of nothing; even the weakest person who is not tried in this struggle is capable of far more than he.

This struggle is not only exhausting but also very terrible (if it is not he himself who has on his own initiative ventured into this, and if that is the case, he is not being tried in the struggle of which we speak) when life at God's direction casts a person out to be strengthened in this annihilation that knows no delusion, permits no evasion, occasions no self-deception, as if he would be capable of more under other circumstances, since when he struggles with himself, circumstances cannot determine the result. This is the annihilation of a person, and the annihilation is his truth. He shall not escape this knowledge, for he is indeed his own witness, his plaintiff, his judge; he himself is the only one who is able to comfort, since he understands the distress of the annihilation, and the only one who cannot comfort, since he himself is indeed the instrument of the annihilation. To comprehend this annihilation is the highest thing of which a human being is capable; to brood over this understanding, because it is a God-given good entrusted to him as the secret of truth, is the highest and the most difficult thing of which a human being is capable, because the deception and the counterfeit are easily produced so that even at the cost of truth he becomes something. This is the highest and the most difficult thing of which a human being is capable—yet what am I saying—he is incapable even of this; at most he is capable of being willing to understand that this smoldering brand only consumes until the fire of God's love ignites the blaze in what the smoldering brand could not consume. —Thus man is a helpless creature, because all other understanding that makes him understand that he can help himself is but a misunderstanding, even though in the eyes of the world he is regarded as courageous—by having

V
92

the courage to remain in a misunderstanding, that is, by not having the courage to understand the truth.

But in heaven, my listener, there lives the God who is capable of all things, or, more correctly, he lives everywhere, even if people do not perceive it. "Indeed, O Lord, if you were a weak, lifeless body like a flower that withers, if you were like a brook that flows by, if you were like a building that collapses in due time—then people would pay attention to you, then you would be an appropriate object for our low and brutish thoughts."[245] But this is not the way it is, and your very greatness makes you invisible, since in your wisdom you are much too far away from man's thoughts for him to be able to see you, and in your omnipresence you are too close to him for him to see you; in your goodness you conceal yourself from him, and your omnipotence makes it impossible for him to see you, since in that case he himself would become nothing![246] But God in heaven is capable of all things, and man of nothing at all.

Is it not so, my listener, that these two correspond to each other: God and man? But if they correspond to each other, then, of course, there is only the question of whether you are going to be happy about this wonderful good fortune—that you two correspond to each other—or whether you prefer to be such a one who does not correspond to God at all, such a one who is capable of something himself and consequently does not correspond completely to God, for indeed you cannot change God, and indeed you do not want to change God so that he would not be capable of all things. To become nothing seems hard—oh, but we speak differently even about human matters. If misfortune taught two human beings that they corresponded to each other in friendship or in love, how negligible the distress caused by the misfortune would seem compared with the joy the misfortune also brought—that these two corresponded to each other! And if two human beings did not understand until the day of death that they corresponded to each other for all eternity—oh, how brief, though bitter, that moment of separation that is death would be compared with an eternal understanding!

Thus a human being is great and at his highest when he corresponds to God by being nothing at all himself, but let us not admire light-mindedly or take the admiration in vain. Did not Moses go as the Lord's envoy to a wicked people in order to free them from themselves, from their servile mentality, and from their servile condition under a tyrant's yoke? Compared with what are called the works of Moses, what is the deed of even the greatest hero; what are demolishing mountains and filling rivers compared with having darkness fall upon all Egypt![247] But these were really only Moses' so-called works, because he was capable of nothing at all and the work was the Lord's. See the difference here. Moses—he is not making decisions and formulating plans while the council of the commonsensical listens attentively because the leader is the wisest—Moses is capable of nothing at all. If the people had said to him, "Go to Pharaoh, because your word is powerful, your voice is triumphant, your eloquence irresistible," he probably would have answered, "Oh, you fools! I am capable of nothing at all, not even of giving my life for you if the Lord does not so will; I am capable only of submitting everything to the Lord." Then he presents himself to Pharaoh, and what is his weapon? The weapon of the powerless—prayers, and even when the last word of his prayers has already reached heaven, he still does not know what is going to happen, even though he believes that whatever happens still happens for the best. Then he returns home to the people, but if they had praised him and thanked him, he probably would have answered, "I am capable of nothing at all." Or when the people are thirsting in the desert and perhaps appeal to Moses,[248] saying, "Take your staff and order the rock to give water," Moses probably would answer, "What is my staff but a stick?" And if the people went on, saying, "But in your hand the staff is mighty," Moses would have to say, "I am capable of nothing at all, but since the people are asking for it and since I myself cannot bear the sight of the misery of this languishing people, I will strike the rock, even though I myself do not believe that water will spring from it"—and the rock did not give water. Consequently, whether the staff he is holding in

v
93

his hand is to be the finger of the Almighty or the stick of Moses, [249]he does not know, not even in the moment the staff is already touching the rock; he does not know it until afterward, just as he never sees anything but the Lord's back.[250] Ah, humanly speaking, the weakest of the Israelites is capable of more than Moses, since that one still thinks he is capable of something, but Moses is capable of nothing at all. At one moment, to seem to be stronger than the strongest, stronger than all others, than the whole world, insofar as the miracle occurs by his hand; in the next moment, indeed, in the very same moment, to be weaker than the weakest, insofar as that one still thinks there is something he is capable of—this kind of greatness will be no temptation to the hankerings of conceit, insofar as it takes the time to understand what constitutes the greatness; otherwise in its loathsome cowardliness it presumably would promptly be ready to wish to be in Moses' place.

If, however, this view, that to need God is man's highest perfection, makes life more difficult, it does this only because it wants to view man according to his perfection and bring him to view himself in this way, because in and through this view *man learns to know himself*. And for the person who does not know himself, his life is, in the deeper sense, indeed a delusion. But such a delusion is rarely due to a person's not discovering the capabilities entrusted to him, to his not trying to develop them as much as possible in conformity with his given situation. He does really sink deep roots into existence and does not deal light-mindedly with himself like the very talented child who does not understand how much has been entrusted to it, like the light-minded rich youth who does not understand the significance of gold—and so it is that we speak of a person's self in terms of monetary value, and he who knows himself knows down to the last penny what he is worth and knows how to exchange himself so that he obtains the full value. If he does not do this, then he does not know himself and is deluded, which the person of good sense will surely tell him and, as life proceeds, will tell him, step by step, that he is not delighting in life in the springtime of life, that he is not affirming himself for what he actually is, that he does not know that people take a person for what he himself claims to be, that he has not known how to make himself important and thereby to give life importance for himself. Alas, but even though a person also knew himself ever so well in this sense, even though he knew how to invest himself in life ever so advantageously and with interest, do you suppose he would therefore know himself? But if he did not know himself, then in a deeper sense his life would indeed be a delusion. Would it then be rare in these sagacious times for a person to be responsible for a delusion like that? What would that sagacious self-knowledge be other than this—that he knew himself in relation to something else [251]but did not know himself in relation to himself; in other words, despite its apparent reliability, all his self-knowledge was altogether vague, since it involved only the relation between a dubious self and a dubious something else. This something else could be changed, so that someone else became the stronger, the more handsome, the richer; and this self could be changed, so that he himself became poor, ugly, powerless; and this change could come at any moment. Once this something else is taken away, he is indeed deceived, and if this something else is of such a nature that it can be taken away, he is indeed deceived even if it is not taken away, since the whole meaning of his life was founded on this something else. In other words, there is no delusion if something that can deceive does so, but instead it is a delusion when it does not.

A self-knowledge of that kind is very imperfect and far from viewing man according to his perfection. Would it not be a strange perfection about which one must finally say, after perhaps having extolled it in the strongest terms: In addition, this is a delusion? Along this road, one never comes to view man according to his perfection, and in order to begin doing that, one must begin to tear oneself loose from any such view, which is just as difficult as tearing oneself out of a dream without making the mistake of continuing the dream: dreaming that one is awake. In a certain sense this is quite complicated, because a person's real self seems to him to be so far distant that the whole world seems much closer to him, and quite

V
95

terrible, because the more profound self-knowledge begins with what someone who is unwilling to understand it might call a shocking delusion: instead of gaining the whole world, to gain himself; instead of becoming the master, to become one in need; instead of being capable of all things, to be capable of nothing at all. Ah, how difficult it is at this point not to fall into dreams again and to dream that one is doing this by one's own power.

[252]When a person turns and faces himself in order to understand himself, he steps, as it were, in the way of that first self, halts that which was turned outward in hankering for and seeking after the surrounding world that is its object, and summons it back from the external. In order to prompt the first self to this withdrawal, the deeper self lets the surrounding world remain what it is—remain dubious. This is indeed the way it is; the world around us is inconstant and can be changed into the opposite at any moment, and there is not one person who can force this change by his own might or by the conjuration of his wish. The deeper self now shapes the deceitful flexibility of the surrounding world in such a way that it is no longer attractive to that first self. Then the first self either must proceed to kill the deeper self, to render it forgotten, whereby the whole matter is given up; or it must admit that the deeper self is right, because to want to predicate constancy of something that continually changes is indeed a contradiction, and as soon as one confesses that it changes, it can, of course, change in that same moment. However much that first self shrinks from this, there is no wordsmith so ingenious or no thought-twister so wily that he can invalidate the deeper self's eternal claim. There is only one way out, and that is to silence the deeper self by letting the roar of inconstancy drown it out.

What has happened? The first self is halted; it cannot move at all. Alas, the surrounding world can actually be so favorable, so tangibly trustworthy, so apparently undeviating, that everyone will vouch for splendid progress if one just begins— it does not help. The person who witnesses that struggle in his inner being must concede that the deeper self is right: in that minute everything can be changed, and one who does not discover this continually runs into the unknown.[253] Never in the world has there been so quick a tongue that it could beguile the deeper self if only it gains a chance to speak. Ah, it is a painful situation. The first self sits and looks at all the beckoning fruits, and it is indeed so clear that if one just makes a move everything will succeed, as everyone will admit—but the deeper self sits there as earnest and thoughtful as the physician at the bedside of the sick, yet also with transfigured gentleness, because it knows that this sickness is not unto death[254] but unto life.

Now the first self has a specific craving; it is conscious of possessing the conditions; the surrounding world, as it understands it, is as favorable as possible; they are just waiting for each other, as it were: the happy self and the favors of fortune—oh, what a pleasant life! But the deeper self does not give ground, does not haggle, does not give its consent, does not compromise; it merely says: Even in this moment everything can be changed. Yet people come to the aid of that first self with the explanation. They call to him; they explain that this is the way it goes in life, that there are some people who are fortunate and are supposed to enjoy life and that he is one of them. Then the heart beats fast; he wants to be off . . . . .

That a child who has a strict father must stay at home is something one must submit to, because the father is indeed the stronger. But the first self is certainly no child, and that deeper self, after all, is himself, and yet it seems stricter than the strictest father, tolerating no wheedling, speaking candidly or not speaking at all. Then there is danger afoot—both of them, both the first self and the deeper self, notice it, and the latter sits there as concerned as the experienced pilot, while a secret council is held on whether it is best to throw the pilot overboard since he is creating a contrary wind. That, however, does not happen, but what is the outcome? The first self cannot move from the spot, and yet, yet it is clear that the moment of joy is in a hurry, that fortune is already in flight. Therefore people do indeed say that if one does not make use of the moment at once, it is soon too late. And who is to blame? Who else but that deeper self? But even this scream does not help.

What kind of unnatural condition is this? What does it all mean? When such a thing occurs in a person's soul, does it not mean that he is beginning to lose his mind? No, it means something altogether different; it means that the child must be weaned. One can be thirty years old and more, forty years old, and still be just a child—yes, one can die as an aged child. But to be a child is so delightful! So one snuggles at the breast of temporality in the cradle of finitude, and probability sits by the cradle and sings to the child. If the wish is not fulfilled and the child becomes restless, then probability calms him and says: Just lie still and sleep, and I shall go out and buy something for you, and next time it will be your turn. So the child goes to sleep again and the pain is forgotten, and the child glows again in the dream of new wishes, although he thought it would be impossible to forget the pain. Of course, if he had not been a child, he surely would not have forgotten the pain so easily, and it would have become apparent that it was not probability that had sat beside the cradle, but it was the deeper self that had sat beside him at the deathbed in self-denial's hour of death, when it itself rose from the dead to an eternity.

When the first self submits to the deeper self, they are reconciled and walk on together. Then the deeper self probably says, "It is true that I had almost forgotten it in our great struggle—what was it now that you so fervently wished; at this moment I do not think there is anything to hinder the fulfillment of your wish if you will only not forget that little secret we two have between us. Now, you see, now you can be gratified." The first self may answer, "Yes, but now I do not care as much about it; no, I shall never be as happy as before, as I was then when my soul craved it, and you do not really understand me." "I do not think so, either, nor would it be desirable for me to understand you in such a way that I craved just as much as you. But have you lost anything by not caring about it in that way? Consider the other side. Suppose, on the other hand, that the surrounding world had deceived you—and you do realize that it could have done that. More I did not say; I merely said that it is possible, and by that I also said that what you regarded as certainty was actually only a possibility. What then? Then you would have despaired, and you would not have had me to rely on. You do recollect, do you not, that the ship's council was almost of a mind to throw me overboard. Would you not be better off now by having lost some of that burning desire and having won the understanding that life cannot deceive you; is not that kind of losing a winning?"

That little secret we two have between us, as the deeper self said. What, presumably, is this secret, my listener? What else but this, that with regard to the external a person is capable of nothing at all. If he wants to seize the external immediately, it can be changed in the same instant, and he can be deceived; on the other hand, he can take it with the consciousness that it could also be changed, and he is not deceived even though it is changed, because he has the deeper self's consent. If he wants to act immediately in the external, to accomplish something, everything can come to nothing in that same moment; on the other hand, he can act with this consciousness, and even if it came to nothing, he is not deceived, because he has the deeper self's consent.

But even if the first self and the deeper self have been reconciled in this way and the shared mind has been diverted away from the external, this is still only the condition for coming to know himself. But if he is actually to know himself, there are new struggles and new dangers. Let not the struggling one himself simply be terrified and frightened by the thought, as if being in need were an imperfection when the discourse is about needing God, as if being in need were a humiliating secret one would rather conceal when the discourse is about needing God, as if being in need were a dismal necessity one would seek to mitigate by enunciating it oneself when the discourse is about needing God. Through more profound self-knowledge, one learns precisely that one needs God, but at first glance the discouraging aspect of this would frighten a person away from beginning if in due time he were not aware of and inspired by the thought that precisely this is

v
98

the perfection, inasmuch as not to need God is far more imperfect and only a misunderstanding. Even though someone had accomplished the most glorious exploits, if he still thought that it was all by his own power, if by overcoming his mind he became greater than someone who captured a city,[255] if he still thought it had happened through his own power, then his perfection would be essentially just a misunderstanding; but a perfection such as that would indeed be scarcely commendable. But the person who perceived that he was not capable of the least thing without God, unable even to be happy about the most happy event—he is closer to perfection. And the person who understood this and found no pain whatsoever in it but only the overabundance of bliss, who hid no secret desire that still preferred to be happy on its own account, felt no shame that people noticed that he himself was capable of nothing at all, laid down no conditions to God, not even that his weakness be kept concealed from others, but in whose heart joy constantly prevailed by his, so to speak, jubilantly throwing himself into God's arms in unspeakable amazement at God, who is capable of all things—indeed, he would be the perfect one whom the Apostle Paul describes better and more briefly: he "boasts of his weakness"[256] and has not even had experiences so numerous and ambiguous that he knows how to express himself more profusely. —People do say that not to know oneself is a deception and an imperfection, but often they are unwilling to understand that someone who actually knows himself perceives precisely that he is not capable of anything at all.

In the external world, he was capable of nothing; but in the internal world, is he not capable of anything there, either? If a capability is actually to be a capability, it must have opposition, because if it has no opposition, then it is either all-powerful or something imaginary. But if he is supposed to have opposition, from whence is it supposed to come? In the internal world, the opposition can come only from himself. Then he struggles with himself in the internal world, not as previously, where the deeper self struggled with the first self to prevent it from being occupied with the external. If a person does not discover this conflict, his understanding is faulty and consequently his life is imperfect; but if he does discover it, then he will once again understand that he himself is capable of nothing at all.

It seems odd that this is what a person is supposed to learn from himself. Then why praise self-knowledge? And yet this is the way it is, and from the whole world a person cannot learn that he is capable of nothing at all. Even if the whole world united to crush and annihilate the weakest, he nevertheless could still continually preserve a very faint idea that he himself was capable of something under other circumstances when the superior power was not as great. That he is capable of nothing at all, he can discover only by himself, and whether he is victorious over the whole world or trips over a straw, it is still the case that by himself he knows or can know that he himself is capable of nothing at all. If someone wants to explain it some other way, then he has indeed nothing to do with others but only with himself, and then every subterfuge is seen through. It is so hard, people think, to know oneself, especially if one is very talented and has a multitude of aptitudes and capabilities and then is supposed to become informed about all these. Oh, the self-knowledge of which we are speaking is really not complicated, and every time a person properly comprehends this brief and pithy truth, that he himself is capable of nothing at all, then he knows himself.

But is one not able, then, to overcome oneself by oneself? This certainly is said at times, but do you suppose that the one who says it has tested and understood himself in what was said: How can I be stronger than myself? I can be stronger than the weakest, and perhaps there lives or has lived someone who might be said to be stronger than all others, but no one was ever stronger than himself. When we speak of overcoming oneself by oneself, by this expression we really mean something external, so that the struggle is unequal. When, for example, someone who has been tempted by worldly prestige conquers himself so that he no longer reaches out for it; when someone who feared life's dangers drives out his fears to such an extent that he no longer flees the dangers; when someone who has lost his bold confidence overcomes himself to the point that he stands his ground and does not retreat from the place of decision—then we shall not depreciate this but praise him instead. But if he will take care not to save his soul in new vanity and drive out the devil with the devil's help,[257] then he will definitely admit that in his innermost being he is not able to overcome himself. But he by no means understands this as if evil had once and for all gained power over him—no, but he is able to do only so much, and this only by extreme effort, in resisting himself, but this, of course, is not overcoming himself. In other words, he creates in his innermost being temptations of glory and temptations of fear and temptations of despondency, of pride and of defiance and of sensuality greater than those he meets in the external world, and this is the very reason he struggles with himself. Otherwise, he struggles with a fortuitous degree of temptation, and the victory proves nothing with regard to what he would be able to do in a greater temptation. If he is victorious in the temptation with which the surrounding world confronts him, this does not prove that he would be victorious if the temptation were as terrible as he is able to imagine it, but not until it appears that immense does he actually learn to know himself. It now appears that immense to him in his inner being, and this is why he knows in himself—something that he perhaps would not come to know in the world—that he is capable of nothing at all.

V
101

My listener, you certainly do not believe that these are the somber thoughts of a "thick-blooded" man; you do not thank God that you are not ravaged by depression [*Tungsindighed*] such as this, do you? If it were depression, is this the way one ought to love God and human beings? [You certainly do not believe] that one thanks God for preferential love, which is indeed to deceive him and give him to understand that if something more oppressive happened one could not believe in his love (because, with this confession, to thank God for not having been tried in the severest conflict becomes something altogether different). [You certainly do not believe] that one shuns the depressed person, as you call him, does not wish to

know that he, too, is a human being, and you dare not say that
he is a criminal, consequently that he is an unhappy human
being, consequently a human being who particularly needs
your sympathy, which you show to him by requesting him to
roam like a leper out among the tombs,[258] while you dare not
acknowledge him as a fellow human being. But if speaking
this way about understanding oneself is regarded by someone
as the somber thoughts of a "thick-blooded" individual, then
it surely must be regarded as foolishness inseparable from his
depression for him to think that this view regarded man according to his perfection and even greater foolishness for him
to rejoice in his perfection. But why should he not be happy,
since one is always made happy by the perfect, and this joy of
his would not rest in a light-minded understanding with
God's preferential love for one individual, and this joy of his
would not shun the sight of the inconsolable one—on the contrary, he would love in him everyone who is inconsolable.
[259]And this is the way it really is, and you, my listener, surely
will not call him depressed, since, on the contrary, he alone is
happy, because someone who is happy in and over God rejoices, and again I say—he rejoices. Why, do you suppose,
does the Apostle Paul, who has given us this beautiful admonition, "Rejoice, and again I say, rejoice,"[260] why, do you suppose, does he pause; why, do you suppose, does he stop before
once again bidding the believer to be happy? Because in an
interlude he took the time to listen, as it were, to everything
terrible that may be uttered, the terrible thought that a person
is capable of nothing at all, in order to allow joy to be totally
victorious—"again I say, rejoice."

This view, that to need God is a human being's highest perfection, does indeed make life more difficult, but it also views
life according to its perfection, and in this view a person,
through the piecemeal experience of [this need], which is the
right understanding with God, comes *to know God*.

Insofar as a person does not know himself in such a way that
he knows that he himself is capable of nothing at all, he does
not actually become conscious in the deeper sense that God *is*
[*er til*]. Even though a person mentions his name at times, calls

V
102

322   *Four Upbuilding Discourses* (1844)

upon him occasionally, perhaps in the more momentous decisions thinks he sees him and is moved (since it is impossible, after all, to catch even a glimpse of God without being moved), he is nevertheless somewhat piously deceived if he therefore believes it is manifest to him that God *is* or that the being [*Tilværelse*] of God would not have another manifestness in this earthly life, the meaning of which is continually confused if God is not implicitly understood. We say that it is a pious deception; we call it by as beautiful a name as possible; we have no intention of plunging into a tirade against it, even though we desire for everyone that it may become manifest with an otherwise decisive certitude that God *is*.

The person who himself is capable of nothing at all cannot undertake the least thing without God's help, consequently without becoming conscious that there is a God. We sometimes speak of learning to know God from the history of past ages; we take out the chronicles and read and read. Well, that may be all right, but how much time it takes, and how dubious the outcome frequently is, how close at hand the misunderstanding that lies in the sensate person's marveling over what is ingenious! But someone who is conscious that he is capable of nothing at all has every day and every moment the desired and irrefragable opportunity to experience that God lives. If he does not experience it often enough, he knows very well why that is. It is precisely because his understanding is faulty and he believes that he himself is capable of something. When he goes into the house of the Lord, he knows very well that God is not there, but he also knows that he himself is capable of nothing at all, not even of inducing a devotional mood, and consequently God must be present if he is actually moved. Alas, there are many who otherwise remain unconcerned about God but who still do not fail to enter the house of the Lord. What a strange contradiction—they gather together there and say to one another: God is not here, he does not dwell in a house built by human hands;²⁶¹ then they go home, but at home God is not there at all. But the person who knows himself in the way mentioned is well aware that God does not dwell in temples, but he also knows that God is with

V
103

him at night when sleep refreshes and when he awakens in an alarming dream, is with him in the day of need when he is searching in vain for comfort, in the tumult of ideas when he listens in vain for a liberating word, in mortal danger when the world does not help, in his anxiety when he is afraid of himself, in the moment of despair when he is working out his soul's salvation in fear and trembling.[262] He knows that God is with him in the moment when anxiety rushes upon him with lightning speed, when it already seems too late and there is no time left to go to the house of the Lord; then he is with him, swifter than the light that pierces the darkness, swifter than the thought that chases away the fog—present—yes, present as swiftly as only one can be who was already present. If this were not so, where would the express messenger be found who would go fast enough for the anxious concern to fetch the Lord, and before he came, more time would again pass! But such is not the case; the only one who thinks that way is the one who thinks that he himself is capable of some thing.

It is certainly true that one can learn to know God in exactly the same way on the day of rejoicing, if one comprehends that one is capable of nothing at all, but to hold on to this on the day of rejoicing is very difficult.[263] When a person is most happy, there is suddenly the tempting thought: Would it not be even more glorious if he himself were capable of all this? Then the rejoicing takes an improper turn, so that it does not rise up to God but swings away from him, and then, then it is a sign that one needs more practice. When everything is shaking again, when thought is confused, when memory wants to terminate its service, when past experience approaches one only alarmingly in the form of terror, when even the most honest intention becomes dishonesty to oneself through the treachery of anxiety—then a person again understands that he himself is capable of nothing at all. But in and with this understanding God is also present immediately, rules the confusion and remembers everything that has been confided to him, which, no doubt, the person being tried has done—in the maelstrom of spiritual trial, the outcome of which would seem to have to be more terrible than death, he has with the greatest haste confided to God what lay especially upon his mind, what would have destroyed him forever and changed the content of his life to a dreadful deception if he himself had forgotten it and God in heaven had also forgotten it. No doubt he has confided it to God, until with God he again fought his way through the terrors, had patience, and gained calmness through trust in God.

If a person whose life has been tried in some crucial difficulty has a friend and sometime later he is unable to retain the past clearly, if anxiety creates confusion, and if accusing thoughts assail him with all their might as he works his way back, then he may go to his friend and say, "My soul is sick so that nothing will become clear to me, but I confided everything to you; you remember it, so please explain the past to me again." But if a person has no friend, he presumably goes to God if under other circumstances he has confided something to him, if in the hour of decision he called God as witness[264] when no one else understood him. And the one who went to his friend perhaps was not understood at times, perhaps was filled with self-loathing, which is even more oppressive, upon discovering that the one to whom he had confided his troubles had not understood him at all, even though he had listened, had not sensed what was making him anxious, but had only an inquisitive interest in his unusual encounter with life. [265]But this would never happen with God; who would dare to venture to think this of God, even if (because he does not dare to think this of God) he is cowardly enough to prefer to forget God—until he stands face-to-face with the judge, who passes judgment on him but not on the one who truly has God as witness, because where God is the judge, there is indeed no judge if God is the witness.

It by no means follows, however, that a person's life becomes easy because he learns to know God in this way. On the contrary, it can become very hard; it may, as stated before, become more difficult than the contemptible easiness of sensate human life, but in this difficulty his life also acquires ever deeper and deeper meaning. Should it mean nothing to him that he continually keeps his eyes on God, that he, although he himself is capable of nothing at all, with God is capable of ever more and more—that he is capable of overcoming himself, since with the help of God he is indeed capable of this! Should it have no meaning for him that he is learning ever more and more to die to the world,[266] to esteem less and less the external, what life gives and takes, what he himself is permitted to achieve in the external world, but to be all the more concerned about the internal, about an understanding with God, about having to remain in it and in it to learn to know God as one who makes everything serve a person for good if he loves God?[267] And should this not even have meaning for him in making the adversities of life lighter, since it is always true that the person who has something else to think about and thereby is kept from being occupied with grief finds it lighter? Finally, should it not have meaning for him and be a blessed reward that he most vividly and confidently understood that God is love,[268] that God's goodness passes all understanding,[269] and that he was not contented with the witness of others or with a view of the order of the world and the course of history, though this may well be far greater, but there is also the question of how one understands this so that one may truly benefit from it.

V
105

We are not saying that knowing God or almost sinking into a dreaming admiration and a visionary contemplation of God is the only glorious thing to do; God does not let himself be taken in vain in this way. Just as knowing oneself in one's own nothingness is the condition for knowing God, so knowing God is the condition for the sanctification of a human being by God's assistance and according to his intention. Wherever God is in truth, there he is always creating. He does not want a person to be spiritually soft and to bathe in the contemplation of his glory, but in becoming known by a person he wants to create in him a new human being.

Suppose, let us just assume this, that a person could be just as ennobled and developed by himself without knowing God. With this presupposition, then I ask you, my listener, would not knowing God in and by itself have the highest meaning, and if a choice is conceivable—that a person could go just as far by himself as by knowing God—what would you choose? Even in human affairs you would probably choose the latter, since if you could be developed just as much in your solitariness, if that were possible, as by learning to know someone to whom you were strongly attracted, your learning to know him would in and by itself indeed have the most beautiful meaning. —The most beautiful meaning? Alas, no, you know very well that it is quite otherwise, at least when we speak of God; to know God is crucial, and without this knowledge a human being would become nothing at all, yes, perhaps would scarcely be able to grasp the first mystery of truth, that he himself is nothing at all, and then even less that to need God is his highest perfection.

II CORINTHIANS 12:7

Since the importance of Holy Scripture is to be an interpreter of the divine to mankind, since its claim is to want to teach the believer everything from the beginning, it follows of itself that its language has shaped the discourse of the God-fearing about the divine, that its words and expressions resound again and again in the holy places, in every more solemn discourse about the divine, whether the speaker seeks to interpret the scriptural text by letting the text speak for itself or is using the scriptural expression in all its brevity as the clear and complete interpretation of the much he has said. But also in everyday and secular speech we sometimes hear a scriptural expression that has wandered from the sacred out into the world—wandered, because the way in which it is used indicates adequately that it did not leave home voluntarily and is now circulating among the secular affairs of men in order to win someone, but that it has been carried off. The person using it is not moved by the biblical expression, does not let his thoughts trace it back to its earnest place in the sacred context, is not dismayed by the idea that it is sacrilegious to use the expression in this way, even though people regard it, far from being an effrontery, as merely a piece of innocent light-mindedness.

One such biblical expression frequently encountered where least expected and at times put to a most inappropriate use[271] is the phrase just read: the thorn in the flesh. But just as this misuse is in itself regrettable (we are thinking not of the presumption of brash mockery but only of the passing use of the phrase as a witticism, the jesting connection that light-mindedness makes with life's trifles), so in a very special way it can also have the sad consequence, if someone suddenly starts to think of the dangers of the lofty life the text speaks about, that one is overwhelmed with anxiety, just as when someone has

v
107

held in his hand and played with a deadly weapon without knowing that it was deadly. And appalling, indeed, just as deadly, the expression really is, inasmuch as it testifies to the deep pain that is the contrast and successor to what is more glorious than any earthly happiness, than the most glorious conception of any merely human thought, the contrast to the supreme blessedness, such as this is experienced when it is inexpressible. The expression has the accent of total earnestness when used by the Apostle Paul, a man who did not experience ups and downs such as that because he had given his life over as prey to the passions, since, on the contrary, this deepest experience and the full assurance of insight had given him an assured spirit.

Is this not appalling! A person is looking for peace, but there is change: day and night, summer and winter, life and death; a person is looking for peace, but there is change: fortune and misfortune, joy and sorrow; a person is looking for peace and constancy, but there is change: the ardor of purpose and the disgust of weakness, the greenwood of expectancy and the withered splendor of fulfillment; a person is looking for peace—where did he not look for it—even in the disquietude of distraction—where did he not look for it in vain— even in the grave!

But an apostle—he uses the strongest expression about a thorn in the flesh, about an angel of Satan who strikes him on the mouth and thereby prevents him from declaring that inexpressible blessedness. Is it so, then, that the more zealously one presses forward, the more dangerous everything becomes? Is it so, then, that every zealousness consumes the zealous, and most appallingly when it is zeal for God in the service of the Lord? No, the apostle does not speak like an incited man who is merely a desperate witness to how he himself has been tumbled about and at best knows how to describe his ups and downs. That he is not permitted to remain in the third heaven, indeed, that it is an angel of Satan who fetches him down again and strikes him on the mouth—this he knows. He knows that in a certain sense the joining of earthly life with beatitude is always an unhappy marriage and that the truly beatific union is concluded only in heaven, just as it was concluded there in the beginning; but he also knows that it is beneficial to him, and that this thorn in the flesh is given him so that he will not be arrogant. The mark of the apostle is that he does not become unsteady, which may happen even to the most honest person who experienced the blessedness of heaven, but who also, when the thorn began to pain and fester, knew of nothing to do but to moan. Not so the apostle. When the angel of Satan darts out from his darkness, when he comes with the speed of lightning to terrify the apostle, it is indeed an angel of Satan, as the apostle says, but if he nevertheless knows that it is beneficial to him, then that terror is no longer an angel of Satan, because no one has ever heard that an angel of Satan came to benefit a human being. It is not the case, as human flabbiness might wish, that the highest life is without dangerous suffering, but it is the case that an apostle is never without an explanation, never without authority.

Having traced the phrase back to the Bible passage, the biblical expression back to its source, the Apostle Paul, we come to our text, where we now read it. Here it has been read repeatedly, again and again. Here the scholars have interpreted it. Who would ever finish if he were to mention the ingenuity and the nonsense that have assisted in or wanted to assist in explaining this passage, which, once it had the reputation of being a riddle, seemed to give everyone an unusually propitious opportunity to become an interpreter of the Bible. — Here a futilely troubled sufferer read it until he found comfort, not in the apostolic upbuilding but in the accidental circumstance that he suffered from the very same physical ailment that the apostle, according to his interpretation of the words, has suggested. —Here a depressed young person read it, although in his reading he did not draw comfort for himself from the book but anxiety into his soul so that he did not even have the courage to ask anyone for the explanation. Alas, he perhaps never found any explanation, but this anxiety about an inexplicable terror became for him his thorn in the flesh. — Here a self-appointed apostle found a prooftext for his being a chosen instrument of God, because he indeed had a thorn in the flesh. —Here a cowardly believer read it and thought that such a thing happened only to an apostle, not to him, who in his own eyes was indeed humble enough not to aspire to something great, all the less so since the thought of the suffering connected with it was already enough for his cowardliness. —Here a simple, devout person read it and read it many times but never thought that he had really understood it, since he had a low opinion of himself and his sufferings compared with an apostle's.[272]

This has now been said,[273] but before anyone looks to an apostle for comfort in his suffering and guidance in his battle, let him search himself thoroughly to see whether his suffering might not have to be judged with a smile, to see whether life has tested him so earnestly that his wanting to be helped by an apostle is not a joke, to see whether he is prepared in earnest to find that an apostle does not have many moments to waste on worldly sorrows, that the apostle hastily leads him from the struggle that may already seem hard enough to the sufferer and leads him into the crucial struggle where the suffering of which the apostle speaks belongs.

Oh, let us never take the sacred in vain. How often have we not coddled the flesh by using the highest and strongest comfort to soothe worldly sorrows and refusing to understand that the word of comfort must first of all wound more deeply before it can heal. Has God ever made a covenant with a person regarding the external? Does it perhaps apply to every suffering that one is to thank God because one has not been tried in it? What about the suffering in which the soul battles through to faith or the one in which faith is victorious over the world?[274] What about the pain in which hope is born or that in which it becomes unshakable? [275]What about the process of being consumed in which self-love breathes its last until love learns to know God, or what about the wretchedness in which the external being fades away until the inner being untangles itself from the corruption?[276] But if praying in this way is not to be called wisdom, if a wisdom of that sort is rather to be called by its proper name, if it is to be called foolishness that has lost the sense of the spirit and cannot under-

stand anything spiritually,[277] if it is to be called cowardliness
that wants to be made happy in a splendid misunderstanding
and wants to remain ignorant that it is a misunderstanding, if
it is to be called effrontery to God because, tempted by human
pitiableness, it wants to remodel him, if it is to be called
treachery to mankind because it wants to defraud the sacred
of its meaning, the struggling one of the other's gratitude, the
victorious one of his reward—then it certainly would be better
to speak in another way of that kind of suffering.

We must warn here against wanting to play the hero,
against wanting to be a warrior at one's own expense,[278]
against wanting to be one's own teacher who determines the
degree of suffering and calculates the advantages. We must
warn that no one is tried in a self-made conflict but is only
cultivated in a new vanity so that the last becomes worse than
the first.[279] But then we are also reminded that suffering is a
component and that no one enters the kingdom of heaven
without suffering.[280] Just to be reminded of it is instructive,
lest the distress of spiritual trial come upon one as unexpectedly as a thief in the night,[281] as birth pangs to one who had
no presentiment of giving birth.[282] See, the apostle has done
this. He himself was the most severely tried, inasmuch as he
experienced sufferings that until then no man had experienced—as surely, that is, as there was a higher life in an apostle   v
than in any previous human being, which of course signifies   110
that the sufferings also are more agonizing. He experienced
them in such a way that he could not seek anyone else's guidance or be strengthened by anyone else's experience. But then
he also left behind him a witness, and "the thorn in the flesh"
became a warning, a reminder, that wherever a person goes
he walks in danger,[283] that even the one who grasps at the
highest is still only aspiring to it, pursued by that angel of Satan, whose assault, just like everything else, must nevertheless
serve the believer for good.[284]

The discourse, however, does not aspire at this time to apostolic comforting or seek to speak to anyone to reassure but
wants, if possible, to speak to terrify. There is a profound and
inscrutable meaning in existence, an agreement entered into

from eternity regarding the earthly and the moment of the heavenly, a marvelous correlation between what belongs together: sorrow and comfort. Therefore, when a person laments that there is no comfort for him, that his suffering is immeasurable, it is because he does not comprehend deeply enough the terror and the distress and because he still prefers to let everything be confused and to seek distraction in the empty solace that there was no comfort, rather than to judge himself and humble himself under the assurance that there is no suprahuman temptation.[285] We shall now, therefore, speak of:

The Thorn in the Flesh.

As everyone knows, the Apostle Paul was a man tried in all kinds of sufferings.[286] Therefore, if the person who suffers, instead of seeking guidance in the comfort offered, becomes crafty, as so often happens, and diverts himself instead by considering whether the speaker is actually tried, tried exactly as he himself is, since otherwise, of course, he lacks experience; if the sufferer, prey to the insidious fabrications of this concealed vanity, would reject the usually reliable testimony of many witnesses—he nevertheless surely will not reject the Apostle Paul. So, then, list your sufferings, or if the sophistry of your sorrow has even made you envious of the apostle and of his intrepidity, then invent sufferings—you no doubt will find the apostle tried in them, even if you do not manage to fashion him to your fancy, to stop him in the race, so that with you he becomes prolix in the prolixity of sufferings. Just as the eye cannot really catch hold of someone who runs, because he is running, so also with sufferings; future sufferings have no time to terrify the apostle, and past sufferings have no time to hold him fast, because he is running. But he nevertheless has experienced suffering, and one is not to teach the apostle that suffering becomes more terrifying if one sits still, enervated by the past, only anxiously occupied with the future, but one shall instead learn from an apostle to run and finish the race.[287]

List, then, the hardships, those that destroy a person by

pouring all the agony into the brevity of a moment, the protracted ones that slowly torture the soul out of the body; list being derided as mentally disordered, being shunned as an offense; list the mortal danger, nakedness, imprisonment, chains;[288] list all the profound indignities of misunderstanding; list finding all asleep[289] except misunderstanding; list being hailed as a false god when one is an apostle;[290] list being forgotten once one is gone, seeing the good cause abandoned by friends who became cowardly and were supported by enemies who aimed at confusion;[291] list being forsaken by the person on whom one is relying, being forsaken by the weakling who wants to help himself,[292] being regarded as a seducer when one is a witness to the truth,[293] as giving sin a pretext for new sin when one is a teacher of truth,[294] being thought of as weak when one is gentle,[295] arrogant when one is vigorous, selfish when one has a fatherly concern.[296] Continue, if you like— you will find the apostle tried in them. But he still does not call all these sufferings the thorn in the flesh.

The difference is that all these sufferings are only in the external world, even the concern about the congregation, even the profound grief of misunderstanding; however oppressive they are to him, he still has nothing for which to reproach himself. During all this suffering, the assurance that he is in harmony with God is dominant. Even though the course of life witnesses against him, as if God is gone from the world and leaves himself without witness, since the witness that everyone, even an apostle, best understands is that the good for which he works is advancing, that the truth he proclaims is triumphant, that the holy cause for which he battles has its blessing, and the work its reward, and the toil its fruitfulness, and the effort its meaning, and the struggle its decision, and the sleepless days and nights a glorious application—even though the world and everything visible seem to be forsaken by God, he still has the witness of the spirit that he is God's co-worker.[297] What, then, is the distress! Everything can change even in the next moment; even if God has gone away, he is still in heaven, where the apostle sees him and the Son of Man at the right hand of power, not sitting there—ah, how could he sit when the apostle is forsaken like this—no, he has arisen, and the apostle sees him as Stephen[298] saw him, standing at the right hand of power, swift to help. Indeed, even if everything is to be rendered futile, is to be blown away like a fantasy, even if nothing, nothing whatever, is to be achieved and the suffering is the one and only actuality, even if the unremitting sacrifice of a long life is to become meaningless like shadowboxing[299] in the air, the apostle is still assured that neither angels nor devils nor things present nor things past nor things future will be able to separate him from the love[300] in which God's witness testifies in his heart! And then what is all earthly suffering compared with this blessedness! Although the apostle is present in the flesh, is he nevertheless not absent, far away, so that those who think to wound him are only deceived! What an empty fancy a prison is when the prisoner it confines is caught up into the third heaven! What is the sense of ridiculing someone who hears nothing but unutterable speech, of executing someone who is absent!

Caught up into the third heaven! On the whole, Paul was not unfamiliar with what is gratifying in life:[301] he dared to hope that he might even reach Spain[302] with the proclamation of the Word, that upon his departure from a congregation he would leave behind some who had been won, some strengthened, some rewon, that he would leave this congregation in order to journey to another, that some would still remain true to him, that occasionally his fatherly concern would also win him a son's devotion. How moved Paul is in speaking of this, how thankful he is! When his desire was fulfilled, when he longed no more to see the loved ones, when he was present with them, when he shared the gifts of the spirit with them and he himself was strengthened by strengthening and enriching others—how glorious his joy must have been, like his words for it! But this expression—to be caught up into the third heaven, to be made a participant in sublime revelations, to sense an inexpressible beatitude—this he cannot use and has not used to describe that beautiful joy he shared with others. But that inexpressible beatitude he could not express—alas, and to prevent it, he was given a thorn in the flesh.

Consequently, that suffering and this beatitude correspond to each other. If that beatitude is reserved only for an apostle, then let no one fear the suffering. But if that is the case, then there is nothing to speak about, and it is not even worth speaking about, and it is inexplicable that the apostle has written about it in the first place. To be sure, he is brief about it, and his description thereby turns out to be vastly different from the fiction and nonsense that are embellished with sacred names, but an apostle is certainly the last person to write riddles that no one can solve, but that at best delay anyone who wants to solve them. An apostle who is trying to be all things to all people[303] is surely the last one to want to be something so singular that with respect to this he would become absolutely nothing to anyone. So banish all curiosity, which is doomed without even knowing it, since its doom is either that it is unable to understand it or that it will be able to understand it, and its sin is either that it neglects lesser matters in order to drop off into reverie about riddles or that it craftily applies its talents to making them ununderstandable and hypocritically pretends that this is a desire for understanding.

Let everyone test himself. With regard to what he has experienced, let him be true to himself, but let no one forget that blessedness of the spirit and suffering of the spirit are not something external of which one can honestly and truly say: The circumstances of my life did not provide me the opportunity to experience this. In the world of the spirit, there is neither sport nor spook; there luck and chance do not make one person a king, another a beggar, one person as beautiful as an Oriental queen, another more wretched than Lazarus.[304] In the world of the spirit, the only one who is shut out is the one who shuts himself out; in the world of the spirit, all are invited, and therefore what is said about it can be said safely and undauntedly; if it pertains to one single person it pertains to all. Why, then, this curiosity in guessing about what God has given every human being the opportunity to experience, indeed, has been made so available that it even may be said: He must have understood it.

If a person died without having understood what it must be

V
113

to be rich, or to be beautiful, or to be a king, or how it must be to be unappreciated, inferior, poor, blind from birth, rejected by his generation, if he died without understanding that venerable wise man's puzzling words about the most beautiful meaning of earthly life, that whether one marries or does not marry, one will regret both[305]—do you suppose that he could therefore be legitimately charged with not having made good use of life? But if a person died and had never experienced what it is to struggle with God, is this a sign that the person being buried had been uncommonly great in the fear of God? Or if he had never experienced what it is to be forsaken by God,[306] would this be a sign that the person being buried had in a special sense been a favorite of the Lord? Or if he had never experienced the Lord's wrath and its consuming fire, indeed, never dreamed that there was any such thing, would this be assumed to be his comfort in death, his righteousness at the judgment, a sign to him that more than anyone else he had been God's friend, or would it be assumed to be adequate for him to answer: I have not had the opportunity to experience anything like this? Alas, suppose such a person nevertheless wanted to explain that expression, suppose that it developed that he had also understood the meaning of a thorn in the flesh, namely, that it was the spirit that had become a thorn in the flesh to him and only when it was gone would he have overcome his pain, cast out his anxiety, which not even love will cast out completely,[307] which faith was not capable of casting out completely, not even in an apostle.

The thorn in the flesh, then, is the contrast to the spirit's inexpressible beatitude, and the contrast cannot be in the external, as if sufferings, chains, the scourges of misunderstanding, and the terrors of death could take it away from him, or as if all the progress of learning and all the victories of faith in the wide world could fully compensate him for the deprivation. As soon as the suffering is perceived and the thorn festers, the apostle has only himself to deal with. The beatitude has vanished, vanishes more and more—alas, it was inexpressible to have it; the pain is inexpressible since it cannot even express the loss, and recollection is unable to do anything but languish in powerlessness! [308]To have been caught up into the third heaven, to have been hidden in the bosom of beatitude, to have been expanded in God, and now to be tethered by the thorn in the flesh to the thralldom of temporality! To have been made rich in God,[309] inexpressibly so, and now to be broken down to flesh and blood, to dust and corruption! To have been himself present before God and now to be forsaken by God, forsaken by himself, comforted only by a poor, demented recollection! It is hard enough for a person to experience the faithlessness of men, but to experience that there is a change in God, a shadow of variation,[310] that there is an angel of Satan that has the power to tear a person out of this beatitude! Where, then, is there security for a human being if it is not even in the third heaven!

But let us not go astray; this is how a worldling would talk who certainly knew what he was talking about and witnessed only to what he had experienced but did not know how to speak as humbly as an apostle, resigned to the will of God in whatever happens. The apostle declares that he knows that this variation is beneficial for him. How simple, how straightforward, how quiet these words! After having spoken of the most beatific and the most oppressive in the strongest terms, after having won and lost, and then to be so composed! My listener, if you are familiar with what others say who have experienced something similar, then you presumably have heard instead a scream of anxiety that now everything was lost forever, a cry of despair that never again would they taste this beatitude.[311] —But woe to the person who wants to be excused from suffering!

That apostolic expression, however, certainly does not indicate only the forsakenness, the suffering of separation, which is even more terrible than the separation of death, since death only separates a person from the temporal and therefore is a release, whereas this separation shuts him out from the eternal and therefore is an imprisonment that again leaves the spirit sighing in the fragile earthen vessel, in the cramped space, in the status of an alien,[312] because the home of the spirit is in the eternal and the infinite. In that very moment, every-

V
115

thing begins, as it were, from the beginning. The person who has been outside himself returns to himself, but this condition, to be by oneself in this way, is not the condition of freedom and of the liberated. So the inexpressible beatitude is gone, and the harvest song of joy is silenced; again there will be sowing in tears,[313] and the spirit will again sit oppressed, will sigh once again, and only God knows what the sigh does not comprehend, to what extent the harp of joy will be tuned again in the secret soul.[314] He has returned to himself; he is no longer beatific by being rescued from himself to himself and to being transfigured in God—so that the past must let go of him and is powerless to condemn him because the self-accusation is mitigated, forgotten in the understanding with Governance's inscrutable wisdom, in the blessed instruction of a reconciliation; so that the eternal fears no future, indeed, hopes for no future, but love possesses everything without ceasing, and there is no shadow of variation. As soon as he returns to himself, he understands this no more. [315]He understands, however, what bitter experiences have only all too unforgettably inculcated, the self-accusation, if the past has the kind of claim upon his soul that no repentance can entirely redeem, no trusting in God can entirely wipe out, but only God himself in the inexpressible silence of beatitude.

The more of the past a person's soul can still keep when he is left to himself, the more profound he is! The brutish comfort that time wipes out everything is even more terrible than the most terrible recollection; and thoughtlessness, which jokes with time and flirts with eternity, helps, as is natural, only the one who "drowsily goes his giddy way";[316] and proud poverty, the glittering squalor of perdition, which lets time go its way, indeed, does not even desire the "boredom" of eternity (although it could be that heaven has contemplated new diversions with which their superior requirements could manage to make shift)—all this is simply anathema, whatever the world wants to call it.

No, time as such will not help a person to forget the past, even though it mitigates the impression; but even if a person— far from self-tormentingly damning himself again and again to consuming its bitterness—allows time, the experienced one, to advise, the past is still not therefore completely forgotten, to say nothing of being entirely annihilated. Only the blessedness of eternity is capable of this, because the soul is entirely filled with it. The reason distraction can help the light-minded forget and a kind of busy activity can help the more thoughtless blot out the past is that distraction and worldly busyness entirely fill their souls. But the more profound a person is, the less this succeeds, and only the blessedness of heaven is adequate to this difficulty, the difficulty of which still requires earnestness for comprehension in the first place. To human understanding, if it is awake at all, to human thought, if it has become at all sober, is it not the most improbable thing of all that anything can be forgotten—indeed, that God can forget anything? In other words, it is not so very difficult to grasp that human thoughtlessness is capable of forgetting even the most important matter. In the moment of blessedness, it is forgotten or it is coexistent with the blessedness, but when a person returns to himself, this is the most improbable of all. And yet this improbability, as is always the case with the improbable, is the beginning of the highest life and is the inscrutable secret. This highest life never attains its perfect form in time, above all not in any meaningless way, as if little by little, perhaps by way of custom and reduction, this improbability would become probable in the understanding of thoughtlessness and according to the conception of spiritlessness. Opposed by probability, to which he must continually die, he can aspire to it only in faith. If faith acquired a probability, then everything would be destroyed and faith would be confused, since this would show that it had not performed the preliminary task and therefore had allowed itself to be confounded with thoughtlessness, which comes most easily to the animal. On the other hand, in an earlier age the meaning of life was assumed to be that one first understood the difficulty before jubilating over the explanation or finding it impossible to stop with the ordinary explanation, that one was first seized with terror before singing victory hymns.

We do not know the life of Paul in great detail, but we do,

however, know Paul, which is the main consideration. That is to say, just as the sensate man is distinguishable by his seeing the speck in his brother's eye but not seeing the log in his own,[317] by his rigorously condemning the same fault in others that he lightly forgives in himself, so the mark of a more profound and concerned person is that he judges himself most rigorously, uses all his ingenuity to excuse another person but is unable to excuse or forgive himself, indeed, is convinced that the other one is more excusable, because there is always still a possibility, since the only one in relation to whom a person is deprived of this possibility is he himself. Bold confidence is a difficult matter, because it is not exactly synonymous with mental weakness. One may very well stop with it and need not go further by even wishing to judge God, that is, if in other respects bold confidence is bold confidence in the judgment,[318] which certainly requires that God's judgment penetrate the thought and heart, that is, if it is bold confidence in God's mercy and these words are not a feigned pious expression of one's own thoughtlessness, which does not trust in God but is consoled by having ceased to sorrow long ago. If no human being is capable of acquitting himself, he is capable of one thing—of indicting himself so terribly that he cannot acquit himself but learns to need mercy. With regard to this, it is difficult for one person to understand another, [319]because the earnest person always lays the stress on himself.

Paul's life had been very dramatic, and just as the apostle's restless activity harvested many, many happy recollections for him, so also his earlier turmoil, when he kicked against the goads with all his might,[320] wounded him for the rest of his life with a recollection that festers in the flesh like a thorn, which like an angel of Satan silences him. Leave it to a worldly admiration to think that Paul was always great, that even in his error there was something extraordinary. Anyone who seeks comfort or instruction from an apostle quickly sees that an apostle aspires not to the lofty and to the extraordinary but to the humble—why, then, has Paul not earnestly conceived the past? True, in a unique sense he had become another man, a new creature;[321] he had not just changed his name, but in another sense he was still the same man. True, the past was shoved back; it could not acquire the power to seize him with its terror when he was running toward the perfect. True, he was not sitting still, spellbound in a ring of memories of the past, since wherever he went he made everything new.[322] True, he had experienced the beatitude of heaven and had kept the pledge of the spirit, but there was nevertheless a memory. And a memory is difficult to manage. At one time it is far away, and then, presto, it is right there as if it had never been forgotten.

When he preached Christ and him crucified[323]—crucified— that was indeed what the Jews shouted. Where was Paul when this happened? We do not know, but when Stephen was stoned he sat there and guarded the garments of the execution- ers.[324] What if he had paused for a moment in the race, what if the recollection had misled him so that he did not hear the preaching but the scream, did not himself preach but threat- ened! When he preached Christ as the Way, as the Way he him- self had trodden and to which he had directed many, this Way had indeed existed before Paul trod it. It had also existed when Saul received permission from the Sanhedrin to imprison those "who were of that Way";[325] consequently, he trod it also at the time when he raved against the Christians with murder and threats.

True, Paul had captured free men since that time, far more and far, far more securely than when he had led them captive to Jerusalem, but those unfortunates—where were they now? [326]What if he had stood still, what if recollection had overtaken him so that he had sunk into apprehensive ruminating about ever being able to find those unfortunates again! What if doubt had become dominant—whether all his activity, whether pro- claiming the Word to all people, was what he was supposed to do! Surely Saul thought that his zeal was an ardor pleasing to God—oh, but precisely this, this having to catch himself or be caught in a self-deception such as that, and consequently hav- ing to repent of what he regarded as pleasing to God [327](what an upheaval in thought and mind, what a sign of terror, what

a difficulty for repentance to grasp its object and to hold it: to
have to repent of the best that one has done, indeed, what one
even regarded as pleasing to God), and consequently in that
connection to have to repent of the screams of the persecuted,
the misery of the prisoners (what a labor for repentance, since
it certainly was not Saul's desire to do this but zeal, as he
thought, for the good cause), and then as reward for his zeal
to have to harvest not only the ingratitude of men but the bitterness of repentance because he had raved! Paul was brought
to Agrippa in chains, and the king said to him: You are raving,
Paul.[328] What if these words—you are raving—had halted
him, [329]had given an opportunity for the confounding of recollection; what if that holy fieriness that burned in him, a well-
pleasing offering to God, had again become raving; what if he
had become a self-torturer in order to praise God, because that
also requires a great soul!

But Paul knew that it was an angel of Satan—alas, therefore
he does not turn aside—but he knew that it was beneficial for
him that it happened and therefore also knew that this angel
of Satan was nevertheless an emissary of God. Is this not a
marvel—to change an angel of Satan into an emissary of
God—would not Satan himself grow weary! When an angel
of darkness arrays himself in all his terror, convinced that if he
just makes Paul look at him he will petrify him, when at the
outset he jeers at Paul for not having the courage to do it, then
the apostle looks at him, does not quickly shrink back in anxiety, does not strike him down in terror, does not reconnoiter
with hesitant glances, but looks at him fixedly and steadfastly.
The longer he looks, the more clearly he perceives that it is an
emissary of God who is visiting him, a friendly spirit who
wishes him well. One almost sympathizes with the poor
devil, who wants to be so terrifying and then stands there un-
masked, changed into the opposite, and thinking only of making his escape.[330]

Then the past was behind; repentance held it captive, cut
away the connection with it, resisted it, whether it wanted to
launch a joint offensive, or a single renegade tried to make a
surprise attack. Faith kept the rebellious thoughts in obedience

under the grace of God, which comforted the apostle beyond
all measure, since he knew that he was indeed an unprofitable
servant, the least of the apostles, unfit to be called an apostle
because he had persecuted the Church of God (I Corinthians
15:9). If Paul had wanted to gauge his apostolic work and let
it try to compensate for the past, the rebellion would have
erupted, and not even Paul would have been able to stop it;[331]
whereas now it became for him a thorn in the flesh, not in
itself, but because the inexpressible beatitude had departed
from him.

    v
    120

But this rebellion continually ponders the past; it will come
again as the future with new terror. There is no security in
time so that a person can say with worldly composure, "peace
and security,"[332] unless he finds comfort in thoughtlessness.
The thing to do, then, is to run—alas, one would so like to
run faster and faster, but as long as one is running in time one
does not run past time.

[333]You who know what the discourse is about—[334]call it an
escape by which you already had almost slipped behind the
curtain that separates you from all the world's terror and distress, rescued from the snare of relapse you left behind long
ago—but there was still a little something lacking. Call it a
struggle in which you already had been almost victorious,
and, [335]although exhausted, you felt all your power in the last
lap, in which you were going to grasp the treasure[336] for all
eternity—but there was still a little something lacking. Call it
a glorious ending of the arduous wandering in the fog of unintelligibility, when the explanation illuminated [*lyste ind*] it
and explained the suffering and the loss and the danger and
the difficulty and the meaning of the anxiety and pronounced
[*lyste*] the blessed peace of understanding upon it—but there
was still one little word lacking.

You who know what the discourse is about, suppose it happened to you in the beginning, when the blessing of fulfillment offered the good intention its dependable arm—but
there still remained one difficulty. Suppose it happened to you
in the course of time, when fulfillment faithfully accompanied
the confident traveler step by step, did not hurry ahead like a

stands that? Here thoughtlessness does not venture to help with its extensive explanations about what is beneficial in life.

We have been speaking about the thorn in the flesh; we have tried to explain the expression in a general sense, that is, in the general sense in which, by pertaining to one single person, it pertains to all. We have not been particularly concerned about ferreting out what Paul may have particularly had in mind with this expression, and we have desired least of all to ask about it in the same sense that someone might ask whether Paul was tall or short, handsome, and the like. We are especially unwilling to suggest the possible accidental something, the possible insignificant something, that may be the single individual's thorn in the flesh. Perhaps a description of this would fascinate a reader, perhaps would even lead a reader to admire the speaker, but it would, of course, be despicable if the speaker wanted to interfere in this way with the upbuilding. The general explanation, on the other hand, is this: that the highest life also has its suffering, has the hardest suffering; that no one is to desire light-mindedly anything from which he mendaciously omits the danger; that no one is to become discouraged by being placed in the danger of which he may have been ignorant; that no one is spiritlessly to prize the cozy and easygoing days of his life. If only a person is really aware of the dangerousness, he is already on the way to begin the good fight.[341] The comfort will surely come, and one must not grasp it too early. The one who has spoken here is just a young person; he is not going to prevent anyone from being terrified, since he will not be able to comfort with the ambiguous experience that a long life has taught him, that the danger was not as an apostle depicts it and as every more profound person at one time in his youth has suspected until the paths are separated—one person fights the good fight of danger and terror; the other becomes sagacious and spiritlessly rejoices over the security of life.

AGAINST COWARDLINESS[342]

II TIMOTHY 1:7

God did not give us a spirit of cowardliness but a
spirit of power and of love and of self-control

If it is really so that there is something in life that has or can
have such power over a person that it little by little makes him
forget everything that is noble and sacred and makes him a
slave in the service of the world, of the moment; if it is really
so that time has or can gain such power over a person that
while it adds days to his life it also every passing day measures
the greater distance of his life from the divine, until he,
trapped in everydayness and habit, becomes alienated from
the eternal and the original; if experience has taught us that
this has also happened to someone who once had a strong
sense of the presence of the eternal—then it certainly would
be beneficial to recommend every means against this and desirable that the recommending be done in an earnest but also
winsome way. God be praised, there are many means, just as
the dangers are many, and every one of these means is trustworthy and tested. One such means is resolution or coming
to a resolution, because resolution joins a person with the eternal, brings the eternal into time for him, jars him out of the
drowsiness of uniformity, breaks the spell of habit, cuts off
the tedious bickering of troublesome thoughts, and pronounces a benediction upon even the weakest beginning,
when it is indeed a beginning. Resolution is a waking up to
the eternal, and someone who has lacked the rejuvenation of
resolution for a long time may very well feel, when he does
make a resolution, as did the widow's son from Nain when he
woke up on the bier—alas, previously he was even more like
the widow's son when he was carried out dead.[343] Therefore,
we praise resolution. But the discourse on this has no inten-

tion of tickling the ears of youth or of sounding like something sensuously and titillatingly different to the sentimental ears of the soft, as is the case with talk occasionally heard, with this effect even if not intended, when it shouts to the world, "The whole thing takes only a moment, just come to a resolution; like the bold swimmer dare to dive into the sea; dare to believe that a person is lighter than all his sufferings, that the swimmer's path goes through all the currents, through the foaming waves, straight to the goal. Observe him, the undaunted swimmer: he climbs to a high place, his eyes delight in the danger, his body rejoices in a shudder of terror—then he dives boldly into the waves; he vanishes as if swallowed by the sea but quickly emerges and has triumphed, triumphed in one single moment. Just so does resolution stand on the mount of transfiguration,[344] rejoices in the danger, then dives into the sea, and in the same moment emerges with the victory!" If this is how the discourse in honor of coming to a resolution sounded, then it surely would make an impression—how the listener would praise the speaker's enthusiasm, admire his eloquence, and how changed the listener would be on returning home: he would sit there surrounded by lofty resolutions, doubtful only about which heroic figure would suit him best, [345]and soon he would long to hear a discourse like that again, and until then he would do what he could—extol the speaker, whose powerful excitement, whose bold imitative gestures as he described the swimmer, were so vivid to him. Alas, let the theater keep what belongs to the theater and the juggling heroes: pretentious words, bold gestures, and the applause of an appraising crowd. Anyone who wants to praise the benefit of making a resolution certainly does not want to be guilty of a deception by which he would delay the listener in acting and give him enough to do in admiring, because admiring, too, is a means of distraction, and to assist in evoking it is—an assassination, or foolishness.

Therefore, the discourse must begin in a different way and above all forswear deception; the devil uses many arts[346] to tempt a human being, and it is always a dangerous assault when the devil, by means of high-minded resolutions, or rather by talk about them and admiration of them, together with the subsequent distaste when a person sees how little he can do, wants to induce him to give up everything. No, we creep before we learn to walk, and to want to fly is always precarious. To be sure, there are great decisions, but even in regard to them the main thing is to activate one's resolution, lest one become so high-flying in the resolution that one forgets to walk.

The deception in that talk was that it seemed as if a person was supposed to deliberate on whether he wanted to dive into the sea. This is already wasted effort, a delay in carrying out something, a nourishment for pride that a person fancies or allows himself to fancy that life is like that, that danger is a celebration to which one is invited, a proposal that is made, whether one wants to or not. This is far from the case. The pompous platitude makes a person forget that he is indeed in danger, that it is a question not of boldly leaping out but of saving himself. Neither has he entered into danger by diving down from high places in the manner of the swimmer or that extolled resolution; on the contrary, it quite simply and naturally has come to pass by his having been conceived in transgression and born in sin,[347] since at birth he was exposed to the danger there where he now is. What thoughtlessness to remain ignorant of the existence of danger, but what perversity to encourage someone with big words and promises of a hero's fame to venture out where he is! [348]Yet even to have dived into danger oneself is a proud thing; it is somewhat more humble for a person to admit that he is there, to confess to himself that he is where circumstance and providence have placed him, without daring to leave this place either to flee or to climb to a high place from which he will dive down into danger. The danger is there; to discover it is not so extraordinary that it would tempt to pride if one considers that the terror of the danger increases in proportion to the pride over discovering it—indeed, that the terror easily gets out of hand if all such deliberation is not in turn cut off by the simple observation that all one has to do is save oneself. It is a proud thing to dive into danger, and it is a proud thing to battle with untold horrors, but it is also wretched (how wretched it is one sometimes learns from the same person) to have an abundance of intentions and a poverty of action, to be rich in truths and poor in virtues.

The danger is there; this is no secret for the wise or for the courageous—the simple person knows it also. We shall not, instead of calling the danger by its true name, speak of the sea and the storm and the thundering roar, which easily tempts the power of the imagination to imagined conceptions and imagined exploits. There is indeed danger to fortune and welfare: that you will lose them and along with them, perhaps, your courage and your faith. There is indeed the danger of soul: that the world will come to be empty and everything a matter of indifference to you, life without taste and nourishment, truth itself a toilsome fabrication, and death a vague thought that neither alarms nor beckons. There is indeed the danger of sin: that you will forget your duty or at least forget that it should be done with joy, forget that one is to endure one's sufferings or at least forget that one should bear them devotedly, the danger that you will fall into sin and lose your bold confidence, go despondent through life and despair in death, so that not even repentance can be a support to you. There is indeed the danger of death, which has its spies everywhere, although it knows that no human being will evade it. Is there, then, no danger, or are you unaware of it, you who perhaps want to climb to the mountain peak in order to throw yourself into it? Do you not know that you are under indictment, and if no earthly court of law accuses you, then you are accused in heaven, where the judgment will be? Do you not know that you are in prison, even if the prison is as spacious as the wide world? But try this: go to the farthest limits of the world, conceal yourself in the abyss,[349] and then see whether the justice that imprisoned you does not know how to go and fetch you out. Do you not know that the witnesses are there (even though far from witnessing against you they are at the moment your most intimate confidants), that these witnesses are your thoughts, that this eyewitness is you yourself, whom the day of reckoning will compel to be your own informer, without being able to hide the most secret counsel or forget the most fleeting thought or keep a single thought so well concealed inside you that your conscience would not know how to wrench open your inclosing reserve [*Indesluttethed*]³⁵⁰ and the involuntary self-appraisal would not know how to tear it from you? Human justice is very prolix, and yet at times quite mediocre; ³⁵¹divine justice is more concise and needs no information from the prosecution, no legal papers, no interrogation of witnesses, but makes the guilty one his own informer and helps him with eternity's memory.

But it was just as much a mirage whereby that deceptive talk made it seem as if everything were decided, everything won, on the battle day of resolution. It is certainly true that much is already won by making a good beginning, but in the same moment the point is to come into stride at the beginning, because there perhaps is nothing more demoralizing for a person than having a good and glorious beginning promptly stand in his way instead of helping him to go on. It is a proud thing to concentrate all the threatening dangers and terrors in one place, to charge forth where the enemy's hosts are most numerous; those are proud words that want to make the sun stand still³⁵² so that twilight may not fall before all the enemies are overcome. On the other hand, it is humble to admit that the struggle, even through no fault of one's own, drags out so that every day has its evening, and because of one's fault drags out in such a way that twilight sometimes falls on a defeat. It is humble to admit that even the progress through life of the most honest contender is difficult, that even the person who walks his way with firm steps³⁵³ nevertheless does not walk with a hero's pace, indeed, that when the evening of life cools the contender after the long day there still is no opportunity for fanfare, since even the person who came closest to the goal does not arrive with the qualifications or the disposition for the rigors of a victory celebration but, weary and worn, desires a grave in which to rest and a blessed departure from here in peace. To be sure, such a person's life was not unfamiliar with great decisions, but he nevertheless admits that his entire life was a struggle, and in conversation with others he is not

v
128

tempted to mention proudly the great decisions he has had the honor of helping to make; he is well aware that his telling about the daily struggle would be wearisome to the inquisitive. And yet this was his life; he perhaps experienced the changeableness of life, perhaps that of people, but danger followed him constantly. But as the danger recurred, he renewed his resolution, and in that way he carried through his battle. Although his step was weak, his gait vacillating, at times going backward instead of forward, resolution helped him again, little by little; he still exhorted himself with a beautiful saying, "Do what you can for God, and he will do for you what you cannot do," until again he came to a resolution, even though his resolution seems to be of humble origin, a cripple compared with that highborn resolution.

If making a resolution is understood in this way to be the constant renewal of a crucial resolution (an apparent contradiction akin to reminding someone to act as if this were the last day of his life and then pointing out that a long life lies ahead of him), then it remains fixed that resolution is a saving means. But if this does remain fixed, then it is in turn worthwhile to be aware of the hereditary enemy of resolution, cowardliness, which, tenacious of life as it is, always contemplates cutting off or harming the good understanding of resolution with the eternal, gnawing asunder the chain of resolution, which is easy to carry and becomes heavy only when it is broken. Therefore, the discourse, as it relates to the apostle's brief words, will be directed against cowardliness. Even though it is sometimes said that fear of God, that religion, that Christianity makes a person cowardly, the opposite certainly cannot be declared more emphatically than here, where the apostle specifically says that God does not give a spirit of cowardliness, which consequently must come from somewhere else and presumably was already present in that objection. No one should plead, therefore, that it is his piety, his humility under the powerful hand of God,[354] that makes him cowardly; no one should fear to entrust himself to God with the idea that this relationship would deprive him of his power and make him cowardly. It is just the reverse. Anyone upon whom God does not confer knighthood with his powerful hand is and remains cowardly in his deepest soul, if for no other reason than that he was too proud to bear the accolade, inasmuch as it, like every accolade that confers knighthood, requires the confession of one's own unworthiness. We shall now, therefore, speak:

Against Cowardliness.

It is supposed to be a sign of a sophisticated age that the inadmissible, the forbidden, and sin are given an absolving, an almost honorable name. Sometimes the falsification is continued so long that the old, earnest, and explicit word is forgotten and goes out of use. If it happens to be heard on occasion, it almost evokes laughter, because it is assumed that the speaker either is a man from the country who speaks an archaic, stilted language that totally lacks the flexibility of the vernacular or is a wag who is using such a word simply to evoke laughter, either at the word itself or at its mimicking of others, of whom it prompts recollection. A similar falsification is perpetrated when someone chooses to use one of two words, both of which refer to something reprehensible, indeed, equally reprehensible, because in the general view it has a connotation of something that in the eyes of the world is not bad.

This is the case with the two words "cowardliness" and "pride." If a preacher, whose work it is to attend to people's lives and to call them to the good, wanted to warn against pride, he probably would find many listeners, and yet the effect of what he said on all of them might be far from what he intended—indeed, there might even be someone who without paying attention to the admonition heard the flattering recognition implied in using this word. But if he wanted to warn against cowardliness, then his listeners would no doubt look around to see whether any such wretch was present, a cowardly soul, the most contemptible of all, the most intolerable, for even a degenerate person can still be tolerated if he is proud—but a coward . . . . . A person really must be without an ear for the thieves' slang of the passions if he does not perceive that there must be something wrong with cowardliness, since it has become so repulsive, so fearful of being named— indeed, has so completely vanished from life. And yet anyone who was much inclined to assume that the polite warning against pride applied to him can be sure that the insulting words about cowardliness apply to him also, because cowardliness and pride are one and the same; he can be sure that the words applied especially to him, that is, if he was very eager to seem proud, since that is precisely cowardliness.

Pride and cowardliness are one and the same. This must not, however, be misunderstood; what is meant in particular here is that what is spoken of under the name of pride is ordinarily cowardliness. Even false pride is rarely to be seen, and if the preacher were to adapt his discourse to the conditions manifest in life, he would rarely warn against pride. False pride requires a high conception of one's own worth and of the responsibility the proud person has for himself, which he fears more than he fears the whole world. The proud person always wants to do the right thing, the great thing, and he is actually struggling not with people but with God, because he wants to do it with his own power; he does not want to sneak out of something—no, what he wants is to set the task as high as possible and then to finish it by himself, satisfied with his own consciousness and his own approval. Therefore, even the falsely proud person must be able to be proud in solitariness, must be able to renounce and reject all reward in the world,[355] the favor of people, and not a living soul, not the defiance of the proudest, not the pleas of the most lovable, may disturb him. No gain, not the whole world, not the most insignificant and secret thing may tempt him. He must concentrate all his thought in order to see the right; he must will it, because he is too proud to admit that people could be in the right in opposition to him, even though no one could convince him of that. But such an existence is sleepless, very exhausting, and pursued by many terrors. Therefore, if we take this requirement out among the people, how rarely is there anyone who has met it. Yes, many have taken pride's first leap into life, many fatuously enough, but when it comes to the next step, then the proud person goes begging to the very same person he proudly disdained; he who tossed his head proudly now bends his knees, he who proudly rejected is now contented; he who wanted to flout everything now begs for life; he who proudly wanted to be unto himself enough is looking around for like-minded people; he who has cunningly altered pride's task lies a little to himself and procures the opinion of others that this is indeed the proudest thing of all—then they band together and are proud in a solidarity that is vanity and cowardliness. We certainly do not say this in order to extol that false pride, but its way nevertheless is terrible and therefore is seldom trodden, which is fine, of course, because the devil lies in wait for false pride, and it becomes his victim, since it is cowardliness. In other words, someone who stands alone this way is bound to discover that there is a God, and if he then is unwilling to understand that it is too little to be alone with a secret, if he is too proud to have an almighty God as co-knower, then he is indeed cowardly. Even though the world and all the terrors that earthly and human life conceal do not succeed in exposing his solitariness as a mirage, the Almighty will quickly do it, and this he cannot bear; consequently he is cowardly.

Since, then, even false pride is very rare in the world and nevertheless pride is so frequently mentioned, it can be concluded that cowardliness must be very common—indeed, this conclusion can be drawn without offending anyone; and without being a judge and a prober of hearts, one can take it for granted that everyone is somewhat cowardly, and in particular it can safely be assumed that anyone who seeks to know himself better will be willing to acknowledge that he has not infrequently caught himself in it, and for that reason he is always a bit dubious about even his boldest enterprise. That the confounding can occur is not difficult to understand, and the discourse will continually call attention to it, because, although it deals with cowardliness, it continually aims at pride. If the subject is to be approached fundamentally, that first lie must be prevented first of all. Even when cowardliness is mistaken for sagacity, with a generally esteemed common sense that secretly is selfishness, even then it is at first mistaken for pride—

V
131

that is, in the sense that being wise about the world and one's own advantage in this way is something great. If a warning is given against such sagacity, then take great care that the admonition does not become tempting, for there just might be someone who would like to hear such an admonition, and not exactly for the sake of the admonition. Only a religious view can speak honestly about and against such a thing, because the religious view knows the one thing needful and knows that it is the one thing needful,[356] and therefore it is not busy with the multifarious or does not become seductive in describing the differences.

Now if it so happened that, just as there is a curse on cowardliness, there was also a curse on it of such a nature that it could not appear in any form other than its actual form, that it could not deceive anyone with any disguise—then it surely would soon become homeless in the world, because who would live in the same house with this contemptibleness! Indeed, it would soon be compelled to flee to the most remote places, and then not even the most degraded and despicable would call it out. But such is not the case. Cowardliness is precisely the most flexible, the most adroit, the most pleasant, so to speak, of all the passions; it is not noisy and strident, but, quiet and suggestive and yet lustful, it attracts all the passions to itself, since in its association with them it is extremely engaging, knows how to maintain a friendship with them, and buries itself deep in the soul like somnolent vapor of stagnant water, from which pestiferous breezes and deceptive phantoms rise, while the vapor still remains. What cowardliness fears most is the making of a resolution, because a resolution always disperses the vapor for a moment. The power cowardliness prefers to conspire with is time, because neither time nor cowardliness finds that there is any reason to hurry. Is it not curious that it is God and the eternal and not time that say: [357]this very day.[358] Then let each day have its own trouble and toil,[359] and also its own pleasures and rewards. This is resolution's ceaseless refrain, its most ceremonious and its most everyday request, its first and its last word, that which it wants every day to signify and wants to give significance to every day: this very day.

But *in the first place,* cowardliness keeps a person from *acknowledging what is the good, the truly great and noble,* which ought to be the goal of his striving and his diligence early and late. If cowardliness had to reveal itself at this point as the wretched vermin it is or come forth in all its grossness, then there would be no danger, but it never appears in this way, or in any case not until later, inasmuch as evil always tempts with a winsome form and then throws off the mask and allows its victim to sink into the abyss with the thought that it is too late. Cowardliness merely wants to prevent the decision of resolution; therefore it gives its conduct a grand name. It zealously opposes precipitousness, immaturity, and haste—no, the continued striving[360] is the great thing; it is a proud task. The continued striving—a marvelous phrase—how disappointing if cowardliness were not to capture one soul for itself! That the continued striving still must have a beginning, especially in view of its presumably coming to an end—this neither cowardliness nor time wants to know about; only resolution knows this, as the phrase indicates, since the resolution [*Beslutning*] is the beginning, and yet it takes its name from its knowing that a conclusion [*Slutning*] is coming. If cowardliness has come along this far with a person, then it can be said to be nicely and cozily settled. What a proud thing to stare constantly into the clouds in this way without ever needing to bend its head to see its feet! If God is to be praised for forming man upright, how much more should cowardliness be praised, because it raised him up even more splendidly! A person such as that now lives with the far-off great goal before his eyes; if he should have misgivings for a moment, then cowardliness is promptly prepared with the explanation that it has to be this way because the goal [*Maal*] is so infinitely far off. He lives in the continued striving; if the concern should awaken about whether it was a striving, whether it was ongoing, then cowardliness dispels every doubt and immediately smooths out the furrowed brow by explaining that the single day, the single week, is too small a category to gauge [*udmaale*]

v
133

such a striving. In truth, is he not striving? Cowardliness calmly goes on with its striving and can see very well that week by week, yes, day by day, it is not striving in vain, and neither is it striving toward an infinitely far-off goal.

But the good, the truly great and noble, is, of course, not just something general and as such the general object of knowledge; it is also something particular in relation to the individual's particular talent, so that one person is capable of more than another, so that one person is capable of it in one way, another in another. The talent itself is not the good, as if exceptional capability were the good and limited capability the bad (what a bane for the fortunate, what despair for the unfortunate!)—no, talent is the indifferent that nevertheless has its importance.[361] If the capability is exceptional, then cowardliness says, "When one is so equipped, there certainly is no rush about beginning. This is much too easy, take your time, take a little loss: the expert player likes to begin when the game is half lost. I know it so well; right now I am idly hanging fire, but shortly, soon now, I will really get under way." How proudly cowardliness does talk! What does it mean to say that the task is too easy—it means that it is difficult, and by calling something more difficult, cowardliness has brought the person choosing to choose that which in the eyes of the world seems to be hardest but is the easier task. In other words, it is more difficult to begin quietly because it is less prestigious, and this bit of humiliation is precisely the difficulty. Consequently, it was not pride but cowardliness that was the counselor. Everyone knows that the moment of danger gives a person greater strength, but note well to what extent and in what way one is thereby greater. Is it such a great thing, after all, to need to have the terror of danger in order to muster one's strength, not to mention that the opposite could also occur, that the terror would certainly be there, but the strength would vanish. It was so easy that he could not resolve to begin. It was proud, but it was cowardly, because actually he was afraid that what he had let himself call a trifle might not turn out to be exactly that, and then he would be in the awkward position of being obliged to feel his own weakness without confronting the colossal name of the supreme terror, of being obliged to stand there in disgrace, deprived of every brilliant exit.

Or the capability is slight. Then cowardliness says, "This is too little to begin with." It is very fatuous, indeed, even foolish, to say this, because if one does not have more to begin with, it must indeed always be enough, and the less one begins with, the greater one becomes; but cowardliness, you see, has won sagacity over to its side, and sagacity declares that this is absolutely right, because the person who begins nothing does not lose anything either. Sagacity of that sort is certainly something of which to be proud, and pride has already discerned that rejecting everything is a much prouder thing than beginning with little, and this the person can do who rejects the little offered to him and in addition everything that was not offered to him at all. It seems proud, but cowardliness was, after all, the original inventor.

Besides all its other good qualities, the good, the truly great and noble, has the quality of not allowing the observer to be indifferent. It elicits a pledge, as it were, from the person who has once caught a vision of it. However deep that person sinks, he never actually forgets it completely; even in his reprobate state, this recollection is certainly a torment to him, but also at times a deliverance. But just as it lifts a person up, so also it humbles him, because it requires of him all his power and yet retains the authority to call him an unworthy servant[362] even when he has done his utmost. Now it is extremely important for cowardliness to prevent this loving understanding, resolution's solemn agreement with the good on such humiliating terms. In that case, pride is promptly on the spot; in agreement with cowardliness, it explains that it is much prouder to be conscious that one could be somewhat more than one is if one only wanted to be. From time to time, this indefinite greatness may be rated as high as one wishes, and one must not let oneself be upbraided as an unworthy servant. Sagacity also supports cowardliness and teaches that one ought to be a little mistrustful at all times, never to devote oneself altogether. This is indeed very sagacious, but just suppose it were foolishness with regard to something in which there is nothing at all to win if one does not stake everything. [363]Moreover, would it be sagacious in daily life to haggle with a merchant who had fixed prices and to offer him a little bit less; would it also be sagacious if he had absolutely fixed prices and one urgently needed what he had to sell? And yet it is indeed sagacious, and cowardliness smiles at the rashly proud one who forces his way to the front to take part in the competition for honor, smiles at him when he stumbles and consoles itself. Yet the cowardly proud one is more sagacious than the rashly proud one only for a moment and is more despicable, or, to put it more accurately, since it is useless to dwell on such differences, they have both lost everything.

If this is what happens, then a person has himself and his cowardliness to thank for it, because God does not give a spirit of cowardliness but a spirit of power and of love and of self-control, such as is necessary in order to know what is the good, what is truly great and noble, what significance it has for him and in relation to him; in order to love the good with the unselfish love that desires only to be an unworthy servant, which is always love's delight, and the opposite of it is a violation that pollutes love for him by making it profitable; and in order to maintain constancy, lest everything become unfruitful without the self-control that tempers the effort and the decision of resolution. This acknowledgment, this assent of resolution, is the first dedication. Alas, how rarely a person experiences this in such a way that even merely in the moment of dedication he renounces all dreams and fancies, every mirage that wants to inflate him and cause him to be amazed at himself, and instead receives the power to envision it as it is, the power to embrace it with self-denying love, the power to make the pact of self-control with it! How rarely a person experiences this in such a way that even merely in the hour of dedication he has the power to hold to the good, which seemingly wants to destroy him, the love not to shrink from it, the self-control not to falsify himself!

Cowardliness does not come from God, but it knows how to assume the appearance of a spirit of power and of love and of self-control. Now it is certainly true, as cowardliness also teaches, that everyone ought to strive for a high and far-off goal—it is high, because it is heaven; it is far off, and who does not know that, far off especially if a person's merit is supposed to reach it. But from the very beginning God himself has divided time, has separated day and night,[364] and in the same way the self-control of resolution will also promptly divide time for a human being, so that morning's renewed resolution and evening's thanksgiving and the quiet celebration of the day of rest—or however resolution has otherwise divided time for you, my listener—will each acquire its significance as division and as goal. If someone is unwilling to understand this in the beginning, he will not actually come to a resolution, and this will actually make his life meaningless, indeed, as suspect as the friendship that continually rejects every opportunity life provides to express itself, meaningless, yes, unlived, like the speech that is never heard, that in its superiority disdained every word and phrase the language offered. Who does not see this? Even the most cowardly would perhaps smile at this discourse as superfluous, because the rendering of the account will show what ought to have been done; but perhaps he does not bear in mind that if the resolution is not the beginning and the beginning the resolution, then the final account can never be rendered, because in a certain sense there is none.

Now it is certainly true that the good, the truly great and noble, is different for different people, but resolution, which is the true acknowledgment, is still the same. This is a very upbuilding [*opbyggelig*] thought. Someone who wants to erect [*opføre*] a tower sits down and roughly estimates how high he can erect the tower.[365] Alas, how different it appears at the time of the rough estimate, but how similar in the moment of resolution, and if there is no resolution, there will be no tower, however imaginary or however really splendid the estimate was! The good resolution, which corresponds to the acknowledgment of the good, is indeed to will to do everything in one's power, to serve it to the utmost of one's capability. To do everything one is capable of doing—what blessed equality, since every human being is indeed capable of that.

V
136

Only in the moment of the rough estimate is there a difference. Or consider someone who wants to do an act of
mercy—can he do more than give all that he possesses—and
did not the widow give infinitely more than the rich man who
gave out of his abundance![366] At times the circumstances can
determine that a penny signifies little more than it usually signifies, but if someone wants to do something marvelous, he
can make the one penny signify just as much as all the world's
gold put together if he gives it out of compassion and the
penny is the only one he has. Indeed, someone who has an ear
for judging how large the gift is detects the difference just by
hearing the jingle of the coins, but compassion and the temple
box understand it differently. [367]Someone who has only an ear
for hearing the whisper of the possibilities in the rough estimate makes an enormous distinction, but resolution understands it differently. When someone who enjoys health and
strength and who possesses the best gifts of the spirit enters
the service of the good with all that he has, with the range of
years that seem to stretch out before him, with expectancy's
every demand upon life, every claim expected and demanded
only for the sake of the good—and when, on the other hand,
someone who sadly sees his earthly frailty and the day of dis-
integration so close that he is tempted to speak of the time
granted him as the pastor speaks of it, when in the hour of
resolution a person like that promises with the pastor's words
"to dedicate these moments" to the service of the good—
whose tower then becomes higher? Or when one person joyfully feels like someone who is going to become a mighty instrument for the winning of many and another sadly considers
himself only a burden to others—when they both nevertheless
resolve to will to be everything, and altogether nothing, for
the good, whose tower then becomes higher? Do they not
both reach to heaven? Or when one person, a stranger to internal enemies, aggressively directs his mind and thought toward humankind in the service of the good and wins thousands, and when another, retreating to internal battles, in the
moment of resolution saves himself, whose tower then becomes higher? If cowardliness could understand this, it would

not be so opposed to resolution, because this is the secret of resolution. It demands everything, that is true; it does not allow itself to be deceived, it tolerates no dishonesty, it is close-fisted down to the last penny[368] toward the person who wants to give almost everything. But it is not petty; it relishes the sight of someone who gives away the little he has and is angry only if he wants to hold back, if he wants to put the blame on his poverty, if he sophistically wants to delude himself into thinking that it is impossible for him to give away everything since he [369]possesses nothing, if he wants to divert himself by wishing that he had much to give away, if he wants to entertain himself by thinking how magnanimous he then would be, wants to satisfy his urge for resolution with dreams until the urge passes. All this is cowardliness and concealed pride, which desires to become in obscurity a little more than one is and to put off the resolution with feigned approval.

In the next place, cowardliness prevents a person from *doing the good*, from accomplishing the truly great and noble to which he has attached himself in a resolution. In the foregoing, we have already directed attention to a kind of superstition that makes a person think that everything is settled by a resolution, which he then is not averse to making, perhaps even in the opinion that through resolutions his life has a superiority that excuses him from being concerned about lesser things. Only on solemn and crucial occasions will he venture everything; lesser things do not occupy him. Alas, but wanting, as it were, merely to dress up in life this way is a glittering delusion. For anyone who allows himself to nourish such ideas about it, the resolution itself becomes a seducer and deceiver instead of a trustworthy guide. It is certainly true and right that the splendor of eternity shines upon the resolution, that in the resolution everything seems decided for eternity, but this is only the first step. Then the resolution changes its clothes and now wants to concern itself specifically with the most everyday matters, and thus in its everyday or, if I may put it this way, in its house clothes the resolution does not appear as divine, but in its innermost nature it is entirely the

V
138

same. In other words, it is the meaning of resolution for human life that it wants to give it coherence, an even and calm progress. For this, resolution has the winsome faculty of concerning itself with little things, so that one neither disregards them nor is lost in them; so that life goes forward in the resolution, strengthened, refreshed, and invigorated by the resolution.

Now resolution is something else. Perhaps it is to be sparing of what poverty alone needs to care about, to hold back a little word of anger, to bring oneself to submit to a minor unpleasantness, to keep on working a little longer, to forget a little insult. How changed! Is it not unfaithfulness on the part of resolution to behave in this way, or is this actually what the resolution was? After all, the resolution was to will not to need earthly things, in contentment to will to become carefree like a bird of the air.[370] Indeed, the resolution was to will to be victorious over one's disposition and over one's enemies by reconciliation; the resolution was that the evening of life should witness that there had been work during the day; the resolution was to lift up one's soul over everything that was petty in life.

Yes, that was the resolution; it is not forgotten. But now this . . . . . Good Lord, are we so close to poverty [371]that we need to be sparing of the little we have; are we so irritable that we have to be so afraid of a little outburst; does half an hour have the power to make one a loafer; are we perhaps mad the minute we are a little depressed; are we irreconcilable when we are willing to forget the greater insults and remember only the lesser ones? Oh, anyone who knows anything about resolution will not deny how beautifully it knows how to speak, almost to plead, for itself, plead that we will simply do what it says, and above all not contaminate ourselves by believing that we entrusted ourselves to a faithless one in entrusting ourselves to the resolution. It admits that what it wants is a trifle, that it should be done precisely as a trifle, since otherwise it is compelled to make life strenuous for a person in an opposite way in that a trifle becomes the most important; therefore that which is a trifle and as such can be disregarded is no trifle when resolution has laid claim to it, and to become unfaithful to one's resolution on the occasion of a trifle is indeed unfaithfulness and no trifle. Finally it becomes jealous of itself and wants to help the person for a time by nagging him and giving him no peace.

Where does the fault lie if the person and the resolution no longer live together in harmony?[372] It lies with his cowardliness. It is quite true that a person's soul can become confused if the trivial continually becomes for him the important. The resolution does not want this either; it wants him to do it as a trifle, do it as an additional consequence of the resolution. Cowardliness, however, always wants to deal with the important, not simply in order to carry out something properly but because it is flattering to be tried in the more important things and because, when one fails, it is consoling that it was something important. It is presumably very rare that a person actually stops making an attempt or at least stops believing that he could accomplish something great and thereby admit his cowardliness (if in other respects the great is something that in its universal validity pertains to every human being, since in relation to the external and the accidental it may very well be wise and sober not to venture too much); no, he first cheats the task, calls it a trifle, and then he abstains from accomplishing it. But the deception is that of cowardliness, and the satisfaction is that of pride—so here again cowardliness is what lies at the base.

If the resolution does not prevail in this struggle, if it more frequently comes to grief in this way, it finally becomes exhausted, and things become worse and worse until the resolution becomes a half-forgotten, aimless thought, a whim of former days that once in a while visits the one who has changed. Instead of the steady progress envisioned by the resolution, there is regression. Deliverance, however, is to be sought again only in the resolution, but the conditions are not the same as at first. Now cowardliness is in opposition; powerless as it is, it nevertheless directs its hatred at the resolution, in its heart thinks baleful thoughts[373] about it, and satisfies itself through the deception of pride. Who could ever count all the evasions, the sophistries, that cowardliness is able to find in such circumstances, all the fraudulent suggestions it knows how to make in order to prove itself right over against the resolution, in order to become assured that the decision is a snare in which one is caught, a self-torturing in which the prisoner scourges himself, a deceiver who still does not help. Did it really help earlier, or have there not been particular moments when one was almost willing to conclude a bargain with it, but see whether it helped right away! Even though the resolution is again victorious in a person, oh, how seldom he really regains his strength. Cowardliness lies in wait everywhere, and if it is capable of nothing else, it sees to it that there is a little discrepancy in the renewal of the resolution. If the resolution is to be truly renewed and to some purpose, it must begin precisely where it left off. This is very painful. Then cowardliness and time help with false friendship. The intervening time places the regression at a distance, distances it in less definite contours; the intervening space deceives the eyes; as past, the wasted time does not seem so long or so empty and barren. Moreover, the weeds sometimes bear magnificent flowers. Then when forgetfulness has provided a little relief, the resolution finally comes again. [374]Alas, but cowardliness has indeed been involved; even though it is not the father of the resolution, which it never is, it nevertheless stood by and in part prevented the resolution from bringing into life a coherence in the deeper sense. Perhaps pride comforts with the bold thought of beginning over again, of letting the past be forgotten and beginning more bravely than ever. But who is it that pride comforts? Such comfort can only violate the resolution. It is cowardliness that is grasping for it; consequently, here again it is cowardliness that lies at the base. If this happens, a person can thank himself and cowardliness for it, because God gives a spirit of power, of love, and of self-control.

Yet perhaps it did not happen this way. Perhaps mention is made of someone who, humanly speaking, dared to resolve to erect the tower high. If the resolution was great, then the implementing of it was also great; the resolution triumphantly steers as if under full sail straight to the goal. But there is still a discrepancy, a little trifle beyond his capability; he knows it, he knew it, he gradually perceives it more and more clearly. If his resolution was the good, then it was to sacrifice everything in the service of the good; if this is not his resolution, then no matter how great it was, all his admired power, his perseverance, his triumphant advance are only of superfluous and self-invented importance—the good and God do not need him. Even someone adequately equipped to transform the world—if he wants to do it on his own account—is not even as important in the eyes of God as a sparrow of the air,[375] which God really does not need. But if it was the good resolution, then it is jealous of itself and scrupulous with a person. What does it mean that he, although actually capable of something great, is incapable of something insignificant? However great he may be, he is still only a servant; when he has promised everything to the good, this has a far more sacred and authentic meaning than the great-in-the-eyes-of-the-world thing he is able to perform. Even if he were capable of teaching all people the truth, if upon discovering weakness and discrepancies in himself he nevertheless concentrated all his might upon himself, then he would really be true to himself and more important to God than if he did the opposite, although people probably would swoon if they could see a world-moving power occupied with what they call a trifle, even if it were not so, since the opposite would be to become a riddle to himself and in the process to do his utmost to make life meaningless.

V
141

But how is this little discrepancy to be explained; why is it there? It is a trifle—hence it is a matter of pride not to be concerned about it. It is a trifle—how strange that life is such that the great men are unable to do the lesser things ordinary people are able to do. It is a trifle—how close the ridiculous is to the most profound earnestness! That the greatest thing and the least thing are connected in this way, that a trifle mocks the great in this way, tags after it like a teasing nisse[376]—how strange this is (really something for the soul expert to ponder), something that could be called life's envy of the prominent, which mockingly indicates to him that he is still a human being like everyone else, like the lowliest, that the human demands its rights!

Of course, every such explanation probably has its significance, especially for the uninvolved, but if the one involved is satisfied with it, then he really will only be diverted and is fundamentally cowardly and does not dare to come to himself in order to endure the contradiction that awaits him, in order to learn what every human being should not just learn by rote but learn very particularly, that he is nothing—which some learn by recognizing that what they are capable of is as good as nothing, others by recognizing that what they are not capable of is as good as nothing but is sufficient to make all their capability essentially nothing. The extensive enterprise can often be dazzling enough, especially when it is not only glorious and lauded by men but beneficial for many, and yet it is only a mirage; the resolution is still not the good resolution, since a person such as that does not completely give himself along with everything to the good, namely, along with his weakness, and leave it up to God whether he wills that through a long life this abundance of power is to work itself weary on a little weakness such as this or whether the one gloriously equipped is to have importance for others. The mirage is due to such a person's becoming a worthy servant in his own eyes, an important instrument, but this is not the good resolution, which is satisfied with being willing to be an unworthy servant. Therefore every person is to test himself.[377] Possibly there has been someone in this world who was admired by men, extolled in his lifetime, missed in death, honored as a benefactor, commemorated with memorials, to whom God nevertheless was obliged to say: Unhappy man, you did not choose the better part.[378] But if this was the case, then a person such as this certainly also noticed time and again the discrepancy, which, properly understood, either merely wanted to be an unremitting disciplinarian[379] to him, and as such also requested access to him at all times, or insisted that he transform this extensive enterprise and renew the good resolution, because God does not give a spirit of cowardliness but a spirit of power, of love, and of self-control. Do what you can for God, and God will do for you what you cannot do. But is this doing what you can an unwillingness to be humbly aware of the weakness in which he perhaps will become understandable to you? Yes, it is hard when it seems as if one could do so very much for the good, but it nevertheless is certain that the only thing and the greatest—something the greatest and the lowliest of men are capable of doing for God—is to give oneself completely, consequently one's weakness also, for obedience is dearer to God than the fat of rams.[380]

There is a foolishness in youth's high-flying resolutions, but in reliance on God one dares to venture everything. Venture it, then, you who became unfaithful to yourself and to your resolution, you who, thereby enfeebled like a childish old man, now drag along without ever trusting in the restitution of the resolution; venture to renew your resolution—it will certainly raise you up again in trust in God, who gives a spirit of power and of love and of self-control! Venture it, you who threw off the chain of resolution and now may be boasting of your freedom like a released prisoner. Venture to understand that this pride of yours is cowardliness; turn yourself in again so that justice may again bind you in the service of the resolution; venture it in trust in God, who will give a spirit of power and of love and of self-control! Venture it, you who once humbled yourself under God in the good resolution but made a mistake and in your own eyes and in the eyes of others became so very important to the good; venture it again in order to become nothing before God—he will surely give you a spirit of power, of love, and of self-control!

Finally, cowardliness prevents a person from acknowledging the good that he does do. Now it is certainly true that it is always preferable to be regarded as lowlier and worse than one is than to be regarded as better than one is, which is a great danger if it happens to a person and terrible if he himself is responsible for it. Oh, even if I were dying, I would still recommend these words: "When you fast, anoint your head and wash your face, so that men will not see you fasting, but your Father who is in secret."[381] Even though a person went astray and sinned,

v
143

there nevertheless are still comfort and trust in God's compassion. But if a person is senseless enough to flirt with the highest, if the sacred words "virtue" and "love" and "piety" have become platitudes that he mouths to the point of nausea, if he has developed this art to the utmost of being able to deal thoughtlessly with even the holiest and most earnest thoughts, of being able to transform even the most earnest subject into bombast, the most sacred subject into a flourish; or if he were so base as to affect a hypocritical appearance, so base as to hold men in contempt by "disfiguring his face,"[382] so base as to assume that God himself is for sale, yes, is purchasable with words and platitudes—where, then, is there deliverance for such a person? Or should language, especially in our day, perhaps consider finding such a new and ceremonious expression for the holy that it could impress one who tried (one would almost think this) his very best to create in every better person an aversion to that which has been received from our more earnest forefathers as a sacred heritage? Or would the holy ever be able to grasp someone who was much too accustomed to dealing with it hypocritically? But if this is the way it is, then attention should be given lest a person himself, out of cowardliness even though doing the good, become a snare for himself and the ruination of others by misleading their judgment. It should be noted that it is cowardliness that wants to prevent a person from acknowledging the good that he does do.

V
144

From the very start, everything that is good in a person is silent, and just as it is essentially God's nature to live in secret, so also the good in a person lives in secret. Every resolution that is fundamentally good is silent, because it has God as its confidant and went to him in private;[383] every holy feeling that is fundamentally good is silent and concealed by a modesty that is holier than a woman's;[384] every pure sympathy for the human that is fundamentally good is silent, because it is hidden in God; every emotion of the heart is silent, since the lips are sealed and only the heart expanded. How dismal if people more and more forget that when everything becomes silent, when no one mentions or relates what is occurring within, when silence grows around a person, that he then can be with God in secret! How dismal if generation after generation the noise and the turbulence of life carry the child and the youth earlier and earlier out into the pandemonium, gather him into the vociferous crowd or make him vociferous, the earlier the better! Let worldly exploits become greater and greater, more and more extraordinary, more and more complicated, but do not forget that what a person gains by taking part in them, indeed, by managing the greatest of human enterprises, is not worth picking up on the beaten path compared with being superfluous in the world but sharing with God.

But if the good is silent this way, how easy for it to be misjudged! Unfortunately, it is frequently the case that the best people, who like that king's daughter[385] certainly possess the heart's gold but have no small change to give away, sometimes suffer the most in the world simply because of others. Alas, if this happens, there is the temptation to break off relations with people and shut oneself in with the good in silence. It is so tempting not only for the falsely proud person but also for someone who, quiet and silent, humbles himself under God in fear and trembling;[386] when all the inauthentic glitter and rouged untruth are held in high honor and even want to judge the one misjudged,[387] then it is so tempting to be silent, to give the appearance that the judgment is correct, to be silent and not to defend oneself with a word but take one's secret into the grave. When pure and warm feelings witness with a person's heart that he loved much,[388] when the sentimentality out there has monopolized the great word and even wants to judge the one misjudged, then it is so tempting to be silent, almost to confirm its judgment, and simply take along the consciousness that in its way the surrounding world acknowledged the good in him; after all, was he not declared to be the only selfish one? [389]When so many people promptly say yes to the good and promise to do the Father's will and let themselves be praised for it, then it is very tempting to say no and secretly try to do it. When the soul is sighing and moaning and fasting, then it is so tempting to anoint one's head and wash one's face[390] and not seek the company of the bighearted but be the

V
145

heartless one. When so many hurry forward with their gifts and are called benefactors, or when they throng together around the injured party who acquired worldly significance by being wronged, or visit the prisoner who acquired worldly fame by his imprisonment, then it is very tempting to be anonymous, unseen to visit the widow, the orphan,[391] and the prisoner[392] who was shut out from society! But this also has its danger; it can become dangerous for oneself, and cowardliness can easily be present covertly or can little by little sneak its way in.

The good retains the right to make a person an unworthy servant even when he does the most. For the selfishness in man, this thought is the most humiliating. It requires from a person the honest confession that he is just like every other human being, even the lowliest, or (for this, unfortunately, is truer) the lowliest that any human being can become. But if he acknowledges the good, the world will perhaps judge differently; it will demand something else from him, and this he perhaps cannot endure, even if he secretly has the honesty to will and the strength to do the good. With his good resolution, he wished only to be an unworthy servant,[393] that is, a servant who asks no reward. But see, the world rewards him; it rewards him with misjudgment. This was not according to the arrangement. Oh, anyone who does not comprehend that he is still an unworthy servant even when he does the most he can for the good and also suffers misjudgment—his thought has not even comprehended the perfect, to say nothing of having fulfilled it. If he fears misjudgment, it is indeed cowardliness that prevents him from acknowledging the good.

But a person may himself contribute to eliciting the misjudgment. Consequently, to that extent he seems not to be asking any reward for the good, even though he does not acknowledge it. But let us look at that. When he suffers misjudgment, it is easy for him to become more self-important; he does not judge others, but he wants his deeds to judge others and in a crafty way, if I dare say so, wants to build up a larger balance with God. He is not entirely content with being an unworthy servant; he wants to be a little more than that.

Now, a person can occasion misjudgment, indeed, the world's persecution, by appearing as the advocate of the good in an exaggerated way, consequently by acknowledging the good too much, if you please, but we are not speaking of this here. What we are speaking of here is the occasioning of misjudgment by failing to acknowledge the good. We shall not say with the Preacher (Ecclesiastes 4:10), "Woe to him who is alone; if he falls, there is no one else to raise him up,"[394] for God is indeed still the one who both raises up and casts down, the one who lives in association with people and the solitary one; we shall not cry, "Woe to him," but surely an "Ah, that he might not go astray," because he is indeed alone in testing himself to see whether it is God's call he is following or a voice of temptation, whether defiance and anger are not mixed embitteringly in his endeavor. How close is the path that leads astray!

Alas, there may have been someone who even called the curse upon himself and who nevertheless was in the right, who had a clear conscience about the matter for which he was judged but was wrong in being silent, wrong in that the essential reason perhaps was that he lacked the courage to admit his weakness, that he preferred to seem evil and be hated rather than to be loved and have his weakness known to others. Alas, there may have been someone who endured purposeless sufferings so hard that they could inspire a poet and who also at times became very self-important because of the anguish of being misunderstood, and yet, if he were really honest, he himself would have to confess that by means of a little confession he could at least have mitigated it! Alas, there may have been someone who bore the yoke of misjudgment years and days, did not become self-important but walked bent under the yoke because he suffered it as his punishment, even though he had allowed a change, so that he was punished not for what he should be punished for but for something else, and he on his own initiative accepted people's misjudgment from God's hands as a divine judgment but allowed people to be mistaken.

Silence and light-mindedness [*Letsind*] can indeed also conceal a heavy-mindedness [*Tungsind*] that gloomily loves the

v
146

good. It will be very exhausting, and what is worse, the heavy-mindedness thrives and is nourished thereby. Silence and indifference to everything can also conceal a bad conscience, which still has this expression of the good, that it will simply suffer its punishment. We are speaking here not of hypocrisy, which wants to appear better, but of the opposite, a hatred of oneself that wrongs the person himself so that he is merely inventive in increasing his own torment. But hatred of oneself is still also self-love, and all self-love is cowardliness.

Let each one test himself to see whether he acknowledges the good that dwells within him, that moves and fills his heart, the good for which he lives. If he does this, not vociferously, not obtrusively, because the acknowledgment should be like the good—reticent, unassuming, decorous, always modest— then he should tolerate the world's misjudgment. He has no responsibility, for then and only then is he actually "open before God."395 But if he does not do this, he had better watch out, because cowardliness only too willingly keeps bad company with pride. Cowardliness's deception is to misrepresent the task and to make the difficult easy and the easier difficult; pride finds satisfaction in choosing the fancied difficulty. Then one becomes self-important, since someone who does the good but does not acknowledge it is still not altogether like other people. But whoever judges in this way is not judging spiritually, because anyone who judges spiritually knows that every human being is only an unworthy servant. To want to renounce the world and the world's opinion and then in turn to pay oneself a worldly tribute for having done so is not renunciation of the world, even if cowardliness and pride can succeed in bringing off a remarkable deception. And if a person actually does love the good, does this not still have one claim upon him, the claim that he acknowledge it? The good certainly is not vain, and that is by no means the reason it makes this claim upon him, but it is the truth, and therefore all vociferousness is also just as detestable to the good. It is the truth, and the acknowledgment is the truth he owes to his neighbor. Is it not a good deed to restrain the arm of someone who wants to commit a misdeed, and is it not also a good deed to restrain the judgment of someone who wants to misjudge and cannot judge otherwise if acknowledgment of the good does not prevent it? Much wrong can be done to a person, but perhaps the worst is to come with belated repentance over a rash, unjust judgment that one nevertheless has oneself helped to occasion.

As you can see, if this happens, if a person goes astray in this way by doing the good, he can thank himself and cowardliness for it, because God gives a spirit of power, of love, and of self-control. Do what you can for God—but is it doing what you can to be unwilling to acknowledge the good, to be exclusive about it, although your life certainly must teach you to believe that a person is better than he seems—then God will give you a spirit of power and of love and of self-control. Therefore, venture it, you who embraced the good and remained true to your resolution; have the courage (since you do know that the discourse is against cowardliness, not against pride) to venture the lesser, if you wish to call it that, to acknowledge the good even if you do not gleam with it! Therefore, venture it, you who in your heart acknowledge the good, venture to do it before people. Do not do it ashamedly and with downcast eyes, as if you were walking a forbidden road;[396] acknowledge it even though you are ashamed because you always feel your own imperfection and lower your eyes before God! Venture it in trust in God, you who endured your punishment and did not flee the judgment of conscience. Venture the lesser (the discourse is against cowardliness, not against pride; yet it still pertains to you), to endure the sympathy of people, you who endured the punishment. Thus let each one acknowledge the good, renewed in his resolution, never led astray by any jugglery that it is more difficult to serve the good when one is misjudged. How, indeed, would it help for it to be more difficult if it was also less true or for it to be more difficult for many if it was easier for him?

[397]ONE WHO PRAYS ARIGHT STRUGGLES IN PRAYER AND IS VICTORIOUS—IN THAT GOD IS VICTORIOUS [398]

Who would engage in a struggle if he did not have the hope of being victorious, but who would not joyfully engage in a struggle if he was sure of victory? So, my listener, stir up the contender, call him forth to battle and make the conditions of the struggle so favorable that the expectancy of victory becomes a certainty. Tell him that he is the stronger. But see, the victory is still uncertain as long as it is not won! Tell him that the mighty ones are his friends, prepared to help. But see, despite that, the victory is still not yet won! Tell him that the opponent is so weak that the struggle is just for the sake of show. But see, the most certain victory is still doubtful as long as it is not won! So, then, is the victory never certain as long as it is not yet won? So, then, does the contender always go into the struggle with a certain doubt? Not at all! There is a condition of the struggle that removes every doubt, consequently a condition of the struggle that makes the contender truly joyful and intrepid, and this is the condition: if he loses, then he is victorious. Would thought, no matter how long it pondered, be able to think out a greater certainty of victory than this—that the loss is a victory!

If a man were to call the people together and say, "I am, to be sure, inviting you to a struggle, but the victory is certain," what a crowd would turn out to take part in the struggle or, rather, to join in the victory. If he added, "The victory is so certain that a loss is a victory and to be overcome is to become the victor," what envy would be awakened, since only one individual would be given the opportunity! If, in order to calm and pacify the tempers of the many, he said, "Everyone can take part; no one is shut out," how expectantly and in what high spirits the whole host would gather around him. But if the one speaking were to be a little more explicit and to the questions of the combat-eager about "the place, the battleground, and the provocative situation" were to answer, "The battleground is in the inner being of everyone, and therefore it is best that everyone go to his own home, so that the battle can begin," probably only one individual, scarcely the multitude, would follow his advice to part company, but they would look at him with different eyes, would stand there like a curious mob to whom a fool by his speech gives something to laugh about. Furthermore, if in reply to the question "What is the nature of the struggle?" he answered, "Praying," no further evidence against him would be necessary,[399] since praying is indeed the very opposite of struggling; praying is a cowardly and fainthearted business, left to women and children, but struggling is to a man's liking. If in reply to the question "What is the nature of the victory?" he answered, "Realization that one has lost," then probably even those less inclined to laughter would not refrain from smiling and from listening with a smile to what the speaker added: that it was correct to use the word "loss," that this was not a figurative expression but simply and plainly designated what human language and the human mind understand by a loss and a defeat, that on the other hand "to be victorious" had to be understood in a high and noble and, to that extent, figurative sense. Then when the multitude was tired of laughing, its spokesman would probably end the whole episode with the presumptuous and not unwitty remark that he held the very opposite view and for his part would rather be the victor in the literal sense and lose in the figurative sense.

My listener, is not this discourse a picture of what happens in life? A random word collects a crowd; the easily bought victory makes them enthusiastic, but the more profound explanation puts them off, and if the price is what it must be in relation to the highest, then mockery gives the signal for retreat and gives the retreat the appearance of a glorious victory. Does not mockery always gain the highest at a bargain price! And yet how despicable to want to think that the price of the highest and the most sacred, just like the price of temporal things, should be determined by an accident, by the scarcity or the abundance of the commodity in the country. On the other hand, how upbuilding it is to consider that this is not the case and that someone who fancies that he has bought the highest at a low price is simply mistaken, since the price is always the same. How sure and cheerful and resolute the soul becomes in the thought that no price is too high when that which one is buying is the highest. It is probably true, as people say, that gold also can be bought at too high a price, but the highest cannot be bought at too high a price. If one has bought at too high a price, then one has not bought the highest!

Therefore, it is beautiful and uplifting to meet in the gospel narrative[400] or in life a man who does not bargain in the marketplace, where the most sagacious, reckoning the conditions, today buys at a high price what the most foolish, aided by an accident, buys cheaply tomorrow—no, a resolute man who has understood what the highest is but is also willing to pay everything to buy it. It is salutary and refreshing to see him standing there, quiet and earnest, with the incorruptible beauty of his eternally conceived resolution: he has collected everything he possesses, he has added to this every earthly desire, everything that could be called a person's claim on life, and he puts it aside—he bids. If you see him tomorrow—unchanged, he repeats the bid unchanged. If the world employs all its cunning and all its flattery and all its terror—he nevertheless holds to his bid, if only he might succeed in buying the highest. But this high-minded resolution, which is a consequence not so much of long deliberation as of the deepest impulse of earnestness, is indeed also necessary if a person is to buy the highest. The sensate person will not understand what the highest is, will not understand what the good fight[401] is, what it is to be victorious and to lose, *will* not, because, praise God, the poorest and simplest child who received the most meager education in the charity school—he knows it very well. Yes, it would be a uniquely great and exceptional person who in his adulthood accomplished merely half of what he knew in his childhood, of what in his boyhood he knew how to develop in an essay. But the sensate person's self-love is too narrow-minded to want to be grasped by the highest; it is use-

v
151

less for anyone to think of making the highest comprehensible
to him by means of fine words, to think of tricking him into
it by a pious fraud or of playing him into its hands by a loving
ruse: in his hands it becomes perverted; in his hands it becomes the opposite. It is true and always will be true that virtue is the highest sagacity. It is also certain that the sensate
person is eager to be sagacious and aspires to sagacity, but
even if someone, in order to win him, were to expound this,
he still would never win him to virtue; if that is to happen, the
sensate person's conception of sagacity would first have to be
completely altered. It is true that a conciliatory spirit is the
hardest revenge; it is true, as an old wise man has said, that
the worst punishment for insults is to forget them.[402] But
what confusion there would be, what atrocious presumptuousness, if a vengeful person were to hide like a wolf[403] in the
garments of a conciliatory spirit, or would he thereby come a
step closer to the beautiful virtue of a conciliatory spirit?
Without fail, the good has its reward, but if the "reward-hun-
gry" sensate person wanted to do the good for that reason,
would he ever put it into practice? Incontestably, it is always
the surest thing in life to do one's duty, but can it really be the
surest thing to do when duty sometimes gives orders to sacrifice life? No, the soul must make a resolution in renunciation
of all calculating, all sagacity and probability; it must will the
good because it is the good, and then it will certainly perceive
that it has its reward; it must continue in duty because it is
duty, and then it will thereby really feel the security; it must
will to be reconciled with its opponent[404] out of the unreckon-
ing impulse of the heart, and then the good fight of reconciliation will also win for him the affection of the vanquished.

The same holds true for the understanding of what is to be
the theme of this discourse—how one who struggles aright in
prayer is victorious by losing. If a person is unwilling to make
a decisive resolution, if he wants to cheat God of the heart's
daring venture in which a person ventures way out and loses
sight of all shrewdness and probability, indeed, takes leave of
his senses or at least of all his worldly mode of thinking, if
instead of beginning with one step he almost craftily seeks to

find out something, to have the infinite certainty changed into a finite certainty, then this discourse will not be able to benefit him. There is an upside-downness that wants to reap before it sows; there is a cowardliness that wants to have certainty before it begins; there is a hypersensitivity so copious in words that it continually shrinks from acting; but what would it avail a person if, double-minded and fork-tongued, he wanted to dupe God, trap him in probability, but refused to understand the improbable, that one must lose everything in order to gain everything,[405] and understand it so honestly that, in the most crucial moment, when his soul is already shuddering at the risk, he does not again leap to his own aid with the explanation that he has not yet fully made a resolution but merely wanted to feel his way. Therefore, all discussion of struggling with God in prayer, of the actual loss (since if the pain of annihilation is not actually suffered, then the sufferer is not yet out upon the deep,[406] and his scream is not the scream of danger but in the face of danger) and the figurative victory cannot have the purpose of persuading anyone or of converting the situation into a task for secular appraisal and changing God's gift of grace to the venturer into temporal small change for the timorous. It really would not help a person (even if the one speaking were capable of it) if the speaker, by his oratorical artistry, led him to jump into a half hour's resolution, by the ardor of conviction started a fire in him so that he would blaze in a momentary good intention without being able, however, to sustain a resolution or to nourish an intention as soon as the speaker stopped talking. Even if an angel spoke with the tongue of an angel[407] in order to describe the beneficial effect of prayer, it would not help the sensate person, because he neither understands nor cares about that for which prayer is beneficial. Of what use would it be, then, if the sensate person was pleased to hear the word "beneficial" and the angel used it, when the two of them, at odds in everything, would not even agree on the use of this word.

Yet the discourse may well have its significance, but to ruminate on this is again precarious and doubtful; therefore, it is best to regard the discourse as a daring venture. In other words, if one person makes comprehensible to another something that is to his advantage in the temporal sense and the latter acts accordingly, then the former may be said to have brought it about. If, however, a person tries to make comprehensible to another his eternal well-being, this does not help straightway in the same manner, inasmuch as the second still has not grasped the eternal on the basis of what the first said. If, however, he makes the eternal resolution and in it grasps the eternal, then he owes no one anything, not the speaker either. To be specific, no human being can give an eternal resolution to another or take it from him; one human being cannot be indebted to another.[408] If someone objects that then one might just as well be silent if there is no probability of winning others, he thereby has merely shown that although his life very likely thrived and prospered in probability and every one of his undertakings in the service of probability went forward, he has never really ventured and consequently has never had or given himself the opportunity to consider that probability is an illusion, but to venture the truth is what gives human life and the human situation pith and meaning, to venture is the fountainhead of inspiration, whereas probability is the sworn enemy of enthusiasm, the mirage whereby the sensate person drags out time and keeps the eternal away, whereby he cheats God, himself, and his generation: cheats God of the honor, himself of liberating annihilation, and his generation of the equality of conditions.

Therefore, the discourse will seek to comprehend what is upbuilding in the thought that: *One Who Prays Aright Struggles in Prayer and Is Victorious—in That God Is Victorious.*[409]

To struggle in prayer—what a contradiction! Would one expression be strong enough to hold together two such opposite thoughts! In every struggle the weapon of combat is designated in advance; therefore, if prayer is designated as the weapon of combat here, then the struggle seems impossible, since prayer, after all, is not a weapon of war but on the contrary the quiet pursuit of peace; prayer is the weapon not of one who attacks another or of one who defends himself but of one who yields. If, as is routine in any struggle, the distance between the contenders is determined in advance, then the struggle again seems impossible, because when there is no praying, God is in heaven and man is on earth, and consequently the distance is too great; but when there is praying, they are indeed too close to each other, then there is no in-between that can be marked out as the battleground. In other words, if a person yields himself completely in prayer, he does not struggle, but if he does not yield himself at all, then he is not praying, even if he were to stay down on his knees praying day and night. It is the same here as with a person who is maintaining a connection with a distant friend. If he does not see to it that the letter is addressed properly, it will not be delivered and the connection will not be made, no matter how many letters he writes; similarly, let the one who prays see to it that the form of the prayer is proper, a yielding of himself in the inner being, because otherwise he is not praying to God; and let the one who prays be scrupulously attentive to this, since no deception is possible here in relation to the searcher of hearts. Whereas kings and princes flee to rural solitude in order to escape the hordes of ill-timed or unreasonable supplicants, God in heaven is better safeguarded, although he is still always the nearest one to every human being; better safeguarded, since every prayer that does not have the right form, which is in the inner being, does not reach his ear at all, although he is near enough to hear the softest sigh, does not pertain to him, since it is not a prayer to him. And even if such a prayer pushes itself to the front, even if it resounds loudly out in the world, there is no living creature who knows to whom these words pertain, to say nothing of an angel's having the idea of bringing it before God[410]—if you can imagine such a thing, my listener, since the angel promptly sees from the form that it is not directed to God. This, you see, is why it seems so impossible that prayer can become a weapon against God, because only the proper prayer reaches him; the improper prayer he does not even hear, and it is even less possible that someone praying in this way would be able to attack or wound him or wrong him. A person can wrong another human being with his prayer, and prayer in this manner is a terrible weapon between man and man, perhaps the most pernicious. The strong man is warned not to misuse his power against the weak, but the weak man is also warned not to misuse the power of prayer against the strong. It may well be that a tyrant who misused his power, a deceiver who misused his shrewdness, never perpetrated as atrocious a wrong as the one who cowardly and slyly prayed in the wrong place, prayed in order to advance his will, [411]flung himself into the weakness of prayer, into imploring misery, in order to shatter another person. But this is not the case in the relationship to God; in his blessedness, he is spared the most forgivable and the basest misuse of prayers, of screams and tears.

But then what is the condition in which the struggle of prayer may be said to take place? Who is the praying one who struggles with God in prayer and therefore simultaneously preserves a relationship of deep and inward devotion to God because he prays but is also so separate from God that they are able to struggle? If we consider the child, presumably everyone is inclined to praise its simple and devout prayer, since the child is poor in spirit and therefore sees God,[412] and its prayer never engages in struggle with him. This is the basis of the child's happiness, but in a later consideration this is also the basis of an ambiguity in the child's devotion to God. The child, if for the most part it is brought up in the admonition of the Lord, prays to God about the good, thanks God for the good. About what good and for what good? About the good according to the child's conception. When the child receives a toy at Christmas time, it thanks God, as it is encouraged to do, and it would have to be a peculiar child who in that season of the year would not be thoroughly convinced of God's goodness, if the parents' circumstances generally support their predisposition toward God and toward the child. So it is with all the good about which the child prays and for which it gives thanks.

On the other hand, the child does not ascribe the painful, the sad, or the unpleasant (and actually the child mind distinguishes almost exclusively between the pleasant and the unpleasant) to God. No wonder, then, that the child thinks God is goodness itself! The unpleasant is explained in another way, probably most often by means of the idea of evil people or a bad man who only makes mischief. If the child sees its mother distressed, it never thinks of tracing the distress back to God as the cause, or that there might be an ambiguity of distress and accordingly that the distress might come from God for the very purpose of drawing the person to God. The child, however, immediately thinks of evil people. If the child loses its father in death and sees the mother's pain, it actually has no conception of what death can be; the child is far removed, even though it becomes aware, because of the seriousness, of the shadow of sorrow that spreads over the whole environment. But the child also receives new clothes and at times is so delighted with them that the mother herself, even if in tears, cannot help smiling at it, and by this the child's view of death is again confused. Now if the mother, despite her sorrow, does not forget her solicitude for the child and explains to it that the father is in heaven with God, then the child is quickly reconciled with God and, as always, is a blessing here also, because the explanation, which in the beginning was perhaps only an invention of mother love intended for the child, little by little, quietly and secretly, satisfies the mother and becomes an explanation for the sorrowing widow.

The child leaps over the difficulty: death. The father was here on earth, and it was very good, for his father love was completely in accord with the child's conception; now the father is in heaven and is comfortable with God. But the child really does not give any thought to how the change came about; in any case, it will scarcely occur to the child to attribute the death to God. Therefore, we should always be a little cautious in the frequent eulogizing of the piety of the child mind. What is laudable, something everyone must desire, must seek to preserve until death, is the child's inwardness, since to the child God is truly living and present every time it thinks of him. In another sense, however, the child's conception of God is really not very godly.

The difficulty begins as soon as the contrasting ideas must be thought together, as when the sorrowing wife must ascribe

v
156

her loss and distress to God, must find another explanation than the one the mother had readily available for the child. The difficulty first appears at a later age, when on the one hand the conceptions of the joyful, the desirable, good, and evil are clearly developed, and on the other hand the conception that ultimately everything must be ascribed to God if there is to be a God and a godly view of life. If the childlike sensibility comes back again unclarified, we call it childishness and are not satisfied with inwardness, because this is required to be related to a larger maturity. [413]Who, indeed, would praise the piety of the adult who did not have a more earnest conception of life than to know how to distinguish between the pleasant and the unpleasant and a more holy conception of God than to dare thoughtlessly to saddle, as it were, God with the same understanding, in which they were agreed that God gave and he thanked? Such a wretch would certainly never reach the point of struggling in prayer, since if everything went according to his wish, he would give thanks for it, and if it went contrary to his wish, he would stop praying, because he would altogether lack the true inwardness of the thought that it must be understood as God wants it to be understood, that everything must be ascribed to him. But this inwardness cannot immediately penetrate the outward, which is in tune with the sensate person's ideas and conceptions, and thereby the struggle is made impossible, because to learn to know God is even more difficult than to know a human being, and if one knows God only through externals, one cannot easily be halted by a disappointment, inasmuch as God is solely spirit. If a person gives up the inwardness of that thought, he no longer reaches the point of struggling in prayer. His struggle becomes something entirely different, for which we dare not promise such a glorious outcome, no matter whether he goes so far as to want to defy God, indeed, to the extreme defiance of wanting to deny God and thereby almost annihilate him, or is so childish as to want to put God in a predicament so that God will have regrets afterward when it is too late. Just as there has never been anyone who has not assumed the existence of a god, but there certainly have been some who have not wanted to let this thought have any power over them, so in a less direct way others demonstrate that they cannot do without God if for no other reason than to be able to become self-important and significant by means of the idea that God cannot manage without them, just like a pampered and spoiled child who wants to do without his father and yet cannot do without the thought that nourishes his own vanity— that it is bound to hurt his father.

How numerous the strugglers are, how varied the struggle in which the one who prays tries himself *with* God (since someone who tries himself *against* God does not struggle in prayer), how varied the means of prayer, the special nature of the prayer, with which the struggler seeks to overcome God! The struggler is indeed so inclined; it is his intention that the struggle be fruitful, that it end with a glorious result, and if anyone were to say to him, in order to calm him down, that God is the unchanging, that God not only lives far off in heaven but is even further away from every human being in his changelessness, [414]this kind of talk would certainly upset the struggler. Just as the worst thing that can be said of a person is that he is an inhuman brute, so it is the worst and the most revolting blasphemy to say of God that he is inhuman, no matter if it is supposed to be very fashionable or bold to talk that way. No, the God to whom he prays is human, has the heart to feel humanly, the ear to hear a human being's complaint; and even though he does not fulfill every wish, he still lives close to us and is moved by the struggler's cry, by his humble request, by his wretchedness when he sits abandoned and as if in prison, by his speedy joy over the fulfillment when in hope he anticipates it. Indeed, this God is moved by the struggler's lament when he is perishing in despondency, by his shout when he is sinking in the maelstrom of change, by the thanksgiving he promises for all time; he is moved, if not earlier, then by the final sigh when, humanly speaking, it already seems to be too late.

So there is a struggle. One person contends in prayer for his share of the good things that fail to come, another for the honor that beckons, another for the happiness he wants to cre-

V
158

ate for his beloved, another for the happiness that will flourish for him at his beloved's side. One person contends in prayer against the horror of the past from which he is fleeing, another against the terror of the future into which he is staring, another with the secret horror that resides in solitude, another with the danger everyone sees. One person contends for the fulfillment of the wish, another against the fulfilled wish, since it was precipitous. One person strains every nerve even though he keeps on praying; another is expecting everything from the prayer even though he keeps on working; one ponders the relation of the fulfillment to the work; another ponders the misrelation. Alas, even though there is peace in the land, health and abundance, alas, even when the sun smiles bright and warm, there is still so much struggle. Alas, even when the overarching night sky is silent and starlit and the fields are at rest, there is still so much struggle!

But what is the issue in the struggle? That God is goodness? Not at all. That God is love? Not at all. No, it is a matter of making oneself clear to God, of truly explaining to him what is beneficial for the one who is praying, of truly impressing it upon his mind, of truly gaining his consent to the wish. And the struggle is well intentioned toward God, because it is about truly being able to be happy in God, truly being able to give him thanks, truly being able to witness to his honor, truly being able to be assured that all fatherliness lives in heaven, truly being able to love him—as people do indeed say when they designate the ultimate, to love as much as one loves God. And the struggler is open toward God, because he dares to testify to himself that he is not a child, does not fragment his soul so that he wishes for one thing this minute and something else the next, so that when the fulfillment arrives he has thoughtlessly forgotten the wish—no, there is only the one. He dares to testify to himself that he is straining all his understanding to become sufficiently foresighted to spy the remotest hint of the fulfillment, that he is straining every thought to conjure forth from the most insignificant event anything it could be hiding, that he welcomes with thanksgiving any hint and invites it to stay. Nor is his prayer some deceitful strategy, his last resort, since he does like to pray and does not want to stop praying. If he catches himself becoming lukewarm[415] and falling away from God, he is not slow to repent and is quick to struggle again in prayer.

This is the struggle. Is it not so, my listener, or was it not this way? The person who falls away and gives up praying—of him and his struggle we do not speak. But now the outcome! But who is it who asks? Is it an inquisitive man who would also like to hear this story? We have no reply for him. If it is a man who has been tested, then he himself knows it better than the speaker, and we shall indeed be glad to receive his guidance. But let the struggler ask, because the person who struggles is indeed the first to ask about the outcome. Perhaps he would prefer that there would be an experience that would guarantee that circumstances are such that prayer is a kind of payment God requires, but for this price the one who prays eventually does obtain what he desires. Do you suppose that this experience would be able to help him; do you suppose that the experience has helped anyone at all except the one who himself had it and consequently was not helped by it? Perhaps he would wish that there would be mention of a marvelous fulfillment of the wish, that it happened as it once did long ago that the wedding guests received the unexpected abundance of good wine, and the blind his sight, and the paralytic his health, and the dead man his life, and the mother her child again, and that unhappy fugitive among the graves regained his participation in the community of men.[416] Do you suppose that it would benefit him, as he construed it, if nevertheless the addition were made that this does not happen anymore? Happy indeed is anyone to whom this happened; blessed indeed is anyone who can rejoice over it, over those glorious days, even though he knows that they are past! But what about the outcome of the struggle, you ask, and this question is not casually tossed out. It is simultaneously afraid and eager to hear the explanation. To look forward to an explanation is still always a comfort, and hope dares to promise itself everything from the explanation as long as it has not been heard. Therefore one is afraid to *have* heard it, but the

explanation is, after all, a comfort, and this is why one is eager
to hear it. The outcome has already been mentioned: *one who
prays struggles* in prayer; we have seen him struggle; he *is victorious*. This, then, is the outcome, but he is victorious *in that*
God is victorious and in this way he becomes one who *prays
aright*.

My listener, have you never talked with a person who although much wiser was nevertheless favorably disposed toward you, indeed, more or at least more soundly (and consequently more) concerned about your welfare than you
yourself? If you have not, then consider what could happen to
you or to me, as I now present it. You see, in the beginning
we were completely at odds. What the wise one said seemed
very strange to me, yet I had confidence in him that he would
not misuse his superiority but would allow himself to be per-
suaded and would himself help me to eliminate the misunderstanding. So we talked together and exchanged many a word
in the struggle of discussion. Presumably the wise one must
have maintained his outlook, for he remained calm, whereas
I, without really noticing how and without feeling ashamed
of it, became almost violent, because it was so important to
me that the wise one should share my view that I did not dare
to adhere to it except in agreement with him—but did dare to
attack him in order to move him to agreement. Indeed, was it
not bound to make me violent; after all, it was self-contradic-
tory to want to win the wise one over to my view in a crafty
way by means of my skill (as if I were the stronger) and then
be really convinced of the correctness of my view only in the
confidence that it was the view of the wise one, since he was
indeed the stronger—I continually had this faith in him—and
to me agreement with him was crucial. Finally, after fitfully
wandering around, as it were, in the conversation for a long
time and after having both attempted and suffered much, I
was suddenly so clear about what I wanted to say that I very
briefly and with unaccountable force set forth my view, assured that it was bound to convince him. And see, the wise
one agreed with me and gave me his approval. But since he
was favorably disposed toward me and believed that I could

bear the explanation, he shook his finger at me and said: Your present view is just what I said from the beginning, when you could not and would not understand me.

[417]Then, of course, modesty awakened in my soul, and I was ashamed of my earlier conduct, but nevertheless it did not take away from me the bold confidence to rejoice over the truth now understood, even though I was far from having vanquished the wise one, since only I myself had become convinced and strengthened by the struggle. How amazing! But it was indeed fortunate that I did not take another road, did not lose my temper, did not discontinue the struggle, did not abuse the wise one as if he were my enemy because he would not yield to me, did not raise a hue and cry about his self-love because he would not indulge me but on the contrary loved me better than I myself understood. And modesty again saved me from doing what I otherwise would have done if I had discontinued the struggle and later discerned the truth myself: that I would have continued to regard the wise one as my enemy, although what I now discerned was just what he had said; that I would even have wanted to insult him by defiantly suggesting that I had now understood the truth without him and in spite of him, although he simply wanted to help me to discern the truth by myself and although he was the only one who could have prevented me from doing this by agreeing with me, whereby he would have ransomed [*løskjøbt*] himself from my insults and bought [*kjøbt*] my thanks.

This is how it is with the struggler if he does not give up the inwardness that is the condition for really being able to say of him that he is struggling in prayer. Do not say, my listener, that this is a pious fancy; do not appeal to experience, that it does not go this way in life. Indeed, that is unimportant if it nevertheless can go this way and you are coercing me, in order to agree with you, only to say that it probably does go otherwise in life, namely, because it does happen that people become lukewarm and cold and indifferent, so that they perceive neither the former nor the latter, and forgetful, so that when they have come to the end they no longer remember how it was in the beginning, and crafty and fraudulent and brash, so that they accuse God of not helping them and flout God, saying that they can help themselves, of which the former is an eternal lie, and the latter, if there is to be any truth in it at all, no one can have learned except from God. But for the person who does not give up his inwardness, does not in his struggling struggle himself out of the relation to God but struggles his way closer to God, it happens as was explained, in that the prayer's inwardness in God becomes the most important to him [418]and not a means for the attainment of an end. Or should praying for something belong so essentially to prayer that the prayer becomes more inward the more one has to pray for or the more copious one is in words? Should not a person who prays, indeed, one who prays aright, be one who says: Lord, my God, I really have nothing at all for which to pray to you; even if you would promise to grant my every wish, I really cannot think of anything—except that I may remain with you, as near as possible in this time of separation in which you and I are living, and entirely with you in all eternity? And insofar as the one who prays turns his gaze toward heaven, would that one, then, be one who prays, or one who prays aright, whose restless eyes continually bring him some comfort for a particular sorrow, some fulfillment of a particular wish—and not rather the one whose calm eyes seek only God? And it must come to this if the inwardness is not given up but is kept unchanged and is guarded as a sacred fire within a person, because the wish, the earthly craving, the worldly concern is the temporal and ordinarily dies before the person dies even if he does not grasp the eternal—how then would it hold out with the eternal! Then the wish becomes less and less ardent, and finally its time is over; then the worm of craving dies[419] little by little, and craving becomes extinct; then the vigilance of concern falls asleep little by little, never to awaken again, but the time of inwardness is never over.

[420]Who, then, has been victorious? It is God, from whom the one praying could not extort fulfillment by his prayers. But the one praying is indeed also victorious. Or is it victory to be acknowledged in the right although one is in the wrong, to obtain the fulfillment of an earthly wish [421]as if it were the

highest, a demonstration that one had prayed to God and prayed aright, a demonstration that God is love and that the one who prays has an understanding with him, when, on the contrary, the one who prays has become a lifelong debtor to the one whom he himself has made into an idol by his prayer and by his thanks.

What, then, is the victory? In what is the condition of the victors different from that of the strugglers? [422]Has God become changed? An answer in the affirmative seems to be a dark saying, and yet it is so, he has become changed, for now it has indeed become manifest that God is unchanging. But this changelessness is not that chilling indifference, that devastating loftiness, that ambiguous distance, which the callous understanding lauded. No, on the contrary, this changelessness is intimate and warm and everywhere present; it is a changelessness in being concerned for a person, and therefore it does not admit of being changed by the scream of the one who prays as if everything were all over now, by his cowardliness when he finds it most convenient not to be able to help himself, by his false contrition [*Sønderknuselse*], of which he promptly repents [*fortryde*] as soon as the momentary alarm of the danger is past.

[423]Has the one who prays become changed? Yes, this is not hard to see, because he has become one who prays aright, and he who prays aright is always victorious, since it is one and the same. In an imperfect way, he was already sure of this, because while he had sufficient inwardness to pray, he was also assured that the wish would be fulfilled if he prayed aright, prayed aright with regard to the wish—this is how he understood it. Now he is changed, but this is still true—indeed, now it has become true that when he prays aright he is victorious. That he prayed was beneficial for him from the very beginning, however imperfect his prayer; it helped him, namely, to concentrate his soul on one wish. Unfortunately, a person usually desires far too many things, lets his soul flutter with every breeze. But he who prays knows how to make distinctions; little by little he gives up that which according to his earthly conception is less important, since he does not really

dare to come before God with it, and because he does not wish to forfeit the goodness of God by always importuning for this and that, but on the contrary wants to give all the more emphasis to the request for his one and only wish. Then before God he concentrates his soul on the one wish, and this already has something ennobling about it, is preparation for giving up everything, because only he can give up everything who had but one single wish. In this way he is prepared to be strengthened in the struggle with God and to be victorious, because he who prays aright struggles in prayer and is victorious in that God is victorious.

On the battlefield, it so happens that if the first line of combatants has been victorious, then the second is not led into battle at all but merely shares in the triumph. In the world of the spirit, it is not this way. If a person has not done his utmost to win a victory, then the victory admittedly means a victory, but it also means that he will soon be led into a new struggle in order to be victorious by losing. [424]How many strugglers there are now; how hidden and private the struggle in a person's inner being frequently is, since the visible betrays nothing. [425]He who prays asks for nothing in the external world, his wish does not center on anything earthly, his mind is not occupied, is not concerned with many things—no, he sits there quietly with his loss, but still he is not idle, for he is ruminating, and still he is not passive, for he is pondering an explanation. Consequently, the struggle has become even more inward. He is not intent upon explaining his wish to God, making himself clear to God in his prayer—far from it: he has given up his wish, he is bearing his loss, he is reconciling himself to the pain, and yet he is a long way from *the explanation*; his struggle in prayer is for God to explain himself to him. And he dares to testify to himself that he is not a child who thinks that the explanation is there for the asking, or a young girl who wants to dream up an explanation—no, he is working. When life is noisy during the day, his thought works at drowning out the noise; when everything is still at night, his thought is working in order to find the explanation. Indeed, even in the moment of weakness, when ordinarily no one is able to work, his thought still works—it works on holidays as well as on workdays, and the day of celebration has not yet arrived. What has happened must, of course, be for the best, the loss and the pain must be efficacious in quite another way than the fulfillment of the one and only wish or of all wishes. Efficacious—yes, that is the name of the bridge he wants to throw from his pain across to his blessedness, but alas, the bridge is continually being cut off! Efficacious—yes, that is the name of the ferryman whose friendship he wants to buy, but alas, he is silent! [426]Efficacious—yes, that is the name of the twilight in which he wants to meet God, but alas, the summons does not come! Efficacious—yes, that is the name of the initiation he covets, that he might be initiated into the understanding that with God is the secret of the sufferings!

Or is this the explanation, that God denies him the understanding and requires only faith and consequently wants only the understanding with him that is in the realm of the ununderstandable? Indeed, this is faith, and let us not mock God and human beings and those who have been tried and the heroes and the language and the successors and those who are troubled and ourselves by wanting to make it into something else. Faith reads the understanding only as in a dark saying;[427] humanly speaking, it does not have the explanation, only in a certain deranged sense, so that, humanly speaking, it is the most foolish business arrangement ever made in the world. But this is the way it is supposed to be, and God in heaven is still unembarrassed; he is not selling out, whatever human beings do. And he is indeed unchanging, as the understanding says in order to mock the troubled one who cries out to God; but see, its mockery recoils on itself, because God truly is unchanged. He has not become a friend of cowardliness and softness; he has not become so debilitated over the years that he cannot distinguish between mine and thine and everything runs together before him; he is himself still the first inventor of language and the only one who holds the blessing in his hands; he is unchanged, even though he would not be able to satisfy the demands of the times! So it is with faith—humanly speaking, it is the most foolish and, humanly speaking, the most difficult business arrangement.

[428]And when is the Comforter coming? "When I have gone away from you,"[429] Christ answered the sorrowful disciples he had trained as shop apprentices to make the good business arrangement. And what was he to them? He was all that they possessed; for them he was their sole, priceless possession; with them he was the daily bread of joy; to them he was the expectancy of blessedness. No rich man became so poor by losing everything, and no lover became so poor by losing the beloved, and no one full of expectancy became so poor as the disciples. Yet Christ had to go away, "and this is beneficial for you."[430] You see, this is faith's explanation—do you suppose that the disciples, humanly speaking, understood it or could understand it? So the Comforter is coming. When? Indeed, when this has happened. But is he coming right away—because this, of course, is what we are asking about by asking when. But was it right away for the disciples, was it right away for Abraham—when it took seventy years for the comfort to come?[431] Blessed be the man who knows how to sing for the one who grieves, who knows how to support the one whose knees have deteriorated and who totters as he walks, to lead someone who stared himself blind because he saw nothing but hopeless wretchedness around him. [432]But let us renounce all the loose talk that wants to shorten time for the sorrowing one but has not itself learned from sorrows what it is to count, all the loose talk that has the form of comfort but not its power, all the verbosity that sounds eloquent to the ear but has the repulsiveness of falsehood in the eater's mouth! No, the Comforter does not come immediately, and the only thing a person dares to tell himself and others is that he is coming, as surely as God lives he is coming.

Then the Comforter comes with the explanation; then he makes everything new,[433] strips the sufferer of his mourning apparel and gives him a new heart and an assured spirit.[434] It may, however, take time. If the struggler—even though he thought that he had lost everything—had deceived himself, if his soul in one regard or another maintained a worldly well-being with the aid of human probability, then there is still time. Then misjudgment can have time to vex him who lost everything; then ingratitude can have time and courage to be obstinate and to defy him who, misguided by the scream that indicated great danger, ventured into the danger and himself stayed there where the one who had screamed imagined himself to be; then mockery can have time to wound by demanding human demonstration from him who has only his sufferings as a demonstration that God is love; then shame has opportunity to seek the company of hurt. How many new pains may still be reserved for him who believed that he had lost everything, how privately and hiddenly they may strike him. But it all helps the explanation!

In this way, the struggle goes on for an explanation, and prayer is the means by which the explanation will correspond to the way he prays about it. One person struggles with all his might against the explanation that would make himself guilty—no, it was all the dispensation of providence, all from God in order to test, to purify, to try the lover. Another struggles in order that the explanation may explain his guilt to him, so that the passion of freedom will not seem an illusion, but that the chasmic separation of guilt may make the blessedness of reconciliation all the more inward. One person asks that the explanation will unite him to the race and that the explanation will lie in the fate common to all, which is meaningful for the whole; another that the explanation will consider him outside the relation to others in order to select him for solitary pain, but also for solitary election. [435]So the struggle goes; the struggler contends with God in prayer, or he struggles with himself and in his prayer calls on God for help against himself. [436]But if the struggler still does not give up his inwardness and consequently stop praying, if he loves God greatly,[437] if he longs for God humbly as one longs for someone without whom one is nothing, fervently as one longs for someone by whom one becomes everything; if he deals honestly with his debt of thanksgiving and adoration to God, which constantly increases because as yet he cannot give thanks aright, cannot understand aright; if he deals with it as a good entrusted to him for better times—then, then he is struggling in prayer. And whatever happens in the meantime, which is concealed even from the angels, and whenever the hour comes that no one knows except God,[438] and even though he must buy new oil for the lamp[439] of expectancy more than once, it nevertheless remains certain that anyone who buys from God will never be deceived by having his purchase later prove to be of lesser worth. Even though a person accidentally bought a trifle at too high a price, if we may speak this way, nevertheless, if he bought it from God and the expensive purchase was made in integrity before God and in trust in the Lord,[440] then he has not bought too dearly, he will not regret the purchase, because what he bought was no trifle—the payment and God vouch for that. If a person cared so much for what the sagacious promptly and the majority the next day would label a trifle that in the loss of it he would have lost everything and in this pain renounced the world and everything that belongs to the world,[441] he will not repent of the purchase when he also sees its insignificance, if his silent pain otherwise brought him into relationship with God, because to scream, to become temporarily important to oneself and to others, is certainly not buying from God; it is only an unfruitful manifestation of the vain nature of the sensual and the sensate. He will not regret the purchase only if he truly did give up everything, and this can be the truth, since otherwise no one could have given up everything except someone who in the opinion of worldly appraisers has lost everything, but to lose everything and to give up everything do not mean one and the same. But someone who even on the occasion of a trifle bought God's confidence and friendship will truly not regret it; on the contrary, he will eternally give thanks to God that he was the kind of child who cared so much for a trifle, the kind of child who simply could not grasp that it was a trifle.

But what about the outcome! [442]My listener, imagine a child sitting and drawing with a pencil, drawing whatever occurs to a child, whatever a child recklessly and disconnectedly dashes off; but behind the child stands an invisible artist who guides his hand so that the drawing that is about to become disordered submits to the law of beauty, so that the line that is about to go astray is called back within the boundary of beauty—imagine the child's amazement! Or imagine that a child puts his drawing aside in the evening, but while he sleeps a friendly hand finishes the jumbled and poorly begun sketch—imagine the child's wonder when he sees his drawing again the next morning! So also with a person; let us never forget that even the more mature person always retains some of the child's lack of judgment, especially if the prayer is to assist the explanation, not as the essential but as a means. The young man is busy considering what he wants to be in the world, whom of the great and outstanding he wants to emulate. The more earnest one has put away childish things;[443] he is not concerned with the external world this way; he only wants to develop himself. Therefore, he sits down and draws. Is he not one who draws, he who struggles in prayer with God for an explanation? Will not the explanation draw a boundary line between him and God so that face-to-face with God he begins to resemble himself? Ah, but now comes the difference, because the child has to be helped by the addition of something, but more and more is taken away from the struggler. The external world and every claim on life were taken away from him; now he is struggling for an explanation, but he is not even struggling his way to that. Finally it seems to him that he is reduced to nothing at all. Now the moment has come. [444]Whom should the struggler desire to resemble other than God? [445]But if he himself is something or wants to be something, this something is sufficient to hinder the resemblance. Only when he himself becomes nothing, only then can God illuminate him so that he resembles God. However great he is, he cannot manifest God's likeness; God can imprint himself in him only when he himself has become nothing. When the ocean is exerting all its power, that is precisely the time when it cannot reflect the image of heaven, and even the slightest motion blurs the image; but when it becomes still and deep, then the image of heaven sinks into its nothingness.

Who, then, was victorious? It was God, because he did not give the explanation requested by the one who prayed, and he did not give it as the struggling one requested it. But the one struggling was also victorious. Or was it not a victory that instead of receiving an explanation [*Forklaring*] from God he was transfigured [*forklaret*] in God, and his transfiguration [*Forklarelse*] is this: to reflect the image of God.

What, then, is the victory; in what is the condition of the victors different from that of the strugglers? [446]Has God become changed? An answer in the affirmative seems to be a hard saying, and yet it is so; at least the one who prays understands him differently and demands no explanation. Has the one who prays become changed? Yes, because he understands himself differently, and yet he does not stop being one who prays, since he gives thanks always. [447]But the one who always gives thanks prays aright, and the one who always gives thanks must also have been victorious continually; otherwise why should he give thanks! [448]And would this giving of thanks ever cease? Certainly not; there is always reason to thank God, and every human being is in debt to him, and eternally in debt. Alas, the debt someone incurs at the gambling table, by throwing dice, in a game of cards, is called a debt of honor; I suppose that because it is meaningless in itself we have to give it an impressive name and then hurry to be rid of it. The debt to God is not a debt of honor like that, but it is, nevertheless, an honor to be in debt to God. It is an honor not to owe fortune anything, but to owe God everything; not to owe fate anything, but to owe providence everything; not to owe caprice anything, but to owe a fatherliness everything. — In this way, he who prays aright struggles in prayer and is victorious in that God is victorious.

We have spoken about struggle. [449]Struggle is usually not joyful; when one person is victorious, the other is crushed— alas, it sometimes happens that both the victor and the one overcome have lost. But this struggle is marvelous, well worth being tested in, eternally worth praising, since here they both are more blessedly victorious than when the lover's argument is transfigured into increased love. [450]Are you saying, my listener, that this discourse is not easy (one who is being tested may find it poor and bland compared with the sufferings)—the struggle itself is not easy either. If someone wants to beguile himself by anticipating the quiet outcome of the struggle, its happy understanding, then this is not the fault of the discourse. The victory is still a victory only in a certain high and noble and therefore metaphorical sense, but the pain is literal. When the hour of victory is coming, we do not know, but this we do know—the struggle is a life-and-death struggle.

SUPPLEMENT

KEY TO REFERENCES

Marginal references alongside the text are to volume and page [III 100] in *Søren Kierkegaards samlede Værker*, I-XIV, edited by A. B. Drachmann, J. L. Heiberg, and H. O. Lange (1 ed., Copenhagen: Gyldendal, 1901-06). The same marginal references are used in Søren Kierkegaard, *Gesammelte Werke*, Abt. 1-36 (Düsseldorf, Cologne: Diederichs Verlag, 1952-69).

References to Kierkegaard's works in English are to this edition, *Kierkegaard's Writings* [*KW*], I-XXVI (Princeton: Princeton University Press, 1978-). Specific references to the *Writings* are given by English title and the standard Danish pagination referred to above [*Either/Or*, I, *KW* III (*SV* I 100)].

References to the *Papirer* [*Pap.* I A 100; note the differentiating letter A, B, or C, used only in references to the *Papirer*] are to *Søren Kierkegaards Papirer*, I-XI³, edited by P. A. Heiberg, V. Kuhr, and E. Torsting (1 ed., Copenhagen: Gyldendal, 1909-48), and 2 ed., photo-offset with two supplemental volumes, I-XIII, edited by Niels Thulstrup (Copenhagen: Gyldendal, 1968-70), and with index, XIV-XVI (1975-78), edited by Niels Jørgen Cappelørn. References to the *Papirer* in English [*JP* II 1500], occasionally amended, are to volume and serial entry number in *Søren Kierkegaard's Journals and Papers*, I-VII, edited and translated by Howard V. Hong and Edna H. Hong, assisted by Gregor Malantschuk (Bloomington: Indiana University Press, 1967-78).

References to correspondence are to the serial numbers in *Breve og Aktstykker vedrørende Søren Kierkegaard*, I-II, edited by Niels Thulstrup (Copenhagen: Munksgaard, 1953-54), and to the corresponding serial numbers in *Kierkegaard: Letters and Documents*, translated by Henrik Rosenmeier, *Kierkegaard's Writings*, XXV [*Letters*, Letter 100, *KW* XXV].

References to books in Kierkegaard's own library [*ASKB* 100] are based on the serial numbering system of *Auktionsprotokol over Søren Kierkegaards Bogsamling* (Auction-catalog of

Søren Kierkegaard's Book-collection), edited by H. P. Rohde (Copenhagen: Royal Library, 1967).

In the Supplement, references to page and line in the text are given as: 100:10-20.

In the notes, internal references to the present work are given as: p. 100.

Three periods indicate an omission by the editors; five periods indicate a hiatus or fragmentariness in the text.

To opbyggelige Taler

af

S. Kierkegaard.

Kjøbenhavn.

Trykt i Bianco Lunos Bogtrykkeri.

1843.

TWO UPBUILDING DISCOURSES

by

S. Kierkegaard.

———————

Copenhagen.

Printed by the Bianco Luno Book Press.

1843.

Tre opbyggelige Taler

af

S. Kierkegaard.

Kjøbenhavn.

Faaes hos Boghandler P. G. Philipsen.

Trykt i Bianco Lunos Bogtrykkeri.

1843.

THREE UPBUILDING DISCOURSES

by

S. Kierkegaard.

Copenhagen.

Available from Bookdealer P. G. Philipsen.

Printed by the Bianco Luno Press.

1843.

Fire opbyggelige Taler

af

S. Kierkegaard.

Kjøbenhavn.

Faaes hos Boghandler P. G. Philipsen.

Trykt i Bianco Lunos Bogtrykkeri.

1843.

FOUR UPBUILDING DISCOURSES

by

S. Kierkegaard.

———————

Copenhagen.

Available from Bookdealer P. G. Philipsen.
Printed by the Bianco Luno Press.
1843.

MDCCCXLIV.

To opbyggelige Taler.

Af

S. Kierkegaard.

Kjøbenhavn.

Faaes hos Boghandler P. G. Philipsen.

Trykt i Bianco Lunos Bogtrykkeri.

MDCCCXLIV.

TWO UPBUILDING DISCOURSES.

by

S. Kierkegaard.

Copenhagen.

Available from Bookdealer P. G. Philipsen.

Printed by the Bianco Luno Book Press.

MDCCCXLIV.

Tre opbyggelige Taler

af

S. Kierkegaard.

Kjøbenhavn.

Faaes hos Boghandler P. G. Philipsen.

Trykt i Bianco Lunos Bogtrykkeri.

MDCCCXLIV.

THREE UPBUILDING DISCOURSES

by

S. Kierkegaard.

———————

Copenhagen.
Available from Bookdealer P. G. Philipsen.
Printed by the Bianco Luno Press.

MDCCCXLIV.

Fire opbyggelige Taler

af

S. Kierkegaard.

Kjøbenhavn.

Faaes hos Boghandler P. G. Philipsen.

Trykt i Bianco Lunos Bogtrykkeri.

MDCCCXLIV.

FOUR UPBUILDING DISCOURSES

by

S. Kierkegaard.

———————

Copenhagen.
Available from Bookdealer P. G. Philipsen.
Printed by the Bianco Luno Press.

Atten opbyggelige Taler

af

S. Kierkegaard.

Kjøbenhavn.

Paa Boghandler P. G. Philipsens Forlag.

Trykt i Bianco Lunos Bogtrykkeri.

1843—1845.

EIGHTEEN UPBUILDING DISCOURSES

by

S. Kierkegaard.

———

Copenhagen.

Bookdealer P. G. Philipsen's Publishing House.

Printed by the Bianco Luno Press.

1843-1845.

Sexten opbyggelige Taler

af

S. Kierkegaard.

Kjøbenhavn.

Paa Boghandler P. G. Philipsens Forlag.

Trykt i BiancoLunos Bogtrykkeri.

1843—1845.

SIXTEEN UPBUILDING DISCOURSES

by

S. Kierkegaard.

Copenhagen.

Bookdealer P. G. Philipsen's Publishing House.

Printed by the Bianco Luno Press.

1843-1845.

SELECTED ENTRIES FROM
KIERKEGAARD'S JOURNALS AND PAPERS
PERTAINING TO
EIGHTEEN UPBUILDING DISCOURSES

It is strange what hate, conspicuous everywhere, Hegel has for the upbuilding,[1] but that which builds up is not an opiate that lulls to sleep; it is the amen of the finite spirit and is an aspect of knowledge that ought not to be ignored.—*JP* II 1588 (*Pap.* III A 6) July 10, 1840

*The Upbuilding That Lies in the Thought That in Relation to God We Are **Always** in the **Wrong**[2]*

Otherwise we might be tempted to despair of providence.

For if there were one man, one single man, no matter if he were the most powerful who ever lived in the world or the most humble, a man who on judgment day could justifiably say: I was not provided for, in the great household I was forgotten, or even if he put much of the blame at his own door yet could justifiably say: I acknowledge that I went astray in the world, I departed from the way of truth, but I did repent of my sin, I honestly intended and strove to the utmost for the good, I lifted up my voice and shouted to heaven for help, but no one answered, there was no constructive solution, not even the remotest relief . . . . . if there were such a man, then everything would be foolishness, where then would the limit be.

—Anyone who has ever yielded to temptation must confess, however, that there was a possibility that in the next moment help was already at hand, and this is an observation, not a sophism, as it might seem to a despairing mind inclined to say: One can always say that.—*JP* V 5486 (*Pap*. III C 5) *n.d.*, 1840-41

Only that which is upbuilding truly unites jest and earnestness. Consequently it is a jest—more priceless than the whole world—that God in heaven is the only great one whom one unceremoniously addresses with *Du*,[3] even though one is ever so insignificant; but this jest is also the deepest earnestness, simply because every human being does it. On the other hand, it is a very mediocre, cheap, and human joke when a particular favorite addresses an earthly majesty with the familiar *Du*; therefore there is no earnestness at all in this jest.—*JP* IV 4924 (*Pap*. IV A 80) *n.d.*, 1843

From sketch; see 31:1, 70:4-5, 109:1-2, 125:1, 141:1, 159:1:

Contents
1. Have a heartfelt love for one another.[4]
2. Every good and every perfect gift.
3. Every good and every perfect gift.
4. The Lord gave, and the Lord took away; blessed be the name of the Lord.
5. Be sober in prayer.
6. Be vigilant in prayer.
7. To save one's soul in patience.

—*Pap*. IV B 161 *n.d.*, 1843

From sketch; see 159:1-3, 205:1-2:

5th Collection of
Upbuilding Discourses.

No. 1. to gain one's soul in patience (popular).
No. 2. to learn from what one suffers (stringent and upbuilding by its stringency).
No. 3. to learn from what one suffers (popular).

No. 4. to learn from what one suffers (lyrical).

(a) No. 5. to be sober in prayer and to become sober through
prayer.

(b) No. 5. patience in expectancies,
on the Gospel for the Sunday after Christmas
Anna.[5]
—*Pap*. IV B 160 *n.d*., 1843-44

From sketch:

Prayer.

Father in heaven! You loved us first.[6] Help us never to forget
that you are love,[7] so that this full conviction might be victorious in our hearts over the world's allurement, the mind's unrest, the anxieties over the future, the horrors of the past, the
needs of the moment. O grant also that this conviction might
form our minds so that our hearts become constant and true
in love to them whom you bid us to love as ourselves.—*JP* III
3394 (*Pap*. IV B 171) *n.d*., 1842-44(?)

From sketch:

You Loved Us First[8]

Father in heaven, let us never forget that you are love, neither when joy claims to make everything comprehensible
without you, nor when sorrow's dark speech . . . . . nor
. . . . .
that nothing may take this assurance away from us, neither
the present nor the future, nor we ourselves with our foolish
desires, but let us hold on to this assurance and you in it. But
then grant also that we might remain in you, convinced that
he who remains in love remains in you and you in him.[9]

And when anxieties seek to terrify us, then hasten, God, to
give us a testimony.

that this assurance might also form our hearts, that our hearts might remain in love and thereby remain in you, convinced that he who remains in love remains in you and you in him.

might be victorious over the lust of the world, over the restlessness of the mind, over the need of the moment, over the anxiety of the future, over the terrors of the past, this full assurance.—*JP* III 2401 (*Pap.* IV B 150) *n.d.*, 1843

From sketch:

To Learn from What One Suffers.
Intro.

It is so difficult to speak about sufferings; one is so reluctant to omit anyone, and yet it seems that, for example, the quiet ones among us, the simple people, really do not suffer very much.
—The limitation—

—*Pap.* IV B 162 *n.d.*, 1843

From sketch:

To Learn from What One Suffers.

The qualification of inwardness, any other qualification of learning is external; the deep impression, in comparison with which all other learning is like writing in sand.—*Pap.* IV B 163 *n.d.*, 1843

From sketch:

Be Vigilant in Prayer

How difficult it is *actually* to be vigilant. One does not know whether one still is awake, actually is awake, is sleeping internally.

This lends itself to allegorical development in terms of physical awakening.

—*JP* III 3392 (*Pap.* IV B 164) *n.d.*, 1843-44

From sketch:

Be Sober in Prayer

To pray (to collect oneself) is a task for the whole soul, no easy matter.[10]
1. Conditions before prayer
2. During prayer and after it
3. About fulfillment
> do not use many words.
> do not anxiously interrupt the prayer
> to see if it is happening now.

—*JP* III 3393 (*Pap.* IV B 165) *n.d.*, 1843-44

From sketch:

How Difficult It Is to Wake Up.

(on the Epistle for the first Sunday in Advent.[11])

to be developed from actual sleeping.—
we finally say to a person: Are you actually awake now? Here each one must call himself, not as someone else calls us in the morning in daily life.

The disciples who could not keep themselves awake in Gethsemane.[12]—*Pap.* IV B 167 *n.d.*, 1843-44

From sketch:

The Gospel about the two sons, one of whom said yes and did not do it, and the other said no and did it.[13]

Yes and No
—*Pap.* IV B 168 *n.d.*, 1843-44

From sketch:

The two ways and the two brothers.
on the Gospel about a father who had two sons; the one
promptly said yes and did not do it, the other promptly
said no and did it.[14]
                                              —*Pap.* IV B 169 *n.d.*, 1843-44

From sketch:

You believe that God is love and that he guides everything
into good for you. But where do you find the image of this,
where an instructive representation of this love, if you yourself do not develop your life accordingly. If you are not moved
by the pleas of the destitute, if you can walk past him and
forget, is it not as if in that moment God forgot you, that it
must go with you in the world the very same way you let it
go with others?—*JP* I 909 (*Pap.* IV B 170) *n.d.*, 1843-44(?)

From sketch:

there he sits in his royal dignity; all the splendor of Phoe-
nicia enhances the glory of his rule over God's chosen people.
The crowd surrounds his throne, a confusion of noise—it is
pride over the king's magnificence, envy, reproaches against
God for having given him what was denied them—it became
still—he is going to stand up—he speaks—but no words come
from his lips—he sinks back powerless, the glory of the
throne, the splendor of the crown, the purple garment are too
heavy for him; he rises again, the people listen—all is vanity,
sheer vanity.[15]—*Pap.* IV B 172 *n.d.*, 1842-44(?)

From sketch:

I know very well that it is not only the poor who hunger,
that there is a hunger that all the treasures of the world cannot
satisfy, and yet this hunger is for them—I know very well that
there is a thirst that all the streams of overabundance cannot

quench, and yet this thirst is for them—I know very well that there is an anxiety, a secret, private anxiety, about losing— — *JP* I 44 (*Pap*. IV B 173) *n.d.*, 1842-44(?)

From sketch:

There was a poor widow; she went up to the temple, she laid her mite in the temple box;[16] she felt how insignificant she was, how insignificant her gift; she hid herself, she did not want anyone to see her, and yet there was a witness, and she became immortalized in history.

There were those who ranked high in the world; they were prodigal with their overabundance, the world admired them—but how could this be compared with the quietness and solemnity.—*Pap*. IV B 174   *n.d.*, 1842-44(?)

From sketch; see 31, 125:

Merciful God! We do know that every good gift and every perfect gift comes from you—but you did not send us empty-handed into the world—let not our hands be closed, our hearts be hardened—but add your blessing so that our gift may be a gift from you above, good and perfect.—*JP* III 3395 (*Pap*. IV B 175) *n.d.*, 1842-44(?)

From sketch:

In sparse but strong strokes, the Holy Gospel describes for us one of the contrasts we often experience in the world. There was a rich man—there was a poor man.[17] Everyone promptly attaches a conception to *he was rich* (here a digression about the glory of wealth, about the individual's independence of earthly cares and thereby a possible striving for something higher—), he was *poor* (digression)—

Still another stroke for the contrast—he was *buried*, the rich man died and was buried (the animal dies—its body rots away, and no one pays any attention to it; this is why the poor want so much to be buried[18]). At his departure, the glory of the world gathers around him; he is again clad in costly linen

IV
B 176
348

IV
B 176
349

a large funeral procession, they *carried him*

—the poor man also died; he was not buried; perhaps was thrown aside because in death he lay in the way, just as he had in life, perhaps in order to clear the way for the magnificent funeral procession—he *was carried away* by angels.

One thing in common—*they died*—

One thing in common—they awakened—

—*Pap*. IV B 176 *n.d.*, 1842-44(?)

From draft of Preface; *see 5:*

Preface.

IV
B 143
331

That a young theological student ventures to do what even renowned clerical speakers seldom do, to publish sermons, is so odd that no doubt everyone will readily understand my remark that it is my opinion, as well as my desire, that literature will totally ignore them. When the matter is perceived in this way, it may not be such a great disaster if one more little superfluous book comes out. If the author himself is so obliging as to acknowledge, as I do, its superfluity, he shows that he recognizes his duties to his neighbor and has at least done his part to prevent anyone from wasting his money, his time, and his trouble.

These sermons [*Prædikener*][19] are not published to draw any attention whatever to themselves, much less to their author. They came into existence in concealment and because of their illegitimate and doubtful origin desire to steal through life secretly and unnoticed. They are not published to be read by an authorized critic, something that is already adequately demonstrated by their form, which in more than one way deviates from the authorized form, yet not by way of accidentality of the form in relation to the thought. Only that which is original is the upbuilding and is that only insofar as it remains in its originality as the present, since only the present is the upbuilding, which more and more vanishes when we want to give the originality and naturalness of the mood time to clothe itself, as it were, in the thought, in order that this conventional or historical attire might be more attractive and respectable.

But enough of this. It would pain me if this casual remark or these two sermons were to become the assuredly innocent cause that would give one or another genuinely speculative pate occasion by way of συγκαταβᾶσις [condescension] even to want to explain to me what it is that the times with categorical necessity demand.[20] For many reasons, I am far from flattering myself with the satisfying thought of having understood the times; indeed, even wanting to understand the times is itself a task that in its very immensity is suitable only for thinkers, not for more limited pates. In view of this, I have chosen the lesser task, one that our age, which is moved only by great ideas, may call an insignificant and foolish task, for example: to want to understand a very particular human being, for example, *oneself.* With regard to this task of mine, I have a wish that our age, which lives only for great and spacious ideas, will call foolishness, the wish to be understood by a very particular human being, by the one I with joy, indeed, with gratitude, will call *my* reader, without concealing that by wanting to be my reader he does more for me than I can do for him by writing for him.

IV
B 143
332

Although this little book wants to be only what it is, a superfluity, and desires only to remain in hiding, I nevertheless have not bidden it farewell without attaching an almost fantastic hope to it. That is, inasmuch as by its publication it is in a figurative sense starting a journey, I let my eyes follow it for a little while. I saw then how it wended its way down solitary paths or walked solitary on public roads. After a few little mistakes, through being deceived by a fleeting resemblance, it finally met that single individual whom I call my reader.— *Pap.* IV B 143 *n.d.*, 1843

Addition to final copy of Three Upbuilding Discourses *(1843); see 5:2-5, 53:2-5:*

. . . . . (which is called "discourses," not sermons, because its author does not have authority to *preach*; "upbuilding discourses," not discourses for upbuilding, because the speaker by no means claims to be a *teacher*)—*JP* V 5686 (*Pap*. IV B 159:6) August 9, 1843

From draft of The Book on Adler; *see 5:3:*

Note. One or another reader perhaps recalls that I have always used this expression about myself *qua* author, that I am *without authority*, and have used it so emphatically that it *has been repeated as a formula in every preface*. Even though as an author I have had no benefit, I have at least done everything finitely possible not to confuse the highest and the holiest. I am a poor individual human being. If I am, as some think, a bit of a genius, about that I would say: Let it go hang. But an apostle is in all eternity qualitatively just as different from me as the greatest genius who has ever lived is different from the most obtuse person who has ever lived.—*Pap*. VII² B 235, p. 144 *n.d.*, 1846-47

In margin of final copy; see 5:1, 53:1:

To the typesetter: this is to be printed in the *smallest possible brevier.*—*Pap*. IV B 159:5 *n.d.*, 1843

From final copy; see 53:28:

Copenhagen, August 9, 1843²¹ [*changed from:* Summer 1843 *and then deleted*].
—*Pap*. IV B 159:7 *n.d.*, 1843

Addition in margin of final copy; see 55:1:

To the typesetter
The headings are to be printed as large as possible.
—*Pap*. IV B 159:8 *n.d.*, 1843

Addition to Pap. IV B 144; *see 55:2, 69:2:*

Above all have a heartfelt love for one another.
I Peter 4:7-12.
—*Pap*. IV B 145 *n.d.*, 1843

From sketch; see 55-78:

III
God's Love Hides a M[ultitude of] S[ins][22]

IV
B 144
332

Is this reason to sin. Christianity is a religion for *all*, for it pardons a woman who was taken in adultery and condemns the man who looks at a woman to lust after her.

When the Pharisees surrounded that woman,[23] they *discovered* a multitude of sins, but Christ wrote in the sand—and hid it.

IV
B 144
333

In Christ everything is revealed—and *everything is* hidden.

Christ's love that indulgently hides a multitude of sins and Christ's love of God, a love that is pleasing to God and under which he hides a multitude of sins.

He who hides a transgression seeks love. Proverbs 17:9.—*JP* III 2397 (*Pap.* IV B 144) *n.d.*, 1843

Addition to Pap. IV B 144:

Love conquers all—more accurately characterized: *struggling love.*

IV
B 146
333

(1) It struggles with itself.[24]

Therefore a clear and definite conception of his own weakness is required of him who is to be possessed [by love]—and then to rejoice in happiness—I wonder if it is so easy.

(2) It struggles with time.[25]

Therefore a concrete conception of time is required of him—and then to rejoice in happiness—Oh! I wonder if it is so easy.

(3) It struggles with vicissitude.

IV
B 146
334

Therefore he must have undergone a religious change—and then really to rejoice in his happiness—I wonder if it is so easy.—*JP* III 2398 (*Pap.* IV B 146) *n.d.*, 1843

Addition to Pap. IV B 144:

(Love Casts Out Fear)

Perhaps you would like to do much for another person whom you think you love, but you want it to succeed for you, you want to be recognized for it, admired if not by others at least by the particular person; but you are honest enough to confess to yourself that even with the greatest effort you are able to do only a little. This little you do not want to do, because it is so humbling—consequently you do not love the other person as yourself.

Perhaps love requires that you shall yield. If a father said to his son: We must be separated—would it be a proof of his love for his father if he said: Should I forsake you?—it is indeed the father's wish.

Self-love is egotism unless it is also love for God—thereby love for others.—*JP* III 2399 (*Pap.* IV B 147) *n.d.*, 1843

Addition to Pap. IV B 144:

IV
B 148
334

Above All Have a Heartfelt Love for One Another[26]

Christianity has been accused of assuming too little in man, of making a clod of him—yet it assumes that man loves himself; for it says that we must love our neighbor as we love ourselves.[27] This is not merely a hard truth but a profound connecting point.

IV
B 148
335

See index to Augustine,[28] first part, under the article *amor probus—improbus* [honorable love—dishonorable].

Love can express itself in many external works, but all these works can also be lacking in love. We can gain friends by unrighteous mammon, but everything disappears; this is not the love being discussed here; it must be an abiding love since it is to have power to hide a multitude of sins.

And only that one is unhappy who is either too vain to be able to love what he must admire or whose inclination governs him so that he loves what he despises.

heartfelt: the qualification of inwardness. Whatever does not proceed from faith is of evil; the same holds for love. Romans 14:23. Psalm 15:4.

The love that, if it has bound itself to its own detriment, nevertheless does not change it [the promise]; but if it has bound itself to another person, to detriment, it changes it.

In margin:

Intro.

When an apostle talks about love, it is something different from the frequently disappointing, frequently confusing talk we generally hear—and yet he adds: a *heartfelt* . . . . . —*JP* III 2400 (*Pap*. IV B 148) *n.d.*, 1843

From sketch; see 69:1:

For No. 2[29]

Lord, our God, you know all, the most secret thought, and when apprehensions would dismay us, when the grief of sin overwhelms us—then hurry, O Lord, and give witness to love, that it may again be victorious in our soul and hide a multitude of our sins.—*JP* III 3391 (*Pap*. IV B 149) *n.d.*, 1843

Deleted from final copy; see 77:17:

Or is not God's heart greater than a human being's?—*Pap*. IV B 159:14 *n.d.*, 1843

From sketch; see 79:3-17:

IV
B 151:1
336   Give what you will—only give the witness along with it
and therein yourself—the joy—be joyful in you—the sorrow—sorrow in you—take everything, if only I may keep the
witness—even death's message, that it comes with greetings
and witness from you.

lest joy tear us away from you in the forgetfulness of pleasure, lest sorrow separate you from us.

You have all the good gifts, and your abundance is greater
than human understanding can grasp; you are willing to give,
IV
B 151:1
337   and your goodness is greater than human understanding
grasps—and yet no human being ventures to request it of you,
but therefore we request it of you, and we have this comfort,
that you grant every prayer in that you give either what we
pray for or that which is far better than that for which we pray.

to be strengthened in the inner being
—*Pap*. IV B 151:1 *n.d.*, 1843

Deleted from sketch; see 80:2-81:6, 84:17-31:

Intro.

The apostle is in prison.

God assigned man to be the lord of nature. He puts a
question to it and demands an explanation from it, a witness.—*Pap*. IV B 151:2 *n.d.*, 1843

Deleted from sketch; see 86:3:

concerned knowledge
—*Pap*. IV B 151:8 *n.d.*, 1843

Deleted from sketch; see 86:31-35:

. . . . . the explanation that creation by itself can give is
very equivocal, can mean this and that and the opposite—it
does not benefit a person—one does not know whether it is

God's mercy or his wrath—therefore the pagans' anxiety and the oracle's mysteriousness.—*Pap.* IV B 151:5 *n.d.*, 1843

Deleted from sketch; see 86:35-87:19:

Every explanation that comes from God is a strengthening in the inner being, be it good fortune and prosperity and joy— the person who builds his barns larger and thanks God for it, should this not be a strengthening

Proclaimer of

That which announces itself in this witness is the inner being, which here is established according to its possibility— *Pap.* IV B 151:7 *n.d.*, 1843

From final draft; see 86:35:

. . . . . and any witness of this kind is deceitful, and any expression of this knowledge is enigmatic and only engenders anxiety in the same way as it dwelt in the soul of the pagans when the secret wisdom attempted to explain the relation of everything to a person.—*Pap.* IV B 152 *n.d.*, 1843

From sketch; see 87:20-89:31, 93:7-98:33, 98:26-101:21:

1. when everything witnesses with.
   the immediate demonstration is no demonstration in the inner being
   when one achieves that for which one has worked, one is to thank not oneself for that but God; otherwise it is no demonstration in the inner being.
2. when everything witnesses against.
   adversity can come from other people; God allows it—or from God—ordeal
   Faith, Hope, Love.
   there is a hope that is the playmate of childhood; it does not persevere in the ordeal. There is another hope that is gained in the ordeal (experience gives hope); it

perseveres, it cannot be put to shame, because it is
strongest when the suffering is greatest.
3. God's assistance.
   the witness is still God's gift, even though a person
   can almost extort it from God, like that widow.[30]
   Conclusion
about God's fatherly love.
—*Pap.* IV B 151:3 *n.d.*, 1843

From sketch; see 88:6-89:3:

We often hear people say
   the world is so deceitful—they are thinking of adversity—only a more earnest individual is almost more
   fearful of prosperity. —And Job was an old man; he
   prayed for his children when they went to parties.
—*Pap.* IV B 153:1 *n.d.*, 1843

In margin of Pap. IV B 153:1:

. . . . . in this respect one person will not believe another.
It is good that one can learn to help oneself in the inner being,
something one cannot learn from others.—*Pap.* IV B
153:2 *n.d.*, 1843

In margin of final draft; see 88:33-37:

. . . . . and thus no discourse, not even the most glorious,
can help another person, because no one, after all, understands
another person except the spirit that is within him.—*Pap.* IV
B 154:1 *n.d.*, 1843

From final draft; see 89:5-11:

Consider him, the fortunate one, the favored one, who does
not sow and does not gather into barns[31]—he walks so lightly,
his life a dance,
The world is always ready with explanation and testimony.

he who has the world is like one who does not have it, and only he who, when he has the world, is like one who does not have the world, only he has the world; otherwise the world has him.—*Pap*. IV B 154:2 *n.d.*, 1843

From sketch; see 90:34-37:

Prosperity can have its basis in his being more sagacious, stronger, etc., in something that lies within himself.—*Pap*. IV B 153:5 *n.d.*, 1843

From sketch; see 90:18-26:

. . . . . but he rejoices over God* more than over all this— he who has the world is like someone who does not have it— he who uses it is like someone who does not misuse it.—*Pap*. IV B 153:3 *n.d.*, 1843

In margin of Pap. IV B 153:3, see 90:38-91:4:

*only he is in *legitimate* possession of it. This is why the fortunate person is uneasy, this is why the powerful man, before whom the whole world trembles, trembles. Then what does the legitimate possession lack.—*Pap*. IV B 153:4 *n.d.*, 1843

Deleted from sketch; see 92:22-24:

. . . . . there were those who gradually lost the inner being—
or those in the moment of good fortune who made the mistake of thinking that they had themselves to thank for it, although earlier they had to confess that they were not capable of it by their own powers.—*Pap*. IV B 151:6 *n.d.*, 1843

From sketch; see 93:36-95:4:

When would the inner being be more likely to awaken than in adversity, when the world withholds itself—but then existence shows itself as anarchy and this evokes a response in a person; he surrenders to it, and then the inner being is lost and all is vanity.—*Pap.* IV B 151:9 *n.d.*, 1843

From sketch; see 95:5-25:

1. the concerned person.

the wish.

the temptation to abandon himself to the apparent anarchy—a kind of despair.

but the person who had the concern in his soul before the external concern came to him, the person whose soul was never satisfied by joy in such a way that it did not retain a concern until the witness came, but neither was it overwhelmed by the concern in such a way that the possibility of joy vanished as long as a witness was possible—he gradually threw overboard the worldly weight of earthly desires.

the earthly desires that once were wings for him

hope.

—*Pap.* IV B 158:1 *n.d.*, 1843

From sketch; see 95:34-96:26:

2. the person who was wronged.

by people

faithlessness—envy, which would like to halt him in the good.

—hate and revenge.

love of God.

whether people rose up against him as brigands or deserted him as deceivers.

a person could win another's love and lose God's

a love that does not weary of doing good.

—*Pap.* IV B 158:2 *n.d.*, 1843

From sketch; see 97:20-98:25:

3. the person who was tried.

the trouble was not external. —People were favorably

disposed toward him—and yet distress—ordeal.   His soul froze.

the temptation to *boast* of being lost.

faith.

—*Pap*. IV B 158:3-4 *n.d.*, 1843

From sketch; see 99:8-19:

. . . . . when we speak of the external gifts and then call God father, it is a metaphorical expression, figurative, but inwardly understood, and indeed the inner being asks not about the gift but about the giver, not about what he gives but about who it is who gives—then it is a literal expression.—*Pap*. IV B 158:7 *n.d.*, 1843

From sketch; see 99:19-20:

. . . . . only the inner being understands that God is father.—*Pap*. IV B 158:6 *n.d.*, 1843

From sketch; see 99:24-28:

. . . . . comes with the gift in a feeling or mood, can give himself essentially and penetrate the whole gift—*Pap*. IV B 158:9 *n.d.*, 1843

From sketch; see 99:19-28:

. . . . . it is a metaphorical expression, and it almost seems inadequate. When you want to raise it up to God, it fades away.—*Pap*. IV B 158:8 *n.d.*, 1843

From sketch; see 99:37-100:27:

When you came to him and had gained the whole world
    But your earthly [father] could rejoice with you only on
    the chance that it would not become a snare for you; since

only God can rejoice totally with you, because if you rejoice with God over it, then the temptation retreats.—
Pap. IV B 158:5 *n.d.*, 1843

From sketch; see 101:7-22:

The person who turned back to his first love is always
happy. Fortunate is the person who truthfully dared to say that
God was his first love. Fortunate the person who, however
tossed about in the world, nevertheless turned back to it
again.—*Pap.* IV B 151:4 *n.d.*, 1843

See 223:6-7:

. . . . . Even if prayer does not accomplish anything here
on earth, it nevertheless works in heaven.—*JP* III 3390 (*Pap.*
IV A 145) *n.d.*, 1843

See 223:6-7:

. . . . . Of course, when prayer is heard here on earth and
mingles with busy human speech, it is idle talk, but it is working in heaven; and frequently prayer does sow in corruption,
but nevertheless it harvests in incorruption.[32]—*JP* III 3396
(*Pap.* IV A 171) *n.d.*, 1844

Deleted from final copy; see 231:9:

He is often reminded of that convict who certainly knew
how to expound on the condition of his fellow prisoners and
say the words that tethered their minds in the sorrowful service of unfreedom but yet was himself a leper just like the
others.—*Pap.* V B 195:4 *n.d.*, 1844

From draft; see 242:1-243:3:

Think *about your* **Creator** in the days of your youth

My listener, perhaps you need a demonstration of the existence of God—indeed, then my discourse will look good be-

fore I am even finished with it, and then I come to the discourse—or do you not feel the mockery of you as the text is
read. —Even though the Preacher ordinarily speaks rigorously to people, he nevertheless is so courteous as to assume
that you understand that there is a God and is not so vain as to
think that he has invented the existence of God.—*Pap.* V B
194 *n.d.*, 1844

Deleted from final copy; see 247:34:

. . . . . because he who heeds the wind will not sow, and he
who regards the clouds will not reap (Ecclesiastes 11:4).—
Pap. V B 195:6 *n.d.*, 1844

Deleted from final copy; see 282:29:

And just as one country keeps a trusted person at another's
court, so the single individual keeps a highly trusted thought
at God's throne in order to know immediately when the servant's time is at an end.—*Pap.* V B 195:7 *n.d.*, 1844

In margin of final copy; see 291:1:

To the typesetter. The entire book is to be printed in the same
types used in 1843 for *Two Upbuilding Discourses* and with the
same number of lines per page.—*JP* V 5734 (*Pap.* V B 232:1)
n.d., 1844

From draft; see 295:2-29:

Though this little book (   ) is now
once again going out into the world, it hopes even less than
the first to draw any irrelevant attention to itself or occasion
new misunderstanding,[*] since it presumably is so familiar
that the passersby who see it only in passing are not further
disturbed by it and let it freely go its way.[**] Now and then
one sees a messenger who goes his way at certain times, and
precisely because those whom it does not concern know that

this is the case, they let it go and know at once that this is no concern of theirs.

[*]*In margin:* since it no doubt has rather accustomed the passersby to letting it shift for itself.

[**]*In margin:* So it is now and then with a child who comes at certain times and occasionally brings food to a prisoner. The first time he perhaps is stopped, but when he comes later, the guard and the superintendent say: Just let him go, and as soon as they see the child, they are not concerned with him and let him go his way.—*Pap.* V B 233:1 *n.d.,* 1844

From draft; see 295:2-14:

V
B 233:2
361

Though this little book (   ) is now going out once again, it is even less fearful than the first of awakening any irrelevant attention but hopes that precisely because of the repetition the passersby have become accustomed to letting it shift for itself. So it is now and then with a child bringing food to a prisoner. The first time he perhaps

V
B 233:2
362

even attracted attention, but soon he is familiar, and no attention is paid to him except to let him go on his errand undisturbed.—*Pap.* V B 233:2 *n.d.,* 1844

From draft; see 295:2-29:

V
B 233:7
362

Though this little book (   ) is again going out into the world, it is even less fearful of drawing irrelevant attention to itself than the first time it went out, hopes rather that the passersby, insofar as they notice it, will let it shift for itself. A messenger now and then goes his way at certain times

The first time he perhaps even attracted someone's attention, but soon he is so familiar that no attention is paid to him except to let him go his way without even turning to look at him. In the same way, it goes out to seek that single individual whom I with joy and gratitude call my reader, in order to pay

V
B 233:7
363

him a visit, indeed, in order to stay with him, not to leave him again as that messenger does. That is, as soon as he has received it, then it has ceased to be, because it is nothing for itself and by itself, but, all that it is, it is only for him and by him. And although the trails always lead ahead to that favorably disposed person, not back, and although the previous messenger never returns home, and although the person who is sending it never discovers anything about its fate—the next messenger nevertheless cheerfully goes its way in order to disappear, never to return home, and this is precisely the joy of him who sends them.—*Pap.* V B 233:7 *n.d.*, 1844

From draft; see 295:2-29:

    Though this little book (   ) is once again going out into the world, it is even less fearful of drawing any irrelevant[*] attention to itself than the first time it started on its journey and hopes rather that because of the repetition the passersby will scarcely notice it, and in any case only[**] to let it shift for itself. A messenger now and then goes his routine way at set times. The first time he perhaps even attracted someone's attention, but soon he is familiar and so familiar that no attention is paid to him[***] except to let him go his way without even turning to look after him. So then the book goes out to seek and to find that single individual whom I with j. and g. c. m. r., in order to pay him a visit,[****] indeed, in order to stay with him and not leave him again, as that messenger does. That is, as soon as he has received it, then it has ceased to be, because it is nothing for itself and by itself, but all that it is, it is only for him and by him. And although the trails always lead ahead to *my* reader, not back, and although the previous messenger never returns home and although the one who sends it never discovers anything about its fate, the next messenger nevertheless goes happily through death to life, cheerfully goes its way in order to disappear, never to return home again—and this is precisely the joy of him who sends it.

    [*]*In margin:* impeding
    [**]*In margin:* as something irrelevant
    [***]*In margin:* he is scarcely noticed

V
B 233:8
363

V
B 233:8
364

[****]*In margin:* as a messenger, yet not like that messenger
in order to turn back again; it
—*Pap.* V B 233:8 *n.d.,* 1844

From sketch; see 295:10:

Only in this way does the one follow the others, and their
author never hears more from them and does not desire
it.—*Pap.* V B 233:5 *n.d.,* 1844

From sketch; see 295:10:

Storks and swallows are, of course, esteemed birds, but
the first starling also signifies spring. Perhaps someone
looks around for the first starling, but the second one—
who cares about it?
—*Pap.* V B 233:9 *n.d.,* 1844

From sketch; see 295:10-21:

Someone who is not a prisoner and to whom it does not
intend to bring food but merely wants to visit, but whom it,
unlike that messenger, does not leave again, because as soon
as he has received it, it has ceased to be, since it is not for itself
and by itself, but all that it is, it is only for him and by him.—
Pap. V B 233:4 *n.d.,* 1844

In margin of Pap. V B 233:4; *see 295:15-16:*

. . . . . and the discourse seeks that single individual whom
I with joy call my reader, whom it does not expect to find as
a prisoner, even less expects to be able to release him, not even
to bring him food, but only wants to visit him—*Pap.* V B
233:6 *n.d.,* 1844

From sketch; see 295:21-27:

. . . . . and although the trails always lead ahead to that
single individual and not back, and although the previous

messenger never returns home, yet it goes almost cheerfully and happily the same way—in order to disappear,
never to return home—and this indeed is the joy of him
who sends it.—*Pap.* V B 233:3 *n.d.*, 1844

Deleted from margin in final copy; see 295:28-29:

. . . . . who here for the last time is sending such a one and
therefore wishes to bid farewell to his reader, since he has
never wished to be remembered but only to be forgotten.—
Pap. V B 232:8 *n.d.*, 1844

From sketch; see 297:1-326:14:

To need God is a human being's highest perfection.   V
                                                          B 196
                                                           340
Text

among those born of women none is greater; yet he who is
least in the kingdom of God is greater than he.[33]
   If a human being did not have absolute need of God, he   V
could not   B 196
                                                             341
   1. know himself—self-knowledge.
   2. be immortal.
                    —*JP* I 53 (*Pap.* V B 196) *n.d.*, 1844

From sketch; see 300:4:

A human being's highest achievement is to let God be able
to help him.—*JP* I 54 (*Pap.* V B 198) *n.d.*, 1844

From sketch:

Great men like Xerxes[34] and others have a slave to remind
them to do this and that, but someone who is eager to thank
God and yet is afraid that ultimately he will forget to do so
has only one to whom he can turn—to God himself—with the
prayer that he will remind him to give thanks. Is it not strange!
So little can a human being do without God that he cannot

even do without God's help in thanking God.—*Pap.* V B
197 *n.d.*, 1844

From draft; see 300:5-16:

Pause now a moment, lest we confuse everything by mixing
things together without noticing the sting of the thought.—
Pap. V B 200 *n.d.*, 1844

From draft; see 302:21-25:

He still had a powerful man who wanted to do everything
good for him. —now have the analogy to God's not helping
him in external ways be that that man cannot (if you think that
the reason God does not do it is that he is unwilling, then you
indeed misunderstand everything).—*Pap.* V B 201 *n.d.*, 1844

In margin of draft; see 308:29-33:

. . . . . if he, before the eye aims at something and makes a
conquest of it, first captures the eye so that it may belong to
him and not he to the eye; if he, before the hand grasps for
something, first grasps the hand so that it may belong to him
. . . . . —*Pap.* V B 205 *n.d.*, 1844

In margin of draft; see 310:5-10:

Fenelon, quoted from Jacobi, *Werke*,[35] I, p. 173 bottom.
                                         —*Pap.* V B 207:1 *n.d.*, 1844

From draft; see 312:2-16:

. . . . . he cannot himself decide.* And if we now, perhaps
out of habit and thoughtlessness, speak about the greatness of
Moses as we speak about all other greatness, there no doubt
would be some contemporary of his who would be foolish
enough to smile at Moses—if he did not come to admire him
by taking his greatness in vain—and be foolish enough to say:

V
B 207:2
342

V
B 207:2
343

If only I were Moses, I certainly would—alas, if he had been Moses he certainly would have understood that he himself was capable of nothing at all. But precisely because Moses had understood this, he was happy and confident in his trust in God, and in whatever happened he was blessed in the understanding that he was suitable to God precisely because he himself was capable of nothing at all.

In margin: *not even in the moment when the staff is already touching the rock.—Pap.* V B 207:2 *n.d.*, 1844

From draft; see 313:12-16:

. . . . . to something else* but did not know himself in relation to himself.

In margin: *there can be changes, and thereby he is changed (another becomes the strongest, the most handsome, the richest, etc.: basically there are implicit in this person's immediate self-relationship to his environment all of the sophistic positions Socrates fought against, that the strongest is the just[36] etc.).—JP* I 914 (*Pap.* V B 207:3) *n.d.*, 1844

In margin of draft; see 314:9-32:

As soon as he turns and faces himself, he will discover that the other to which his first self relates is changeable. As soon as he wants to relate to it, the other self will form him in such a way that it retains the upper hand. Now he comes to a standstill. It is difficult, to be sure, just like rising from sleep to hard work; indeed, it is far easier to go on sleeping and let oneself be lulled by the lullabies of other people.—*Pap.* V B 207:4 *n.d.*, 1844

From draft; see 321:18-29:

Indeed, he truly did become happy, as we shall now show more explicitly.—*Pap.* V B 207:5 *n.d.*, 1844

In margin of draft; see 323:23:

..... like the spiritual trial of sorrow—since once one has become unhappy, one really prospers—but whether it would not have been better not to have become unhappy at all . . . . .
—*Pap.* V B 207:6 *n.d.,* 1844

From draft; see 324:26-32:

..... but this never would have happened with God. [*] But from this it does not follow that such a person's life always becomes easy; on the contrary, it can become very hard, but even when he suffers most, he will not for all the world change places with anyone whom suffering does not place in relation to God.
[*]*In margin:* and the person who truly has God as witness seldom has him as judge, as it is in the earthly—*Pap.* V B 207:7 *n.d.,* 1844

From draft;[37] *see 330:9:*

So it perhaps also happens at times in life, and since we are supposed to talk about sufferings, and since it seems to be characteristic of the times that one is not as likely to become self-important through honor, power, and superiority as by sufferings, and since there is a profound truth in regarding suffering as the true means of education, it would perhaps be helpful to bring to mind the untruth in this view. But since we do not have the authority to admonish, we choose another means. Smile only a little at what I will now tell you, my listener; it still is and continues to be an upbuilding discourse, and if by hearing it you are brought to smile at yourself, then the discourse has in fact induced you to admonish yourself. There was once a man who had a riding horse; every time he came home after having ridden, he was somewhat fatigued but was nevertheless pleased with the horse, pleased with riding. Then one day another man borrowed his horse and quickly turned back, explaining in the strongest terms that the horse jolted terribly. The owner answered, "Does it really? I never knew that, for since I have never ridden another horse, I believed that this was the way riding was supposed to be and that the rough motion was part of the fun." Yet from that moment on a change came over him; he never rode anymore because he could not find a horse that was sufficiently smooth-riding, and because finally he wanted the impossible—that the horse should move without one's detecting it. In the same way, my listener, there is perhaps many a one who bears life's sorrows and tribulations in the belief [*] that they are part of living, indeed, that they are part of the enjoyment—until someone tells him that living is dreadful, and he is never happy anymore but at most becomes self-important by not being happy and by being able to reject everything in life.

[*]*In margin:* since I have never lived before, I believed that this was the way life was supposed to be and that this was part of the enjoyment.—*Pap.* V B 209:2 *n.d.*, 1844

From draft; see 330:10:

This has been said; let it now also be forgotten [*changed from:* But if the suffering is true and deep, then it does not help to want to smile]—*Pap.* V B 209:3 *n.d.*, 1844

From draft; see 330:31-331:9:

. . . . . does it perhaps also apply to the suffering in which faith is born, in which faith is victorious, in which hope is developed and acquires its eternal object and love learns to grasp God.

V
B 209:4
344

It is this, the highest of life's sufferings, about which the apostle speaks. Even though it is painful that they exist, they are still unable to overwhelm a person who has the apostle's guidance and explanation, because the very fact that before he is tried in them he learns that they exist is already a counterweight against them. Not so with the apostle, who himself first experienced the suffering that hitherto no human being had known, as surely, that is, as there otherwise was a higher life in an apostle than there had ever been in any human being

V
B 209:4
345

before him and as surely as life, the higher and more devout it
becomes, causes deeper pains. What the apostle has experienced primitively can be experienced frequently, experienced
again and again; and therefore it is of benefit to speak of it but,
please note, in such a way that it signifies something universal,
and we are not concerned about learning merely historically
what kind of illness P. suffered from.[*] This is of minor importance, and of course the dissimilar in the individual can become the designation for it, but what is described there is
something universal

[*]*In margin:* in the same sense as whether P. was tall or
short—*Pap.* V B 209:4 *n.d.,* 1844

From draft; see 337:1-14:

. . . . . when he was caught up into the third heaven, when
he was hidden in the bosom of beatitude, and as if there were
no more strife for him, no presentiment of strife, but all victory—but that this can vanish again![*] What confidence can
one have in that? And what shall a person do in order to grasp
it again? There is nothing to do; it is God's grace itself that
overshadows a person. And can it ever come again? No one
knows that. But faith? Yes, if it has not already grasped it—
but to have grasped it and now to be thrust back.

[*]*In margin:* It is hard enough for a person to experience the
faithlessness of human beings—but God's faithlessness—*Pap.*
V B 211:2 *n.d.,* 1844

From draft; see 337:28:

And it is indeed also true that it may seem this way to a
person, but an apostle is recognized by his knowing that it is
beneficial for him.—*Pap.* V B 213:1 *n.d.,* 1844

From draft; see 338:18-23:

Then he understands, however, only the self-accusation if
the past has the kind of claim upon his soul that no repentance
can redeem but only make more terrible, that no trusting in

God entirely wipes out, but only God himself—that is, when he is again with God.—*Pap.* V B 212:1 *n.d.*, 1844

From draft; see 340:25-26:

. . . . . because what the earnest person lays the stress on particularly is that it is he who is the guilty one, and he is not comforted by having been willing himself to forgive and acquit all other human beings if they were in the same situation. Therefore, for the individual person, something that we ordinarily would call a minor fault can be sufficient, not for him to despair but for him to be unable to acquit himself and for him to keep a bygone in his soul that in time can always find an opportunity to alarm him now and then. In this way, every human being can experience the same thing, and the difference between people lies not so much in the different things that they experience as in the modes in which they experience them, because every human being experiences the essential. Thus no person has ever lived who has not had occasion to experience that he was a sinner, but is it therefore experienced by everyone! But a past sin is not therefore annihilated and can never be entirely annihilated in time; it is still a part of him, and something that once had power over him can indeed still acquire it.—*Pap.* V B 212:2 *n.d.*, 1844

V
B 212:2
346

V
B 212:2
347

From draft; see 341:29-34:

What if he had stood still in the race, what if recollection had seized him, what if apprehensive ruminating had overwhelmed him, whether he would be able to find them again, to rescue them again, to do something good again—and perhaps it could not be done.—*Pap.* V B 212:3 *n.d.*, 1844

In margin of draft; see 341:37-342:9:

. . . . . (what an upheaval in thought and mind † I place a cross here so that no one will light-mindedly slip by).—*Pap.* V B 213:3 *n.d.*, 1844

From draft; see 342:12-13:

. . . . . had given recollection time to wound him with the thought of the terror, what if he had not had the humility to understand that it was forgiven him, what if he had made the mistake of wanting to let his work night and day, his apostolic task, make satisfaction for it, and from this viewpoint all this work showed itself to be nothing—*Pap.* V B 213:4 *n.d.*, 1844

From draft; see 342:34:

. . . . . so that he would not pride himself.—*Pap.* V B 212:4 *n.d.*, 1844

In margin of draft; see 343:7:

Psychological detail in the single individual.—*Pap.* V B 213:5 *n.d.*, 1844

From draft; see 343:18-345:15:

And the person who has been caught up into the third heaven has indeed grasped this; for him the rest of beatitude has begun, and now he has to run again.

In margin: In an old devotional book, it says that God deals with a human being as the hunter deals with game in hunting—he gives it a little time to rest and catch its breath, and then the chase begins again. The truth and the falsity of this.—*Pap.* V B 212:5 *n.d.*, 1844

From draft; see 343:18-22:

. . . . . call it a glorious ending to misunderstanding's arduous wandering, when the explanation illuminated [*lyste ind*] it and explained the suffering and the loss[*] and the meaning of the anxiety and pronounced [*lyste*] the blessed peace of understanding upon it; but there was still one little word lacking,

call it a glorious ending to the arduous wandering in the desert of unintelligibility,
[*]*In margin:* and the danger and the difficulty—*Pap.* V B 215 *n.d.*, 1844

From draft; see 343:24-26:

. . . . . had already grasped at the treasure, and you still have enough strength to reach it with your last effort, but it is still a finger-breadth away—*Pap.* V B 214:1 *n.d.*, 1844

From draft; see 344:22-345:15:

This discourse is true in a sense,[*] but its upbuilding value is doubtful. The apostle, however, knows that it is beneficial for him. He who had been caught up into the third heaven had already entered into rest and now again perceived that the thorn in the flesh festered with new pain; he knows it is beneficial for him in that every temporal anxiety that desires must be consumed, every self-confidence[**] that wants to be complete must burn out in the distress of the future; it is beneficial for the apostle so that he will not become proud, he who did indeed fight the good fight; it is beneficial for many that the apostle is with them once again.[***]

[*]*In margin:* This chase, if it is true, will also be a race toward the perfect, so that every time one pauses for breath, one advances.

Here the part about the relapse. After some time, everything becomes milder, the sin less terrible, sadder; finally one is almost unable to understand that it was possible for a person, but the relapse teaches one again.

[**]*In margin:* that craves to be deceived in order to become what it is

[***]*In margin:* One is not unacquainted with the relapse but thinks that nevertheless now everything has become better, but a new relapse will place a leaden weight upon one.—*Pap.* V B 214:2 *n.d.*, 1844

Deleted from draft; see 358:14:

Let us pause a moment at this point. Someone who wants to erect a tower sits down and makes a rough estimate—*Pap.* V B 218:1 *n.d.*, 1844

From draft; see 360:3-6:

Or is it not just as when doubt congratulates itself on having rooted out all superstition, and knows that it does not believe anything untrue, but has forgotten that it is just as great a misfortune not to believe what is true.—*Pap.* V B 218:2 *n.d.*, 1844

From draft; see 362:13-16:

And someone who makes a rough estimate of his life understands it differently, and cowardliness helps him to drink the good wine first and then be sickened by the dregs or to perish because he has nothing but water to drink; but the person who makes a resolution no longer makes a rough estimate—he understands everything differently.—*Pap.* V B 218:3 *n.d.*, 1844

From draft; see 363:10-16:

. . . . . possesses nothing.* No, do what you can; you can come to a resolution, and then God will do for you what you cannot do.

Venture all, therefore, only in trust in God (to be developed).

In margin: *which again is a hidden pride, because he fears that in the moment of resolution it will appear how little it is—so it is nevertheless better to fool oneself and entertain obscure conceptions while one holds off the decision and deceives oneself as if one did not entertain these conceptions.— *Pap.* V B 218:4 *n.d.*, 1844

From draft; see 364:23-28:

. . . . . so that one needs to hold back
To be developed.
In margin: is one then so close to madness because one is a
little depressed—*Pap.* V B 218:5 *n.d.*, 1844

From draft; see 366:22-33:

But in this way cowardliness has indeed disturbed the con-
tinuity of life, which the resolution wanted.
Who does not see now that it is cowardliness and this cowardliness a concealed pride.—*Pap.* V B 218:6 *n.d.*, 1844

From draft; see 370:33:

. . . . . a woman's, since this modesty conceals that in this
feeling he is with God, and in truth to be in understanding
with God is something so high that one does not dare to name
it, lest one defile it, and if one named it, one is almost afraid
of smiling at the thought that it actually would be so—that is,
if being in understanding with God has not become a *geläufig*
[current] idiom—*Pap.* V B 220:1 *n.d.*, 1844

From draft; see 371:21-23:

. . . . . when thoughtlessness and gibberish and half-baked
feelings and hasty resolutions and misunderstanding and
prinked-up self-love and the sickly intoxication of promises
and intentions attack someone like that.—*Pap.* V B
220:3 *n.d.*, 1844

In margin of draft; see 371:33-36:

. . . . . when all are willing to give the good their words
and yet not do it, then it is tempting to say no and yet do it,
like the son in the Gospel (the one brother).[40]—*Pap.* V B
220:4 *n.d.*, 1844

From draft; see 373:9:

About Solitude

    Ecclesiastes 4:10. Woe to him who is alone; if he falls, there is no one else to raise him up.

                                     —*Pap.* V B 235 *n.d.*, 1844

Deleted from final copy; see 377:1:

No. 4.

                                 —*Pap.* V B 232:11 *n.d.*, 1844

From draft; see 377:1-3, 382:27-29:

    By struggling aright in prayer, the marvel comes to pass that God in heaven and you are victorious, because you are victorious in that God is victorious.—*JP* III 3397 (*Pap.* V B 221) *n.d.*, 1844

From draft; see 384:8-12:

    . . . . . flung himself as something miserable and thereby caused new pain to the person who wished him well, was so weak and base as to appeal to the sympathy of the one whose kindness and solicitude he refused to understand, did all he could by his prayer to bewilder the understanding of the person who, strained to the utmost, worked for the welfare of the one praying.—*Pap.* V B 227:1 *n.d.*, 1844

From draft; see 386:10-22:

    The misrelation between inwardness and maturity is to find fault—for example, if someone in the same way as a child would thank God because he won in the lottery but could not endure the least little thing. Now the possibility of conflict is apparent, because deep within there nevertheless lives the thought that everything must be ascribed to God, and it is the inwardness of this innermost thought that nourishes prayer.— *Pap.* V B 227:2 *n.d.*, 1844

From draft; see 387:19-30:

. . . . . in that case he might, and rightfully so, turn his back on you lest what you say go like a sword through his heart, nail him to a cross of bleak common sense, trap him in the powerlessness of a supercilious sagacity.—*Pap.* V B 227:3 *n.d.*, 1844

From draft; see 391:4-26:

. . . . . but since you did have this confidence in me and although you disagreed with me you had in your innermost being an integrity that made you stick with me, I was also convinced that in the end you would yourself perceive it, perceive it with all joy, as if you yourself had thought it up.

In margin: then for the first time modesty awakened
by his struggle he had strengthened me
—*Pap.* V B 227:4 *n.d.*, 1844

From draft; see 392:9-33:

Inwardness is the eternal, and desire is the temporal, but the temporal cannot hold out with the eternal. Desire glows less and less fervently, and at last its time is over, but the time of inwardness is never over. Inwardness, its need for God, has then conquered, and the supplicant does not seek God in the external world, does not create him in his desires, but finds him in his inner being, and finally believes that he himself never did desire so vehemently, never has been in such a misunderstanding, and believes that such as he now has become he was from the beginning. But he does not therefore pray less than before, because that which made him pray was inwardness, and it has now conquered.—*JP* II 2114 (*Pap.* V B 227:5) *n.d.*, 1844

In margin of draft; see 392:34-36:

It was an illusion that they contended; they were friends.—
Pap. V B 228:2 *n.d.*, 1844

From draft; see 392:38-393:6:

. . . . . as if this were a demonstration and the genuine demonstration of God's love, and as if by the aid of this alone one
had an understanding with God. Indeed, it is to lose oneself
and lose God, because he who has no more certain demonstration than the uncertain does not possess God and is not
possessed by him. Now see how changed.

In margin: that one learns to thank a god, indeed, has become a lifelong debtor to him whom one has oneself made
into an idol by one's prayer and by one's thanks.—*Pap.* V B
227:6 *n.d.*, 1844

From draft; see 393:8-22:

b. God has become changed, for now it has indeed become
manifest that he is unchanging. —Not the cold changelessness
of the understanding.—*Pap.* V B 229:2 *n.d.*, 1844

From draft; see 393:23-394:11:

The change
a. The one who prays has become one who prays aright,
and he was convinced that if he only understood how to pray
aright then everything would be good.

> that before God he began to concentrate on one single
> wish, since otherwise all dying to the world is only de-
> lusion.

—*Pap.* V B 229:1 *n.d.*, 1844

From draft; see 394:21-35:

2.

How many strugglers there are, how hidden and private the
struggle in a person's inner being frequently is.

> The one whom God has selected out of the relationship
> with other human beings and selected for solitary pain.
> The struggle here is to obtain an explanation from God—

not to explain God—which is beneficial. He does not himself hit upon something and wish, but he bears the privation and the loss and prays only for an explanation of why he must suffer it. —But God refuses to give him the whole explanation.*

—*Pap.* V B 229:3 *n.d.*, 1844

Addition to Pap. V B 229:3; *see 396:3-4:*

*God cannot give him the whole explanation, for when is the Comforter coming? Just as in the past, when Christ had gone away, that is, when all earthly joy and certainty had vanished, which is why Christ said: It is beneficial for you that I go away, since otherwise the Comforter cannot come.—*Pap.* V B 229:4 *n.d.*, 1844

From draft; see 394:21-395:14:

His plans do not range widely abroad, his thoughts are not busy in the world; he is pondering only an explanation. And he dares to testify to himself that he is not a child who thinks that all that is needed is to ask a passerby about it or a young girl who thinks that the pastor may explain it in passing. No, he works, and in the daytime when life is noisy, his thought works at drowning out the noise; when everything is still at night, his thought is working. That he could find an explanation so that the whole thing may be efficacious for him—efficacious, yes, that is the name of the bridge he wants to throw from his pain across to his blessedness, but see, the storm of sufferings cuts it off.

"efficacious," that is the name of the friend he wants to win for himself, but, alas, this friend is so inclosed [*indesluttet*].*

—*Pap.* V B 229:12 *n.d.*, 1844

Addition to Pap. V B 229:12; *see 395:13-14:*

*if only he might be initiated into the comfort that with God is the secret of the sufferings

is this the explanation, that the explanation fails to come
—*Pap.* V B 229:14 *n.d.*, 1844

From draft; see 395:10-12:

efficacious—yes, that is the name of the friendship he wants
to buy for himself, the name of the inclosed [*indesluttet*] friend
who refuses to open himself to him
In margin: the rendezvous
—*Pap.* V B 230:1 *n.d.*, 1844

From draft; see 396:3-4:

And Christ Became **Invisible** to Them

. . . . . understood as a higher spiritual qualification in relation to seeing the visible form—in contrast to the mistaken
use of the words: Blessed are they who saw what you saw[41]—
which does not hold true in the external sense, because this is
paganism, and Judaism is further advanced inasmuch as it did
not even allow any likeness of God (because God is *invisible*,
consequently not because the likeness is objectionable, but because there is none, since there is no likeness to or of invisibil-
ity).[42]—*Pap.* V B 236 *n.d.*, 1844

From draft; see 396:4:

V
B 237
364

An Ascension Discourse

Just as in teaching a child to walk one covertly gets in front
of the child and turns toward it—consequently does not walk
alongside the child but is oneself the goal (how lovely if it is
the mother!) toward which the child is to walk alone—so also
Christ in his Ascension covertly gets in front, does not walk
beside the disciples; he is himself the goal toward which the
believer strives while he is learning to walk alone. There he
stands at the goal, turns toward the believers, and stretches out
his arms just as the mother does. Even though she stands so

V
B 237
365

far away that she cannot reach the child, she stretches out her arms and motions with them as if she already embraced the child, although there is still some distance between them. That much solicitude she has, but more solicitous she cannot be, since then the child does not learn to walk.[43]—*JP* II 1835 (*Pap.* V B 237) *n.d.*, 1844

From draft; see 396:24-32:

but cursed be all the loose talk that comes in the guise of sympathy and yet does not have the power of truth,[*] that offers itself and yet sinks to its knees as soon as the sufferer wants to lean on it for support, that sounds so delightful to the listener but has the repulsiveness of falsehood to the cater, all the deceitful comfort that thinks that the Comforter is coming immediately[**]

[*]*In margin:* has not learned from sorrow to count
[**]*In margin:* to be developed: the forty days the disciples had to wait[44] (their reflections during those days)—*Pap.* V B 230:3 *n.d.*, 1844

From draft; see 397:28-30:

Struggles with himself in prayer (not with God), prays to God for help against himself.—*Pap.* V B 229:5 *n.d.*, 1844

From draft; see 397:30-398:1:

If he still does not give up his inwardness (and as a consequence stop praying), if he loves God greatly, longs for him—indeed, how shall I say it—not as a young man for his beloved, no, as one who in all eternity is nothing without God; if he deals honestly with the debt of thanksgiving that runs on because he cannot rightly understand and consequently cannot give thanks aright, but deals with it honestly as a good entrusted to him for better times.— —*Pap.* V B 229:13 *n.d.*, 1844

From draft; see 398:34-399:7:

> Just as the adult stands behind a child and guides his hand while it is drawing, so that gradually something beautiful and great emerges from the drawing.
>
> —*Pap.* V B 229:7 *n.d.*, 1844

From draft; see 399:26-30:

What the child wants to be in the external world, what he wants to resemble, whom he wants to resemble—to resemble God.

if someone wants to be something himself, then this something is enough to frustrate the resemblance and to make the mistaken identity impossible. He must himself want to be nothing.

In margin: if it has now come so far with him that he thinks he cannot become anything at all, then the moment is there—*Pap.* V B 229:16 *n.d.*, 1844

From draft; see 399:27-29:

> Himself wanting to be something—Stoicism.
>
> —*Pap.* V B 229:6 *n.d.*, 1844

From draft; see 400:7-13:

> *The change*
> Either he comes to understand himself differently
> Or to understand God differently.
>
> —*Pap.* V B 229:8 *n.d.*, 1844

From draft; see 400:13-16:

> The one who prays aright always gives thanks and consequently is always victorious; otherwise why should he always give thanks.
>
> —*Pap.* V B 229:11 *n.d.*, 1844

From draft; see 400:10-29:

He can always thank God. One forgets this. The debt one incurs at the gambling table, by throwing dice, in a game of cards, is a debt of honor, but not the debt one is in to God for the solicitude of his providence, for the wisdom of his governance.—*Pap.* V B 229:10 *n.d.*, 1844

From draft; see 400:30-36:

Conclusion

Struggle is not pleasant; usually only one is victorious; sometimes both lose—this struggle is joyful and upbuilding, because they are both victorious.—*Pap.* V B 229:9 *n.d.*, 1844

From draft; see 400:36-401:8:

Perhaps you are saying, my listener, that this discourse is not easy (one who is being tested may find it poor and bland compared with the sufferings)—the struggle itself is not easy, either, and if someone should brashly want to waltz himself into it and play like a child with the name of the terror, he will know, if he understands it at all, that here it is a matter of a life-and-death struggle, of pain and spiritual trial, and sleeplessness.—*Pap.* V B 229:15 *n.d.*, 1844

Perhaps my upbuilding discourses could be made even more specific: Upbuilding Discourses for Kings and Queens —for Beggars—etc.— —*JP* V 5735 (*Pap.* V A 39) *n.d.*, 1844

Now I am going to write occasional discourses instead of upbuilding discourses, wedding addresses and communion addresses or funeral addresses.[45]—*JP* V 5741 (*Pap.* V A 62) *n.d.*, 1844

The journal[46] will be divided as follows:
Praemonenda [Preface]
1. *Examinatio* [Examination]

How does a new quality emerge through a continuous quantitative determination?[47]
2. *Contemplatio* [Contemplation]
de omnibus d.[48]
3. *Exaedificatio* [Upbuilding]
concerning the expectancy of faith.[49]
Miscellanea [Miscellany]
The question to Prof. Martensen[50] regarding the Aristotelian doctrine of virtue.
—*JP* V 5712 (*Pap.* V A 100) *n.d.*, 1844

Addition to Pap. V A 100:

Second Number

1. *Examinatio* [Examination]
to what extent is being a category—a quality.[51]
2. *Contemplatio* [Contemplation]
P. Møller[52] poetically diffused.
3. *Exaedificatio* [Upbuilding]

a.) on the upbuilding in always thanking God.[53]
b.) on the advantage of studying the sources.[54]
their significance for the personality.
Miscellanea [Miscellany]
Question to Prof. Heiberg,[55] what is poetry.
The hidden (a young girl has said it).
Weisse,[56] something similar at the beginning of part one.
—*JP* V 5713 (*Pap.* V A 101) *n.d.*, 1844

The Relation between *Either/Or* and the *Stages*[57]

In *Either/Or*[58] the esthetic component was something present battling with the ethical, and the ethical was the choice by which one emerged from it. For this reason there were only two components, and the Judge was unconditionally the winner, even though the book ended with a sermon and with the observation that only the truth that builds up is the truth for me (inwardness—the point of departure for my upbuilding discourses).

In the *Stages*[59] there are three components and the situation is different.

1. The esthetic-sensuous is thrust into the background as something past (therefore "a recollection"), for after all it cannot become utterly nothing.

The Young Man (thought—depression); Constantin Constantius (hardening through the understanding). Victor Eremita, who can no longer be the editor (sympathetic irony); the Fashion Designer (demonic despair); Johannes the Seducer (damnation, a "marked" individual). He concludes by saying that woman is merely a moment. At that very point the Judge begins: Woman's beauty increases with the years; her reality [*Realitet*] is precisely in time.[60]

2. The ethical component is polemical: the Judge[61] is not giving a friendly lecture but is grappling in existence, because he cannot end here, even though he can with pathos triumph again over every esthetic stage but not measure up to the esthetes in wittiness.

3. The religious comes into existence in a demonic approximation (Quidam[62] of the imaginary construction) with humor as its presupposition and its incognito (Frater Taciturnus).[63]—*JP* V 5804 (*Pap.* VI A 41) *n.d.*, 1845

VI
A 41
17

See journal, p. 158 n., p. 130 [*Pap.* VI A 1; V A 47].

VI
A 147
60

1. A little about the contradictions in the upbuilding address.

The relationship to scholarship—which categories may be used.

> Here a little about my upbuilding discourses,[64] that they were not sermons.[65] (Objections have been made to this without bearing in mind that for this reason the title was not put that way—but upbuilding discourses.)

It is of equal merit to be a good speaker and a good listener:

in scholarship as many results as possible, in religious ad‐
dress as few results as possible, just as strong in the im‐
mediate as the reflective, and one must above all have ex‐
isted [*existeret*] in both.

The one is a work of art; the other a work of scholarship.

Situation: that Hegel in punishment for his attack upon
the religious would have to deliver an upbuilding dis‐
course.

—*JP* I 630 (*Pap*. VI A 147) *n.d.*, 1845

From draft of Postscript *(SV VII 229):*

Magister Kierkegaard's four most recent upbuilding dis‐
courses took on a certain humorous touch,[66] perhaps as a sign
that here what he wanted to achieve was achieved—the hu‐
morous is lightly brought about by using immanence and
having time wrongly reflect itself in it, so that eternity lies
behind. The religious consists in this, that eternity is behind;
the essential is this, the humorous consists in this, that time is
like a simulated motion.

Seen from my point of view, this is the direct transition
to the paradox.

—*Pap*. VI B 41:7 *n.d.*, 1845

From draft of preface to proposed "Minor Writings":[67]

Although by their very difference in both essence and struc‐
ture* the different parts of this work have a relation to one
another that will be able to occupy someone who happens to
have the time and talent and wish to think about such things,
yet each particular part so lends itself to being read separately
for upbuilding that in order to suggest this I have arranged it
in such a way that each part can be purchased separately.
Something that is supposed to serve for upbuilding must
never contain a split, as if there were one kind of upbuilding
for the simple and another for the wise. I have perceived, how‐

ever, the relational unity in such a way that what the simple can understand should covertly contain what can engage the wise and more educated. Consequently, it ought to be present but concealed so that only reflective self-activity itself can generate it again, since to be more educated, more developed, is still something accidental—the upbuilding is essentially the same for all.

*for reflective comparison

—*Pap*. VII¹ B 220 *n.d.*, 1846-47

From draft of The Book on Adler:

Let us now recapitulate and see what Adler has done and bear in mind the words of Paul as a motto: "All that is done is done with the aim of upbuilding; whether someone speaks in tongues or prophesics, he does it for upbuilding."[68] These words contain the demand for sober-mindedness and the ethical responsibility, so that no one should chaotically think that it is a person's, to say nothing of a chosen person's, task to be like a troll-witch.—*Pap*. VII² B 235 *n.d.*, 1846-47

VII²
B 235
72

From draft of The Book on Adler:

. . . in the early summer of 1846, he altogether unexpectedly appeared in the *Adresseavisen* with four new books[69] at one time . . .

VII²
B 235
128

But primarily the four books must objectively have a deeper purpose—for example, if possible, maieutically to cover a specific terrain on all sides at the same time. It must then be important to the author of the four books—for him a half-poetic artistic task—that each book, which essentially *in itself* is different from the others, be kept *characteristically* distinct from the others. The author must poetically know how to support the illusion, which consists essentiallly in the special point of departure in the particular book. By way of the announcement, he himself must see to splitting them up, so that the impact of the four books at the same time actually is a product of the reader's self-activity. Above, all, no one is obliged to

VII²
B 235
129

know that there are four books at the same time. Therefore, the art connoisseur, if he discovers in a roundabout way that there is one author, still can have a certain enjoyment in entering into the illusion that there are not four books by one author but by four authors. Thus, even in *Adresseavisen*, the one and the same author does not introduce and offer himself as the author of four books at one and the same same. As a matter of fact, not long ago such a thing was done in Danish literature in a more artistic manner . . ..[70]—*Pap.* VII² B 235 *n.d.*, 1846-47

What is the essentially Christian and the point in the fifth of the *Christian Discourses*[71] is specifically that the authority of the Bible is affirmed, that it is not something one has thought out but something commanded, something with authority, the requirement that adversity is the task. Consequently the analogy of the child of whom the parents require something is continually used: in the same way the Bible, God's Word, commands the elders. In an upbuilding discourse [*opbyggelig Tale*], I could not so rigorously maintain that the Bible says this.—*JP* I 207 (*Pap.* VIII¹ A 20) *n.d.*, 1847

The essentially Christian, the point in the sixth discourse,[72] is specifically that it does not enter into a development of the temporal and the eternal, that when placed together they must yield the concept "suffering"; instead, the presentation is strictly from the apostolic word. An upbuilding discourse, which functions with the aid of reflection, could never be structured in this way.—*Pap.* VIII¹ A 21 *n.d.*, 1847

VIII¹
A 32
19

VIII¹
A 32
20

N.B.

One suffers only once—but is victorious eternally.[73] Insofar as one is victorious, this is also only once. The difference, however, is that the one time of suffering is momentary[74] (even though the moment were seventy years)[75]—but the one time of victory is eternity. The one time of suffering (even though it lasted seventy years) can therefore not be pictured or portrayed in art. On the altar in Vor Frelsers Church there is a work that presents an angel who holds out to Christ the cup of suffering.[76] The error is that it lasts too long; a picture always endures for an eternity. It appears interminable; one does not see that the suffering is momentary, as all suffering is according to the concept or in the idea of victory. The victory, however, is eternal; this (insofar as it is not spiritual) can be portrayed, because it endures.

Meanwhile, the first impression of the upbuilding is *terrifying*[77]—if men take time to understand it properly, since in this case to suffer once is like being sick once—that is, for a whole lifetime. But the wisdom and impatience of this world must not demand, either, that one should be able to comfort the sufferer—at least if one is to speak of the essentially Christian, because the comfort of Christianity begins first of all where human impatience would simply despair. This is how deep the essentially Christian is—*first of all* one must scrupulously try to find the *terrifying* and then scrupulously once again—then one finds the *upbuilding*. Alas, as a rule we try scrupulously in neither the first instance nor the second.—*JP* IV 4594 (*Pap.* VIII[1] A 32) *n.d.*, 1847

Invitation

VIII[2]
B 188
295

Gratified to learn that my upbuilding writings, addressed to the single individual, are still read by many individuals, I have considered obliging these my readers, and perhaps gaining more individuals as readers, by publishing such works in the future in smaller sections on a subscription basis.[78] The possible advantages are, first, that the books will be read better if they are read in smaller sections; second, that a certain calmness of understanding may enter into the relation between author and reader, so that a beginning need not be made each time; and finally, that the publication can properly take place quietly and unnoticed, avoiding all irrelevant attention.

From July 1 of this year, I plan, then, to publish under the more general title

Upbuilding Reading

a section of six, at most eight, sheets [*Ark*][79] every three months. Lest the fortuitous division of time arbitrarily cause a disturbing interruption and sometimes let the reader wait three months for an installment or the concluding installment, I have in mind rounding out each section lyrically or dialectically as a little entity by itself so that it may be regarded and read as a separate book.

In my opinion, culture by no means makes upbuilding superfluous: it just makes it more and more necessary, not that culture in itself entails this or leads directly to this. But because the *cultured person*, if he understands himself (and if not, then his culture may well be purely imaginary, which, since a continuation is rarely lacking, fosters new and worse fancies), will become aware that what we call culture leaves a whole side of the soul unsatisfied, without nourishment and care—therefore, aware of this, he will respond to the need whose claims he perceives, and he will make it his concern to see to it that this need for upbuilding will increase equally with his increasing culture. With regard to culture, the need is *immediate*, the immediate that *perhaps not everyone has*. With regard to upbuilding, the explicit task is precisely *to develop* deeper and deeper the need that everyone *ought to have*. —For the *simpler people*, however, who also have the advantage neither of the time nor of the circumstances for the cultivation of the spirit, the upbuilding becomes that which cultivates, that which genuinely and nobly cultivates one who nevertheless remains uninitiated into that which cultivates intellectually and esthetically. —Genuine education never makes one grow away from the upbuilding as something one needs less and less, but makes one grow up to the upbuilding as something one needs more and more and of which one needs more and more. Lacking all other culture, a person can be cultivated by the upbuilding; eternally understood, all other culture devoid of the upbuilding is miseducation. Indeed, upbuilding does not want to set at variance any more than love does, even though it always requires two. The upbuilding does not want to consolidate differences between people any more than the ocean wants to separate. Just like love, the upbuilding wants to unite, if possible, the most different in essential truth.

Since this is so, it is my hope and desire that for the sake

VIII²
B 188
296

of the plan and for mine—but certainly also for their own sakes—a good number of individuals will sympathetically participate. If I am granted the strength and energy to keep on, and in that case if there is also continued support from without, it would indeed be a great and encouraging joy for me that there might be in our native land one more recognizable expression that people need upbuilding, that the upbuilding is a necessity of life. This certainly can be recognized by the fact that in the course of a year many upbuilding books are published; but it is even more decisive to have an ongoing periodical for upbuilding reading (especially if many participate)—one among the many for light reading.

S. Kierkegaard.

January 1848

at the end of the year, the common title page, the table of contents, the list of subscribers.—*JP* V 6095 (*Pap*. VIII² B 188) *n.d.*, 1847-48

This is how it is used. The subject of the single individual appears in every book by the pseudonymous writers, but the price put upon being a single individual, a single individual in the eminent sense, rises. The subject of the single individual appears in every one of my upbuilding books, but there the single individual is what every human being is. This is precisely the dialectic of "the single individual" [*changed from:* the particular]. The single individual can mean the most unique of all and it can mean everyone. Now if one desires to stimulate attention, one will use this category in rapid succession but always in double-stroke. The pride in the one thought incites a few, the humility in the other thought repels others, but the confusion in this doubleness provokes attention, and yet this is the idea of "the single individual." The pride in the one thought eggs on a few who in that sense of the word could very well desire to be the single individual of the pseudonyms. But then they are repelled in turn by the thought of "the single individual" in the sense of the upbuilding.*

In margin: *That is, the point of departure of the pseudonymous writers is continually in the differences—the point of
departure in the upbuilding discourses is in the universally human.—*Pap.* VIII² B 192 *n.d.*, 1847-48

VIII¹
A 486
216

Some Discourses to Be Written for Awakening[80]

Thoughts That $\frac{\text{Attack}}{\text{Wound}}$ from Behind[81]—for Upbuilding.[*]

"Watch your step when you go to the house of the Lord"
(Ecclesiastes).[82] See one of the earlier journals [*Pap.* VIII¹ A
256].[**]
        This will be the introduction.
    In the following discourses the text is to be chosen in such
a way that it appears to be a Gospel text, and is that also, but
then comes the stinger.

No. 1.   "What shall we have, we who have left all?" And
         Christ answers: You will sit on thrones[83] etc.

The satire for us in this question—we who have probably
not left anything at all.

No. 2.   All things serve us for good, *if* we love God.[84] If
         we love God. (The irony.)

No. 3.   There will be the resurrection of the dead, of both
         the righteous and the unrighteous.[85]

VIII¹
A 486
217
Rejoice, you are not to ask for three demonstrations[86]—it is
certain enough that you are immortal—it is absolutely certain—because you must come up for judgment.[87] This is a
new argument for immortality.

No. 4.   It is blessed—to be mocked for a good cause.[88]
         (Rejoice when men speak all sorts of evil about
         you.[89])

So rejoice, then—but perhaps there is no one present to
whom this discourse applies.[90] You, my listener, rejoice perhaps because you are highly honored, esteemed, and regarded. Yes, then indeed for you it is a meal like the stork's at
the fox's house.[91]

The satirical.

"Woe to you if everyone speaks well of you."[92] Here is not appended "and lies"; it is not necessary, since if everyone speaks well of a person, it must be a lie.

No. 5. "We are nearer to salvation now than when we became believers."[93] But are you sure you have become a believer.

No. 6. He (Christ) was believed in the world[94] (I Timothy 3:16). But this is perhaps merely a bit of historical information.

[*]*In margin:* "An assault by thoughts"
[**]*In margin:* Journal NB², pp. 147-48 [*Pap.* VIII¹ A 256]. Ditto, pp. 242, bottom, and 243, top [*Pap.* VIII¹ A 367].—*JP* V 6096 (*Pap.* VIII¹ A 486) *n.d.*, 1847

Yes, it had to be this way. I have not become a religious author; I was that: simultaneously with *Either/Or* appeared two upbuilding discourses[95]—now after two years of writing only religious books there appears a little article about an actress.[96]

IX
A 216
112

Now there is a moment, a point of rest; by this step I have learned to know myself and very concretely.

So the publication must proceed (that is, of course I have more, I have finished what is to be used: (1) A Cycle of Ethical-Religious Essays, (2) The Sickness unto Death, (3) Come Here, All You . . . . .), if I do not happen to die beforehand. My health is very poor, and the thought of dying has gotten the upper hand with me as I use this half year to sorrow for my sins and work further in the presentation of Christianity. Perhaps it is a despondent thought, perhaps also because I have become disinclined to make the finite decisions involved in publication—in any case I have now been prodded by it.

IX
A 216
113

The next publication will be very decisive for my outer life. I always have held on to the remote possibility of seeking a pastoral call[97] if the worst comes to worst financially.[98] When I publish the last books, this may well be denied me even if I were to seek it, so the problem will not be as before, if I do dare to undertake it, but rather that it will not even be given to me.

This is one more heavy burden added to my inner suffering and outer mistreatment, but no doubt it will be beneficial so that I do not rush on but come to need God more and more. The more God entrusts to me, the more burdens he lays upon me.

So the work goes on, given time, if I do not die before that, carrying the enormous column of reflection as I virtually do every moment—and yet trustful as a child in my inner being. Oh, I can never sufficiently thank God for what he has done and is doing for me, so indescribably much more than I had expected, he who helps one, step by step, if one honestly tells him the situation and then allows oneself to be helped, helps one by taking away the burdens one may not be able to bear, helps one little by little to carry the burdens from which one once shrank. He who loves God is loved forth[99] by God in such a way that this is an education. At all times there is a world of help possible, because for God everything is possible: if I have done something wrong, even though I honestly considered it, there is at all times a world of help, because for God everything is possible[100]—how blessed that he is also love,[101] that for the loving one everything is possible, and that he for whom everything is possible is love. And if I stumble, if sin wins a temporary victory over me, oh, at all times for the honest penitent there is a world of help in the Atonement for all our sins[102] with him, our Savior and Redeemer.

To be surrounded everywhere by love in this way, oh, who would not feel blessed in the midst of all his sufferings, which no doubt come so that one may not take salvation in vain but also to make one even more blissfully aware of salvation.—*JP* VI 6229 (*Pap.* IX A 216) *n.d.*, 1848

But on the other hand, the understanding, reflection, is also a gift of God. What shall one do with it, how dispose of it if one is not to use it? And if one then uses it in fear and trembling not for one's own advantage but to serve the truth, if

IX
A 216
114

IX
A 222
117

one uses it that way in fear and trembling and furthermore believing that it still is God who determines the issue in its eternal significance, venturing in trust in him, and with unconditional obedience yielding to what he makes of it: is this not fear of God and serving God the way a person of reflection can, in a somewhat different way than the spontaneously immediate person, but perhaps more ardently. But if that is the case, does not a maieutic element enter into the relation to other men or to various other men. The maieutic is really only the expression for a superiority between man and man. That it exists cannot be denied—but existence presses far more powerfully upon the superior one precisely because he is a maieutic (because he has the responsibility) than upon the other.

As far as I am concerned, there has been no lack of witness. All my upbuilding discourses are in fact in the form of direct communication.

IX
A 222
118

Consequently there can be a question only about this, something that has occupied me for a long time (already back in earlier journals[103]): should I for once definitely explain myself as author, what I declare myself to be, how I from the beginning understand myself to be a religious author.

But now is not the time to do it; I am also somewhat strained at the moment. I need more physical recreation.—*JP* VI 6234 (*Pap.* IX A 222) *n.d.*, 1848

N.B. N.B.

IX
A 227
124

Yes, it was a good thing to publish that little article.[104] I began with *Either/Or* and two upbuilding discourses;[105] now it ends, after the whole upbuilding series—with a little esthetic essay. It expresses: that it was the upbuilding—the religious—that should advance, and that now the esthetic has been traversed; they are inversely related, or it is something of an inverse confrontation, to show that the writer was not an esthetic author who in the course of time grew older and for that reason became religious.

But it is not really to my credit; it is Governance who has

held me in rein with the help of an extreme depression and a troubled conscience.

But there still would have been something lacking if the little article had not come out; the illusion would have been established that it was I who essentially had changed over the years, and then a very important point in the whole productivity would have been lost.

It is true I have been educated by this writing, have developed more and more religiously—but in a decisive way I had experienced the pressures that turned me away from the world before I began writing *Either/Or*. Even then my only wish was to do, as decisively as possible, something good to compensate, if possible in another way, for what I personally had committed. That I have developed more and more religiously is seen in my now saying goodbye to the esthetic, because I do not know where I would find the time that I could, would, or would dare fill up with work on esthetic writings.

IX
A 227
125

My energies, that is, my physical energies, are declining; the state of my health varies terribly. I hardly see my way even to publishing the essentially decisive works I have ready ("A Cycle of Essays," "The Sickness unto Death," "Come Here, All You Who Labor and Are Burdened," "Blessed Is He Who Is Not Offended"[106]). It is my judgment that here I am allowed to present Christianity once again and in such a way that a whole development can be based on it. The emphasis upon the situation of contemporaneity, that Christ's life is infinitely more important than the result; the unrecognizability or the incognito in relation to the God-man; the impossibility of direct communication etc.—in my opinion all the essays contain such a wealth of ideas that again and again I cannot praise God enough for having granted me so infinitely much more than I had expected. And, moreover, I am convinced that it will serve for the inward deepening of Christianity—it has been taken in vain, made too mild, so that people have forgotten what grace is; the more rigorous it is, the more grace becomes manifest as grace and not a sort of human sympathy.

Just one wish for this endeavor of mine if I happen to be separated from it. I live in the faith that God will place the accent of Governance on the life of an extremely unhappy, humanly understood, man who nevertheless by the help of God has felt indescribably blessed—but my wish is that now R. Nielsen[107] might be relied on. The same cause that has cost me my health and an enormous strain, the same cause that as long as I live occasions only insults and humiliation because in so many ways I am the object of envy, the same cause, as soon as I am dead, will be a triumphant cause!—if only he does not sell too cheap.

So I turn to the other side,[108] forgetting all these many thoughts, mindful only of my sins and entrusting myself to the Atonement of Jesus Christ.—*JP* VI 6238 (*Pap.* IX A 227) *n.d.*, 1848

IX
A 227
126

N.B. N.B.

IX
A 241
135

Strange, strange about that little article[109]—that I had so nearly gone and forgotten myself. When one is overstrained as I was, it is easy to forget momentarily the dialectical outline of a colossal structure such as my authorship. That is why Governance helped me.

Right now the totality is so dialectically right. *Either/Or* and the two upbuilding discourses*[110]—*Concluding Postscript*—for two years only upbuilding discourses and then a little article about an actress. The illusion that I happened to get older and for that reason became a decisively religious author has been made impossible. If I had died beforehand, then the writing I did those two years would have been made ambiguous and the totality unsteady.

In a certain sense, of course, my concern is superfluous when I consider the world of actuality in which I live—since as a matter of fact I have not found many dialecticians.

In margin: *Note. And these two discourses quite properly did not appear at the same time as *Either/Or* but a few months later—just as this little article now.—*JP* VI 6242 (*Pap.* IX A 241) *n.d.*, 1848

IX
A 241
136

"Let not the heart in sorrow sin"[111]

Under this title I would like to write a few discourses[112] dealing with the most beautiful and noble, humanly speaking, forms of despair: unhappy love, grief over the death of a beloved, sorrow at not having achieved one's proper place in the world, the forms the "poet" loves and that only Christianity dares to call sin, while the human attitude is that the lives of such people are infinitely more worthwhile than the millions that make up the prosy-pack.—*JP* VI 6277 (*Pap.* IX A 421) *n.d.*, 1848

. . . *The Sickness unto Death* appears at this time, but pseudonymously and with me as editor. It is said to be "for upbuilding." This is more than my category, the poet-category: upbuilding.[113]

Just as the Guadalquibir [*sic*] River (this occurred to me earlier and is somewhere in the journal[114] [*Pap.* X¹ A 422]) at some place plunges underground, so is there also a stretch, the upbuilding, that carries my name. There is something (the esthetic) that is lower and is pseudonymous and something that is higher and is also pseudonymous, because as a person I do not correspond to it.

The pseudonym is Johannes Anticlimacus [*sic*] in contrast to Climacus, who said he was not a Christian. Anticlimacus is the opposite extreme: a Christian on an extraordinary level—if only I myself manage to be just a simple Christian.

"Practice in Christianity" can be published in the same way, but there is no hurry.

But nothing about my personality as a writer; it is false to want to anticipate during one's lifetime—this merely converts a person into the interesting.

On the whole, I must now venture in quite different directions. I must dare to believe that through Christ I can be saved from the power of depression in which I have lived; and I must dare to try to be more economical.—*JP* VI 6431 (*Pap.* X¹ A 510) *n.d.*, 1849

[*In margin:* About *The Sickness unto Death.*]
The book is characterized as being "for upbuilding";[115] the preface speaks of it as upbuilding.[116] It really should say: for awakening. [*In margin:* see p. 259 in this journal (*Pap.* X¹ A 529)] This is its basic character, and this is the forward step in the writings. Essentially it is also for awakening, but this does not need to be said yet. This will come out decisively for the first time in the next book, "Practice in Christianity."—*JP* VI 6436 (*Pap.* X¹ A 520) *n.d.*, 1849

The two works by Anti-Climacus[117] ("Practice in Christianity") can be published immediately.
With this the writing stops;[118] essentially it has already stopped (that which is wholly mine) with "The Friday Discourses."[119] The pseudonymous writer[120] at the end is a higher level, which I can only suggest. The second-round pseudonymity is precisely the expression for the halt. *Qua* author I am like the river Guadalquibir [*sic*], which at some place plunges underground; there is a stretch that is mine: the upbuilding;[121] behind and ahead lie the lower and the higher pseudonymities: the upbuilding is mine, not the esthetic, nor that for upbuilding, and even less that for awakening.[122]—*JP* VI 6461 (*Pap.* X¹ A 593) *n.d.*, 1849

[*In margin:* Peter's remarks at the convention.]
Peter's Remarks at the Convention.[123]

X²
A 273
201

After all, there is some confusion-compounding to take a passage from Paul and then exhibit Martensen[124] and me as the two positions.[125] If Martensen is to be compared to Paul, then Paul (and also his σωφροσύνη [soundness of mind, self-control]) becomes ecstasy pure and simple. The Martensenian-Petrian concept of composure is a partially irreligious concept of mediocrity and indolent comfortableness.
Moreover, Peter should also have pointed out that it is especially difficult these days to represent ecstasy. Mediocrity, worldly haggling, etc. are preponderant. It should also be

X²
A 273
202

pointed out that my ecstasy is characterized by an equally great composure. The very fact that I use pseudonyms, invented characters (consequently not myself) to represent the ecstatic, while in the upbuilding discourses I myself speak gently and quietly. The difference between the category of the single individual as it is used by the pseudonyms and as I use it etc.

But what does Peter care about all this. He self-complacently expounds mediocrity (and of course to the jubilation of the rural clergy): that there are two trends (that is, the achievers)—and they are one-sided; but we, who achieve nothing, we are of the truth, and we are also the majority. Just believe me, I know; should I not know it—after all, I am eight years older than my brother.—*JP* VI 6553 (*Pap.* X² A 273) *n.d.,* 1849

X²
A 560
402

Reduplication

Every striving that does not apply one-fourth, one-third, two-thirds, etc. of its power to *working against* itself systematically is essentially secular striving, in any case unconditionally not a *reforming* effort.

Reduplication means to work also against oneself while working; it is like the pressure on the plow-handles, which determines the depth of the furrow—whereas a striving that while working does not work also against itself is merely a superficial smoothing over.

What does it mean to work against oneself? It is quite simple. If the established, the traditional, etc., in the context of which a beginning is to be made, is sound, thoroughly sound—well, then apply *directly* what is to be applied; in any case there can be no talk or thought of reforming, because if the established is sound, then there is nothing, after all, to reform.

To the same degree, however, that the established, consequently *there* where one's striving begins, is corrupt, to the same degree the dialectical begins: to work against oneself becomes more and more necessary, so that the new, by being

applied directly, is not itself corrupted, does not at once suc- x^2
ceed etc., and thus is not maintained in its heterogeneity.   A 560
    403

Again the difference is between the direct and the inverted, which is the dialectical. Working or striving directly is to work and strive. The inverted method is this: while working also to work against oneself.

But who dreams that such a standard exists, and that I use it on such a large scale! Understood I will never be. People think I am involved in a direct striving—and now they believe that I have achieved a kind of breakthrough! Oh, such ignorance! The publication of *Either/Or* was a huge success; I had it in my power to continue. After all, what is the origin of all the problems in my striving; I wonder if it is not in myself? It is public knowledge that not one single person has really dared to oppose me. But I have done that myself. What a wrong turn on my part, if my striving was to be direct, to publish *Two Upbuilding Discourses* after *Either/Or*, which could only have a disturbing effect, instead of letting *Either/Or* stand with its glittering success, continuing in the direction that the age demanded, only in slightly reduced portions. What a counter effort by myself that I, the public's darling, introduce the single individual, and finally, that I plunge myself into all the dangers of insults!

But such things can be understood only by someone who himself has risked something essentially similar. Someone else cannot conceive it or believe it.

R. Nielsen[126] is actually confused about this, for he interprets my striving as direct striving.—*JP* VI 6593 (*Pap.* X^2 A 560) *n.d.*, 1850

A Possible Preface to the Upbuilding Discourse "The x^5
Woman Who Was a Sinner."   B 117
    312

If neither "The Accounting" nor *Two Discourses at the Communion on Fridays* is published but only the upbuilding discourse, which is to be dedicated to my father, the following preface could perhaps be used.[127]

X⁵
B 117
313

Preface

What was said in my first book of upbuilding discourses, in the Preface to *Two Upbuilding Discourses* in 1843, that this book "seeks that single individual [*hiin Enkelte*]"; what was repeated verbatim in the Preface to each new collection of upbuilding discourses; what was pointed out, after I had exposed myself to the laughter and the insults of the crowd and thus, as well as I could, contributed to evoking awareness by dedicating the next large work, *Upbuilding Discourses in Various Spirits*, 1847, to "the single individual [*den Enkelte*]"; what world revolution in 1848 certainly did not witness against or render untrue—emphasis upon the single individual—let me repeatedly remind [readers] of this. [*In margin:* If for the sake of recollection it is possible for a thinker to manage to concentrate all his thinking in one single idea, this has been granted to me, the upbuilding author, whose entire thinking is essentially contained in this one thought: the single individual.]

"The single individual"—of course, the single individual religiously understood, consequently understood in such a way that everyone, unconditionally everyone, yes, unconditionally everyone, just as much as everyone has or should have a conscience, can be that single individual and should be that, can stake his honor in willing to be that, but then also can find blessedness in being what is the expression for true fear of God, true love to one's neighbor, true humanity [*Menneskelighed*], and true human equality [*Menneske-Lighed*]. Oh, if only some might achieve it, if it is not, although the task for all, nevertheless too high for all of us, yet not too high in such a way that it should be forgotten, forgotten as if it were not the task or as if this task did not face us in November 1850, so that we may at least learn to forsake not only the mediocre but also the indifferent half measures that reject an established order, yet without driving through to become in an extraordinary sense the single individual, but rather schismatically organize parties and sects, which are neither the one nor the other.

November 1850
—*JP* II 2033 (*Pap.* X⁵ B 117)

From draft of "The Accounting," in On My Work:

. . . The directly religious was present from the beginning; for *Two Upbuilding Discourses* of 1843 are, after all, concurrent with *Either/Or.* . . .[128]—*Pap.* X[5] B 191, May [*changed to: April, changed to:* March] 5, 1849

X[5]
B 191
377

From draft of "The Accounting," in On My Work:[129]

. . . The movement it [the authorship] describes is: from "the poet," from the esthetic—from the philosopher, from the speculative—to the intimation of the most inward interpretation of the essentially Christian; **from** the **pseudonymous** *Either/Or*, which was immediately accompanied by *Two Upbuilding Discourses* with *my name* as author, **through** *Concluding Postscript* with my name as editor, to *Discourses at the Communion on Fridays* [*here a double dagger in red crayon, in margin a double dagger and: see the attached*], the lastest work I have written, and "of which two have been delivered in Frue Kirke." . . .[130]—*Pap.* X[5] B 201 *n.d.*, 1849

X[5]
B 201
382

From draft of "The Accounting," in On My Work:

Yet I owe it to the truth to admit that in the beginning it was by no means my thought to become a religious author in the sense I have become that; on the contrary, it was truly my intention in the beginning to become a rural pastor the moment I laid down my pen. I profoundly understood that I belonged to the religious, that it was a deception on my part, albeit a pious deception, to pass myself off as an esthetic author, and I sought an energetic expression for my belonging in the strictest sense to the religious and thought to find this in leaping away from being an esthetic author—and at once becoming a rural pastor. My first thought was to stop with *Either/Or*—and then at once a rural pastor. It did not happen; but since it did not happen, there was promptly a religious signaling (*Two Upbuilding Discourses*). . . . My thought was to deceive by becoming an esthetic author and then promptly to become a rural pastor, accentuating the religious doubly

X[5]
B 217
404

X[5]
B 217
405

strongly by the contrast. Something else happened: the religious found its expression in my becoming a religious author, but consequently a religious author who began with an esthetic productivity as a deception. The point was that the religious found its expression unconditionally at the same time the esthetic deception was initiated—otherwise there would have been a show of justification in saying that originally I was not conscious that the esthetic productivity was a deception and that the explanation would be that in the beginning I wanted to be an esthetic author and then later changed. But the presence of the religious at exactly the same time found its expression not as I had thought, by my becoming a rural pastor, but by the publication of *Two Upbuilding Discourses.—Pap.* X⁵ B 217 *n.d.*, 1849

X⁵
B 217
406

From draft of reply to a pamphlet on Kierkegaard's writings:[131]

X⁶
B 145
217

. . . Let us look at this a little more closely. I certainly do think that my presentation or illumination of the essentially Christian comes some points closer to the truth than the proclamation of Christianity hereabouts ordinarily does—but I am only a poet. If he so wishes, "the pastor" can make capital of this; he can say: To be a pastor is something far higher; a poet, and Magister Kierkegaard is right here, is inadequate when it comes to the essentially Christian, and Mag. K. is only a poet—oddly enough, says so himself. But I have not said that. I have not said that I, measured against "the pastor," that is, every pastor as such, am only a poet, but measured against the ideal, I am only a poet. For example, in order to jack up the price of preaching, in the preface to my "Upbuilding Discourses,"[132] I have continually repeated that they are not sermons or have pointed to "the sermon" as something higher. If he so wishes, "the pastor" may make capital of this. He can sermonize or hold forth like this: A pastor preaches; that is far higher. But in a way it may be good to have Magister Kierkegaard with us, since he illuminates what we pastors do. His upbuilding discourse is not poor work, but, as he himself says, it still is not a sermon. There, my little children, you see

X⁶
B 145
218

what we pastors do and the truth of what you read as little children in the verse: "Who can do it best? Our pastor can do it best."[133] But I have not said that, I have not said that I, measured against "the pastor," that is, every pastor as such, cannot preach; I have said that, measured against the ideal, my upbuilding discourse is still not a sermon. I have also said "that before God I regard my whole work as an author as my own education";[134] I am not a teacher but a learner. Every teacher of religion, every music teacher, every gymnastics coach, every part-time teacher may make capital of this if he wishes and say: There you see what it is to be a teacher if Magister Kierkegaard, who is for all that a gifted person, is only a learner, as he himself says. But I have not said that I, measured against every part-time teacher, could not be called a teacher, but that before God, measured against the ideals for being a teacher, I call myself a learner. . . . —*JP* VI 6786 (*Pap.* X⁶ B 145) *n.d.*, 1851

EDITORIAL APPENDIX

ACKNOWLEDGMENTS

Preparation of manuscripts for *Kierkegaard's Writings* is supported by a genuinely enabling grant from the National Endowment for the Humanities. The grant includes gifts from the Dronning Margrethes og Prins Henriks Fond, the Danish Ministry of Cultural Affairs, the Augustinus Fond, the Carlsberg Fond, and the Lutheran Brotherhood Foundation.

The translators-editors are indebted to Grethe Kjaer and Julia Watkin for their knowledgeable observations on crucial concepts and terminology.

John Elrod, Per Lønning, and Sophia Scopetéa, members of the International Advisory Board for *Kierkegaard's Writings*, have given valuable criticism of the manuscript on the whole and in detail. Jack Schwandt, Jørgen Hansen, Margaret Hansen, Craig Mason, and Julia Watkin helpfully read the manuscript. Kathryn Hong, associate editor for *KW* at St. Olaf, scrutinized the manuscript. Regine Prenzel-Guthrie, assistant editor for *KW*, also scrutinized the manuscript and prepared the index.

Acknowledgment is made to Gyldendals Forlag for permission to use the texts and to absorb notes in *Søren Kierkegaards samlede Værker* and *Søren Kierkegaards Papirer*.

Inclusion in the Supplement of entries from *Søren Kierkegaard's Journals and Papers* is by arrangement with Indiana University Press.

The book collection and the microfilm collection of the Kierkegaard Library, St. Olaf College, have been used in preparation of the text and of the Supplement and Editorial Appendix.

The original manuscript was typed by Dorothy Bolton and Kennedy Lemke. The final manuscript and composition tape were prepared by Francesca Lane Rasmus. The volume has been guided through the press by Cathie Brettschneider.

COLLATION OF THE SIX VOLUMES
OF *UPBUILDING DISCOURSES* IN THE DANISH
EDITIONS OF KIERKEGAARD'S COLLECTED WORKS

TWO UPBUILDING DISCOURSES (1843)

Vol. III Ed. 1 Pg.	*Vol. III* Ed. 2 Pg.	*Vol. 4* Ed. 3 Pg.	*Vol. III* Ed. 1 Pg.	*Vol. III* Ed. 2 Pg.	*Vol. 4* Ed. 3 Pg.
11	15	13	33	40	33
15	19	15	34	41	34
16	20	15	37	45	35
17	21	16	38	46	35
18	22	17	39	47	36
19	23	18	40	48	37
20	24	19	41	49	38
21	26	20	42	50	39
22	27	21	43	51	40
23	28	23	44	52	41
24	29	24	45	54	42
25	30	25	46	55	43
26	32	26	47	56	44
27	33	27	48	57	45
28	34	28	49	58	46
29	35	29	50	59	47
30	36	30	51	60	48
31	38	31	52	62	49
32	39	32			

THREE UPBUILDING DISCOURSES (1843)

Vol. III Ed. 1 Pg.	Vol. III Ed. 2 Pg.	Vol. 4 Ed. 3 Pg.	Vol. III Ed. 1 Pg.	Vol. III Ed. 2 Pg.	Vol. 4 Ed. 3 Pg.
271	301	55	294	325	75
273	303	57	295	327	76
274	304	57	296	328	78
275	305	58	297	328	78
276	306	59	298	329	79
277	307	60	299	331	80
278	308	61	300	332	81
279	309	62	301	333	82
280	310	63	302	334	83
281	311	64	303	335	84
282	313	65	304	336	85
283	314	66	305	338	86
284	315	67	306	339	87
285	316	67	307	340	88
286	317	68	308	341	89
287	318	69	309	342	90
288	318	69	310	343	91
289	320	70	311	345	92
290	321	71	312	346	93
291	322	72	313	347	94
292	323	73	314	348	95
293	324	74	315	349	96

FOUR UPBUILDING DISCOURSES (1843)

Vol. IV *Ed. 1* Pg.	*Vol. IV* *Ed. 2* Pg.	*Vol. 4* *Ed. 3* Pg.	*Vol. IV* *Ed. 1* Pg.	*Vol. IV* *Ed. 2* Pg.	*Vol. 4* *Ed. 3* Pg.
7	7	101	39	41	130
9	9	103	40	43	131
10	10	103	41	44	132
11	11	104	42	45	133
12	12	105	43	46	134
13	13	106	44	47	135
14	14	107	45	48	136
15	15	108	46	49	137
16	16	109	47	51	138
17	18	110	48	52	139
18	19	111	49	53	140
19	20	112	50	54	141
20	21	113	51	55	142
21	22	114	52	57	143
22	23	115	53	58	144
23	24	116	54	59	145
24	25	117	55	59	145
25	26	117	56	61	146
26	27	118	57	62	147
27	28	119	58	63	148
28	29	120	59	65	149
29	30	121	60	66	150
30	31	122	61	67	151
31	33	123	62	68	152
32	34	124	63	69	153
33	35	125	64	71	154
34	36	126	65	72	156
35	37	127	66	73	157
36	38	128	67	74	158
37	39	129	68	75	159
38	41	130			

Editorial Appendix

TWO UPBUILDING DISCOURSES (1844)

Vol. IV	*Vol. IV*	*Vol. 4*	*Vol. IV*	*Vol. IV*	*Vol. 4*
Ed. 1	*Ed. 2*	*Ed. 3*	*Ed. 1*	*Ed. 2*	*Ed. 3*
Pg.	*Pg.*	*Pg.*	*Pg.*	*Pg.*	*Pg.*
73	81	163	94	105	183
75	83	165	95	107	185
76	84	165	96	108	185
77	85	166	97	109	186
78	86	167	98	110	187
79	87	168	99	111	188
80	88	169	100	112	189
81	89	170	101	114	190
82	91	171	102	115	191
83	92	172	103	116	192
84	93	173	104	117	193
85	94	174	105	118	194
86	95	175	106	120	195
87	97	176	107	121	196
88	98	177	108	122	198
89	99	178	109	123	199
90	100	179	110	125	200
91	101	180	111	126	201
92	103	181	112	127	202
93	104	182	113	128	203

THREE UPBUILDING DISCOURSES (1844)

Vol. IV Ed. 1 Pg.	Vol. IV Ed. 2 Pg.	Vol. 4 Ed. 3 Pg.	Vol. IV Ed. 1 Pg.	Vol. IV Ed. 2 Pg.	Vol. 4 Ed. 3 Pg.
121	137	209	147	167	235
123	139	211	148	168	235
124	140	211	149	169	236
125	141	212	150	171	237
126	142	213	151	172	238
127	143	214	152	173	239
128	144	215	153	174	240
129	146	216	154	175	241
130	147	217	155	176	242
131	148	218	156	177	243
132	149	219	157	179	245
133	150	220	158	180	245
134	151	221	159	181	246
135	152	222	160	182	247
136	154	223	161	183	248
137	155	224	162	184	249
138	156	225	163	185	250
139	158	227	164	187	251
140	158	227	165	188	252
141	160	228	166	189	253
142	161	229	167	190	254
143	162	230	168	191	255
144	163	231	169	192	256
145	165	233	170	194	257
146	166	233			

FOUR UPBUILDING DISCOURSES (1844)

Vol. V Ed. 1 Pg.	Vol. V Ed. 2 Pg.	Vol. 4 Ed. 3 Pg.	Vol. V Ed. 1 Pg.	Vol. V Ed. 2 Pg.	Vol. 4 Ed. 3 Pg.
79	85	263	115	127	299
81	87	265	116	128	299
82	88	265	117	130	301
83	89	266	118	131	301
84	90	267	119	132	302
85	91	268	120	133	303
86	93	270	121	134	304
87	94	270	122	135	305
88	95	272	123	137	306
89	96	272	124	138	307
90	97	273	125	138	307
91	99	275	126	140	308
92	100	276	127	141	309
93	101	277	128	142	310
94	102	278	129	143	311
95	103	279	130	145	312
96	105	280	131	146	313
97	106	281	132	147	314
98	107	282	133	148	315
99	108	283	134	150	316
100	110	284	135	151	317
101	111	285	136	152	318
102	112	286	137	153	319
103	113	287	138	154	320
104	114	288	139	156	321
105	115	289	140	157	323
106	117	290	141	158	324
107	117	290	142	159	325
108	119	291	143	160	326
109	120	292	144	162	326
110	121	294	145	163	328
111	122	295	146	164	329
112	124	296	147	165	330
113	125	297	148	167	331
114	126	298	149	168	332

Vol. V Ed. 1 Pg.	Vol. V Ed. 2 Pg.	Vol. 4 Ed. 3 Pg.	Vol. V Ed. 1 Pg.	Vol. V Ed. 2 Pg.	Vol. 4 Ed. 3 Pg.
150	169	332	160	181	343
151	170	333	161	182	344
152	171	334	162	183	345
153	172	335	163	185	346
154	173	336	164	186	347
155	175	337	165	187	348
156	176	338	166	188	349
157	177	340	167	189	350
158	178	341	168	191	351
159	180	342			

NOTES

TWO, THREE, FOUR UPBUILDING DISCOURSES (1843)

1. See Historical Introduction, p. xxi; *JP* V 5328, 5335, 6073, 6135; VI 6164, 6167, 6173, 6178, 6627 (*Pap.* II A 231, 243; VIII¹ A 397, 650; IX A 68, 71, 85, 106; X³ A 128).

2. See Supplement, pp. 430-31, 432 (*Pap.* IV B 143, 159:5).

3. The Danish *opbyggelig* has been variously translated as "edifying," "devotional," and "upbuilding." The last of the three options has been chosen for the present volume primarily because of the too limited meanings of the other two. They are specialized words with quite circumscribed applicability. "Edify" has lost its meaning of "to make a building." Furthermore, its specialized meaning is, if not archaic, obsolescent and mildly objectionable. As T. H. Croxall observes, "Now if we set out to 'edify' an Englishman, it is enough to put him off forthwith. In Danish, however, the word *opbyggelig* carries no such repulsion" (*Johannes Climacus, or De omnibus dubitandum est*, tr. T. H. Croxall [London: Adam and Charles Black, 1958], pp. 90-91). At best, "edify" has an aura of mustiness, remoteness, and fragile preciosity and at the same time lends itself readily to an ironical tone. One never hears the word used in its elementary sense; very rarely does one hear it used in its positive specialized sense; occasionally it has an ironical touch. The first volume of *Either/Or* uses *opbyggelig* ironically in "Diapsalmata" and in "The Seducer's Diary" (*Either/Or*, I, pp. 38, 419, *KW* III [*SV* I 22, 386]), as might be expected, but in the discourses *opbyggelig* is elemental, strong, and positive.

An early use of *opbygge* by Kierkegaard cannot be translated in any other way than "build up": "But at the same time that he [Faust] is building up her faith in this way, he is also undermining it" (*Either/Or*, I, p. 209, *KW* III [*SV* I 184]). In the discourses, Kierkegaard's use of the verb *opbygge* is like the use of "build" and "build up" in modern translations of the New Testament, whereas the King James Version ordinarily uses "edify" (but also "build up" in a few instances). The Phillips and New English Bible translations consistently have a form of "build" or "build up" or some other term, like "help" or "fortify," but not "edify." The Revised Standard Version has "build," "build up," or "upbuilding" about twice as frequently as some form of "edify." For example: "Let us then pursue what makes for peace and for mutual upbuilding" (Romans 14:19); " 'Knowledge' puffs up, but love builds up" (I Corinthians 8:1); " 'All things are lawful,' but not all things build up" (I Corinthians 10:23); "On the other hand, he who prophesies speaks to men for their upbuilding and encouragement and consolation" (I Corinthians 14:3).

Kierkegaard keenly appreciated language and the root meanings of words, as is evident, for example, in the last of the eighteen upbuilding discourses, where an upbuilding thought [*opbyggelig Tanke*] is immediately associated with the analogy of one who plans to erect [*opføre*] a tower (p. 361). *Opbygge* is directly and more extensively discussed in *Works of Love* (*KW* XVI [*SV* IX 201-04]) in a long passage on language and metaphor, the opening pages of the chapter "Love Builds Up."

> All human speech, even the divine speech of Holy Scripture, about the spiritual, is essentially metaphorical [*overført*, carried over, transferred] speech. . . .
>
> One of the metaphorical expressions that Holy Scripture frequently uses, or one of the phrases that Holy Scripture frequently uses metaphorically, is: "to build up." And it is already upbuilding [*opbyggelig*]—indeed, it is very upbuilding to see how Holy Scripture does not become weary of this simple phrase, how it does not ingeniously strive for variety and new turns of phrase but, on the contrary and in keeping with the true nature of spirit, renews the thought in the same word! . . .
>
> "To build up" is a metaphorical expression; yet with this secret of the spirit in mind, we shall now see *what this word signifies in ordinary speech.* "To build up" is formed from "to build" and the adverb "up," which consequently must receive the accent. Everyone who builds up does build, but not everyone who builds does build up. For example, when a man is building a wing on his house we do not say that he is building up a wing but that he is building *on*. Consequently, this "up" seems to indicate the direction in height, the upward direction. Yet this is not the case either. For example, if a man builds a sixty-foot building twenty feet higher, we still do not say that he *built up* the structure twenty feet higher—we say that he built *on*. Here the meaning of the word already becomes perceptible, for we see that it does not depend on height. . . . This "up" in "build up" indicates height, but it indicates height inversely as depth, since to build up is to build from the ground up. . . . It is commendable that before beginning a man calculates "how high he can erect the tower," but if he is going to build up, then by all means have him be careful to dig deep, because even if the tower reached the sky, if this were possible, if it lacked a foundation, it would not actually be built up. To build up without a foundation at all is impossible—it is building in the air. Therefore, one is linguistically correct in speaking of "building air castles"; one does not say "build up air castles," which would be careless and incorrect use of language. Even in a phrase denoting something insignificant there must be congruity between the separate words; there is none between "in the air" and "to build up," since the former takes away the foundation and the latter refers to this "from the ground up." The combination, therefore, would be a false overstatement.
>
> So it is with the expression "to build up" in the literal sense; let us now bear in mind that it is a metaphorical expression and proceed to the subject of this deliberation: **Love Builds Up.**

It is obvious that the only suitable English translation of *opbygge* in the above long passage is "build up." "Build," "build up," and "upbuilding" may not be elegant and not always idiomatic English terminology in the construction industry, but they are strong and faithful especially as metaphor, and they are in the company of good modern English translations of the New Testament. And here is also an instance attesting to the soundness of the view that wherever an adequate English word with a Germanic root is available as a translation of a word in Danish (also a Germanic language), it is usually to be preferred to an English word with a Latin root. See *JP* IV 4923-26 and pp. 759 62; VII, p. 99.

4. See Historical Introduction, pp. xiv-xvii, and Supplement, pp. 482-83 (*Pap*. X¹ A 510, 520, 593); *Sickness unto Death*, title, *KW* XIX (*SV* XI 113).

5. See Supplement, pp. 431-32, 488-89 (*Pap*. IV B 159:6; VII² B 235; X⁶ B 145).

6. "That single individual," initially specific, became Everyone, the universal singular to whom the entire authorship is addressed. See Historical Introduction, pp. xvii-xxi.

7. Kierkegaard's thirtieth birthday.

8. See Matthew 10:29. In *The Concept of Anxiety* (p. 54, *KW* VIII [*SV* IV 325]), Kierkegaard states, "It is not my intention to write a learned work or to waste time in search of literary proof texts." Consequently he is at times somewhat free in quoting various works. This same freedom is often exercised in his quoting of biblical texts. Furthermore, the Danish Bible translation of his time (1830; *ASKB* 7) has some terminology at variance with twentieth-century English translations. Therefore, translations of Bible-related passages in the discourses are of Kierkegaard's Danish text and frequently have some terminology not found in the RSV and other current English translations. See Niels Munk Plum, "*Lidt om Søren Kierkegaards Citationsmaade*," *Teologisk Tidsskrift, Række* IV, VIII, 1927, pp. 42-49.

9. The discourses were intended to be read aloud. See Historical Introduction, pp. xx-xxi.

10. See Mark 12:30-33.

11. See John 5:1-9.

12. See Galatians 3:24-25.

13. See Matthew 15:27; Luke 16:21.

14. Note the change from the plural on p. 8 to the singular here.

15. Cf. Job 9:3.

16. Ecclesiastes 1:9.

17. See Romans 8:28.

18. Luke 10:42.

19. Cf. James 1:17. See pp. 32, 125.

20. See Psalm 33:4; I Corinthians 1:9, 10:13.

21. See Mark 12:30-33.

22. See *Practice*, *KW* XX (*SV* XII 181).

23. Cf. *The Concept of Irony, with Continual Reference to Socrates*, p. 67, *KW* II (*SV* XIII 160 fn.).

24. See Supplement, p. 424 (*Pap*. IV B 161).
25. See I Corinthians 3:19; Job 5:12-13.
26. See Psalm 145:16.
27. See Luke 17:5.
28. See James 5:7.
29. Cf. John 3:8.
30. Cf. I Corinthians 13:12. The Danish New Testament of the time (1830; *ASKB* 7) has *mørk Tale* [dark saying].
31. See I John 5:8.
32. See Luke 21:19.
33. See I John 5:4.
34. See I Peter 3:4; Romans 2:7.
35. See II Corinthians 11:1,17,21; Romans 3:5.
36. See James 1:13.
37. See I Peter 5:6.
38. The source has not been located.
39. See Psalm 14:2.
40. See John 16:16.
41. See Psalm 104:30.
42. See Supplement, p. 478 (IX A 216). See also note 100 below.
43. See James 1:14.
44. See Hebrews 1:14.
45. See Isaiah 66:18; Psalm 94:11, 139:2-5.
46. See John 14:2-3.
47. See II Corinthians 9:7.
48. See Luke 21:19.
49. See Acts 1:9.
50. See Genesis 1:31.
51. See Ephesians 6:12.
52. See I Timothy 4:4.
53. See I Timothy 4:3.
54. See Romans 8:28.
55. See I Thessalonians 5:17.
56. See Acts 2:3.
57. See Luke 8:15.
58. See I John 4:10,19.
59. See II Timothy 2:13.
60. See I John 4:19.
61. See Luke 18:11.
62. On jest as the expressive, indicative ethics of the gift, see *JP* II 2137-40 and p. 605. In *JP* I 993 (*Pap*. X³ A 734) the same conception of jest is expressed as "a striving born of gratitude."
63. See I John 4:10.
64. See I John 3:20.
65. See Isaiah 42:3.

66. See II Corinthians 4:16.

67. See Luke 23:43.

68. See p. 340 and note 318.

69. See note 1 above.

70. See notes 3, 4, 5 above.

71. With reference to the Preface, see Supplement, p. 432 (*Pap*. IV B 159:5).

72. With reference to the following parenthesis, see Supplement, pp. 431-32 (*Pap*. IV B 159:6; VII² B 235).

73. See note 6 above.

74. See note 9 above.

75. With reference to the end of the Preface, see Supplement, p. 432 (*Pap*. IV B 159:7).

76. See note 8 above. With reference to the heading, see Supplement, p. 432 (*Pap*. IV B 159:8).

77. See Supplement, p. 432 (*Pap*. IV B 145).

78. With reference to the remainder of the paragraph, cf. I Corinthians 13.

79. See Mark 12:42-44.

80. The idea is attributed to Solon (c. 639-559 B.C.), Athenian statesman. See, for example, Aristotle, *Nicomachean Ethics*, 1100 a; *Aristoteles graece*, I-II, ed. Immanuel Bekker (Berlin: 1831; ASKB 1074-75), II, p. 1100; *The Complete Works of Aristotle*, I-II, ed. Jonathan Barnes (rev. Oxford tr., Princeton: Princeton University Press, 1984), II, p. 1738; Herodotus, *History*, I, 32-34; *Die Geschichten des Herodotos*, I-II, tr. Friedrich Lange (Berlin: 1811-12; *ASKB* 1117), I, pp. 18-20; *Herodotus*, I-IV, tr. A. D. Godley (Loeb, Cambridge: Harvard University Press, 1981-82), I, pp. 39-41:

> ". . . Thus then, Croesus, the whole of man is but chance. Now if I [Solon] am to speak of you, I say that I see you very rich and the king of many men. But I cannot yet answer your question, before I hear that you have ended your life well. For he who is very rich is not more blest than he who has but enough for the day, unless fortune so attend him that he ends his life well, having all good things about him. Many men of great wealth are unblest, and many that have no great substance are fortunate. Now the very rich man who is yet unblest has but two advantages over the fortunate man, but the fortunate man has many advantages over the rich but unblest: for this latter is the stronger to accomplish his desire and to bear the stroke of great calamity; but these are the advantages of the fortunate man, that though he be not so strong as the other to deal with calamity and desire, yet these are kept far from him by his good fortune, and he is free from deformity, sickness, and all evil, and happy in his children and his comeliness. If then such a man besides all this shall also end his life well, then he is the man whom you seek, and is worthy to be called blest; but we must wait till he be dead, and call him not yet blest, but fortunate. Now no one (who is but man) can have all these good things together, just as no land is altogether self-suffing in what it produces: one thing it has, another it lacks, and the best land is that which has most; so too no single person is

sufficient for himself: one thing he has, another he lacks; but whoever continues in the possession of most things, and at last makes a gracious end of his life, such a man, O King, I deem worthy of this title. We must look to the conclusion of every matter, and see how it shall end, for there are many to whom heaven has given a vision of blessedness, and yet afterwards brought them to utter ruin."

So spoke Solon: Croesus therefore gave him no largess, but sent him away as a man of no account, for he thought that man to be very foolish who disregarded present prosperity and bade him look rather to the end of every matter.

But after Solon's departure, the divine anger fell heavily upon Croesus: as I guess, because he supposed himself blest beyond all other men.

Later, Croesus (fl. 560 B.C.), king of Lydia, recalled and expressed the idea when Cyrus, king of Persia, was about to have him burned to death; whereupon Cyrus reprieved him. See *Herodotos*, I, pp. 86-87; Loeb, I, pp. 109-13; *JP* III 2739 (*Pap.* IV A 3).

81. See Deuteronomy 32:35; Romans 12:19.
82. See Exodus 20:5.
83. See, for example, *Works of Love, KW* XVI (*SV* IX 69).
84. See Hebrews 1:1.
85. See Philippians 3:13-14; I Corinthians 9:24.
86. See Galatians 4:3.
87. See I John 3:20.
88. See Matthew 20:1-16.
89. See Luke 7:41.
90. See Tobit 4:7.
91. See Matthew 7:1-5; Romans 2:5.
92. See Titus 1:15.
93. See Mark 7:22 (marginal reference in Kierkegaard's manuscript). The King James translation and the Danish translation of the time (1830; *ASKB* 7) have "an evil eye," but this is omitted in the Revised Standard Version.
94. See Matthew 20:15 (marginal reference in Kierkegaard's manuscript).
95. See Matthew 5:8 (marginal reference in Kierkegaard's manuscript).
96. See Matthew 6:22-23 (marginal reference in Kierkegaard's manuscript).
97. See Proverbs 10:10.
98. See Matthew 5:22 (marginal reference in Kierkegaard's manuscript).
99. T. Kingo, *"Ak, Herre, se Min Hjerte-Vee,"* stanza 8, *Psalmer og aandelige Sange af Thomas Kingo*, ed. Peter Andreas Fenger (Copenhagen: 1827; *ASKB* 203), no. 221, pp. 491-92 (ed. tr.).
100. Danish: *opelske* [to raise, cultivate, encourage]. In Kierkegaard's writings it means to love up, to love forth. See, for example, *Works of Love, KW* XVI (*SV* IX 208), in which *opelske* is used along with *opbygge* [to build up] and *opdrage* [to draw upward, to bring up, to educate; cf. Latin *educere*, to lead out, to lead forward]. In *Works of Love* and *Eighteen Discourses, fremelske* and *opelske* are synonymous. See also *JP* V 5526 (*Pap.* III A 171).

101. See Genesis 4:7.
102. See Galatians 5:20-23.
103. See Matthew 13:12.
104. See James 5:20.
105. See Isaiah 42:3; Matthew 12:20.
106. See Luke 15:20-24.
107. See II Corinthians 6:14.
108. See I Corinthians 13:7.
109. See I Peter 3:9.
110. See Romans 12:14.
111. See Matthew 5:39-41.
112. See Matthew 18:22.
113. See Psalm 32:1.
114. Bias (fl. 550 B.C.), one of the Seven Wise Men of Greece. See Diogenes Laertius, *Lives of Eminent Philosophers*, I, 5, 86; *Diogen Laërtses filosofiske Historie*, I-II, tr. Børge Riisbrigh (Copenhagen: 1812; *ASKB* 1110-11), I, p. 38; *Diogenis Laertii de vitis philosophorum*, I-II (Leipzig: 1833; *ASKB* 1109), I, p. 41; *Diogenes Laertius*, I-II, tr. R. D. Hicks (Loeb, Cambridge: Harvard University Press, 1979-80), I, p. 89:

> He was once on a voyage with some impious men; and, when a storm was encountered, even they began to call upon the gods for help. "Peace!" said he, "lest they hear and become aware that you are here in the ship."

115. See Acts 27:22.
116. See Matthew 24:22; Mark 13:19-20.
117. See Hebrews 4:12.
118. See James 5:16.
119. See Genesis 18:22-33.
120. See I Corinthians 6:3.
121. With reference to the following paragraph, see Supplement, p. 433 (*Pap.* IV B 144).
122. See John 8:3-11.
123. See Supplement, p. 435 (*Pap.* IV B 149).
124. See Supplement, pp. 432, 435 (*Pap.* IV B 145, 148).
125. See Philippians 2:12.
126. See I Corinthians 9:26.
127. See I Corinthians 9:22.
128. See Romans 13:12; I Thessalonians 5:4-8.
129. See John 9:4.
130. See I Peter 4:7.
131. See I Peter 4:8; Supplement, p. 424 (*Pap.* IV B 161).
132. See Hebrews 9:27.
133. See I Corinthians 13.
134. See James 2:13.
135. See John 5:44.

136. See Luke 18:9-14.

137. See Mark 12:17.

138. See Job 9:3.

139. See Horace, *Carminum*, III, i, 40; *Q. Horatii Flacci opera* (Leipzig: 1828; *ASKB* 1248), p. 145; *Horace The Odes and Epodes*, tr. C. E. Bennett (Loeb, Cambridge: Harvard University Press, 1978), p. 171: "But Fear and Threats climb to the selfsame spot the owner does; nor does black Care quit the brass-bound galley and even takes her seat behind the horseman."

140. Hans Adolph Brorson, "*Flye min Aand, og bryd med Styrke,*" stanza 1, *Psalmer og aandelige Sange*, ed. Jens Albrecht Leonard Holm (Copenhagen: 1838; *ASKB* 200), 203, p. 604 (ed. tr.). The Brorson text has *Satans* [of Satan] instead of *Syndens* [of sin].

141. See Luke 7:36-50. *An Upbuilding Discourse*, in *Without Authority*, *KW* XVIII (*SV* XII 243-59), is an extended consideration of this theme.

142. See Supplement, p. 435 (*Pap.* IV B 159:14).

143. With reference to the following paragraph, see Supplement, p. 433 (*Pap.* IV B 144).

144. See Luke 7:41-43.

145. See Luke 7:47.

146. With reference to the following paragraph, see Supplement, p. 436 (*Pap.* IV B 151:1).

147. See II Corinthians 4:16.

148. With reference to the following paragraph, see Supplement, p. 436 (*Pap.* IV B 151:2).

149. See Galatians 1:15-16, 2:2.

150. See I Peter 2:20.

151. See II Timothy 4:9-16.

152. See II Corinthians 6:10.

153. See Ephesians 3:13.

154. See Mark 2:20.

155. See I Corinthians 9:26.

156. See I Corinthians 1:18.

157. See II Corinthians 1:23; I Thessalonians 2:5.

158. See Ephesians 3:16.

159. With reference to the remainder of the paragraph, see Supplement, p. 436 (*Pap.* IV B 151:2).

160. See Matthew 16:2-3.

161. See James 4:13.

162. See Luke 12:16-21.

163. See James 4:14.

164. See I Corinthians 3:9.

165. With reference to the following three paragraphs, see Supplement, p. 436 (*Pap.* IV B 151:8).

166. With reference to the remainder of the sentence, see Supplement, pp. 436-37 (*Pap.* IV B 151:5); *Works of Love*, *KW* XVI (*SV* IX 218-19).

167. See Supplement, p. 437 (*Pap.* IV B 152).

168. With reference to the remainder of the paragraph, see Supplement, p. 437 (*Pap.* IV B 151:7).

169. With reference to the following three paragraphs, see Supplement, pp. 437-38 (*Pap.* IV B 151:3).

170. See Acts 14:17; I Corinthians 10:13

171. See John 4:24.

172. With reference to the following six sentences, see Supplement, p. 438 (*Pap.* IV B 153:1-2).

173. See Mark 10:23.

174. Matthew 7:13-14.

175. With reference to the following sentence, see Supplement, p. 438 (*Pap.* IV B 154:1).

176. See Job 1:5.

177. With reference to the following two sentences, see Supplement, pp. 438-39 (*Pap.* IV B 154:2).

178. See Matthew 4:8-9.

179. With reference to the following two sentences, see Supplement, p. 439 (*Pap.* IV B 153:3-4).

180. See I Corinthians 7:31; II Corinthians 6:10.

181. See Luke 12:18.

182. With reference to the following three sentences, see Supplement, p. 439 (*Pap.* IV B 153:4).

183. See Luke 16:2.

184. With reference to the following sentence, see Supplement, p. 439 (*Pap.* IV B 151:6).

185. See Exodus 13:21-22.

186. With reference to the following paragraph, see Supplement, pp. 439-40 (*Pap.* IV B 151:9).

187. With reference to the following eight sentences, see Supplement, p. 440 (*Pap.* IV B 158:1).

188. See Romans 5:3-4.

189. See Hebrews 5:8.

190. See Genesis 23:17-20.

191. With reference to the following paragraph, see Supplement, p. 440 (*Pap.* IV B 158:2).

192. See I Corinthians 2:9; *Fragments*, p. 109, *KW* VII (*SV* IV 271).

193. With reference to the following paragraph, see Supplement, pp. 440-41 (*Pap.* IV B 158:3-4).

194. See Ephesians 2:3.

195. See *JP* I 744 (*Pap.* IV A 165), reference to *Die deutsche Theologie mit einer Vorrede von Dr. M. Luther und Johann Arnd*, ed. Friedrich C. Krüger (Lemgo: 1822; *ASKB* 634), p. 41. Cf. *Sickness unto Death*, pp. 72-74, *KW* XIX (*SV* XI 183-85).

196. See II Peter 3:8.

197. See Hebrews 12:6.

198. See Ephesians 3:13-19.

199. See James 1:17.

200. With reference to the following three sentences, see Supplement, p. 441 (*Pap.* IV B 158:7-8).

201. With reference to the preceding clause, see Supplement, p. 441 (*Pap.* IV B 158:6).

202. With reference to the remainder of the sentence, see Supplement, p. 441 (*Pap.* IV B 158:9).

203. With reference to the following sentence, see Supplement, pp. 441-42 (*Pap.* IV B 158:5).

204. See Romans 12:15.

205. Ibid.

206. See Romans 8:38.

207. With reference to the following paragraph, see Supplement, p. 442 (*Pap.* IV B 151:4). Cf. "The First Love," *Either/Or*, I, pp. 231-79, *KW* III (*SV* I 205-51).

208. See Historical Introduction, p. xxi.

209. See note 3 above.

210. See note 4 above.

211. See note 5 above.

212. See Mark 12:41-44.

213. See Supplement, p. 424 (*Pap.* IV B 161); *Postscript*, *KW* XII (*SV* VII 231-32 fn.).

214. See *Repetition*, pp. 204-13, *KW* VI (*SV* III 238-46).

215. See Job 7:11.

216. See I Corinthians 10:13.

217. Cf. the trial sermon in *JP* IV 3916 (*Pap.* IV C 1, pp. 360-69).

218. See II Timothy 4:7.

219. See Ecclesiastes 1:18.

220. See I Corinthians 13:12.

221. See I Corinthians 15:42.

222. See Job 4:4.

223. See Job 29:4.

224. See Job 1:20.

225. Job 1:21.

226. See Genesis 41:29-30.

227. See James 1:17.

228. See Job 4:3-4.

229. See Job 29:8.

230. See Job 29:13.

231. See Mark 9:43-48.

232. See Job 1:1.

233. See Luke 8:15.

234. See Job 1:15.

235. See Job 1:16.
236. See Matthew 7:26.
237. See Exodus 33:23.
238. On this theme, see *The Changelessness of God*, in The Moment *and Late Writings*, KW XXIII (*SV* XIV 276-94).
239. See I Peter 5:7.
240. See Mark 4:9.
241. See I Corinthians 13:1.
242. See Job 2:9.
243. See pp. 31-48; Supplement, p. 424 (*Pap* IV B 161).
244. See Genesis 2:16-17.
245. See Ecclesiastes 1:18.
246. See Genesis 1:4,10,12,18,21,25,31.
247. See Genesis 2:21-22.
248. Aristotle's definition of God. See *Metaphysics*, 1072 b; Bekker, II, p. 1072; *Works*, II, p. 1694:

That that for the sake of which is found among the unmovables is shown by making a distinction; for that for the sake of which is both that *for* which and that *towards* which, and of these the one is unmovable and the other is not. Thus it produces motion by being loved, and it moves the other moving things. Now if something is moved it is capable of being otherwise than as it is. Therefore if the actuality of the heavens is primary motion, then in so far as they are in motion, in *this* respect they are capable of being otherwise,—in place, even if not in substance. But since there is something which moves while itself unmoved, existing actually, this can in no way be otherwise than as it is.

249. See Isaiah 11:6.
250. See Genesis 2:19-20.
251. See Psalm 85:11.
252. See Genesis 3:8-9.
253. See Genesis 3:6.
254. See Genesis 3:18-19.
255. See, for example, *Anxiety*, pp. 31, 33, 98, KW VIII (*SV* IV 303-04, 305, 368).
256. See Matthew 12:29; Mark 3:27; Luke 11:21-22.
257. See Philippians 2:10.
258. See Proverbs 16:8,19; Psalm 37:16.
259. See Luke 10:42.
260. Cf. Psalm 103:13.
261. See I Corinthians 3:1-2.
262. See Luke 15:16.
263. See Matthew 13:25.
264. See Matthew 13:24-28.
265. See Matthew 6:3.

266. See Matthew 19:17.
267. See *Fragments*, pp. 14–18, 58–59, 62–66, 68–69, *KW* VII (*SV* IV 184–87, 224, 227–30, 232–33).
268. See Philippians 2:13.
269. See Philippians 1:6.
270. See Acts 17:28.
271. See Matthew 12:30.
272. See Galatians 1:16.
273. See I Corinthians 12:31.
274. See Acts 1:9.
275. See Romans 11:34.
276. See pp. 297–326.
277. See Acts 7:55–56.
278. See John 8:9.
279. See Psalms 141:1, 143:7.
280. See James 1:19–20.
281. See Mark 8:36.
282. See Ephesians 4:26.
283. See I Thessalonians 4:5–7.
284. See Matthew 15:33–37; Mark 8:1–8.
285. See Matthew 11:12; Luke 16:16.
286. Cf. Sirach 4:18.
287. See Colossians 4:2.
288. See Luke 11:13.
289. See note 243 above.
290. See James 2:1.
291. See James 2:2–4.
292. See Matthew 22:30.
293. See I Corinthians 7:29–31.
294. See James 1:9–10.
295. See John 8:1–11.
296. See Matthew 5:28.
297. See Mark 12:31; James 2:8.
298. See Psalm 23:4.
299. See Exodus 3:2.
300. See Ephesians 6:12.
301. See Job 1:21.
302. See Ephesians 4:30.
303. See I Corinthians 7:21.
304. See Matthew 15:5; Mark 7:11.
305. See II Corinthians 9:7.
306. See Matthew 26:53.
307. See Luke 14:12.
308. Croesus (fl. 560 B.C.), wealthy king of Lydia. See note 80 above.
309. See Matthew 4:1–9.
310. See Romans 14:17.

311. With a kiss, Judas betrayed Christ to the Roman soldiers. See Matthew 26:49; Mark 14:45; Luke 22:48.
312. See Matthew 10:28.
313. See Matthew 16:26; Mark 8:36.
314. See Philippians 2:12.
315. See Matthew 6:3.
316. Cf. Matthew 6:2.
317. See I Corinthians 4:2.
318. See Luke 18:1-5.
319. See Matthew 5:23-24
320. See Kingo, "*Far, Verden, far vel,*" stanza 2, *Psalmer*, 93, p. 253.
321. See Matthew 11:5.
322. See I John 4:20.
323. See John 9:6-11.
324. See John 18:15-17,25-27.
325. See Luke 16:21.
326. See Matthew 6:26.
327. See Matthew 6:28-29.
328. See Luke 16:9.
329. Cf. Leviticus 25:10,13,28,40.
330. See Matthew 10:24.
331. Acts 20:35.
332. See, for example, Plato, *Symposium*, 212 b-c; *Platonis quae exstant opera*, I-XI, ed. Friedrich Ast (Leipzig: 1819-32; *ASKB* 1144-54), III, pp. 20-21; *The Collected Dialogues of Plato*, ed. Edith Hamilton and Huntington Cairns (Princeton: Princeton University Press, 1963), p. 563 (Socrates speaking):

This, Phaedrus—this, gentlemen—was the doctrine of Diotima. I was convinced, and in that conviction I try to bring others to the same creed, and to convince them that, if we are to make this gift our own, Love will help our mortal nature more than all the world. And this is why I say that every man of us should worship the god of love, and this is why I cultivate and worship all the elements of Love myself, and bid others do the same. And all my life I shall pay the power and the might of Love such homage as I can. So you may call this my eulogy of Love, Phaedrus, if you choose; if not, well, call it what you like.

333. See John 9:4.
334. See Matthew 6:19-20.
335. See Romans 13:8.
336. The text follows the Danish Bible (1830; *ASKB* 7) of Kierkegaard's time. See Supplement, pp. 424-25 (*Pap.* IV B 160).
337. From a children's rhyme. See *Børnerim*, illus. Frants Henningsen (Copenhagen: Gyldendal, 1919), n.p. (ed. tr.):

The rich bird comes swishing,
Comes flaunting

> Over the fields and the meadows,
> 'And do you see, you poor bird,
> You poor bird,
> How my feathers do shine?'
> The poor bird comes limping,
> comes hobbling
> Over the fields and the meadows,
> 'And do you see, you rich bird,
> You rich bird,
> How my feathers do hang?'

338. See I Peter 3:4.

339. Cf. Johann Wolfgang v. Goethe, *Faust*, I, 208-09; *Goethe's Werke. Vollständige Ausgabe letzter Hand*, I-LX (Stuttgart, Tübingen: 1828-42; *ASKB* 1641-68 [I-LV]), XII, p. 37; *Faust*, tr. Bayard Taylor (New York: Random House, 1950), p. 22 (Wagner speaking):

> Ah, God! but Art is long,
> And Life, alas! is fleeting.

340. See Matthew 24:15; Mark 13:14.

341. See Mark 8:36-37.

342. See Job 1:21.

343. See I Timothy 6:7.

344. See James 5:7.

345. See Luke 5:5.

346. An echo of the language but not of the thought of Hegel. Cf., for example, G.W.F. Hegel, *Phänomenologie des Geistes*, *Georg Wilhelm Friedrich Hegel's Werke. Vollständige Ausgabe*, I-XVIII, ed. Philipp K. Marheineke et al. (Berlin: 1832-45; *ASKB* 549-65), II, pp. 124-25; *Sämtliche Werke. Jubiläumsausgabe* [*J.A.*], I-XXVI, ed. Hermann Glockner (Stuttgart, Frommann: 1927-40), II, pp. 132-33; *The Phenomenology of Mind* (tr. primarily of *P.G.*, 3 ed., 1841; Kierkegaard had 2 ed., 1832), tr. J. B. Baillie (New York: Harper, 1967), pp. 206-07:

We have to think pure flux, opposition within opposition itself, or Contradiction. For in the distinction, which is an internal distinction, the opposite is not only one of two factors—if so, it would not be an opposite, but a bare existent—it is the opposite of an opposite, or the other is itself directly and immediately present within it. No doubt I put the opposite here and the other, of which it is the opposite, there; that is, I place the opposite on one side, taking it by itself without the other. Just on that account, however, since I have here the opposite all by itself, it is the opposite of its *own* self, that is, it has in point of fact the other immediately within itself. Thus the supersensible world, which is the inverted world, has at the same time reached out beyond the other world and has in itself that other; it is to itself conscious of being inverted (*für sich verkehrte*), i.e. it is the inverted form of itself; it is that world itself and its opposite in a single unity. Only thus is it distinction as internal distinction, or distinction *per se*; in other words, only thus is it in the form of *Infinity*.

347. See *Sickness unto Death*, p. 13, *KW* XIX (*SV* XI 127).
348. See Mark 12:17.
349. See Luke 10:42.
350. See Luke 8:15.
351. See, for example, *JP* III 3660-64 and pp. 908-09; VII, p. 80.
352. See, for example, *Repetition*, *KW* VI (*SV* III 171-264); *JP* III 3791 95 and pp. 920-21; VII, p. 81.
353. See Hebrews 10:39; James 1:21, 5:20.
354. See Luke 21:25-26.
355. See II Peter 3:10,12.
356. See Isaiah 34:4; Psalm 102:26.
357. See Luke 21:26.
358. See I John 3:2.
359. See James 1:22-25.
360. See James 2:19.
361. See Matthew 11:12.

TWO, THREE, FOUR UPBUILDING DISCOURSES (1844)

1. See p. 5 and notes 3-6.
2. See Ecclesiastes 7:2.
3. See I Thessalonians 5:3.
4. See Hans Adolph Brorson, *"Jeg gaaer i Fare, hvor jeg gaaer,"* stanza 1, *Psalmer og aandelige Sange*, ed. Jens Albrecht Leonhard Holm (Copenhagen: 1838; *ASKB* 200), 168, p. 513.
5. See Philippians 2:12.
6. See, for example, Exodus 9:15; Numbers 14:12.
7. The Danish phrase *"for Livs og Døds Skyld"* [literally, "for the sake of life and of death," or "since life is uncertain"] was commonly used in private business in Kierkegaard's time to designate a desire for written documentation. See, for example, C. A. Reitzel's statement of account covering the sale of some of Kierkegaard's books in Frithiof Brandt and Else Rammel, *Søren Kierkegaard og Pengene* (Copenhagen: Munksgaard, 1935), p. 15.
8. See I Thessalonians 5:2.
9. See James 1:23-24.
10. See I Corinthians 9:26.
11. See Matthew 6:34.
12. See Luke 16:2.
13. See Luke 14:28-30.
14. See Matthew 6:27; John 3:27.
15. See I Corinthians 3:2.
16. An allusion to Julius Caesar's *"Veni, vidi, vici."* See Suetonius, "Julius

Caesar," 37, *The Lives of the Caesars; Caji Suetonii Tranquilli Tolv første Romerske Keiseres Levnetsbeskrivelse*, I-II, tr. Jacob Baden (Copenhagen: 1802-03; *ASKB* 1281), I, p. 35; *Suetonius*, I-II, tr. J. C. Rolfe (Loeb, New York: Macmillan, 1914), I, p. 51:

> Having ended the wars, he celebrated five triumphs, four in a single month, but at intervals of a few days, after vanquishing Scipio; and another on defeating Pompey's sons. The first and most splendid was the Gallic triumph, the next the Alexandrian, then the Pontic, after that the African, and finally the Spanish, each differing from the rest in its equipment and display of spoils. As he rode through the Velabrum on the day of his Gallic triumph, the axle of his chariot broke, and he was all but thrown out; and he mounted the Capitol by torchlight, with forty elephants bearing lamps on his right and his left. In his Pontic triumph he displayed among the show-pieces of the procession an inscription of but three words, "I came, I saw, I conquered," not indicating the events of the war, as the others did, but the speed with which it was finished.

17. See Horace, *Carminum*, I, i, 35-36; *Q. Horatii Flacci opera* (Leipzig: 1828; *ASKB* 1248), p. 2; *Horace The Odes and Epodes*, tr. E. C. Bennett (Loeb, Cambridge: Harvard University Press, 1978), p. 5: "But if you rank me among lyric bards, I shall touch the stars with my exalted head."

18. See James 4:13-15.

19. See Genesis 22:16; Hebrews 6:13.

20. See Matthew 20:3-6.

21. See I Corinthians 9:24-26; Philippians 3:14.

22. See John 3:21.

23. See Hebrews 6:4.

24. See, for example, Matthew 8:12.

25. See Psalm 1:1; Luke 16:3.

26. Cf. Matthew 4:5-8.

27. See *Repetition*, pp. 131-32, *KW* VI (*SV* III 174).

28. Ibid., pp. 131-33 (173-75).

29. See Adelbert v. Chamisso, *Peter Schlemihl's wundersame Geschichte* (Nuremberg: 1835; *ASKB* 1630), pp. 7-9; *Peter Schlemihl's forunderlige Historie*, tr. Frederik Schaldemose (Copenhagen: 1841), pp. 9-11; *Peter Schlemihl*, tr. Leopold von Loewenstein-Wertheim (London: Calder, 1957), pp. 21-23:

> "In the short time in which I had the good fortune to find myself in your presence I have, my dear sir, repeatedly—if you will permit me to say so—observed with truly inexpressible admiration the magnificent shadow which you, standing in the sun, with a certain noble contempt and without being aware of it, cast from you—this wonderful shadow there at your feet. Forgive this truly daring imposition but would you not perhaps consider disposing of your shadow?"
>
> I was silent, my head in a whirl. What was I to make of this strange

request to buy my shadow? He must be crazy, I thought, and in a tone that contrasted forcibly with the humility of his own I answered:

"Come, come, my good friend, will not your own shadow do? This seems a deal of a most unusual kind."

"Will the gentleman deign to inspect and try out this purse." He put his hand in his pocket and produced a firmly stitched leather purse of moderate size with two strong leather strings and handed it to me. I dipped into it and took out ten pieces of gold and ten more, ten more, and yet another ten. I quickly held out my hand to him and said:

"Done, the deal is on. For this purse you may have my shadow."

We shook hands on it, he knelt down and I watched him as, with astounding dexterity, he silently detached my shadow from head to foot from the lawn. He lifted it up, carefully folded it and finally put it into his pocket. He then stood up, bowed deeply and withdrew to the rose-grove. I thought I heard him softly laughing to himself. I firmly held the purse by its strings—the sun was shining brightly around me—as I stood there dazed by what had happened.

30. See *Either/Or*, I, pp. 33-34, *KW* III (*SV* I 18).
31. See Matthew 23:4; Luke 11:46.
32. See Luke 10:30-35.
33. See Matthew 25:21.
34. Cf. *Letters*, Letters 167, 196, *KW* XXV.
35. See Revelation 3:15-16.
36. See Genesis 19:26.
37. See Romans 8:28.
38. See Romans 15:5.
39. See Matthew 10:28.
40. See Romans 12:15.
41. Valdemar Atterdag (1320-1375), king of Denmark.
42. See Johann Ludvig Heiberg, *Syvsoverdag*, III, 5 (Copenhagen: 1840), p. 132 (ed. tr.): "As for me, God may keep paradise if he will only let me keep Gurre [castle]."
43. See Luke 12:20, 23:43; Hebrews 4:7.
44. See Matthew 19:3.
45. See I Timothy 6:12; II Timothy 4:7.
46. See I Corinthians 10.13.
47. See Mark 15:31.
48. See Supplement, pp. 424-25 (*Pap.* IV B 160).
49. See Psalm 90:4.
50. See Genesis 8:22.
51. See John 5:2-7.
52. See Genesis 3:15.
53. See John 8:56.
54. See Ephesians 2:19; Hebrews 11:9,13.
55. See Galatians 4:4; Ephesians 1:10.

56. See Matthew 2:9-11.
57. See Luke 2:25-38.
58. See Romans 12:12.
59. See p. 61 and note 100.
60. See Mark 12:25; Matthew 22:30; Galatians 3:28.
61. See Luke 23:28.
62. See "The Work of Love in Commemorating One Who Is Dead," *Works of Love, KW* XVI (*SV* IX 327-39).
63. See Genesis 29:18-30.
64. See Matthew 21:18-20; Mark 11:13-14; Luke 13:6-9.
65. Cf. I Timothy 2:12; Luke 2:38.
66. See Luke 10:42.
67. See I John 2:17.
68. See Matthew 25:1-13.
69. See p. 56 and note 80.
70. See Matthew 10:29.
71. See I Thessalonians 5:19.
72. See I Peter 5:7.
73. See Acts 24:15.
74. Cf. *Sickness unto Death*, pp. 14, 49, 101, 131, *KW* XIX (*SV* XI 128, 160, 211, 240).
75. See I John 4:18.
76. See Luke 2:38.
77. See Matthew 25:21; Luke 19:17.
78. See Matthew 6:21; Luke 12:34.
79. See Luke 10:23-24.
80. See Matthew 11:3.
81. See Genesis 25:29-34.
82. See Proverbs 25:11.
83. See Matthew 25:14-29; Luke 19:12-26.
84. See Supplement, p. 442 (*Pap.* IV A 145, 171).
85. See Matthew 17:21; Mark 9:29.
86. See Proverbs 16:32.
87. See Psalm 126:5.
88. See Matthew 5:1-12.
89. See Luke 23:29.
90. *Beundring* is usually translated as "admiration." For a discussion of the special use of *Beundring* as "wonder" in the writings from 1843 to 1844, see *Fragments*, p. 80, *KW* VII (*SV* IV 244) and note 35.
91. Horace, "*Nil admirari,*" *Epistolarum*, I, 6, 1; *Opera*, p. 232; *Horace Satires, Epistles and Ars Poetica*, tr. H. Rushton Fairclough (Loeb, Cambridge: Harvard University Press, 1978), p. 287:

"Marvel at nothing"—that is perhaps the one and only thing, Numicius, that can make a man happy and keep him so. Yon sun, the stars and seasons that pass in fixed courses—some can gaze upon these with no strain of fear:

what think you of the gifts of earth, or what of the sea's, which makes rich far distant Arabs and Indians—what of the shows, the plaudits and the favours of the friendly Roman—in what wise, with what feelings and eyes think you they should be viewed?

And he who fears their opposites "marvels" in much the same way as the man who desires: in either case 'tis the excitement that annoys, the moment some unexpected appearance startles either. Whether a man feel joy or grief, desire or fear, what matters it if, when he has seen aught better or worse than he expected, his eyes are fast riveted, and mind and body are benumbed? Let the wise man bear the name of madman, the just or unjust, should he pursue Virtue herself beyond due bounds.

92. See I Corinthians 13:11.
93. See Ecclesiastes 1:9.
94. See p. 5 and notes 3-6.
95. See Supplement, p. 442 (*Pap.* V B 195:4).
96. See I Corinthians 15:42,53-54.
97. See *Works of Love, KW* XVI (*SV* IX 221-25).
98. See Ecclesiastes 1:1.
99. See Matthew 16:26; Mark 8:36-37.
100. See Ecclesiastes 1:14.
101. See Luke 11:26.
102. See Ecclesiastes 11:9-10.
103. See Job 38:11.
104. See Ecclesiastes 12:1.
105. See Matthew 18:3.
106. See Romans 12:15.
107. With reference to the following paragraph, see Supplement, pp. 442-43 (*Pap.* V B 194).
108. See, for example, *Fragments*, pp. 39-44, 94-96, *KW* VII (*SV* IV 207-11, 257-58).
109. See Genesis 3:8-10.
110. See Benedict Spinoza, *Tractatus theologico-politicus*, VI; *Opera philosophica omnia*, ed. August F. Gfroerer (Stuttgart: 1830; *ASKB* 788), pp. 142-44; *Philosophy of Benedict de Spinoza*, I-II, tr. R.H.M. Elwes (London: Bell, 1909), I, pp. 94-97; *Fragments*, pp. 41-42, *KW* VII (*SV* IV 208-09 fn.); *JP* II 1333 (*Pap.* IV A 190).
111. See Nicolai Edinger Balle, *Lærebog i den Evangelisk-christelige Religion indrettet, til Brug i de danske Skoler*, I, 1, 2 (Copenhagen: 1824; *ASKB* 183), p. 5; *Repetition*, p. 203, *KW* VI (*SV* III 237).
112. Lucilio (Julius Caesar) Vanini (1585-1619), Italian pantheistic philosopher, burned at the stake in Toulouse. See W. D. Fuhrmann, *Leben und Schicksal des Lucilio Vanini* (Leipzig: 1800), p. 112. See also Hegel, *Geschichte der Philosophie*, III, *Georg Wilhelm Friedrich Hegel's Werke. Vollständige Ausgabe*, I-XVIII, ed. Philipp Marheineke et al. (Berlin: 1832-45; *ASKB* 549-65), XV, p. 244; *Sämtliche Werke. Jubiläumsausgabe* [*J.A.*], I-XXVI, ed. Hermann

Glockner (Stuttgart, Frommann: 1927-40), XIX, p. 244; *Hegel's Lectures on the History of Philosophy*, I-III (tr. of G.P., 2 ed., 1840-44; Kierkegaard had 1 ed., 1833-36), tr. E. S. Haldane and Frances H. Simson (New York: Humanities Press, 1955), III, p. 137.

113. See Psalm 90:4.

114. See Genesis 1:31.

115. See, for example, *Fear and Trembling*, pp. 5-7, *KW* VI (*SV* III 57-59).

116. See Acts 17:28.

117. See Luke 15:8.

118. See Luke 15:3-4.

119. Diogenes of Sinope (412-323 B.C.). See Diogenes Laertius, *Lives of Eminent Philosophers*, VI, 2, 40-41; *Diogen Laërtses filosofiske Historie*, I-II, tr. Børge Riisbrigh (Copenhagen: 1812; *ASKB* 1110-11), I, p. 247; *Diogenes Laertii de vitis philosophorum*, I-II (Leipzig: 1833; *ASKB* 1109), I, pp. 266-67; *Diogenes Laertius*, I-II, tr. R. D. Hicks (Loeb, Cambridge: Harvard University Press, 1979-80), II, p. 43:

> Plato had defined Man as an animal, biped and featherless, and was applauded. Diogenes plucked a fowl and brought it into the lecture-room with the words, "Here is Plato's man." In consequence of which there was added to the definition, "having broad nails." To one who asked what was the proper time for lunch, he said, "If a rich man, when you will; if a poor man, when you can."
> At Megara he saw the sheep protected by leather jackets, while the children went bare. "It's better," said he, "to be a Megarian's ram than his son." To one who had brandished a beam at him and then cried, "Look out," he replied, "What, are you intending to strike me again?" He used to call the demagogues the lackeys of the people and the crowns awarded to them the efflorescence of fame. He lit a lamp in broad daylight and said, as he went about, "I am looking for a man."

120. See *Irony*, p. 46, *KW* II (*SV* XIII 141) (*in mente*).

121. See Matthew 18:10.

122. See Matthew 23:14; Mark 12:40; Luke 20:47.

123. See Deuteronomy 19:14, 27:17.

124. See Matthew 24:36,42; Mark 13:32; Revelation 3:3.

125. See "On the Occasion of a Confession," *Three Discourses on Imagined Occasions*, *KW* X (*SV* V 177-203).

126. See Ecclesiastes 1:18.

127. See Matthew 6:34.

128. See Supplement, p. 443 (*Pap*. V B 195:6).

129. "Genesis" means beginning, "exodus" going out.

130. Cf. II Corinthians 5:7.

131. See *Stages on Life's Way*, pp. 9-15, *KW* XI (*SV* VI 15-20).

132. See I John 2:17.

133. See Romans 4:18, 8:24; *For Self-Examination*, pp. 82-83, *KW* XXI (*SV* XII 365-66).
134. See p. 46 and note 62.
135. See John 6:12.
136. See II Corinthians 7:9-10; *JP* I 443; IV 3915, p. 53 (*Pap.* II A 360; III C 1).
137. See Psalm 103:16.
138. See Matthew 6:7.
139. See reference to Adam Oehlenschläger's *Aladdin*, *Either/Or*, I, p. 22, *KW* III (*SV* I 6).
140. See Matthew 6:20-21.
141. See Luke 16:9.
142. See John 14:2-3.
143. See Luke 16:23.
144. See Matthew 11:12.
145. See Luke 10:42.
146. See Matthew 6:26,28; Luke 12:24,27; cf. *The Lily in the Field and the Bird of the Air*, in *Without Authority*, *KW* XVIII (*SV* XI 3-46).
147. See I Corinthians 13:12.
148. See I Thessalonians 4:13.
149. See II Corinthians 4:17.
150. The Danish *Bedested* [biding place] means a tarrying or resting place on a journey and a place of prayer.
151. See Acts 9:1-30; II Corinthians 12:2-5; Galatians 1:13-16.
152. See Acts 26:24.
153. See I Corinthians 1:22-23.
154. See II Corinthians 6:4-5.
155. See Philippians 4:7.
156. See I Corinthians 2:9; *Fragments*, p. 109, *KW* VII (*SV* IV 271); *JP* IV 3916 (*Pap.* IV C 1).
157. See I Corinthians 9:26.
158. A play on the Danish *vænne sig fra* [wean oneself from] and *vænne sig til* [accustom oneself to].
159. See Matthew 19:21-22; Mark 10:21-22.
160. See Matthew 8:21-22; Luke 9:59-60.
161. Cf. Deuteronomy 25:4; I Corinthians 9:9; I Timothy 5:18. The not uncommon practice of muzzling the working oxen is opposed in the O.T. and N.T. passages.
162. See Matthew 6:4,6,18; Luke 15:20; Revelation 7:17.
163. See Isaiah 25:8.
164. See Philippians 3:10.
165. See Mark 10:9; Genesis 1:28.
166. See Matthew 22:21; Mark 12:17; Luke 20:25.
167. See Matthew 19:24; Mark 10:25.
168. See II Corinthians 4:18.

169. See Mark 3:24-25.
170. See Matthew 9:17; Mark 2:22.
171. See John 11:4; *Sickness unto Death*, pp. 8-9, 17-21, *KW* XIX (*SV* XI 122-23, 131-35).
172. See Job 8:14. The source of the quotation as given has not been located, but it may be from Schopenhauer through Joachim Dietrich Brandis (1762-1845). See Nelly Viallaneix, "*Schopenhauer et Kierkegaard*," *Romantisme*, 32, 1981, pp. 47-64, especially pp. 49-50. See also G. E. Lessing, *Eine Duplik, Gotthold Ephraim Lessing's sämmtliche Schriften*, I-XXXII (Berlin, Stettin: 1825-28; *ASKB* 1747-62), V, p. 113 (ed. tr.): "to want to suspend no less than all eternity on the thread of a spider."
173. See I Samuel 5:3-4.
174. See Herodotus, *History*, VII, 83; *Die Geschichten des Herodotos*, I-II, tr. Friedrich Lange (Berlin: 1811-12; *ASKB* 1117), II, p. 178; *Herodotus*, I-IV, tr. A. D. Godley (Loeb, Cambridge: Harvard University Press, 1981-82), III, p. 391:

> These were the generals of the whole land army, saving the Ten Thousand; Hydarnes son of Hydarnes was general of these picked ten thousand Persians, who were called Immortals for this reason, that when any one of them fell out of the number by force of death or sickness, another was chosen, and so they were never more or fewer than ten thousand.

175. Cf. Matthew 6:2. The Danish Bible (1830; *ASKB* 7) of Kierkegaard's time has a negative clause.
176. See Luke 17:10.
177. See Matthew 20:1-12.
178. See Mark 10:20.
179. See Luke 23:43.
180. Pilate's question; see John 18:38.
181. See Lessing, "*Eine Duplik*," *Schriften*, V, p. 100; *Postscript, KW* XII (*SV* VII 86).
182. See Job 9:3.
183. See Matthew 14:24-29.
184. See Matthew 11:7-8.
185. Isaiah.
186. See Matthew 3:3; John 1:23.
187. See Matthew 3:11; John 1:27.
188. See Matthew 11:11.
189. See Luke 1:5-25.
190. See Matthew 1:18-25; Luke 1:26-56.
191. See Mark 1:6.
192. See Luke 10:24; John 8:56.
193. See Matthew 3:11.
194. See John 3:26.
195. See Genesis 17:20.

196. Cf. *Letters*, Letter 8, *KW* XXV.

197. See Joshua 10:13.

198. See II Timothy 4:7.

199. See John 1:19.

200. See John 16:21.

201. See, for example, Philippians 2:7; *Fragments*, pp. 30-34, *KW* VII (*SV* IV 199-201).

202. See Luke 12:42-48, 19:12-27.

203. See I Corinthians 3:9.

204. See Supplement, p. 443 (*Pap.* V B 195.7).

205. See Matthew 20:28; Mark 10:45.

206. See John 1:15.

207. See Matthew 11:11.

208. See Matthew 3:3; John 1:23.

209. See Matthew 11:3.

210. See Matthew 2:16.

211. See Exodus 1:8.

212. See Psalm 1:3.

213. See Isaiah 66:24; Mark 9:48.

214. See Matthew 12:34.

215. See Matthew 3:7-10; Luke 3:7-9.

216. Cf. I Kings 19:12.

217. See Ecclesiastes 7:2.

218. See Matthew 11:16-17.

219. Plutarch, "How a Man May Become Aware of His Progress in Virtue," 79; *Plutarchs moralische Abhandlungen*, I-V, tr. Johann Friedrich S. Kaltwasser (Frankfurt: 1783-93; *ASKB* 1192-96), I, p. 258; *Plutarch's Moralia*, I-XV, tr. Frank Cole Babbitt et al. (Loeb, Cambridge: Harvard University Press, 1967-84), I, p. 425: "Aeschylus at the Isthmian games was watching a boxing-match, and when one of the men was hit the crowd in the theatre burst into a roar. Aeschylus nudged Ion of Chios, and said, 'You see what a thing training is; the man who is hit says nothing; it is the spectators who shout.' "

220. See Supplement, p. 443 (*Pap.* V B 232:1).

221. Cf. Preface to *Two Upbuilding Discourses* (1843), p. 5 and notes 3-6; Supplement, pp. 443-47 (*Pap.* V B 233:1-9).

222. Cf. John 14:23.

223. Cf. Mark 12:1-9.

224. With reference to the remainder of the sentence, see Supplement, p. 447 (*Pap.* V B 232:8).

225. See, for example, *JP* VI 6157 (*Pap.* IX A 54).

226. Kierkegaard's father, Michael Pedersen Kierkegaard, died August 9, 1838. See also date on p. 5 and note 7.

227. See Supplement, p. 447 (*Pap.* V B 196).

228. See Brorson, "*Her vil ties, her vil bies*," stanza 2, *Psalmer*, 44, p. 863.

229. See I Timothy 6:6-8.

230. In Scandinavia, burial plots in cemeteries are leased, and later, if new payment is not made, the plot is used for another burial.

231. See II Corinthians 12:9; Supplement, p. 447 (*Pap.* V B 198).

232. With reference to the preceding part of the paragraph, see Supplement, p. 448 (*Pap.* V B 200).

233. See Luke 13:29.

234. With reference to the preceding part of the paragraph, see Supplement, p. 448 (*Pap.* V B 201).

235. See, for example, Philippians 2:6-7.

236. See II Corinthians 5:17.

237. Diogenes of Sinope. See Diogenes Laertius, *Lives*, VI, 9, 105; Riisbrigh, I, p. 276; *Vitis*, I, p. 296; Loeb, II, p. 109:

> Hence it has been said that Cynicism is a short cut to virtue; and after the same pattern did Zeno of Citium live his life.
>
> They also hold that we should live frugally, eating food for nourishment only and wearing a single garment. Wealth and fame and high birth they despise. Some at all events are vegetarians and drink cold water only and are content with any kind of shelter or tubs, like Diogenes, who used to say that it was the privilege of the gods to need nothing and of god-like men to want but little.

238. See II Corinthians 4:17.

239. See II Corinthians 11:29-30.

240. See John 2:1-11.

241. See Matthew 19:22.

242. With reference to the following two clauses, see Supplement, p. 448 (*Pap.* V B 205).

243. See Mark 9:43,47.

244. See *JP* I 46 (*Pap.* V A 16).

245. The text is a compacted Danish translation of a quotation in German. See Supplement, p. 448 (*Pap.* V B 207:1).

246. See *JP* I 6 (*Pap.* V A 78).

247. See Exodus 10:22.

248. See Exodus 17:3-6.

249. With reference to the remainder of the paragraph, see Supplement, pp. 448-49 (*Pap.* V B 207:2).

250. See Exodus 33:17-23.

251. With reference to the remainder of the sentence, see Supplement, p. 449 (*Pap.* V B 207:3).

252. With reference to the following paragraph, see Supplement, p. 449 (*Pap.* V B 207:4).

253. Cf. I Corinthians 9:26.

254. See John 11:4.

255. See Proverbs 16:32.

256. See II Corinthians 11:30, 12:5.
257. See Matthew 12:24; Mark 3:22-23.
258. See Matthew 8:28; Mark 5:2-3.
259. With reference to the remainder of the paragraph, see Supplement, p. 449 (*Pap.* V B 207:5).
260. See Philippians 4:4.
261. See I Kings 8:27; Acts 7:48.
262. See Philippians 2:12.
263. See Supplement, p. 450 (*Pap.* V B 207:6).
264. See I Thessalonians 2.3, II Corinthians 1.23; Romans 1:9.
265. With reference to the remainder of the paragraph, see Supplement, p. 450 (*Pap.* V B 207:7).
266. See Colossians 2:20; Galatians 6:14. See also, for example, *For Self-Examination* and *Judge for Yourself!*, pp. 76-81, 116, 131-133, *KW* XXI (*SV* XII 360-64, 396, 409-10).
267. See Romans 8:28.
268. See I John 4:8,16.
269. See Philippians 4:7.
270. See *Postscript, KW* XII (*SV* VII 395); *Sickness unto Death*, pp. 70-71, 78, *KW* XIX (*SV* XI 181, 190); *Point of View, KW* XXII (*SV* XIII 560, 568, 571).
271. See, for example, *Either/Or*, I, p. 237, *KW* III (*SV* I 211).
272. See Supplement, pp. 450-51 (*Pap.* V B 209:2).
273. See Supplement, p. 451 (*Pap.* V B 209:3).
274. See I John 5:4.
275. With reference to the remainder of the paragraph, see Supplement, pp. 451-52 (*Pap.* V B 209:4).
276. See II Corinthians 4:16.
277. See I Corinthians 2:13-15.
278. See I Corinthians 9:7.
279. See Luke 11:26.
280. See Acts 14:22.
281. See I Thessalonians 5:2.
282. Cf. *Fear and Trembling*, p. 27, *KW* VI (*SV* III 80).
283. See p. 183 and note 4.
284. See Romans 8:28.
285. See I Corinthians 10:13.
286. See II Corinthians 6:3-10, 11:23-27.
287. See I Corinthians 9:24.
288. See II Corinthians 11:23-27.
289. See Matthew 26:40; Mark 14:37.
290. See Acts 14:11.
291. See Galatians 2:4.
292. See II Timothy 4:10.
293. See II Corinthians 6:8.

294. See Galatians 2:17.
295. See II Corinthians 10:10.
296. See II Corinthians 12:14-18.
297. See I Corinthians 3:9.
298. See Acts 7:55-56.
299. See I Corinthians 9:26.
300. See Romans 8:38-39.
301. See, for example, Romans 1:11-12, 15:24; Philippians 1:3-8; II Timothy 1:2; Philemon 10.
302. See Romans 15:24,28.
303. See I Corinthians 9:22.
304. See Luke 16:20-22.
305. Attributed to Socrates. See Diogenes Laertius, *Lives*, II, 5, 33; Riisbrigh, I, p. 71; *Vitis*, I, p. 76; Loeb, I, p. 163; *Either/Or*, I, p. 38, *KW* III (*SV* I 22-23); *Stages*, p. 157, *KW* XI (*SV* VI 149).
306. See Psalm 22:1.
307. See I John 4:18.
308. With reference to the remainder of the paragraph, see Supplement, p. 452 (*Pap*. V B 211:2).
309. See Luke 12:21.
310. Cf. James 1:17.
311. See Supplement, p. 452 (*Pap*. V B 213:1).
312. See Romans 8:26; II Corinthians 4:7; Hebrews 11:9.
313. See Psalm 126:5.
314. See Psalm 137:1-6; Brorson, "*I denne søde Juletid*," stanza 6, *Psalmer*, 9, p. 27; *JP* I 800 (*Pap*. III A 12).
315. With reference to the following sentence, see Supplement, pp. 452-53 (*Pap*. V B 212:1).
316. The source of this quotation has not been located.
317. See Matthew 7:3.
318. See I John 4:17. The King James Version has "boldness" and the Revised Standard Version "confidence." The Danish *Frimodighed* combines both meanings.
319. With reference to the remainder of the sentence, see Supplement, p. 453 (*Pap*. V B 212:2).
320. See Acts 26:14.
321. See II Corinthians 5:17; Galatians 6:15.
322. Cf. II Corinthians 5:17.
323. See I Corinthians 1:23.
324. See Acts 7:58.
325. See Acts 9:1-2.
326. With reference to the following two sentences, see Supplement, p. 453 (*Pap*. V B 212:3).
327. With reference to the remainder of the sentence, see Supplement, p. 453 (*Pap*. V B 213:3).

328. Cf. Acts 26:24 (Festus speaking, not Agrippa).
329. With reference to the remainder of the clause, see Supplement, p. 454 (*Pap.* V B 213:4).
330. See Supplement, p. 454 (*Pap.* V B 212:4).
331. See Supplement, p. 454 (*Pap.* V B 213:5).
332. See I Thessalonians 5:3.
333. With reference to the following four paragraphs, see Supplement, p. 454 (*Pap.* V B 212:5).
334. With reference to the remainder of the sentence, see Supplement, pp. 454-55 (*Pap.* V B 215).
335. With reference to the remainder of the sentence, see Supplement, p. 455 (*Pap.* V B 214:1).
336. See Philippians 3:14.
337. See Johann Arndt, *Sämtliche geistreiche Bücher vom wahren Christenthum* (Leipzig: 1832; *ASKB* 276 [Tübingen: n.d.]), III, 23, p. 842; *True Christianity*, rev. and ed. Charles F. Schaeffer (Philadelphia: General Council Publication House, 1917), p. 421.
338. With reference to the remainder of the paragraph, see Supplement, p. 455 (*Pap.* V B 214:2).
339. With reference to the remainder of the paragraph, see Supplement, p. 456 (*Pap.* V B 212:6).
340. With reference to the remainder of the paragraph, see Supplement, p. 456 (*Pap.* V B 214:3).
341. See I Timothy 6:12; II Timothy 4:7.
342. See Supplement, p. 456 (*Pap.* V B 232:10).
343. See Luke 7:11-16.
344. See Matthew 17:1-2; Mark 9:2.
345. With reference to the remainder of the paragraph and the first clause in the next paragraph, see Supplement, p. 456 (*Pap.* V B 216:2).
346. See Ephesians 6:11.
347. See Psalm 51:5; Romans 5:12-21.
348. With reference to the remainder of the paragraph, see Supplement, pp. 456-57 (*Pap.* V B 216:3).
349. See Psalm 139:7-10.
350. See, for example, *Anxiety*, pp. 123-25, *KW* VIII (*SV* IV 391-92).
351. With reference to the remainder of the paragraph and the following paragraph, see Supplement, p. 457 (*Pap.* V B 216:4).
352. See Joshua 10:12.
353. See Hebrews 12:13.
354. See I Peter 5:6.
355. The manuscript (*Pap.* V B 232; B. Pk. 13, Kierkegaard Arkiv, Royal Library, Copenhagen) has a comma here, not a semicolon as in the printed Danish text.
356. See Luke 10:42.

357. With reference to the remainder of the paragraph, see Supplement, p. 457 (*Pap.* V B 234).

358. See Luke 23:43.

359. See Matthew 6:34.

360. See *Postscript*, *KW* XII (*SV* VII 87-88, 99-100); *JP* IV 4519-33; VII, p. 92.

361. See Supplement, p. 458 (*Pap.* V B 218:1).

362. See Luke 17:10.

363. With reference to the following sentence, see Supplement, p. 458 (*Pap.* V B 218:2).

364. See Genesis 1:4-5.

365. See Luke 14:28-30; Supplement, p. 458 (*Pap.* V B 218:1).

366. See Mark 12:41-44.

367. With reference to the following sentence, see Supplement, p. 458 (*Pap.* V B 218:3).

368. See Matthew 5:26.

369. With reference to the remainder of the paragraph, see Supplement, p. 458 (*Pap.* V B 218:4).

370. See Matthew 6:26.

371. With reference to the remainder of the sentence, see Supplement, p. 459 (*Pap.* V B 218:5).

372. Cf. Psalm 133:1.

373. Cf. Matthew 9:4.

374. With reference to the remainder of the paragraph, see Supplement, p. 459 (*Pap.* V B 218:6).

375. See Luke 12:6-7.

376. In Scandinavian folklore, a pixylike invisible creature, helpful when treated properly and mischievous when ignored or mistreated.

377. See Galatians 6:4.

378. See Luke 10:42.

379. See Galatians 3:24.

380. See I Samuel 15:22; Micah 6:7-8; *JP* V 5385, 5893, 6108 (*Pap.* II A 422; VII¹ A 106; VIII¹ A 452, 549).

381. See Matthew 6:17-18.

382. See Matthew 6:16.

383. See Matthew 6:6.

384. For continuation of the sentence, see Supplement, p. 459 (*Pap.* V B 220:1).

385. Cordelia in Shakespeare's *King Lear*, I, 1; *William Shakspeare's Tragiske Værker*, I-IX, tr. Peter Foersom and Peter Frederik Wulff (Copenhagen: 1807-25; *ASKB* 1889-96), II, pp. 8-22; *W. Shakspeare's dramatische Werke*, I-VIII, tr. Ernst Ortlepp (Stuttgart: 1838-39; *ASKB* 1874-81), VII, pp. 5-13; *Shakspeare's dramatische Werke*, I-XII, tr. August Wilhelm v. Schlegel and Ludwig Tieck (Berlin: 1839-41; *ASKB* 1883-88), XI, pp. 5-14; *The Complete Works of Shakespeare*, ed. George Lyman Kittredge (Boston: Ginn, 1936), p. 1198.

386. See Ephesians 6:5; Philippians 2:12.
387. With reference to the previous clause, see Supplement, p. 459 (*Pap.* V B 220:3).
388. See Luke 7:47.
389. With reference to the following sentence, see Supplement, p. 459 (*Pap.* V B 220:4).
390. Cf. Matthew 6:16-17.
391. See James 1:27.
392. See Matthew 25:36-44.
393. See Luke 17:10.
394. See Supplement, p. 460 (*Pap.* V B 235).
395. See II Corinthians 5:11.
396. See John 3:1-2.
397. See Supplement, p. 460 (*Pap.* V B 232:11).
398. See Supplement, p. 460 (*Pap.* V B 221).
399. Cf. Matthew 26:65.
400. Cf. Matthew 13:44-46.
401. See I Timothy 6:12; II Timothy 4:7.
402. The source of this reference has not been located.
403. See Matthew 7:15.
404. See Matthew 5:25.
405. See Mark 8:34-37; Luke 9:24-25.
406. See "70,000 fathoms," *Stages*, pp. 444-45, 470-71, 477, *KW* XI (*SV* VI 414-15, 437-38, 443); *Postscript*, *KW* XII (*SV* VII 114, 171, 195, 246); *Works of Love*, *KW* XVI (*SV* IX 344). See also *JP* II 1142, 1402; IV 4937; V 5792, 5961 (*Pap.* X⁴ A 114; X² A 494; X⁴ A 290; VI B 18; VII¹ A 221).
407. See I Corinthians 13:1.
408. See, for example, *Fragments*, pp. 9-11, *KW* VII (*SV* IV 180-81).
409. See Supplement, p. 460 (*Pap.* V B 221).
410. See Tobit 12:12.
411. With reference to the remainder of the paragraph, see Supplement, p. 460 (*Pap.* V B 227:1).
412. See Matthew 5:3,8.
413. With reference to the following two sentences, see Supplement, p. 460 (*Pap.* V B 227:2).
414. With reference to the remainder of the sentence and the following sentence, see Supplement, p. 461 (*Pap.* V B 227:3).
415. See Revelation 3:16.
416. See, for example, John 2:1-11; Mark 10:46-52, 2:1-12; Luke 7:11-16; Mark 5:1-13.
417. With reference to the following paragraph, see Supplement, p. 461 (*Pap.* V B 227:4).
418. With reference to the remainder of the paragraph, see Supplement, p. 461 (*Pap.* V B 227:5).
419. Cf. Mark 9:48.

420. With reference to the following three sentences, see Supplement, p. 461 (*Pap.* V B 228:2).

421. With reference to the remainder of the paragraph, see Supplement, p. 462 (*Pap.* V B 227:6).

422. With reference to the remainder of the paragraph, see Supplement, p. 462 (*Pap.* V B 229:2).

423. With reference to the following paragraph, see Supplement, p. 462 (*Pap.* V B 229:1).

424. With reference to the following four sentences, see Supplement, pp. 462-63 (*Pap.* V B 229:3).

425. With reference to the remainder of the paragraph, see Supplement, pp. 463-64 (*Pap.* V B 229:12,14).

426. With reference to the following sentence, see Supplement, p. 464 (*Pap.* V B 230:1).

427. See I Corinthians 13:12.

428. With reference to the following ten sentences, see Supplement, pp. 463, 464 (*Pap.* V B 229:4, 236).

429. See John 14:3,16,26, 15:26; Supplement, pp. 464-65 (*Pap.* V B 237).

430. See John 16:7.

431. See Genesis 12:4.

432. With reference to the remainder of the paragraph, see Supplement, p. 465 (*Pap.* V B 230:3).

433. See Revelation 21:5.

434. See Psalm 51:10-12.

435. With reference to the following sentence, see Supplement, p. 465 (*Pap.* V B 229:5).

436. With reference to the following sentence, see Supplement, p. 465 (*Pap.* V B 229:13).

437. See Luke 7:47.

438. See Mark 13:32.

439. See Matthew 25:1-10.

440. See Susanna 35.

441. See I John 2:15.

442. With reference to the following two sentences, see Supplement, p. 466 (*Pap.* V B 229:7).

443. See I Corinthians 13:11.

444. With reference to the following three sentences, see Supplement, p. 466 (*Pap.* V B 229:16).

445. With reference to the following sentence, see Supplement, p. 466 (*Pap.* V B 229:6).

446. With reference to the following four sentences, see Supplement, p. 466 (*Pap.* V B 229:8).

447. With reference to the following sentence, see Supplement, p. 466 (*Pap.* V B 229:11).

448. With reference to the remainder of the paragraph, see Supplement, p. 467 (*Pap.* V B 229:10).

449. With reference to the following two sentences, see Supplement, p. 467 (*Pap.* V B 229:9).

450. With reference to the remainder of the paragraph, see Supplement, p. 467 (*Pap.* V B 229:15).

SUPPLEMENT

1. See, for example, G.W.F. Hegel, *Phänomenologie des Geistes, Georg Wilhelm Friedrich Hegel's Werke. Vollständige Ausgabe,* I-XVIII, ed. Philipp K. Marheineke et al. (Berlin: 1832-45; *ASKB* 549-65), II, pp. 6-8; *Sämtliche Werke. Jubiläumsausgabe* [*J.A.*], I-XXVI, ed. Hermann Glockner (Stuttgart, Frommann: 1927-40), II, pp. 14-16; *The Phenomenology of Mind* (tr. primarily of 3 ed., 1841; Kierkegaard had 2 ed., 1832), tr. J. B. Baillie (New York: Harper, 1967), pp. 71-72:

When we state the true form of truth to be its scientific character—or, what is the same thing, when it is maintained that truth finds the medium of its existence in notions or conceptions alone—I know that this seems to contradict an idea with all its consequences which makes great pretensions and has gained widespread acceptance and conviction at the present time. . . . Philosophy is thus expected not so much to meet this want by opening up the compact solidity of substantial existence, and bringing this to the light and level of self-consciousness—is not so much to bring chaotic conscious life back to the orderly ways of thought, and the simplicity of the notion, as to run together what thought has divided asunder, suppress the notion with its distinctions, and restore the *feeling* of existence. What it wants from philosophy is not so much insight as edification [*Erbauung*]. The beautiful, the holy, the eternal, religion, love—these are the bait required to awaken the desire to bite: not the notion, but ecstasy, not the march of cold necessity in the subject-matter, but ferment and enthusiasm—these are to be the ways by which the wealth of the concrete substance is to be stored and increasingly extended.

2. See *Either/Or,* II, pp. 346-54, *KW* IV (*SV* II 312-18).

3. The familiar form in Danish of the second personal pronoun, used among family and close friends. In recent years, it has come to be used in wider circles.

4. See I Peter 4:8.

5. Luke 2:22-38.

6. See I John 4:19.

7. See, for example, *Works of Love, KW* XVI (*SV* IX 8); *Christian Discourses, KW* XVII (*SV* X 195-96).

8. See I John 4:19.

9. Cf. John 18:21.

10. See *Postscript, KW* XII (*SV* VII 134).

11. Romans 13:11-13.

12. See Matthew 26:40; Mark 14:37; Luke 22:45-46.

13. See Matthew 21:28-32.

14. Ibid.

15. See Ecclesiastes 1:2; *Stages*, pp. 251-52, *KW* XI (*SV* VI 237).

16. See Mark 12:42-44; Luke 21:1-4.

17. See Luke 16:19-25.

18. The text has *beerdiges*, a German word with a Danish ending, meaning literally "to be placed in the earth."

19. Cf. Preface to *Two Upbuilding Discourses* (1843), p. 5.

20. See Johan Ludvig Heiberg, "*Gjensvar paa Herr Professor Hauchs Svar,*" *Kjøbenhavns flyvende Post*, no. 37, 1830, col. 6 fn. See also, for example, *Irony*, p. 207, *KW* II (*SV* XIII 286); *Either/Or*, I, p. 140, *KW* III (*SV* I 119); *Prefaces, KW* IX (*SV* V 17); *Two Ages*, pp. 9-11, 21, *KW* XIV (*SV* VIII 8-11, 20).

21. See p. 295.

22. Cf. *Works of Love, KW* XVI (*SV* IX 267).

23. See John 8:3-11.

24. See *Works of Love, KW* XVI (*SV* IX 37-41).

25. Ibid. (34-35).

26. See I Peter 4:8.

27. See *Works of Love, KW* XVI (*SV* IX 20-27).

28. See Augustine, *Sancti Aurelii Augustini opera*, I-XVIII (Venice: 1797-1807; *ASKB* 117-34), I, col. 1026.

29. The second of *Three Upbuilding Discourses* (1843).

30. See Luke 18:2-5.

31. See Matthew 6:26; Luke 12:24; cf. *The Lily in the Field and the Bird of the Air*, in *Without Authority, KW* XVIII (*SV* XI 3-46).

32. See I Corinthians 15:42.

33. See Luke 7:28.

34. The reference is to Darius, king of Persia, who was succeeded by Xerxes. See Herodotus, *History*, V, 105; *Die Geschichten des Herodotos*, I-II, tr. Friedrich Lange (Berlin: 1811-12; *ASKB* 1117), II, p. 59; *Herodotus*, I-IV, tr. A. D. Godley (Loeb, Cambridge: Harvard University Press, 1981-82), III, p. 127:

> Onesilus, then, besieged Amathus. But when it was told to Darius that Sardis had been taken and burnt by the Athenians and Ionians, and that Aristagoras the Milesian had been leader of the conspiracy for the weaving of this plan, at his first hearing of it (it is said) he took no account of the Ionians,—being well assured that they of all men would not go scatheless for their rebellion,—but asked who were the Athenians; and being told, he called for his bow, which he took, and laid an arrow on it and shot it into the sky, praying as he sent it aloft, "O Zeus, grant me vengeance on the Athenians," and therewithal he charged one of his servants to say to him

thrice whenever dinner was set before him, "Master, remember the Athenians."

See also *Stages*, p. 295, *KW* XI (*SV* VI 276).

35. *Allwills Briefsammlung; Friedrich Heinrich Jacobi's Werke*, I-VI (Leipzig: 1812-25; *ASKB* 1722-28), I, pp. 173-74.

36. See, for example, Plato, *Republic*, 344 c; *Platonis quae exstant opera*, I-XI, ed. Friedrich Ast (Leipzig: 1819-32; *ASKB* 1144-54), IV, pp. 42-43; *The Collected Dialogues of Plato*, ed. Edith Hamilton and Huntington Cairns (Princeton: Princeton University Press, 1963), p. 594 (Thrasymachus speaking). "Thus, Socrates, injustice on a sufficiently large scale is a stronger, freer, and more masterful thing than justice, and, as I said in the beginning, it is the advantage of the stronger that is the just, while the unjust is what profits a man's self and is for his advantage."

37. In *JP* IV 4585 (*Pap.* V A 43), the draft passage (*Pap.* V B 209:2) is quoted with the observation: "*Too humorous.*"

38. Presumably Louis de Ponte (1554-1624), writer and follower of Ignatius de Loyola. The source of the observation has not been located.

39. The source has not been located.

40. See Matthew 21:28-31.

41. See Luke 10:23.

42. See *Fragments*, p. 66, *KW* VII (*SV* IV 230-31).

43. See *Discourses in Various Spirits*, *KW* XV (*SV* VIII 307-08).

44. See Acts 1:3.

45. This was done in *Discourses on Imagined Occasions*, *KW* X (*SV* V 171-253).

46. The journal was not published.

47. See *Anxiety*, p. 30, *KW* VIII (*SV* IV 303).

48. See *Johannes Climacus, or De omnibus dubitandum est*, *KW* VII (*Pap.* IV B 1).

49. See pp. 7-29, 205-26, 253-73.

50. *Grundrids til Moralphilosophiens System* (Copenhagen: 1841; *ASKB* 650), by Hans Lassen Martensen (1808-1884).

51. See *Fragments*, pp. 40-41, *KW* VII (*SV* IV 208-09).

52. It is not clear whether the reference is to Poul Martin Møller (1794-1838), Kierkegaard's favorite professor of philosophy at the University of Copenhagen, or to a fellow university student and later literary critic, Peder Ludvig Møller (1814-1865).

53. See pp. 42-43; *Postscript*, *KW* XII (*SV* VII 147-49).

54. See *JP* V 5601-02 (*Pap.* IV C 97-98).

55. Johan Ludvig Heiberg (1791-1860), Hegelian philosopher and the leading Danish literary critic at the time.

56. Christian Hermann Weiss[z]e, *System der Æsthetik von der Idee der Schönheit*, I-II (Leipzig: 1830; *ASKB* 1379-80).

57. *Stages* was published April 30, 1845.

58. See *Postscript*, *KW* XII (*SV* VII 252).

59. Ibid. (246-53).
60. Ibid. (256).
61. Ibid. (253-54).
62. Someone. See *Stages*, pp. 446-51, *KW* XI (*SV* VI 415-20).
63. See *Postscript*, *KW* XII (*SV* VII 249-50).
64. See ibid. (216-17).
65. See Supplement, pp. 488-89 (X⁶ B 145).
66. See *Postscript*, *KW* XII (*SV* VII 229-30 fn.).
67. This proposed volume was to include *Two Ages, Discourses in Various Spirits*, and *The Book on Adler*. The first two were published separately; *Adler* first appeared in *Efterladte Papirer* (1822), II, pp. 451-704.
68. The text is a free rendering of I Corinthians 14:26. All the Danish translations from Kierkegaard's time have *Opbyggelse* [upbuilding].
69. Adolph Peter Adler, *Nogle Digte; Studier og Exempler; Theologiske Studier; Forsøg til en kort systematisk Fremstilling af Christendommen i dens Logik* (Copenhagen: 1846; *ASKB U* 9, 11, 12, 13).
70. In June 1844, *Three Upbuilding Discourses, Fragments, Anxiety*, and *Prefaces* were published.
71. *Discourses in Various Spirits, KW* XV (*SV* VIII 370-84).
72. Ibid. (385-97).
73. See *Christian Discourses, KW* XVII (*SV* X 103).
74. See II Corinthians 4:7.
75. See Psalm 90:10.
76. See *Christian Discourses, KW* XVII (*SV* X 108-09).
77. Ibid. (102-03).
78. This plan was not carried out.
79. A printing sheet that folded twice gives four sheets of quarto size and folded three times gives eight pages of octavo.
80. This precise plan was not carried out. See notes 81, 90, 93 below on *Christian Discourses*.
81. See *Christian Discourses, KW* XVII (*SV* X 163).
82. See Ecclesiastes 4:17 in Danish Bible, 5:1 in RSV; *Christian Discourses, KW* XVII (*SV* X 167-78).
83. Ibid. (179) (Matthew 19:27-28).
84. Ibid. (190-202) (Romans 8:28).
85. Ibid. (203-13) (Acts 24:15).
86. Ibid. (204).
87. Ibid. (206).
88. Ibid. (222-32).
89. See Matthew 5:11; Luke 6:22.
90. See *Christian Discourses, KW* XVII (*SV* X 225-27).
91. See Aesop, "*Vulpis et Ciconia*," *Phaedri Augusti Liberti Fabularum Aesopiarum Libri V* (Leipzig: 1828), XXVI, pp. 12-13; "The Fox and the Stork," *Babrius and Phaedrus*, ed. and tr. Ben Edwin Perry (Loeb, Cambridge: Harvard University Press, 1965), pp. 221-23.
92. See Luke 6:26.

93. See *Christian Discourses, KW* XVII (*SV* X 214-21) (Romans 13:11).

94. Ibid. (233-44).

95. See pp. 1-48.

96. *The Crisis and a Crisis in the Life of an Actress* (1848), with *Christian Discourses, KW* XVII (*SV* X 319-44).

97. See, for example, *JP* VI 6157 (*Pap*. IX A 54).

98. See, for example, *JP* V 6134; VI 6596 (*Pap*. VIII¹ A 648; X² A 544).

99. See p. 61 and note 100.

100. See Genesis 18:14; Luke 1:37.

101. See I John 4:8,16.

102. See I John 2:2.

103. See, for example, *JP* I 1038; V 6094, 6152 (*Pap*. VI A 40; VIII² B 186; IX A 42), in which Kierkegaard considers the possibility of a direct statement about his work. Subsequently, *On My Work as an Author* was published (1851), and *The Point of View* was published posthumously (1859). *Armed Neutrality* remained unpublished until it appeared in *Efterladte Papirer* (1880, VI, pp. 556-70) and *Papirer* (1932, X⁵ B 107). These three works are found together with *The Point of View, KW* XXII.

104. See note 96 above.

105. Pp. 1-48.

106. The last two pieces are Part One and Part Two of *Practice, KW* XX (*SV* XII 1-134).

107. Rasmus Nielsen (1809-1884), professor of philosophy at the University of Copenhagen. See, for example, *JP* VI 6233, 6415 (*Pap*. IX A 220; X¹ A 406).

108. See *Works of Love, KW* XVI (*SV* IX 14); *Two Discourses at the Communion on Fridays*, in *Without Authority, KW* XVIII (*SV* XII 267); *JP* VI 6382 (*Pap*. X¹ A 247).

109. See note 96.

110. Pp. 1-48.

111. See *Tillæg til den evangelisk-christelige Psalmebog* (Copenhagen: 1845), no. 610, Appendix, p. 51. The author is Aurelius Clemens Prudentius (348- c. 410), Spanish poet.

112. This plan was not carried out. *Sickness unto Death*, pp. 77-131, *KW* XIX (*SV* XI 189-241), embodies some of the themes. See also, for example, *JP* VI 6278-80 (*Pap*. IX A 498-500).

113. For Kierkegaard's distinction, see Supplement, pp. 431-32 (*Pap*. IV B 159:6).

114. See *Irony*, p. 198, *KW* II (*SV* XIII 279); *JP* V 5397; VI 6416 (*Pap*. II A 497; X¹ A 422).

115. See Supplement, p. 482 (*Pap*. X¹ A 510).

116. See *Sickness unto Death*, pp. 5-6, *KW* XIX (*SV* XI 117-18).

117. The first two parts of *Practice*.

118. See *JP* V 5873, 5877 (*Pap*. VII¹ A 4, 9).

119. See *Christian Discourses, KW* XVII (*SV* X 247-317). The reference may

be to *Three Discourses at the Communion on Fridays*, in *Without Authority*, *KW* XVIII (*SV* XI 245-80), ready for publication (published November 13, 1849).

120. Anti-Climacus.

121. See Supplement, pp. 431-32 (*Pap.* IV B 159:6).

122. *Sickness unto Death* and Part One of *Practice*.

123. Pastoral convention in Roskilde, October 30, 1849. Six years later, on July 5, 1855, again in Roskilde, four months before Søren Kierkegaard died, his brother Peter C. Kierkegaard gave another address, under the title "Remarks on the Famous Pseudonyms of the Day and the Theology of Their Author," in which Peter discussed the "misgivings I, for my part, have long entertained against the theology, or what could better be called the nontheology, that an academy of pseudonyms has developed these last years in the literature of our fatherland . . ." (quoted by Otto Holmgaard, *Exstaticus* [Copenhagen: 1967], p. 57 [ed. tr.]). In the *Papirer* there is no reference to this second Roskilde address, but it was the cause of the rift between the brothers during the last days of Kierkegaard's life.

124. Hans Lassen Martensen (1808-1884), professor of theology and successor to Bishop Jakob Peter Mynster in 1854.

125. See II Corinthians 5:13.

126. See note 107 above.

127. The discourse was published (1850) without the contemplated Preface. The other works mentioned were published in 1851.

128. *Either/Or* was published on February 15, 1843, and *Two Upbuilding Discourses* on May 16, 1843.

129. See *Point of View*, *KW* XXII (*SV* XIII 494).

130. See *Christian Discourses*, *KW* XVII (*SV* X 251).

131. *Om Magister Kierkegaards Forfattervirksomhed. Iagttagelser af en Landsbypræst* (Ludvig J. M. Gude) (Copenhagen: 1851). The reply was not published.

132. See pp. 5, 53, 107, 179, 231, 295.

133. From a children's rhyme. See *Moment*, *KW* XXIII (*SV* XIII 38); Evald Tang Kristensen, *Danske Börnerim, Remser og Lege* (Aarhus: 1898), p. 19:

> Sko min Hest
> hvem kan bedst
> det kan vor Præst
> nej det kan han ej
> det kan vor Smed
> som boer ved vort Led
> og ta'r kun to Skilling for 'et
> [Shoe my horse / Who can do it best /
> Our pastor can / No, he cannot /
> Our blacksmith can do it / Who lives near our gate
> And takes only two shillings for it].

134. *On My Work*, with *Point of View*, *KW* XXII (*SV* XIII 501).

BIBLIOGRAPHICAL NOTE

For general bibliographies of Kierkegaard studies, see:

Jens Himmelstrup, *Søren Kierkegaard International Bibliografi*. Copenhagen: Nyt Nordisk Forlag Arnold Busck, 1962.
Aage Jørgensen, *Søren Kierkegaard-litteratur 1961-1970*. Aarhus: Akademisk Boghandel, 1971. *Søren Kierkegaard-litteratur 1971-1980*. Aarhus: privately published, 1983.
François H. Lapointe, *Sören Kierkegaard and His Critics: An International Bibliography of Criticism*. Westport, Connecticut: Greenwood Press, 1980.
Kierkegaard: A Collection of Critical Essays, ed. Josiah Thompson. New York: Doubleday (Anchor Books), 1972.
Kierkegaardiana, XII, 1982.
Søren Kierkegaard's Journals and Papers, I, ed. and tr. Howard V. Hong and Edna H. Hong, assisted by Gregor Malantschuk. Bloomington: Indiana University Press, 1967.

For topical bibliographies of Kierkegaard studies, see *Søren Kierkegaard's Journals and Papers*, I-IV (1967-75).

INDEX

Abraham, 278, 396; burial place of, 95; and Sodom and Gomorrah, 66

accidental, the: vs. the universal, 250

accounting: death and, 198; before God, 16; on judgment day, 73; and salvation, 272; of self, 44

Adam, 225; and Eve, 126; and serpent, 127

Adler, Adolph Peter: as author, 471-72

admonition: concern in, 238; concerned truth of, 239; as good gift, 149-50; and humility, 150; of Paul, 321; of Preacher, 236-40; and single individual, 238-40

Adresseavisen, 471

adult: and Job, 112; piety of, 386

Advent, 427

adversity: courage in, 92; faith in, 26; hope in, 94; and inner being, 93-98, 439; and prosperity, 98, 438; and single individual, 88. *See also* anxiety; despair

Aesop: *Phaedri Augusti Liberti Fabularum Aesopiarum Libri*, 536; "*Vulpis et Ciconia*," 536

Agrippa: and Paul, 342

analogy: bird, 159, 267; drawing child, 398-99, 466; hiker, 160-61, 174; hunter, 344, 454; messenger, 295, 443-47; price of commodity, 378-79; prisoner, 9, 17, 444-47; riding horse, 450-51; stars, 19; sundial, 276; tower, 188, 361-62, 366, 458, 504; warrior, 269

angel(s), 282, 398; and death, 430; at pool of Bethesda, 11; and prayer,

381, 383; of Satan, 328-29, 331, 340, 342, 456

anger: and life, 37-39; vs. love, 56; unrighteousness of, 138

Anna, 425; in expectancy, 208-13, 219, 222-25; and patience, 213; as prophet, 217-18; and Simeon, 208, 219; in temple, 217, 222-23; widowhood of, 209-10; as witness, 208, 225

anon., *Tillæg til den evangelisk-christelige Psalmebog*, 537

anxiety: in defiance, 110-11; and love, 60; single individual in, 110-11; soul in, 184-86, in spiritual trial, 97; and wish, 12. *See also* adversity; despair

apostle: authority of, 70, 329; and congregation, 70-71, 141-43; as God's co-worker, 333; as guide, 135-36; humility of, 340; and love, 435; and single individual, 82, 136-38; speech of, 70; and spiritual trial, 331; suffering of, 330-35; upbuilding by, 329; weakness of, 305-06; as witness, 82-84. *See also individual apostles*

Aristotle: doctrine of virtue of, 468; on God, 513; *Metaphysics*, 513; *Nicomachean Ethics*, 507; *Works*, 507

Ark of the Covenant, 267

Arndt, Johann, *Die deutsche Theologie mit einer Vorrede von Dr. M. Luther und Johann Arnd*, 511; *Sämtliche geistreiche Bücher vom wahren Christenthum*, 529

art: suffering in, 472-73

Augustine: on love, 434; *Opera*, 534

Aurelius Clemens Prudentius, 537
authority: of apostle, 70, 329; in authorship, 179; of Bible, 472; of
experience, 238; of the good, 359.
See also without authority
awakening, 430; discourses for, 476;
of inner being, 439; and sleeping,
427; vs. upbuilding, 483

Balle, Nicolai Edinger, *Lærebog i den
Evangelisk-christelige Religion in-
drettet, til Brug i de danske Skoler,*
521
baptism, 278
beatitude, 454; of heaven, 345; silence of, 338; and suffering, 335
Bethesda: pool of, 11, 207
Beundring, 225
Bias, 509
BIBLE, 472
　Apocrypha
　　Sirach 4:18, 139; 19:26-27, 60;
　　　28:8, 63
　　Susanna 35, 532
　　Tobit 4:7, 508; 12:12, 531
　　Wisdom of Solomon 2:1, 241;
　　　2:6, 241; 2:8, 241
　New Testament
　　Acts 1:3, 535; 1:9, 506, 514; 2:3,
　　　506; 5:9, 283; 7:48, 527; 7:55-
　　　56, 514, 528; 7:58, 528; 9:1-
　　　30, 523; 9:1-2, 528; 14:11,
　　　527; 14:17, 511; 14:22, 527;
　　　17:28, 514, 522; 20:35, 515;
　　　24:15, 520, 536; 26:14, 528;
　　　26:24, 523, 529; 27:22, 509
　　Colossians 1:11, 222; 2:8, 268;
　　　2:20, 527; 3:1-2, 136; 4:2, 514
　　I Corinthians 1:9, 505; 1:18,
　　　510; 1:22-23, 523; 1:23, 528;
　　　2:9, 511, 523; 2:13-15, 527;
　　　3:1-2, 513; 3:2, 517; 3:9, 510,
　　　525, 528; 3:19, 506; 4:2, 515;
　　　6:3, 509; 7:21, 514; 7:29-33,
　　　514; 7:31, 511; 8:1, 503; 9:7,

527; 9:9, 523; 9:22, 509, 528;
9:24-26, 518; 9:24, 508, 527;
9:26, 509, 510, 517, 523, 526,
528; 10:13, 505, 511, 512,
519, 527; 10:23, 503; 12:31,
514; 13, 507, 509; 13:1, 513,
531; 13:7, 509; 13:11, 521,
532; 13:12, 506, 512, 523,
532; 14:3, 503; 14:8, 239;
14:26, 536; 15:2, 239; 15:9,
343; 15:19, 263; 15:42, 512,
521, 534; 15:53-54, 521
　　II Corinthians 1:23, 510, 527;
　　　4:7-18, 253-73; 4:7, 215, 528,
　　　536; 4:16, 507, 510, 527; 4:17,
　　　523, 526; 4:18, 523; 5:7, 522;
　　　5:11, 531; 5:13, 538; 5:17,
　　　526, 528; 6:3-10, 527; 6:4-5,
　　　523; 6:8, 527; 6:10, 510, 511;
　　　6:14, 509; 7:9-10, 523; 9:7,
　　　506, 514; 10:10, 528; 11:1,
　　　506; 11:17, 506; 11:21, 506;
　　　11:23-27, 527; 11:29-30, 526;
　　　11:30, 527; 12:2-5, 523; 12:5,
　　　527; 12:7, 327-46; 12:9, 526;
　　　12:14-18, 528
　　Ephesians 1:10, 519; 2:3, 511;
　　　2:19, 519; 3:13-19, 512; 3:13,
　　　80-101, 510; 3:16, 510; 4:26,
　　　514; 4:30, 514; 6:5, 531; 6:11,
　　　529; 6:12, 506, 514; 6:13, 121
　　Galatians 1:13-16, 523; 1:15-16,
　　　510; 1:16, 514; 2:2, 510; 2:4,
　　　527; 2:17, 528; 3:24-25, 505;
　　　3:24, 530; 3:28, 520; 4:3, 508;
　　　4:4, 519; 5:20-23, 509; 6:4,
　　　530; 6:7, 258; 6:14, 527; 6:15,
　　　528
　　Hebrews 1:1, 508; 4:7, 519;
　　　4:12, 509; 5:8, 511; 6:4, 518;
　　　6:13, 518; 9:27, 509; 10:39,
　　　517; 11:9, 519, 528; 11:13,
　　　519; 12:6, 512; 12:13, 529;
　　　13:9, 302
　　James 1:9-10, 142; 1:13, 506;

bird, 258, 364. *See also* analogy
blasphemy, 387
Børnerim, 515
Brandis, Joachim Dietrich, 524
Brandt, Frithiof, and Else Rammel,
Søren Kierkegaard og Pengene, xxi,
xxii, 517
bridesmaids: foolish and wise, 213
Brorson, Hans Adolph: "*Flye min
Aand, og bryd med Styrke*," 510;
"*Her vil ties, her vil bies*," 525; "*I
denne søde Juletid*," 528; "*Jeg gaaer i
Fare, hvor jeg gaaer*," 517; *Psalmer
og aandelige Sange*, 510

Caesar, Julius, 517–18
Cana: wedding in, 306, 389
Canaan, 95

servant: Christ as, 282; as God's co-
worker, 282; single individual as,
281-82, 443; unfaithful, 282; unworthy, 372-73
service: in expectancy, 222-23; of
the good, 362-69; of world, 308,
347
70,000 fathoms, 531
Shakespeare, William: *King Lear*,
530; *Works*, 530
sickness: unto death, 267, 315
Siloam: pool of, 153
Simeon, 224; and Anna, 208, 219; as
witness, 208, 225
sin(s): danger of, 350; euphemism
for, 353; and guilt, 453; and hate,
61; and love, 55-68, 69-78, 433,
434; multitude of, 62-63, 433;
power of, 75; powerlessness of, 64
single individual, 57, 454, 485; and
admonition, 238-40; in adversity,
88; in anxiety, 110-11; and apostle, 82; vs. congregation, xviii;
and divine equality, 143; and divine justice, 91; vs. generality,
304; and God, 246, 304, 443; and
grace, 269; and Job, 113; life of,
207; and love, 72; and patience,
193; and pseudonymous writers,
475; as reader, 5, 53, 107, 179,
231, 295, 431, 444-47, 486; as receiver of good gifts, 134, 136-38;
and salvation, 268-69; and self-denial, 288; as servant, 281-82, 443;
in terror, 182-83; and thorn in
flesh, 346, and truth, 233-34;
uniqueness of, 475; universality
of, xvii-xx, 475, 486; upbuilding
for, 276, 473
sleeping: and awakening, 427
sobriety: in prayer, 424, 427
Socrates: on Governance, xix; on
love, 515; maieutic approach of,
x, xii, 479; against sophism, 449
Sodom and Gomorrah: and Abraham, 66

Solomon, 89
Solon, 507
Son of Man, *see* Christ
sorrow: and comfort, 34-35, 396; of
Job, 114-15, 122; and joy, 122;
and spiritual trial, 450
soul: anxiety of, 184-86; as child,
316; concern in, 440; in danger,
185, 350; and death, 184-85; expectancy in, 220; gaining of, 159-
75, 424; and the good, 380; inwardness in, 267; knowledge of,
172-75; loss of, 186; and patience,
159-75, 181-203, 424-25; possession of, 166; and prayer, 427; as
self-contradiction, 163, 166-67,
172; strength of, 181-82. *See also*
inner being; inwardness
Spain: Paul in, 334
sparrow, 214; of air, 154, 367
Spinoza, Benedict: *Opera*, 521; *Tractatus theologico-politicus*, 521
spirit: of cowardliness, 347, 360-61,
368-69; God as, 88; of power and
love and self-control, 347, 360-
61, 366, 368-69, 375; of power
and self-control, 219; as thorn in
flesh, 336-37; witness to, 333;
world of, 335, 394
spiritlessness: vs. patience, 198
spiritual trial: apostle and, 331; comfort in, 98; God and, 323-24; hope
in, 95; of inner being, 84, 97-98;
Paul in, 261-63; of sorrow, 450
star(s): as witness, 207. *See also* analogy
Stephen, 334; and Paul, 341
stewardship: and death, 91-92
Stoicism, 466
strength: of soul, 181-82; in suffering, 95; out of terror, 182; in
weakness, 171-72
striving: continued, 357-58
Suetonius (Cajus Suetonius Tran-
quillus), "Julius Caesar," 517-18;
Lives of the Caesars, 517-18

558   *Index*

suffering(s): of apostle, 330-35; in
art, 472-73; and beatitude, 335;
and comfort, 463; as education,
179, 424-25, 426, 450; and faith,
330, 451; of Job, 110-11; and love,
74, 478; of Paul, 82-83, 332-34,
451-52; of separation, 337; in spiritual trial, 97-98; and strength, 95;
and time, 472-73; witness to, 332-
34; and understanding, 454; upbuilding in, 424
sun: rising vs. setting, 275, 277, 289
sundial, *see* analogy
superstition, 458; and expectancy,
259
sympathy: as good gift, 150

teacher: faith in, 12-13; God as, 12-
13, 28; Job as, 109-10, 112, 124;
and pupil, 156
temporality: as deception, 175; as
desire, 461; vs. eternity, 27, 163,
185, 211, 215, 218, 266-67, 356-
57, 392, 461, 470, 472; expectancy
in, 259; and the external, 166; life
of, 265-66. *See also* time
temptation, 440-41; anxiety of, 96;
by God, 33, 38-39, 40, 111; of
God, 35-37, 38-39, 40, 46; by
good gifts, 146-47; hardship as,
94; of John the Baptizer, 280-81;
punishment as, 47-48; struggle
over, 201-02, 320
Teologisk Tidsskrift, 505
terror: cowardliness and, 358-59;
single individual in, 182-83;
strength out of, 182
test: by God, 98
thanksgiving: for good gifts, 42-48,
90, 116, 152-56, 254; of Job, 115-
16, 118; Kierkegaard and, 478; in
prayer, 43, 400, 462, 465, 466-67;
and witness, 93
thorn in flesh, 327-46, 455; and future, 456; of Paul, 328, 336-37,

346; past as, 343-46; single individual and, 346; spirit as, 336; and
upbuilding, 468; as warning, 331
thoughtlessness, 339-40; and danger, 349-50
*Tillæg til den evangelisk-christelige
Psalmebog,* 537
time: and cowardliness, 356-57; fullness of, 219; and love, 433; and
past, 338-39, 456; and suffering,
472-73. *See also* temporality
Total-Anlæg, ix, xiii
tower, *see* analogy
tree: of knowledge, 125-27; of life,
148
truth: concerned, 233-34, 239; and
deception, x, xii-xiv, 306; dialectic of, xvii; general, 276; as good
gift, 150-51; indifferent, 233; and
Pharisee, 152; and upbuilding,
468-69; and witness, 83; word of,
137

understanding: and faith, 395-96;
with God, 459, 462; and reflection, 478-79; of self, 431; and suffering, 454-55
unhappiness: vs. happiness, 20-21,
117
universal, the: vs. the accidental,
250
upbuilding, 423-24, 503-05; apostolic, 329; vs. awakening, 483;
and culture, 474; and direct communication, 479; discourse(s) for,
239-40, 344, 346, 450, 467, 469-
71, 472, 476, 479, 484; in divine
equality, 143; and earnestness,
424; and education, 474; vs. the
esthetic, 479, 482; vs. generality,
276; Hegel and, 423; and humor,
470; and jest, 424; need for, 474-
75; in New Testament, 503; in
observation, 253; Paul on, 471; by
pseudonyms, 482; and reflection,

ADVISORY BOARD

KIERKEGAARD'S WRITINGS